International Economics and Policy

An Introduction to Globalization and Inequality

World Scientific Lecture Notes in Economics and Policy

ISSN: 2630-4872

The World Scientific Lecture Notes in Economics and Policy series is aimed to produce lecture note texts for a wide range of economics disciplines, both theoretical and applied at the undergraduate and graduate levels. Contributors to the series are highly ranked and experienced professors of economics who see in publication of their lectures a mission to disseminate the teaching of economics in an affordable manner to students and other readers interested in enriching their knowledge of economic topics. The series was formerly titled World Scientific Lecture Notes in Economics.

Published:

For the complete list of volumes in this series, please visit
www.worldscientific.com/series/wslnep

World Scientific Lecture Notes in Economics and Policy – Vol. 18

International Economics and Policy

An Introduction to Globalization and Inequality

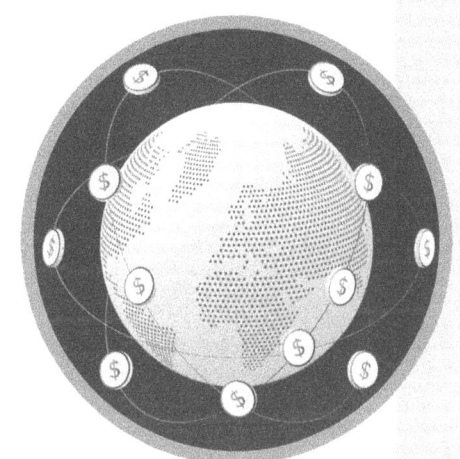

Keith E Maskus
University of Colorado Boulder, USA

W♭ World Scientific

NEW JERSEY · LONDON · SINGAPORE · BEIJING · SHANGHAI · HONG KONG · TAIPEI · CHENNAI · TOKYO

Published by

World Scientific Publishing Co. Pte. Ltd.

5 Toh Tuck Link, Singapore 596224

USA office: 27 Warren Street, Suite 401-402, Hackensack, NJ 07601

UK office: 57 Shelton Street, Covent Garden, London WC2H 9HE

Library of Congress Cataloging-in-Publication Data

Names: Maskus, Keith E. (Keith Eugene), author.

Title: International economics and policy: an introduction to globalization and inequality /
    Keith E Maskus, University of Colorado Boulder, USA.

Description: Singapore ; Hackensack, NJ : World Scientific, 2024. | Series:
    World scientific lecture notes in economics and policy, 2630-4872 ; vol. 18 | Includes index.

Identifiers: LCCN 2023033209 | ISBN 9789811282287 (hardcover) |
    ISBN 9789811283079 (paperback) | ISBN 9789811282294 (ebook) |
    ISBN 9789811282300 (ebook other)

Subjects: LCSH: International trade. | Economics. | Business logistics. | Commerce.

Classification: LCC HF1379 .M37 2024 | DDC 382--dc23/eng/20230825

LC record available at https://lccn.loc.gov/2023033209

British Library Cataloguing-in-Publication Data

A catalogue record for this book is available from the British Library.

For any available supplementary material, please visit
https://www.worldscientific.com/worldscibooks/10.1142/13568#t=suppl

Desk Editors: Aanand Jayaraman/Geysilla Jean

Typeset by Stallion Press
Email: enquiries@stallionpress.com

Preface

This text is aimed at giving students who are not economics majors a comprehensive introduction to the workings of international economics and policy. Ideally, it will help students in international relations, international business, and related fields who take just one course in global economics to achieve a thorough understanding of these matters.

It is organized into "19 chapters" that are comprised of lecture notes, rather than fully developed text. This approach offers both students and instructors a more streamlined approach to understanding the complexities of the global economy.

The notes rely on economic theory where necessary to build a sound knowledge foundation. However, the emphasis is on translating that theory into practical applications that will help students appreciate the clear importance of understanding how countries, businesses, workers, and governments interact with each other.

The text offers in-depth analysis, empirical evidence, and practical examples arising from all the forms of international exchange, including the following:

1. international trade or the exchange of goods and services across borders;

2. international finance or the roles that currencies, exchange rates, prices, and monetary systems play in facilitating global investment and trade;
3. global migration, through which workers move from lower-wage countries to higher-wage countries;
4. the international flows of capital and knowledge through multinational enterprises and global supply chains; and
5. the global policy architecture underlying these flows.

A particular emphasis is explaining clearly how these factors and others, such as technological change, interact to change the global income distribution and expand economic inequality within some countries and reduce it in others.

The author, Professor Keith Maskus of the University of Colorado Boulder, has taught various courses in international economics, economic development and technical change, and global economic policy for over 40 years. In that time, he has taught students in the United States, Germany, Australia, Italy, China, and several other countries. He also has published over 200 articles and books on these subjects, using the tools of fundamental economic theory, statistical analysis, and policy reviews.

Further, Maskus has extensive experience in the global policy community, having spent a year as a Lead Economist at the World Bank and a year as the Chief Economist of the U.S. Department of State. Maskus also has research appointments with the Peterson Institute for International Economics, a prominent think tank in Washington DC, and other institutions.

He consults widely for such international organizations as the World Trade Organization and the World Intellectual Property Organization. All this experience has contributed to the preparation of this text, which is the culmination of his own class notes developed over many years of teaching.

Organization of the Text

The text is organized into 19 chapters, each of them a self-contained set of lecture notes, practical and illustrative examples, and study questions. Each chapter begins with an introduction that explains clearly what the subject matter is about and why it is important to study and understand. The notes also set out the logical progression of the subject matter from one chapter to the next.

Dispersed through the chapters are study questions, which can be used during class to test the understanding students are achieving. They are useful for assessing whether a particular topic has been mastered or whether it needs additional emphasis.

There are also numerical examples of key international economic concepts that students should be sure to work through. Successful completion of these examples will cement the lessons being discussed.

Chapter 1

International economics covers a wide range of topics that can be broadly categorized as follows: (1) international trade; (2) international movements of capital and labor; (3) global trade policy; (4) markets for currencies and exchange rates; and (5) monetary systems, which incorporate a choice between fixed and flexible exchange rates.

The text is organized along these lines. Chapter 1 offers a comprehensive introduction to international economics, explaining how the subject matter is organized and best studied. A major part of the chapter is devoted to understanding the massive economic globalization that took place from the 1980s until quite recently.

Globalization generates both benefits and costs, which may be distributed differently among nations, locations, and people. Thus, Chapter 1 analyzes in broad terms the sources of these benefits and costs and how they affect economic welfare and inequality.

The forces of globalization have been massively important in the world economy, generally raising incomes and productivity. However, many lower-skilled workers have suffered stagnant incomes and the chapter examines the recent political backlash against globalization in the United States and the United Kingdom. This backlash seems likely to persist for many years to come.

Chapter 2

Chapter 2 presents the basic tools of microeconomic analysis that will be used to study the theory of international trade in subsequent chapters. Using supply and demand diagrams, the chapter explains the nature of an *international trading equilibrium* between two countries involving two goods.

The primary point is that a country's exports are the difference between its production and consumption of a good at various relative prices and incomes, while its imports equal the difference between consumption and production of a second good. To understand that idea, notes and diagrams are provided on how consumers and firms reach their decisions on quantities demanded and supplied, both without trade (in "autarky") and with free trade.

Using these concepts, the notes develop the idea of an *international general equilibrium*, in which the trading pattern of both countries and both goods is in equilibrium. The chapter concludes by analyzing the concept of *balanced trade* for a country and the *gains from trade*. These are fundamental and powerful concepts that students should understand thoroughly.

Chapter 3

Chapter 3 explains the next major concept: What a country exports and what it imports depend on *comparative advantage*, the idea that each nation will produce one good relatively more cheaply (in terms of the opportunity cost of the other good) than will other countries. The theory is based on the *Ricardian* or *classical model of trade*. Stripped to its essence, the workers of each country will be relatively efficient at producing one good and inefficient at the other.

Free trade will push countries to specialize their production in the efficient good, which raises global output and consumption opportunities. Through specialization and trade, each country gains both a higher income and greater consumption than in autarky. These gains are shared equally among workers, who enjoy higher real wages in trade. The chapter also analyzes the critical role played by the international price ratio, or *terms of trade*, at which goods are exchanged in determining how much each nation gains from trade.

Chapter 4

Chapter 4 moves to the next great theory of international trade, the *Heckscher–Ohlin model*, also known as the *factor proportions model*. Countries differ widely in their endowments of capital, labor, and other productive resources. This means that, in autarky, capital and labor will be relatively cheap where they are in abundant supply but relatively expensive where they are scarce. This difference implies that, in free trade, countries will export goods that make intensive use of the abundant (cheap) factor and import goods that make intensive use of the scarce (expensive) factor.

For example, a low-wage economy like Mexico will export labor-intensive goods, such as clothing, while a capital-abundant country like the US will export capital-intensive goods, such as machinery and chemicals. This form of specialization also raises overall income in both economies.

This model is extremely important for it explains how trade affects income distribution between labor and capital. Exporters of labor-intensive goods will see the real wages of labor rise due to the extra demand from abroad. However, because they import capital-intensive goods, trade will drive down the real incomes of capital owners.

The process is reversed in capital-abundant nations. Thus, in the US and Europe, for example, a policy of open trade would reduce the real wages of lower-skilled workers while raising the real returns to capital investors, increasing economic inequality. This fundamental insight is extremely important for helping students understand why some people favor open trade and others oppose it.

Chapter 5

Rising economic inequality is a critical feature of modern economies. Chapter 5 analyzes the various sources of this trend, including empirical evidence on the extent of inequality.

The chapter begins with an extensive discussion of the complex processes of *economic globalization* and their sources. Globalization involves increasing integration of countries through liberalized trade, investment, technology flows, and labor migration.

Globalization has many effects on economic well-being and has been a source of poverty reduction in poor countries. However, it can also contribute to inequality within and across nations, which the chapter explains fully.

Inequality arises also from technological change that raises the demand for technically skilled workers in creative jobs and reduces the demand for lower-skilled workers in more routine jobs. This change also pushes higher-skilled workers to concentrate in high-technology urban areas, which increases inequality between growing cities and rural areas.

Other sources of growing inequality in the globalized world include increased offshoring of jobs, expanded market power of large corporations, tax policies that shift the burden of taxes onto labor, and inadequate educational opportunities. Chapter 5 concludes with an extensive review of empirical evidence on these various factors and a discussion of potential policy approaches to reducing inequality over time.

Chapter 6

Chapter 6 introduces recent theories of the nature of international trade. The first idea reflects the fact that goods and services are *differentiated products*, meaning that consumers see varieties of machinery, computers, cars, wine, financial services, and others as varying in quality or style. Firms compete on these variations to earn profits.

In this framework, countries engage in *intra-industry trade*, or the two-way trade in varieties of goods and services. The US both exports and imports varieties of furniture, automobiles, and intermediate inputs, as do other countries.

Here, both demand and supply factors matter for explaining trade. Specifically, firms produce varieties of goods subject to economies of scale, raising a trade-off between preferences for differentiation and the lower costs of large-scale production. The result is two-way trade that both benefits consumers and lowers production costs.

International trade also is *dynamic* in that the characteristics of goods change over time. Newly innovated products are initially exported from countries with advanced technologies but eventually become standardized and exported from labor-abundant countries with lower wages.

This *product cycle* occurs for many industries, and it is an important reason why production and technical information shift from developed countries to emerging and developing countries in a cycle of innovation and international diffusion and learning. The product cycle model is one important explanation for the tendency of real incomes to converge somewhat between rich nations and emerging countries over time.

Chapter 7

The text next moves from theories of how countries trade with each other to analyzing the policies they use to regulate such flows. It is the first of four chapters on *trade policy* or, more broadly, *commercial policy*.

Chapter 7 begins by discussing various reasons why countries choose to interfere with trade, both for economic and non-economic reasons. The chapter is primarily concerned with taxes on imports, called *tariffs*, and subsidies to exports. An important distinction is made between a small country, which must take international prices as given, and a large country, whose decisions about how much to import or export can alter world prices.

Basic theory demonstrates that a small country makes itself worse off by imposing any tax or subsidy on trade. An import tariff, for example, harms consumers more than it benefits domestic producers, even accounting for government tax revenues. The reason it may impose such a tariff is to increase domestic production of the product protected by the tariffs, an example of the *political economy of trade policy*.

However, a large country can reduce the world price of its imported good with a tariff, leading to a possible *terms-of-trade gain* that must be balanced against the efficiency costs of the tariff. But the policy makes foreign countries worse off, raising the prospect of *tariff retaliation* or a tariff war. Both countries would lose welfare from imposing an export subsidy, with a large country especially harming itself because it suffers a term-of-trade loss.

Chapter 8

Chapter 8 analyzes *import quotas*, which are limits on the amount of a good a country can import, and other forms of non-tariff barriers (NTBs) to trade. Tariffs and import quotas have similar effects on prices, output, and consumer and producer welfare. However, there are significant differences between them. One example is that quotas engineer an artificial scarcity of the import good, giving whoever imports it ownership of *quota rents* and encouraging inefficient activity by firms seeking to own such rents.

Governments may not capture quota rents as revenue. It is also possible that foreign firms could benefit from a domestic import quota if they get to keep these quota rents by raising their export prices.

Tariffs permit more flexible market responses than quotas if demand or supply shifts. Quotas also support domestic monopolies and artificially encourage imports of higher-value goods, which is distortionary. For all these reasons, international trade rules attempt to discourage the use of import quotas in favor of tariffs, which are less costly in welfare terms and generate government revenues.

Chapter 8 goes on to analyze whether it makes sense to use trade barriers to achieve non-economic goals, such as increased domestic production of a good to support national defense, or to address market externalities, such as pollution. In general, tariffs and quotas are not appropriate for these goals. The chapter concludes by explaining how tariffs on imported inputs raise the costs of final goods, with an empirical illustration from the recent US tariff imposed on imported steel, which raised the costs of automobiles.

Chapter 9

Chapter 9 offers practical information about how US trade policy works and the nature of the World Trade Organization (WTO), which is the international body governing international trade rules. The first part of the chapter overviews major US trade laws and the conditions under which they permit the country to impose or raise tariffs and other forms of trade policy.

The discussion covers tariffs for protecting national security, offering temporary "safeguards" protection to domestic industries, tariffs taken against other nations in response to "unfair practices", and anti-dumping tariffs and countervailing duties. The notes discuss the structure and operation of the WTO, starting with the logic of why such an institution is needed for regulating and encouraging global trade liberalization.

The WTO is organized around six defining principles, including consensus decision-making, rules governing government-imposed trade barriers, requirements for non-discrimination between domestic firms and foreigners, the reciprocal negotiation of market access, the importance of keeping markets open, and the need for dispute settlement procedures between nations. The WTO has been highly successful at facilitating global trade growth, but it now faces several threats to its existence and legitimacy, including conflicts between trade openness and global environmental protection. The chapter fully discusses these threats.

Chapter 10

Recent decades saw a major increase in the number and importance of preferential trade agreements (PTAs). These are agreements among two or more countries to offer each other free trade without extending those tariff cuts to other countries.

Chapter 10 provides the essential theoretical framework for understanding the impacts of PTAs. A basic observation is that PTAs are discriminatory because they only cut tariffs among member countries. This implies that they can be movements toward more open trade or toward more restricted trade.

The essential trade-off is between *trade creation (TC)*, efficiently raising trade among the PTA members, versus *trade diversion (TD)*, inefficiently reducing trade with non-members. The chapter indicates conditions under which the economic gains from TC are likely to exceed the losses from TD under various circumstances.

Chapter 10 also analyzes various dynamic impacts of PTAs, including growing foreign direct investment into the larger market size, larger economies of scale, more innovation, and greater international negotiating power for PTA members. These are the gains most countries joining PTAs hope to achieve. Finally, the chapter discusses the crucial fact that recent PTAs extend far beyond tariff reductions to agreements among members to adopt regulatory rules governing major elements of their economies, including trade in services, international investment policy, intellectual property rights, digital trade, labor rights, and environmental standards.

Chapter 11

Chapter 11 comprehensively covers theory and empirical evidence about the effects of international labor migration, a subject that rarely receives this much treatment in basic texts. International migration is a critical policy issue in today's world economy and will grow larger in importance as pressures for migration from poor countries to rich countries become stronger over time.

The chapter begins by explaining the various forms of *international factor flows*, including capital, labor, technology, and foreign aid.

Factor movements introduce the need to distinguish between a country's gross national income (GNI) and its gross domestic product (GDP), which differ due to income earned by capital and labor working abroad. GNI is what matters for economic welfare.

The notes provide a clear theoretical framework for understanding the effects of labor flows on GNI in both the origin and destination countries, including the distribution of income between capital and labor. Accounted properly, both countries see a rise in their GNI, meaning they both gain from labor migration. A key factor is the *labor remittances* sent by migrants back to their home nations.

If both nations are better off, why is migration so controversial? People believe that immigration reduces domestic wages and may require costly payments to migrants for public services.

The chapter discusses these issues in considerable detail for the United States, including empirical evidence on immigration flows, wage impacts, and the assimilation of migrants. Perhaps surprisingly, evidence suggests that low-skilled immigration into the US and EU likely raises the wages of native workers by freeing them to work in higher-wage activities.

The chapter concludes by looking at remittances data for several countries and discussing their importance. It also discusses the concepts of brain drain and brain gain among developing countries as skilled workers move to richer nations.

Chapter 12

Another major form of international factor flow is analyzed fully in Chapter 12. This is *foreign direct investment* (FDI) by *multinational enterprises* (MNEs), including *offshoring* and production within *vertical supply chains*.

The chapter opens by explaining key characteristics of FDI and MNEs, including what ownership means and how such firms are organized. A key insight is that, while MNEs invest capital abroad, their activities essentially involve the use of their proprietary technologies abroad, whether in foreign subsidiaries or firms that license the rights to use technologies and trademarks. Students should understand that *MNEs are largely vessels for diffusing technological information abroad*. MNEs often are characterized as either *horizontal* (producing similar goods and services in multiple locations) or *vertical* (producing inputs and outputs at various locations) in an integrated firm, though they are often both.

An essential question is why MNEs exist, despite the high costs of operating abroad. The main answers are found in the *Ownership-Location-Internalization* (OLI) framework, which explains why owning technological advantages encourages MNEs, where they choose to locate, and why they may produce internally through integration or externally through outsourcing.

The chapter analyzes incentives for offshoring jobs through FDI and building global supply chains. This form of FDI can raise economic inequality in both the high-wage parent country and the low-wage recipient country. The reason is that the offshored jobs are relatively low-skilled in the former and high-skilled in the latter. This explains the increasing outsourcing of medium-skilled, routine jobs from the US, the EU, and Japan.

Chapter 13

Chapter 13 introduces students to the basics of international finance: current account balances, international borrowing and lending, currencies, and exchange rates. The notes emphasize two critical issues. First, at its core, "international finance" refers to individuals, firms, banks, governments, and other agents using global asset markets to borrow and lend funds to pay for consumption and investment. Thus, international financial markets efficiently extend domestic markets, increasing opportunities for *intertemporal trade*. Countries gain considerably from such opportunities.

Second, such trades are intermediated through foreign exchange markets, in which currencies are traded. For example, a US firm needing to import a German machine must offer dollars in return for euros to make that payment. There are many complexities in such trades, which are explained in later chapters.

Here, the notes focus on various definitions of exchange rates, how they are computed, and the effects of exchange rate changes. Students should understand that an exchange rate is the price of one currency in units of another currency. For example, if the US dollar- British pound rate is 1.30\$/£, it takes \$1.30 to buy 1 pound. Thus, an *appreciating* currency goes up in price, while a *depreciating* currency goes down in price.

Chapter 14

Flexible (or "floating") exchange rates are highly variable in the short run, changing from month to month and even in a day. Chapter 14 analyzes the reasons for such variations.

The essential insight is that because investors can buy and sell short-term international financial assets in different currencies, changes in the exchange rate are an important component of the returns to portfolio investments. Most people, firms, and investors transact in the spot foreign exchange (FX) market, where currencies are traded for immediate delivery at prices called *spot exchange rates*.

The notes explain how spot rates make possible international trade in goods, services, and such assets as stocks and bonds, along with short-term borrowing. An important feature of floating currencies is that they may be traded instantaneously (through electronic means) in many financial markets. *Spatial arbitrage*, which involves traders buying currencies where they are cheap and simultaneously selling them where expensive, ensures that spot rates are identical around the world.

A second important concept is the *forward exchange rate*, which is a currency price, known today in organized forward FX markets, for delivery at a later date. Forward rates permit firms to hedge, or eliminate, the risk they would face by waiting to buy or sell currencies in the future. The existence of forward rates permits *forward arbitrage*, in which investors use the spot and forward FX markets, plus the ability to borrow or lend at known short-term interest rates, to eliminate any difference in financial returns over time across currencies.

Forward arbitrage establishes an important equilibrium condition, called *covered interest parity* (CIP), that links spot and forward rates with interest rates across countries that permit completely free international capital mobility. This condition establishes important relationships among these asset prices and explains how they vary in the short run.

It is possible also for investors to take risks by buying or selling foreign currency assets and waiting for future exchange rates to become known. Such investments will drive the forward rate to equality with the expected future spot exchange rate, plus a possible risk premium.

Again, these short-run relationships explain the high variability of exchange rates. For example, if there were an unexpected change in a country's monetary policy, raising expectations of higher interest rates in the future, both the current spot and forward exchange rates would move quickly in response.

These relationships are extremely important in international finance, for they establish a close link between monetary policy and exchange rate policy. The notes also discuss other *asset derivatives* in FX markets, including futures contracts and options.

Chapter 15

Due to their volatility, exchange rate changes are not predictable in the short run. In the long run, however, they tend to move in broadly predictable ways that depend on the economic fundamentals of countries, such as inflation and productivity.

Chapter 15 thoroughly analyzes this point. The key insight is that exchange rates must move to offset relative changes in price levels (rates of inflation) among countries and maintain approximate parity in differential costs of living. This concept is called *purchasing power parity* (PPP).

The notes explain the concepts of price levels, or the costs or purchasing a given basket of goods and services. Since these are computed in each country's currency, exchange rates convert these costs into a common currency, such as the US dollar. The result is a *relative cost of living* for a common basket, showing where standards of living are higher or lower.

The spot exchange rate is an important component of these relative costs. However, because it can change in the market, it does not provide a reliable indicator of the true differences in living costs.

Economists define the *purchasing-power-parity exchange rate* as the currency price that would make living costs the same in two countries. Since wages and the costs of land and other factors tend to be much lower in poor countries than in rich ones, it is misleading to compare living costs with the market exchange rate.

Calculations using PPP rates show that actual living standards in poor countries are considerably higher than market rates would suggest. The notes offer several examples of this phenomenon, including the famous "Big Mac Index" computed by *The Economist* magazine.

PPP exchange rates tell us how to compare true living costs, which is important. They also offer an indirect, but crucial, way of understanding how market exchange rates move over time. Specifically, even if it is absolutely cheaper to live in Mexico than in the US for many structural reasons, it is likely that the market exchange rate over time will move to keep this difference the same.

If, for example, Mexico experienced higher price inflation over five years than the US, that would reduce the demand for Mexican goods and services compared to American ones. Over time, this process would depreciate the peso and appreciate the dollar to restore the relative balance in living costs. Thus, PPP theory tells us that in the long run, the exchange rate will move to offset differences in inflation rates, a fundamental economic factor. Also important are changes in productivity levels.

The chapter goes on to relate this insight to monetary policy and aggregate supply policy in each country. Briefly, the country with faster monetary growth will, other things equal, experience higher inflation and a depreciating currency. An example is provided in terms of "quantitative easing", the large monetary expansions undertaken by central banks in major economies during the financial crisis of 2008–2010.

Chapter 16

Chapter 16 introduces the macroeconomic side of international finance, studying how national income accounts are computed in an open economy that trades financial assets. The basic ideas of GDP and GNI are adjusted for the *trade balance*, the *current account*, and the *financial account*.

The current account (CA) balance, which includes trade in goods, services, incomes earned and payments made for the use of foreign capital and labor, and unilateral international grants and gifts, is the best measure of a country's net income from the international economy. The financial account (FA) includes all purchases and sales of domestically owned and foreign-owned assets, such as bank deposits, stocks, bonds, real estate, and production facilities. It is a comprehensive measure of net international asset trade, equivalent to net international borrowing or lending.

The notes show how the CA and the FA are closely linked. If a country has a CA deficit, it must borrow from abroad to pay for those net income payments, which means selling more assets to foreigners on net. This generates an FA surplus and reduces the country's net wealth. If a country has a CA surplus, it has excess funds to lend abroad, meaning purchasing more assets from foreigners on net. This is consistent with an FA deficit and a higher net wealth.

Importantly, the current account balance also must equal an economy's net domestic savings or total savings minus total investment. An economy with savings below investment spending will have a CA deficit and therefore must borrow from abroad to finance the excess investment.

The chapter also discusses the *balance of payments* (BOP), which is the statistical record of the flow of inward receipts and outward payments of a country with the rest of the world in a year, accounting for both income-based transactions and asset trades. There is an important difference between the "accounting BOP" and the "economic BOP". The former must, by definition, be zero because double-entry bookkeeping requires the total of all receipts to equal the total of all payments (or credits equal debits).

But it is possible to account only for those international transactions people and firms choose to make, ignoring the offsetting bookkeeping entry. Doing so generates the economic BOP.

The economic BOP is critical because it determines the net demand for foreign currencies and the domestic currency. In turn, a BOP deficit is likely to depreciate the home currency and a surplus would appreciate it.

However, if the exchange rate were fixed by policy, the central bank would have to buy and sell foreign currency reserves to avoid a change in the exchange rate. Since such transactions by central banks directly change the economy's money supply, it follows that exchange rate policy and monetary policy are directly related to each other under fixed rates. Chapter 16 fully explores the logic of these relationships, offering practical examples.

Chapter 17

Chapter 17 explores these insights in more detail by thoroughly analyzing differences between fixed and flexible exchange rates. The notes begin by showing that developed countries adopt flexible rates, while most developing countries opt for fixed rates, with their currencies tied to the dollar, euro, or other *anchor currencies*. The notes explain why these choices are made, relating to trade and investment patterns, concerns about economic stability, and the degree of capital mobility.

To illustrate the workings of fixed exchange rates, the notes discuss the gold standard, which operated in the late 19th and early 20th centuries. Under the gold standard, countries must exchange gold for the domestic currency at given rates. This directly ties an economy's money supply to the balance of payments.

Countries with BOP deficits, say due to high inflation, would lose gold reserves as they bought domestic currency with gold. In turn, this would reduce the money supply and spending, bringing down inflation in an automatic balancing mechanism.

However, this system collapsed in the 1930s and was replaced after World War II by a fixed-rate system organized around the US dollar. This system failed in the 1970s, leading to the current mixture of flexible and fixed exchange rates.

Chapter 18

An important feature of the modern global economy is that there are increasing numbers of macroeconomic crises in developing and emerging countries, often triggered by the collapse of a country's currency under a fixed exchange rate. Chapter 18 discusses how such crises emerge and what their macroeconomic roots are. It is somewhat more technically advanced than the other chapters in the text.

The notes begin by explaining how central banks (CBs) intervene in FX markets to fix an exchange rate. For example, to fix the Argentine peso to the US dollar, the Argentine CB must agree to exchange dollar-based assets for peso-based assets (including currency) at the fixed rate.

This means the CB's stock of foreign (dollar) reserves can fall quickly if people and investors lose confidence in the peso and don't want to hold them. This could happen in a highly inflationary environment, which itself could be caused by excessive government fiscal deficits financed by the CB purchasing government debt.

Such a system could collapse as foreign reserves are lost, forcing the government to depreciate the currency. In the short term, such crises can significantly cut GDP and employment.

Exchange rate crises also may be the result of changes in the world economy. For example, if the interest rates on dollar assets were to rise, it would be more difficult for Argentine investors to meet payment obligations, leading to government defaults and a collapse in the currency value.

Chapter 19

The final chapter discusses an item of interest to students of international relations and economics: the organization and functioning of the euro system. The euro is a common currency shared by several nations in the European Union. The system therefore sets a rigidly fixed exchange rate among those countries, which eliminates exchange rate risk and raises trade and investment among them.

Countries in the system are supposed to meet macroeconomic targets for low government debt, low inflation, and other factors. Often, they do not meet these goals.

While the euro system ordinarily offers economic stability in the region, under some macroeconomic circumstances, it can raise costs and come under pressure. For example, during the financial crisis that began in 2008, countries with higher indebtedness, such as Greece, Portugal, and Italy, suffered higher unemployment, which could not be relieved by a depreciation of a national currency. This uncertainty caused capital to flow out of these stressed nations, an additional problem. Restoration of normal economic conditions remains elusive, many years later.

The notes explain that the structure of the euro system is considerably flawed and needs major reforms in monetary regulation, financial markets, and national fiscal policies. Such reforms are under discussion now.

About the Author

Keith E Maskus is Professor Emeritus of Economics at the University of Colorado, Boulder. He was Chief Economist of the US State Department from 2016 to 2017 and a Lead Economist at the World Bank from 2001 to 2002. He is a Research Fellow at the Peterson Institute for International Economics and a consultant for international organizations. Maskus has written extensively about various aspects of intellectual property rights, international trade and investment, and technology. His most recent book is *Private Rights and Public Problems: The Global Economics of Intellectual Property in the 21st Century*.

Contents

Chapter 1

Introduction to International Economics

Objectives of the Text

Students will learn an analytical framework for analyzing the basics of international trade and financial linkages among countries, involving cooperation and competition, global markets, and the resulting gains and losses from global engagement.

Students will gain a better appreciation of complicated economic interrelationships among countries. Following are some examples:

- China's entry into world trade in the 1990s and its entry into the World Trade Organization (WTO) in 2001 had large impacts on labor markets in the United States and Europe. How can that be explained?
- Do international trade and foreign direct investment (FDI) harm or benefit the global environment? On what factors does that depend?
- What determines why firms become multinational enterprises? What are their real functions?
- Why do several countries in the European Union share a currency, the euro? What opportunities and problems does that raise?
- Where do foreign exchange crises come from? How costly are they?

Students will become better informed about the world economy and international relations and get used to thinking about facts and evidence.

Why We Study International Economics

Introduction to international economics

The subject of international trade essentially studies the movement of goods and factors, such as capital and labor, from where they are in excess supply to where they are in excess demand.

Trade can be thought of as microeconomics (supply and demand) extended across borders. This book also studies the policies that encourage or deter such movements.

The subject of international finance essentially analyzes how national economies interact at the aggregate level. International finance can be thought of as macroeconomics (inflation, GDP, interest rates, and so on) extended across borders.

The text considers how goods and assets are traded in the aggregate, determining various international macroeconomic balances, such as the current account balance. It also analyzes factors that determine exchange rates, which are the prices of national currencies, and why these prices are so important. Also analyzed is how economic and financial conditions in one country may affect other nations.

Why is international economics a separate field of study?

1. The natural mobility of goods and especially factors is generally more limited across national borders than within countries.

   - There are costs of trading goods and services.
   - Family ties and customs make people less willing to move internationally.
   - There are costs of migration and investing capital abroad.

     Observation: The mobility of capital and technology is very high now. Labor (migration) is far less mobile internationally.

2. National governments use policies to regulate cross-border trade in goods, services, and factors. What kinds of policies?

   - border taxes (tariffs) and quotas on trade;
   - domestic regulations that might restrict trade and FDI, such as product-safety rules, patent laws, antitrust regulation, state-owned enterprises, corporate taxation, poor infrastructure, corruption, and many others;
   - limits on labor immigration;
   - controls on the inward and outward flows of financial capital.

     Observation: We think (or hope) such policies and regulations are in the national interest, but they may be harmful. And they have complex effects we want to study.

3. The existence of national currencies and exchange rates deeply affects international trade and financial flows.
4. Welfare calculations are different comparing national versus international interests.

   - Should policymakers worry about how the country's trade restrictions affect the welfare of trade partners?
   - Should national policymakers care about how the country's regulatory policies, such as environmental protection and capital requirements in banking, change conditions abroad? Should other governments respond?
   - Should a large nation such as the US conduct its own monetary and fiscal policy without thinking about how it will affect macroeconomics in other regions?

Primary questions addressed in international trade

1. What factors explain the patterns and volumes of a country's international trade?
2. What are the gains from trade (GFT)? Can countries be made worse off by engaging in trade?
3. How are the GFT distributed among countries? How about within countries between capital and labor?

4. Does open trade make things better or worse when there are weak domestic regulations?
5. What are the effects of trade barriers on different people, such as consumers and producers, or skilled and unskilled workers?
6. Why do trade restrictions exist and what explains which industries are protected?
7. What are the institutions of the global trading system, such as the WTO and preferential trade agreements?
8. What explains factor movements, including labor, portfolio capital, FDI, and technology, and what are their effects?

Primary questions studied in international finance

1. What determines a country's balance of payments and balance of trade? How do we analyze national income accounts in the open economy?
2. How do foreign exchange markets work?
3. What are the costs and benefits of fixed versus flexible exchange rate systems?
4. What causes movements in exchange rates?
5. Why are there exchange rate and banking crises?
6. What are the effects of exchange rates on trade, income, inflation, and employment? And vice versa?
7. How do countries undertake macroeconomic policy when they know their economies are interrelated?

Globalization: Sources, Channels, and Effects

Motivation: History in the making

The era since the 1980s is generally considered the greatest expansion of economic globalization in history. What are the most significant policy changes in the global economy since 1990?

- the establishment of the WTO (formerly the General Agreement on Tariffs and Trade or GATT) in 1995 and the North American Free Trade Agreement (NAFTA) in 1994;

- the adoption of the euro as a common currency in 1999–2002;
- China joining the WTO in 2001;
- the global great recession of 2008–2014;
- the COVID-19 pandemic that began in 2019;
- the emergence of nationalism and a major pushback against globalization, beginning in the 2010s.

Globalization: Basic comments

What is "globalization"?

Economics definition: Globalization is the continuing integration of markets across borders through reductions in the costs of trading and investing.

What are the major sources of globalizing markets?

- reductions in trade and investment barriers since 1945, including from international trade agreements, such as the GATT and WTO; free trade agreements; international investment treaties; and decisions by emerging economies, to open their national financial markets;
- reductions in transportation and trade costs, from the development of containerization in shipping and the falling costs of air transport;
- massive improvements in information and communication technologies (ICT) associated with software, semiconductors, and computing power.

What are the primary channels of globalization?

- international trade in goods and services;
- FDI by multinational firms as a conduit for technology and capital;
- offshoring of jobs and the fragmentation of production stages into global supply chains;
- massive international financial capital flows;

- labor migration and mobility, especially temporary movements of skilled labor;
- trade in technologies, which diffuses knowledge from R&D and innovation to locations abroad.

Study question 1

Which of the following is not a major source of globalization?

A. Declining barriers to international trade and investment.
B. Rapidly falling costs of engaging in international trade.
C. Reductions in barriers to immigration of low-skilled workers.
D. Improvements in ICT.

Discussion of study question 1

The answer is C. As discussed in these notes, there has been very little relaxation of restrictions against international migration of low-skilled workers. A, B, and D all refer to extremely important factors in globalization.

Globalization data trends: International trade in merchandise

According to the United Nations, in 2021, the global value of world trade in goods reached $28.5 trillion, while trade in services amounted to around $6 trillion.

Growth in the world volume of exports, with 1990 as the base year, is depicted in Figure 1.1. These figures are adjusted for price inflation and the effects of exchange rates, and therefore measure growth in the real quantity of exports.

Between 1990 and 2015, the real volume of world merchandise exports grew by around 350%. By 2021, it had quadrupled. This growth in trade has been considerably more rapid than the increase in real output (GDP). Data from the International Monetary Fund indicate that from 1980 to 2016 global international trade rose by a factor of seven, while world GDP rose by a factor of 3.8.

In recent years, trade in services has expanded faster than GDP as well. These facts demonstrate the increasing reliance of nations on international trade, an outcome of globalization.

Globalization data trends: Trade

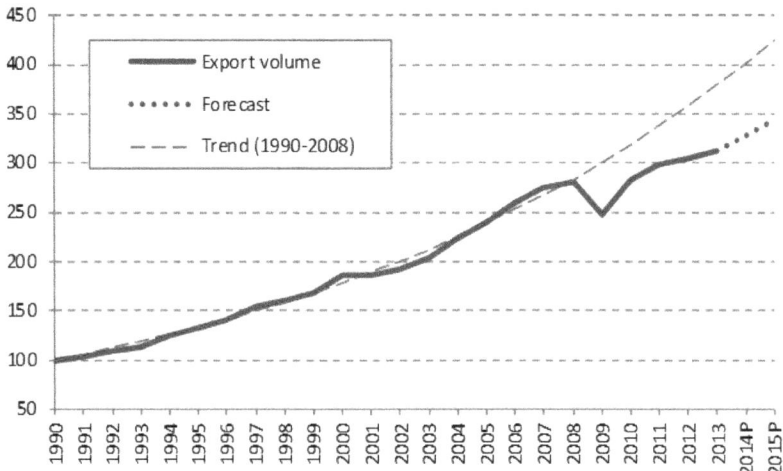

Figure 1.1   World trade volume has nearly quadrupled since 1990.

Source: World Trade Organization, https://www.wto.org/english/news_e/pres14_e/pr721_e.htm.

Globalization data trends: FDI

Table 1.1 shows that the massive increase in the importance of FDI in GDP has been widespread among countries. Since 1990, FDI has grown much faster than GDP and even faster than international trade. Currently, global affiliate sales are estimated to be twice the amount of global merchandise trade. Global affiliate sales (pre-COVID) were around $48 trillion, which may be compared to the estimated world GDP of $88 trillion.

Note in Table 1.1 the extreme integration of the NAFTA countries through FDI. To a great degree, this reflects the development of cross-border supply chains in automobiles. This is a top example of a major reason for the growth in FDI: the huge increase in international production networks.

Table 1.1   Measures of globalization for individual countries.

Country	Total Merchandise Trade (% of GDP)		FDI Stocks Inward (% of GDP)		FDI Stocks Outward (% of GDP)	
	1990	2017	1990	2017	1990	2017
USA	20	28	9.0	40	12	40
Canada	50	64	19	66	14	42
Mexico	38	78	7.6	42	0.9	16
UK	47	62	19	60	21	58
Germany	46	87	13	25	17	44
Australia	32	42	25	47	12	32
Japan	20	31	0.3	4.3	6.4	31
Korea, Rep.	51	81	1.9	15	0.8	23
Singapore	344	322	78	414	20	271
China	24	38	5.2	12	1.1	12
India	16	41	0.5	15	0	6
Brazil	15	24	9.1	38	10	17
Ghana	43	91	3.2	71	0.0	0.8
World	39	56	10	39	10	39

Sources: World Bank, *World Development Indicators* and UN Conference on Trade and Development, *World Investment Report*.

Globalization data trends: International labor migration

Generally, labor flows are far less globalized than capital and trade. But we have seen notable increases in certain measures since 1990, as shown in Table 1.2. For example, the proportion of foreign-born people in Canada's population rose from 15.6% to 20.5%.

Study question 2

Major channels of globalization include the following:

A. Trade in high-technology goods and services.
B. FDI.
C. Migration of skilled labor.
D. Technology licensing.
E. All the above.

Table 1.2   Foreign-born people as a percentage of local population.

Country	1990	2000	2010	2015
USA	7.9	10.7	12.9	13.5
Canada	15.6	17.7	19.9	20.5
Australia	22.8	23.0	26.7	28.2
UK	8.8	10.2	11.2	13.0
Italy	2.5	3.7	9.7	9.7
Mexico	0.4	0.5	0.8	0.8
Japan	0.9	1.3	1.7	1.6
World	2.9	2.8	3.2	3.3

Source: Compiled by author from World Bank, *World Development Indicators*.

Discussion of study question 2

The answer is E. All the factors listed in A through D have contributed significantly as vessels through which globalization occurs.

A brief history of economic globalization

Economists often write about three "waves" of globalization, with an interruption. Roughly, they are as follows:

- **Wave 1:** 1850–1910 was the era of industrialization and mass labor and capital migration to the "New World".
- **Retreat:** 1910–1945 saw a major retreat associated mostly with wars and the Great Depression.
- **Wave 2:** 1945–1980 trade and FDI grew rapidly among developed countries, mainly due to tariff cuts.
- **Wave 3:** 1980-now global economic integration massively increased with more emerging countries linked to global financial markets and complex regional production networks.

Some of these changes are illustrated in the following charts and tables:

Figure 1.2 depicts measures of globalization from 1870 to 2000. The ratio of the foreign capital stock to GDP rose dramatically in

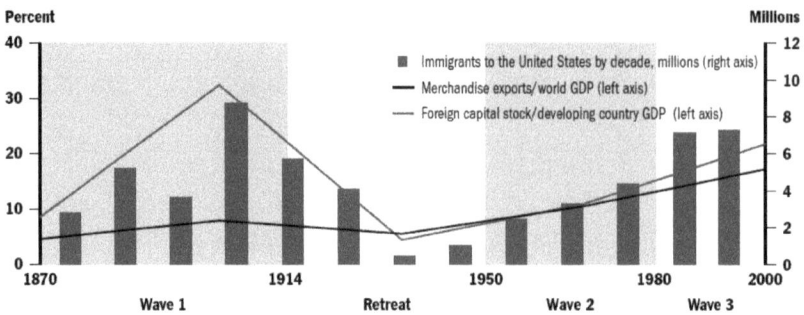

Source: Foreign capital stock/developing country GDP: Maddison (2001), table 3.3; Merchandise exports/world GDP: Maddison (2001), table F-5; Migration: Immigration and Naturalization Service (1998).

Figure 1.2   Globalization waves in history.
Source: World Bank, 2002 Globalization, Growth and Poverty: Building an Inclusive World Economy ©World Bank, http://hdl.handle.net/10986/14051 License: Creative Commons Attribution license (CC BY 3.0 IGO).

the late 1800s before retreating and then rose steadily after 1950. Immigration followed a similar pattern.

Table 1.3 shows the high levels of US immigration from 1880 to 1919, followed by a large decline and then much higher figures in the 1990s and 2000s.

Figure 1.3 shows estimates of total trade divided by GDP for the world, 1500–2011, taken from various sources. Note that globalization through trade is a rather recent phenomenon in world history. Nearly all the increase in this ratio occurred after the late 1800s and especially after the 1930s.

What explains these waves of globalization?

Hint 1: There were no major periods of globalization before about 1850.
Hint 2: Globalization involves expanding foreign trade, meaning that goods must be produced in different places from where they are consumed.

Answers:

• Massive technological changes that made it efficient to produce goods at high volumes in specific places and ship them to others.

Table 1.3 Persons gaining US permanent residence, in millions.

	1870–1879	1880–1889	1890–1899	1900–1909	1910–1919	1920–1929	1930–1939	1940–1949	1950–1959	1960–1969	1970–1979	1980–1989	1990–1999	2000–2009
Permanent residents	2.74	5.25	3.69	8.20	6.35	4.30	0.70	0.86	2.50	3.21	4.25	6.24	9.78	9.24

Source: Compiled by the author using data from US Department of Homeland Security.

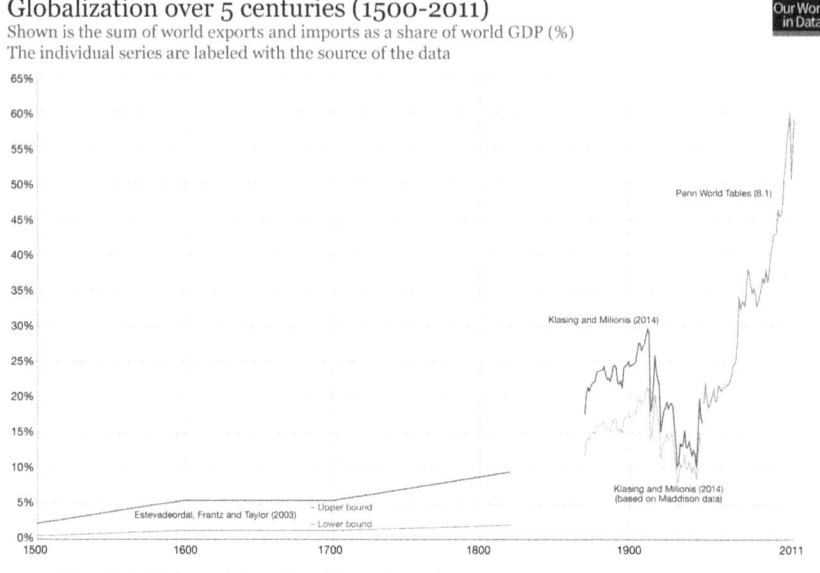

Globalization over 5 centuries (1500-2011)

Shown is the sum of world exports and imports as a share of world GDP (%)
The individual series are labeled with the source of the data

Figure 1.3   Globalization trends since 1500.

Source: Our World in Data, https://ourworldindata.org/grapher/globalization-over-5-centuries?country= OWID_WRL.

- Dramatically reduced costs of transporting goods, due to lower tariffs and better shipping infrastructure.
- With respect to growing FDI, there were much lower costs of managing production across borders and lower investment barriers. These lower costs came mainly from great improvements in information and communication technologies (ICT).

What happened may be described as two great technological "unbundlings" and one long period of cuts in trade and investment barriers. (The concept of unbundling is discussed further in R Baldwin, *The Great Convergence*, 2016.)

The first great unbundling

Prior to around 1850, production could not be very distant from consumption due to high transportation costs and the absence of automated production under economies of scale. The first great unbundling came in roughly around 1850–1920. There were rapid cuts in trade and transportation costs, which meant that production could be concentrated in particular locations (factories) and shipped around the world. What cuts?

- introduction of steamships and centralized ports;
- expanded and standardized railroads;
- improved highway systems;
- containerization of shipping (after 1950);
- improved air freight (after 1970).

Also important was that production concentrated in large factories permitted efficient production due to scale economies, lowering costs and prices. As noted above, there followed a retreat from globalization, roughly from 1915 to 1945. There were two world wars and the Great Depression. Tariffs were raised and countries erected severe limits on immigration.

Market opening and the second great unbundling

After World War II, there was an extended period in which the more developed economies and many major emerging economies systematically opened their markets to more trade and FDI. This was roughly from 1945 to 2018.

There were major tariff cuts and other policy liberalizations through the GATT and WTO. There was also a proliferation of preferential trade agreements like NAFTA and the European Community. From the 1970s through the 2000s, the so-called "Washington Consensus" raised pressures on developing and emerging countries to reform and open their economies. Another important factor was the increasing integration of China and India with the global economy. The second great unbundling can be dated roughly from 1980 to now. It featured two primary characteristics:

1. the ongoing revolution in software, information, and communication technologies;

2. the development of large global production networks through vertical supply chains, often associated with the "offshoring" of jobs from high-wage countries to low-wage countries.

Primary economic gains from globalization

If globalization is the integration of markets, it must change the prices of goods, services, and factors (wages, capital, and land). When prices change permanently, there will be gainers and losers, as later notes discuss.

What are the typical gains from greater trade and investment? Economists identify these major impacts that raise overall incomes:

- Trade encourages specialization, which efficiently allocates resources, raises productivity, and raises aggregate incomes and living standards.
- Imports offer consumers a greater variety of goods at lower prices.
- Open markets give domestic firms more access to global technologies, which improves productivity.
- Trade establishes larger market sizes and opportunities for exporters. Here are two examples:

1. Vietnamese farmers gained higher incomes when the country ended its rice export ban in 2001. The expanded exports raised the price of rice, generating higher rural incomes.
2. Bangladesh garment factories expanded output considerably after trade agreements with the EU, which raised employment rates and wages for female workers.

These and other gains from globalization will be studied in later chapters. But for now, look at what the last 30+ years of globalization have achieved, and at what cost.

Wider social gains from globalization

There were large real-income gains in those emerging and developing economies (EDEs) that reduced barriers to trade and investment, improving living standards and reducing poverty. For example, World Bank data show that the percentage of people living in extreme poverty, defined as $1.90 per day in 2011 prices, declined greatly from 39.6% in 1984 to 8.7% in 2018. Rising real incomes also have improved educational achievement. In the case of Vietnam, primary school enrollment rates increased considerably after liberalization of the rice export ban because children were needed less on the farm. There have been related gains in health status, with countries registering longer life expectancies, lower child mortality, and reduced disease burdens.

It is evident that a significant portion of these gains may be attributed to the impacts of globalization because those EDEs who were "globalizers" (such as China, Malaysia, Thailand, South Korea, and Indonesia) experienced them far more than countries that did not liberalize trade barriers as much.

But here are two important qualifications:

- First, countries where economic growth and social gains have been the greatest generally have paired tariff cuts with other important policies and conditions, such as investments in education, high savings rates, lower corruption, and economic mobility. It is a mistake to attribute a large share of these income gains to trade opening.
- Second, these aggregate gains in income were often accompanied by higher wage and wealth inequality.

The international economic transition

An important source of these income gains associated in part with trade liberalization is the rapid shift of manufacturing and employment from developed economies to major EDEs as the latter became more globalized.

This change was accompanied by a large shift in the share of global GDP production from the G7 countries (the largest seven developed economies) to major "globalizers" among the EDEs. As shown in Figure 1.4, the G7 share of global GDP fell from 67% in 1993 to under 50% in 2012. This shift was due to much faster economic growth rates in the EDEs than in rich countries.

The second panel in Figure 1.4 indicates that there was a similar shift in the share of manufacturing output over the period. Much of this was associated with the offshoring of production and employment by multinational enterprises, which is discussed further in Chapter 12.

Thus, the globalization era is sharply characterized by a transition of GDP and manufacturing from the rich countries to the liberalizing EDEs, raising incomes in the latter. However, this shift suggests that workers in developed economies whose jobs were transferred abroad have suffered costs, as discussed next.

How did this happen?

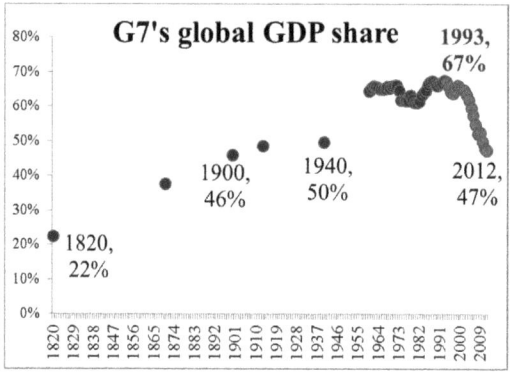 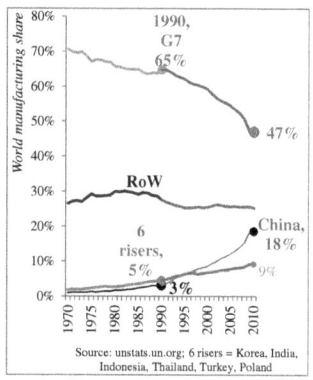

Figure 1.4   The major shifts in the distribution of global income and manufacturing production shares from the G7 (industrialized) countries to the "Globalizing Risers" (RoW refers to the "rest of the world").

Source: Richard Baldwin and Javier Lopez-Gonzalez, National Bureau of Economic Research working paper w18957, 2013.

Primary economic costs of globalization

These impacts will be covered in detail in later chapters. At this point, consider three major costs.

Income redistribution and growing inequality

In rich countries, more open trade and investment markets tend to increase the incomes of higher-skilled workers and capital owners, while reducing the real incomes of lower-skilled workers. The process is that as those economies have rapidly increased their imports of labor-intensive goods from China and other emerging countries, the prices of such imports have been driven down. This has reduced the demand for low-skilled workers in rich countries because they produce similar goods that must compete with imports. As a result, their real wages and incomes have stagnated as jobs have disappeared during the globalization era.

This impact is illustrated in Figure 1.5. It shows what happened to the real incomes of people around the world at different percentiles of the world income distribution from 1980 to 2016. Specifically,

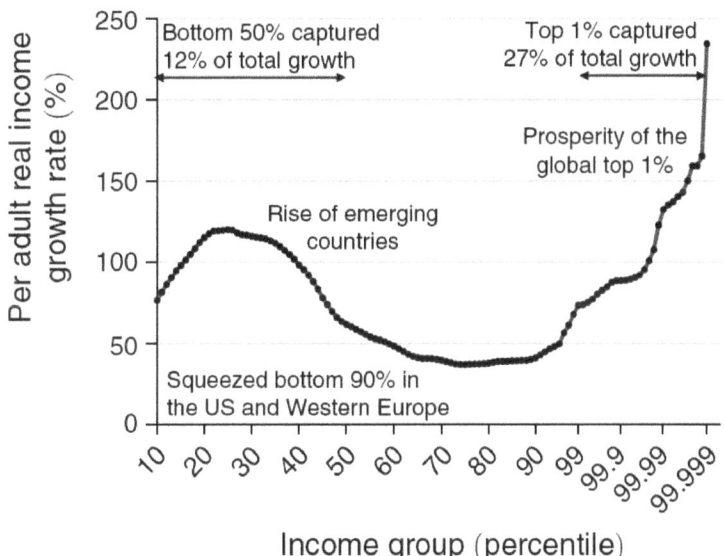

Figure 1.5   Total income growth by percentile of world income distribution, 1980–2016.

Source: Reproduced with permission from Alvaredo *et al.*, The elephant curve of global inequality and growth, *American Economic Association, Papers and Proceedings*, May 2018. Copyright American Economic Association.

workers are arrayed along the horizontal axis by where they ranked in the global income distribution in 1980, based on surveys of income and tax reports around the world. The vertical distance to the curved line shows how much those workers gained in real income over the period.

The figure shows that the main net beneficiaries from this globalization era have been workers in the emerging economies, who saw large increases in real income (those from about the 10th to the 40th percentile). These gains came in China, India, South Korea, Malaysia, Mexico, and other "globalizers".

A group of massive beneficiaries is the "global elite" at the top of the income scale, which shows that the top 1% of income earners gained 27% of global income. These are corporate CEOs, top software developers, financiers, lawyers, and other professionals with considerable technical and managerial skills.

In contrast, low-income and middle-income workers in developed countries were squeezed by these extreme changes in incomes and saw relatively little income growth themselves. These are lower-skilled manufacturing workers and service workers with routine jobs that could be readily offshored.

Figure 1.5 consists of a large "hill" on the left, capturing workers in the emerging economies, followed by a "valley" in the middle, capturing lower-wage and middle-income workers in developed economies, and then a sharp increase upward. The chart is sometimes called the "elephant curve", for its resemblance to an elephant with a raised trunk on the right.

There are additional reasons why globalization and other factors have tended to raise economic inequality:

- Since capital is highly mobile, it can move to where taxes are lower. This has generated lower global capital taxation as countries compete to attract capital. But in turn, countries have raised taxes on labor, which is not as mobile internationally.
- Globalization favors the most efficient (often the biggest) manufacturing and service firms and their locations, which can generate more market power and higher prices.

- As developed economies have shifted more into producing services and away from manufacturing, the importance of labor unions has considerably declined.
- Globalization tends to concentrate economic activity on high-wage services in urban areas with high-skill endowments but to reduce such activity in rural areas. Greater rural–urban inequality results.
- All this combines with skill-biased technical change (SBTC) to raise inequality. SBTC refers to the fact that in recent decades, technological improvements have increased the demand for highly skilled workers but reduced the demand for poorly skilled workers. A clear example is *automation* or the replacement of workers with industrial robots and smart machines.

The global nature of the reduction in labor income as shares of GDP is shown in Figure 1.6.

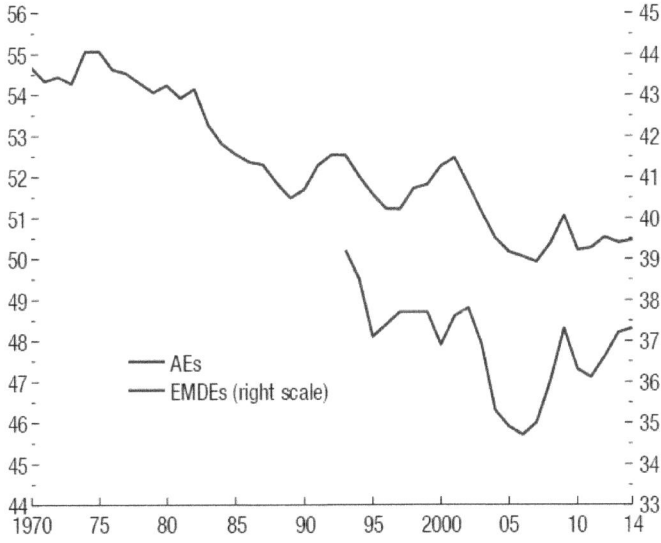

Figure 1.6   The share of GDP paid to labor has fallen in both advanced economies (AEs) and emerging and developing economies (EMDEs).

Source: Reproduced with permission from Dao *et al.*, *Why Is Labor Receiving a Smaller Share of Global Income?* IMF Working Paper 17/169, Washington DC: International Monetary Fund.

Additional economic problems

Exposure to financial crises: Financial liberalization brings significant benefits from more access to capital in developing countries, leading to faster growth. But there are also potential costs:

- In countries with high risks of corruption and expropriation, the capital flows to well-connected interests rather than productive investments.
- Financial liberalization can generate outflows (capital flight) from risky countries.
- High inward capital flows (building up debt in foreign currencies) can be destabilizing when a crisis occurs, leading to high defaults. Taxpayers are often left with the bills to pay.
- High public and private debt in a financial crisis in a country with a fixed exchange rate can reduce employment and real wages.

Some other problems from globalization

- The expansion of trade (which implies growth in production also) has put stresses on resource use and the environment, especially where environmental regulation is weak.
- Economic and social globalization can dilute local cultural preferences, perhaps causing the disappearance of local customs and languages.
- Competition among countries to attract FDI can pressure governments to relax their regulatory policies in ways that may be controversial. This process is called a "race to the bottom", which can happen, though it depends on circumstances.
- More open trade and transportation can transmit domestic problems abroad through travel and trade. Examples include pandemics, plant and animal diseases, financial crises, and others.

Architectural problems in the global trading system

The modern system that attempts to facilitate international trade and investment is highly complex. As discussed in Chapter 9, the WTO establishes rules among countries about cutting tariffs and settling trade disputes, as do numerous "mega" preferential trade agreements, such as NAFTA, the EU, the EU-Canada agreement, and others. These rules and agreements currently go well beyond tariff cuts to rules on "behind the border" regulations. Following are a few major examples:

- Countries must be non-discriminatory in their regulatory treatment and taxes.
- Technical and safety standards of products and inputs cannot be a barrier to trade.
- The use of subsidies and other industrial policies may be limited if they interfere with trade and investment.
- Countries must protect foreign-owned intellectual property rights.
- Many trade agreements feature investor protection rights, which give firms the right to sue governments for regulatory actions. Lawsuits are heard in international tribunals, not domestic courts.

Such rules encourage trade and FDI but are often seen as restricting the ability of national governments to exercise their own policy choices.

The Emerging Backlash against Globalization

Globalization reversal?

These various problems have raised increasing opposition to the globalized system, posing an important question: Can the recent long-term wave of globalization be reversed? Such a reversal happened before in the 1920s and 1930s when tariffs were raised and immigration was slashed among the major economies of the time.

It was hoped that such policies would offset the significant unemployment and deflationary pressures in the Great Depression. If anything, the higher tariffs made the economic situation worse by reducing growth and prolonging the depression.

While time will tell, it does seem that a backlash against globalization is underway in the 2020s, associated with the rise of economic populism and nationalism, which in part have emerged from the job and income losses noted above. Prominent examples include the following:

- the 2016 Brexit vote in the UK, which caused the UK to leave the European Union in 2021;
- the 2016 election of Donald Trump to the US Presidency on his campaign promises to raise tariffs and reduce immigration;
- the fact that many countries raised trade barriers after the Great Recession of 2008, and again during the COVID-19 pandemic (*Source*: https://www.globaltradealert.org/reports/21);
- the growth in political support for populist parties around the world (Figure 1.7).

Measuring the political backlash

In the United States, it is commonly thought that many Americans have become weary of globalization, worried about the job losses from imports and automation, and concerned about the potential impacts of immigration.

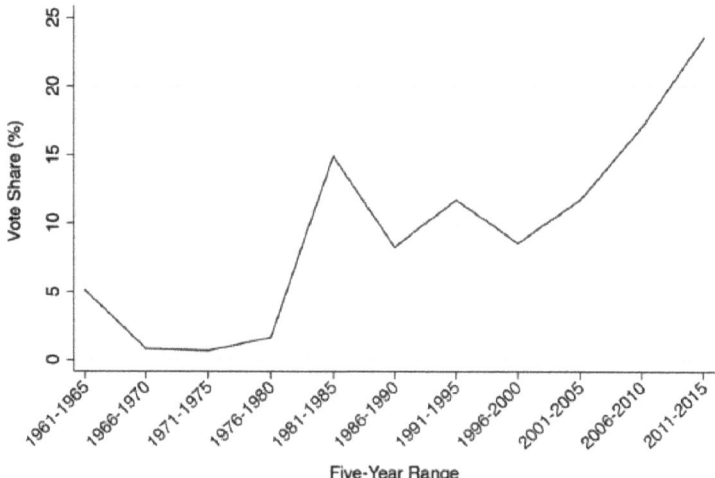

Figure 1.7   Growth in support for populist political parties around the world.

Source: Reproduced with Permission from Dani Rodrik, *Populism and the Economics of Globalization*, National Bureau of Economic Research Working Paper 23559, July 2017.

But in fact, going into the 2016 Presidential election, 72% of Americans saw trade as a positive opportunity, reflecting a significant increase after 2012. This positive attitude peaked in 2020 at 79% before declining sharply by 2021 during the Trump Administration. Despite this fall, the majority attitude remains pro-trade. (Data are from https://news.gallup.com/poll/342419/sharply-fewer-view-foreign-trade-opportunity.aspx.)

It is also interesting that by 2019, a majority of Americans (62%) had a positive view of legal immigration as a benefit to the economy, as shown in the Pew Foundation research poll results (Figure 1.8). The bottom curve on the left side shows that this difference closely tracks the opinions of Democrats (largely pro-immigration) and Republicans (largely anti-immigration).

It is remarkable that there is such a striking age-related difference in opinions toward immigration, as noted in the right panel. Older Americans generally have more negative views and younger Americans have more positive views.

Reconciling these findings

These results suggest that, at least in the United States, there is strong majority support for trade and immigration. Yet, in 2016,

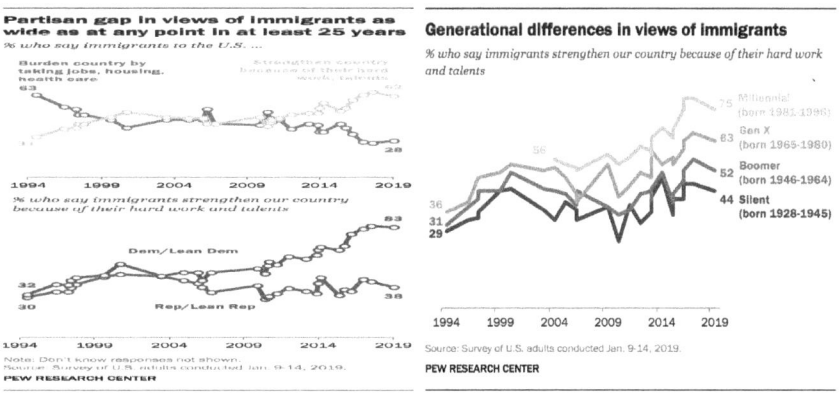

Figure 1.8   US attitudes toward immigration.

Source: https://www.pewresearch.org/fact-tank/2019/01/31/majority-of-americans-continue-to-say-immigrants-strengthen-the-u-s/.

voters there elected a President who ran on a campaign to restrict imports and reduce immigration. What might explain these outcomes?

Figure 1.9, again from the Pew Foundation, indicates that, when asked a broad question, there is clear support for open trade in principle ("trade is good") among countries at all levels of income.

But fewer than half the respondents believe that "trade creates jobs", "trade raises wages", or "trade reduces prices". These are among the primary GFT discussed by economists.

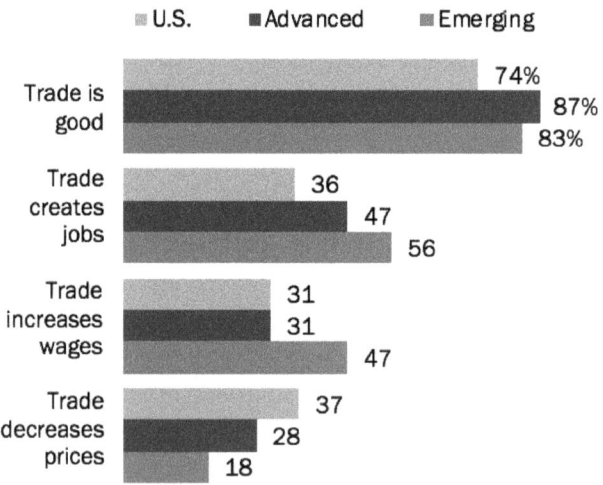

International publics back trade in principle, but many question its benefits

Note: Medians by country economic categorization. Advanced median excludes U.S.
Source: Spring 2018 Global Attitudes Survey. Q25–Q28.

PEW RESEARCH CENTER

Figure 1.9   Global attitudes and understanding of trade.

Source: Pew Research Center, https://www.pewresearch.org/global/2018/09/26/americans-like-many-in-other-advanced-economies-not-convinced-of-trades-benefits/.

Perhaps, this means that people favor trade in the abstract but may not fully understand its benefits or that the public is more aware of the costs of trade than of its benefits. If so, it would raise political susceptibility to vote for candidates and policies opposed to globalization, including trade and immigration.

Backlash episode one: The Brexit vote

The word "Brexit" refers to the vote, by a narrow majority, in 2016, in the UK, to leave membership in the European Union and to the country's ultimate departure from the EU in 2021 after long negotiations. Brexit is revealing for many reasons but here are a few notes of interest.

First, there was a dramatic split in voting for Brexit by age group. 73% of voters aged 18–24 preferred to remain in the EU, as did 62% of those aged 25–34. However, close to 60% of those over age 45 voted to leave the EU. This reflected the facts that older citizens work (or worked) in more traditional sectors that have been pressured by competition within the EU and were more skeptical about the benefits of free labor circulation in the region. Younger voters saw their futures in advanced UK-based service and financial industries, which thrived in the EU, and were more open to immigration.

It is important to note that there was a lower turnout by younger people and a higher turnout by older people. Had more younger voters participated, the result could have been to remain in the EU.

Second, voters were also solidly split by geography within the UK. Within England, regions with older voters and manufacturing declines strongly voted to exit. In the cities, the vote was strongly to remain.

Northern Ireland Catholics voted to remain, as did Scotland overwhelmingly. The former group worried that leaving the EU would raise economic barriers with the Republic of Ireland, which remains in the EU. Scottish voters may have believed that their future economic prospects would be brighter in an integrated Europe than within the smaller UK. Northern Ireland Protestants voted to leave, along with the UK majority.

Third, studies find that within the areas voting for Brexit, those with the highest share of votes to leave the EU had higher shares of immigrants in the population. How it is that higher local immigration presence affects attitudes toward globalization and labor mobility is an interesting and complex question that will be addressed in a later chapter.

Backlash episode 2: The 2016 US Presidential election

Figure 1.10 shows that voters for Donald Trump (the Republican and anti-trade candidate) were overwhelmingly from rural areas and lower-income counties of the US. Voters for Hilary Clinton (the Democratic candidate) were primarily from urban areas and higher-income counties.

There is strong evidence from economic research that regions of the United States that suffered the largest negative employment

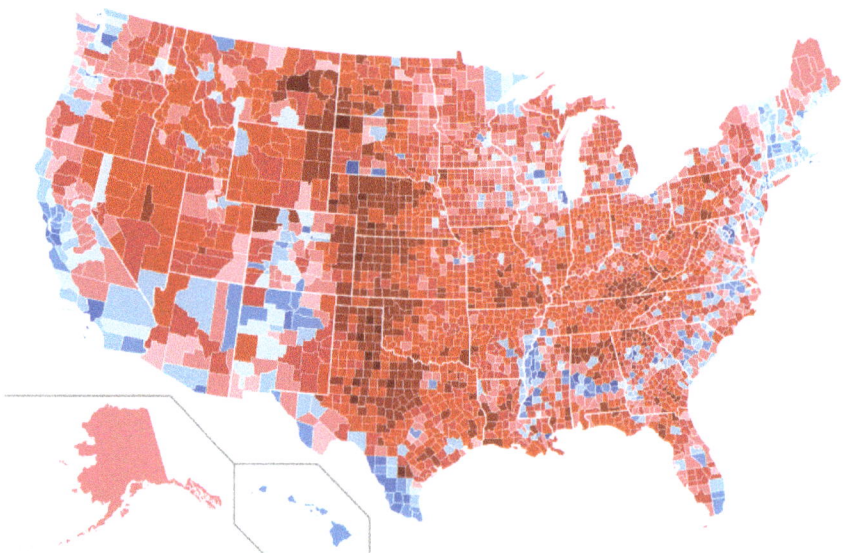

Figure 1.10   2016 votes for Trump (in red shades) and Clinton (in blue shades). Trump won about 2600 counties and Clinton won about 500, including 88 of the largest 100 counties and Washington DC.

Source: https://en.wikipedia.org/wiki/File:2016_Nationwide_US_presidential_county_map_shaded_by_vote_share.svg.

and wage effects from competition with imports from China strongly supported Trump. Candidate Trump promised to fix such problems with higher tariffs, reduced regulation, departures from major trade agreements, and lower immigration. These are the primary policies of economic nationalism.

These results and the voting patterns in Brexit suggest that there is a strong economic basis involved in voting for populist politics and policies. Many other demographic and cultural factors are important also, but they generally correlate with economic gains and losses.

Chapter 2

Basic Theoretical Tools Used in International Trade

The Basic Concept of an International Trade Equilibrium

Depicting an international trade equilibrium

International trade is inherently a general-equilibrium concept, involving at a minimum two goods, two factors, and two countries. This calls for developing some extended microeconomic theory, which we do in later notes.

But we will often use basic partial-equilibrium tools (supply and demand for one good or factor) to illustrate ideas. In this set of notes we work on these tools.

Showing a trade equilibrium for one good with two countries:

Consider the familiar idea of a basic supply and demand diagram (Figure 2.1).

The no-trade equilibrium, which we call "autarky", shows the quantity and price at point A for good X for one country, called Home. This is the diagram studied in principles of economics as a market equilibrium in a single country.

Students may have studied the idea of a price ceiling at $\overline{P}_x$, generating a shortage in this good of quantity BC.

But now observe that this shortage could be filled by importing good X from a second country, called Foreign.

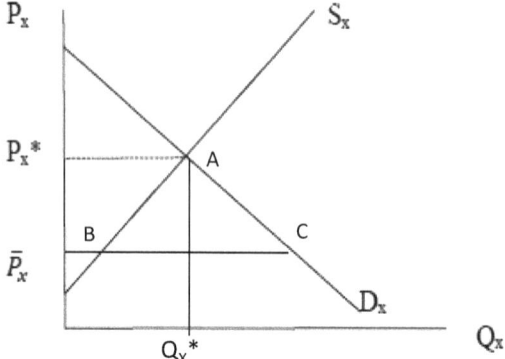

Figure 2.1 Autarky equilibrium.

Note: The "autarky" (no trade) equilibrium exists where domestic demand and supply are equal, at point A.

Notes on the trade equilibrium

To analyze a trade equilibrium, bring together the S and D curves for Home and Foreign. The essential question is which country has a higher autarky price of X (it will be the importer) and which has the lower autarky price (it will be the exporter).

To see this, consider two countries, US (Home) and Thailand (Foreign), in Figure 2.2.

We can see that Thailand has the lower autarky price and US the higher price of good X. If they now trade with one another Thailand would export X in the amount $C_x^T Q_X^T$ and the US would import X in the amount $Q_X^{US} C_X^{US}$. These quantities are equal.

If there are no remaining barriers or costs of trade there would be established an equilibrium price in free trade, labeled P_X^*. This price would hold in both countries.

Note that US imports are the difference between consumption and production, while Thai exports are the difference between production and consumption.

Comparing autarky points to free trade, the price of X falls in the US (imported) and rises in Thailand (exported). These price changes cause output of X to fall in the US and to rise in Thailand, while consumption of X rises in the US and falls in Thailand.

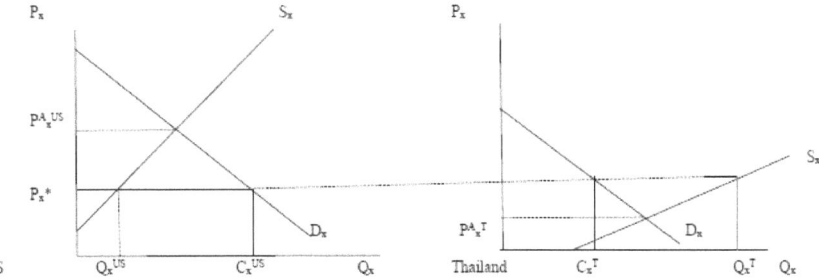

Figure 2.2 International trade equilibrium.

Note: The "A" superscripts refer to "autarky" prices, or the equilibrium prices if countries cannot trade (autarky means a condition of isolation, so no trade in goods or factors).

This is a general equilibrium (GE) of a sort because it links two national markets for good X. But there are several elements missing:

- Trade must involve at least two goods, X and Y.
- Trade must be balanced, meaning the dollar value of X imported must equal the dollar value of Y exported for the US, and the opposite for Thailand. (Of course, countries do run trade deficits and surpluses, which we will ignore until we get to the notes on international finance.)
- These elements mean we need to get two goods and two prices into the model.

Fundamental economic concept: Relative prices

Let there be two goods, Bicycles (B) and Nuts (N). Usually, we think of nominal prices:

$$\text{Let } P_B^{US} = \$500 \text{ per bike} \quad P_B^T = 16{,}000 \text{ Baht (B) per bike}$$
$$P_N^{US} = \$100 \text{ per ton} \quad P_N^T = 2{,}000 \text{ B per ton}$$

Economists argue that rational consumers and producers do not really care about nominal prices since those do not mean much in the context of the economy generally. That is, assume that consumers and producers do not have *money illusion,* meaning they realize that if their income goes up by 10% and both prices go up by 10%, they are not any better off or worse off. Nothing important has changed in the economy in real terms.

Consumers and producers do care about *relative prices*, because they indicate the *opportunity cost* of buying or producing 1 unit more of a good in terms of the sacrifice of the other good. Thus, if P_B rises by 10% but P_N rises by 20% a consumer would buy more B and less N because bikes have become *relatively* less expensive. But producers would produce more N and less B because nuts now command a *relatively* higher price.

This example was given with prices in different currencies, raising the immediate question of which currency to use. Or does that matter?

Relative prices and comparative advantage

We resolve and analyze these issues by using *relative prices*

$$p_B^{US}/P_N^{US} = 5 \text{ and } p_B^T/P_N^T = 8$$

.

Note that bikes are more expensive, and nuts are cheaper, in Thailand in relative terms compared to the US.

- Stated as *opportunity costs* (OC), in the US $1B$ is worth $5N$. So, the OC of buying 1 more B is not being able to buy $5N$. That is, for a consumer with a given income to buy 1 more bike she must buy 5 fewer units of nuts. Similarly, the OC of buying 1 more N is $1/5B$.
- In Thailand, the OC of 1 more B is $8N$ and the OC of 1 more N is $1/8B$.
- These relative prices (OC) are what matter for determining *comparative advantage* (CA) and the pattern of trade.

Concept: Define a country's comparative advantage as the product in which it has the lower relative price:

- US has the CA in bikes and T has the CA in nuts. This is because $p_B^{US}/P_N^{US} < p_B^T/P_N^T$.

The models of international trade we develop in later notes essentially explain the sources of these price differences.

Study question 1

Consider two countries, Japan and France, and two goods, textiles (T) and machines (M). We have these prices:

> In Japan: $P_T = 100,000$ yen and $P_M = 600,000$ yen
> In France: $P_T = 150$ euros and $P_M = 450$ euros

Which of the following statements is true?

A. Japan has a higher OC for textiles than France.
B. France has a lower OC for machines than Japan.
C. Japan has a comparative advantage in machines.
D. France has a comparative advantage in textiles.

Discussion of study question 1

The correct answer is B. The opportunity cost of a machine in France is 3 textiles but in Japan it is 6 textiles.

A is false because the OC of textiles in Japan is 1/6 machine, while it is 1/3 machine in France.

These OC figures show that machines are relatively more expensive in Japan, implying that Japan's CA lies in textiles. Similarly, France has the CA in machines, making D false.

Analyzing the Demand Side of the Equilibrium

Utility maximization: The budget constraint

Consider a consumer in the US, with income of $\$M$ (Figure 2.3). Her budget constraint (b.c.) is: $M = p_B B + p_N N$. Rewrite the equation as $N = {}^{M}/_{P_N} - \frac{p_B}{p_N} B$. This is the b.c. expressed as a straight line, with intercept ${}^{M}/_{P_N}$ and slope $-\frac{p_B}{p_N}$. The slope is the negative of the relative price of bikes.

Let's map this line assuming $M = \$50,000$. Recall that the price of a bike is $\$500$ and the price of a unit of nuts is $\$100$ in the US.

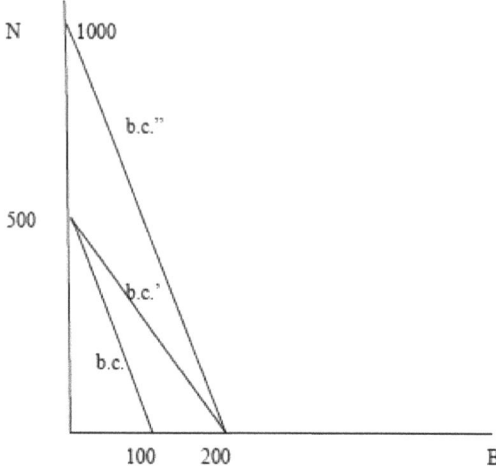

Figure 2.3 Individual budget constraints and prices.

Note: The slope of the initial b.c. $= -p_B/p_N = -5$. It is easier to think of the absolute slope: $|slope| = \frac{p_B}{p_N} = 5$, which is the relative price of B in terms of N. We use this absolute slope in our analysis.

Then Max $B = 100$, Max $N = 500$ are the endpoints, which are the amounts of B and N that could be purchased if the entire income were spent on either good.

The b.c. is the straight line between these endpoints and shows the combinations of N and B that the consumer can buy by spending all her income.

Important note: we've shown the slope as the rise/run, or 5/1. This means the consumer gives up 5N per 1B along the b.c. But the slope is the relative price of B. That is, since $P_B/P_N = 5$ it follows that $1B = 5N$ in the market. Don't get confused by units versus prices.

This price ratio is the market rate of exchange at which consumers and producers buy and sell B and N. It is the price of the good on the horizontal axis divided by the price of the good on the vertical axis.

Here are some comparative statics (simple changes within the model):

- Let P_B fall to $250, then $P_B/P_N = 2.5$ and Max B rises to 200. This means the b.c. gets flatter (lower slope) and consumers have a better opportunity to buy both goods (see b.c.').
- Let income M rise to $100,000. This shifts the b.c. out in parallel (showing the same relative price) by a factor of 2. At the same nominal prices consumers can buy more of both goods (see b.c.'').
- Clearly for consumers lower prices and higher incomes are beneficial in shifting out the b.c. The larger is the available (B, N) bundle the better off is an individual consumer.

Utility maximization: Indifference curves

We need to figure out how many units the consumer chooses to buy of B and N, which determines her quantities demanded for the given prices and income.

This is a deeper issue than it seems, but to focus on the basics we will assume that individual consumer preferences are given by *indifference curves* (Figure 2.4).

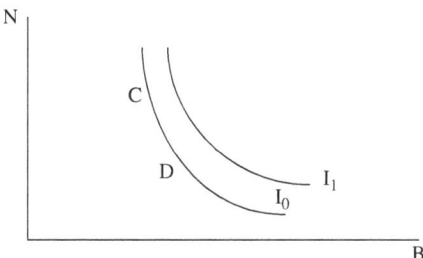

Figure 2.4   Individual indifference curves.

Note: The slope of an IC is negative. Define the *marginal rate of substitution* (MRS) as the absolute slope of an IC. $MRS = |^{\Delta N}/_{\Delta B}|$ for a given level of utility along any IC. This figure shows how this slope diminishes as more B and less N are consumed. For example, at point C the MRS might be 3, meaning the consumer would give up $3N$ for $1B$ and feel equally well off. But at point D the MRS might be 1, so she gives up $1N$ for $1B$. This idea reflects *diminishing marginal utility*: the more B a person has the less she wants more of it at the margin and the fewer are the units of N she is willing to give up.

An indifference curve shows the combinations of goods
B and N which make the consumer equally well off. The idea
comes from assuming a person has a well-defined utility function:
$U = U(C_B, C_N)$.

Indifference curves have these properties:

- ICs are downward-sloping, because if the consumer has less B, she
  must get more N to be indifferent. Note this assumes goods are
  substitutes in demand.
- ICs are *convex* (curved away from origin), which means there is
  diminishing marginal utility for each good. See Figure 2.4.
- Higher ICs (those further from the origin) indicate higher levels of
  utility.
- Logically, ICs cannot intersect. Imagine 2 ICs intersecting at some
  point C in Figure 2.4. To the left of C points on the steeper IC
  would be preferred to points on the flatter IC. But just the opposite
  would be true to the right of C. This situation is inconsistent with
  the idea of unchanged utilities along any single IC.

Utility maximization: Indifference curves and the budget constraint

The consumer maximizes her utility (welfare) by choosing the IC that
is the highest available for the given b.c. In Figure 2.5 this would be
at point C^* on the original b.c.

Now if the relative price of bikes falls to 2.5 there is a higher b.c.,
permitting the consumer to move to $C^{*\prime}$, with higher utility. The
consumer is better off.

In this depiction she consumes more of both goods, though that
isn't necessary depending on her preferences. But she does get to a
higher indifference curve and has gained welfare.

The diagram depicts a fall in the relative price of bikes. But it
is also true that a lower relative price of nuts, which would pivot
the b.c. to a steeper line from the B endpoint to above the initial N
endpoint, would raise consumer welfare.

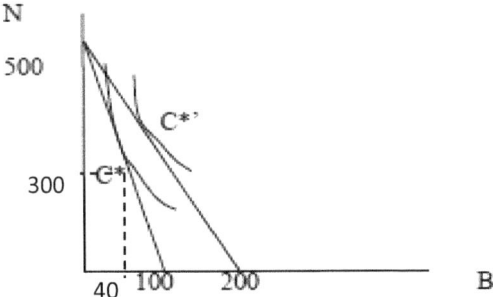

Figure 2.5 Utility maximization.

It is evident that an increase in the consumer's income M would raise the b.c. and make her better off as well by permitting her to consume on a higher IC.

An important implication is that in equilibrium MRS $=^{P_B}/_{P_N}$.

The MRS equals the market price ratio.

If this were not true, the consumer could choose a different bundle. Imagine an indifference curve that cuts the original b.c. rather than is tangent to it. That curve must lie below the one tangent at C^*, so it would imply a lower utility level for the given income.

Finally, because C^* is the consumption equilibrium, its ordinates on the two axes show the quantities demanded by this consumer, which are shown as $40B$ and $300N$. Thus, quantities demanded are determined by this tangency for the given level of income ($M) and prices of the two goods.

Utility maximization: Individual demand curves

Now we can define *demand curves* for this individual. Note that consumption of both goods changes when the price of B falls. What really matters is the relative price change. Therefore, demand curves are defined by

$$D_B = D_B\left(\frac{p_B}{p_N}, M\right) \quad \text{and} \quad D_N = D_N\left(\frac{p_B}{p_N}, M\right)$$

In general, if M rises, we expect both D_B and D_N to rise (positive impacts).

If the price ratio rises (higher relative price of bikes) we expect a lower quantity demanded for B (negative impact) and a higher quantity demanded for N (positive impact).

This is all just like regular demand theory for one good, except that we have relative prices in these demand curves, not just the individual good price.

Demand in the national economy

Can we do the same thing for the total economy?

First, think about the national budget constraint. To do this, begin with a brief aside on Gross National Income (GNI) versus Gross Domestic Product (GDP).

- Gross National Income, which used to be called GNP, is the total income earned by factors (labor, capital, land) of one country, no matter where they produce or sell things (at home or abroad).
- Gross Domestic Product is the total final output produced in a country, no matter whether the factors of production are domestic or foreign-owned.

In a world where factors do not move across borders, GNI and GDP are the same. This is what we will assume until later in the course.

Countries that have a lot of workers abroad who send remittances home generally have GNI > GDP.

Countries that invest a lot abroad and own intellectual property abroad also have GNI > GDP.

Just the opposite cases for GDP < GNI.

Here are some countries with large inward personal remittances (as % of GDP) in 2016:

- Nepal 31.3%; Kyrgyz Republic 30.4%; Haiti 29.4%; Liberia 26.1%; Honduras 18.0%; El Salvador 17.1%; Philippines 10.2%.

What about Mexico? Inward remittances are 2.7% of GDP, but that's a large number: \$35.1 billion at the 2016 exchange rate.

For now, we assume there are no international factor movements, so that GNI = GDP.

National budget constraint

Here, GNI will indicate the national budget constraint, determined by total income. But because GNI = GDP, we can substitute GDP. In our simple two-good case we then have:

$$\text{GDP} = P_N N + P_B B. \text{ Then } N = \frac{\text{GDP}}{P_N} - \left(\frac{P_B}{P_N}\right) B$$

$$\text{Or} \quad \frac{\text{GDP}}{P_N} = N + \left(\frac{P_B}{P_N}\right) B$$

This says that the ratio $\frac{\text{GDP}}{P_N}$ is *real GDP* measured in units of nuts. It is the maximum number of N that could be consumed if all the country's GDP were spent only on N (that is, if $B = 0$).

And $\frac{\text{GDP}}{P_B}$ would be *real GDP* measured in bicycles.

Example: Suppose there are 1 million identical people in the US, each with an income of $50,000. Then GDP per capita is $50,000. We compute that

- Nominal GDP = 1m*50,000 = $50 billion.
- Real GDP in N = ($50 billion/100) = 500 million N; Real GDP in B = ($50 billion/500) = 100 million B.

Next, we need to figure out how many of each good the national economy would choose to consume given these prices and GDP (Figure 2.6).

Can we add up individual preferences (utility functions) to get a set of *community indifference curves* (CICs)? And would that define aggregate demand curves?

Yes, we can do this in the very special case that, at all times and in all situations, every person has the same income (that is, there is perfectly equal income distribution) and also every person has the same preferences for B and N.

Then CICs would just be "blown up" parallel versions of any individual person's ICs and total (national) demand curves would be the number of people times each person's demand curves.

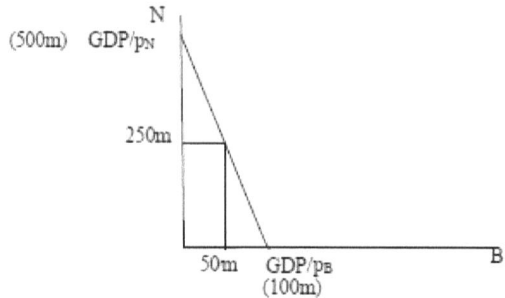

Figure 2.6 The national budget constraint. Thus, *real GDP is given by the national budget constraint*. At the midpoint, $\frac{GDP}{P_N} = N + (\frac{P_B}{P_N})B = 250m + 5(50m) = 500m$ nuts. Indeed, real GDP would be the same at any point on the GDP line. *Real GDP is the same anywhere along the national budget constraint.*

But in cases that are more general than this it becomes virtually impossible to precisely define community utility functions or CICs. That is because (1) income distributions can be different as the economy changes; and (2) individual taste patterns are different.

Thus, in general, when prices change or aggregate income goes up, how much demand for the goods changes in the total economy depends on both the new income distribution and the structure of individual preferences. And, in general, we do not know all these utility functions, nor can we predict precise changes in income distribution.

This is a real problem in analyzing the gains and losses from international trade. It is also true for any branch of economics that pays attention to welfare. And it is a problem for political science, sociology, philosophy, and so on.

We are not in a position in this class to resolve this complex issue. Rather, we will make the following highly simplifying assumption, which boils down to the case of identical preferences and identical incomes mentioned above. (In economics, this is called the "representative agent" model and is widely used, especially in macroeconomics.)

The assumption is that we can characterize national utility function by a set of *community indifference curves* (CICs), which have the same characteristics as individual ICs. Then we have these implications:

Aggregate demands are defined by points where CICs are tangent to GDP lines, as in the next diagram. Thus, as before we can write national demand curves as

$$D_B = D_B\left(\frac{p_B}{p_N}, GDP\right) \quad \text{and} \quad D_N = D_N\left(\frac{p_B}{p_N}, GDP\right)$$

We would ordinarily expect the same effects. Higher GDP would raise the demand for both N and B but a rise in the relative price ratio would reduce the quantity demanded of B and raise the quantity demanded of N.

Since a higher real GDP (higher national b.c.) generates consumption on a higher CIC we are willing to say that going from a lower to a higher CIC raises national welfare (see Figure 2.7 where GDP rises for the same relative price).

This theory determines both the national demand for goods and how welfare changes as incomes and prices change. But keep the following issues in mind:

In general, a higher GDP does not mean that all people are better off. It depends on how income is distributed in the new cases versus the original case. That makes it hard to argue unambiguously that the economy in total is better off, even with a higher real GDP. This

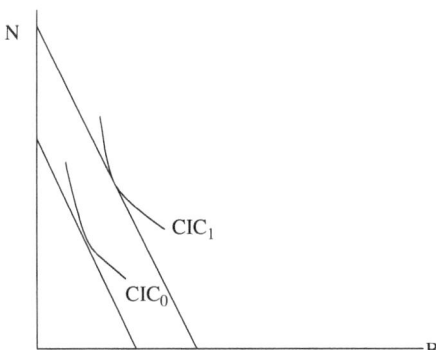

Figure 2.7   Changes in real GDP and welfare.

Note: The straight lines are GDP levels, which operate as national budget constraints. A higher real GDP (higher b.c.) places the economy on a higher CIC, implying a higher level of economic welfare.

is unsatisfying because we do wish to understand demand curves and think about welfare changes.

However, there is a defensible and useful way to think about this problem. Note that if there is higher real GDP, it is possible, at least in principle, to tax those who gain income and use those proceeds to compensate the losers through redistribution policies, such that nobody is made worse off by the policy change and some are made better off.

Thus, in economics our basic welfare criterion comes down to this *compensation principle: If a change in the economy (due to changes in policy, technology, factor supplies, and the like) generates a higher real GDP so that the gainers could in principle compensate the losers, society is better off.*

Actual compensation policies are not common. There is one in the trade area for the US. The Trade Adjustment Assistance (TAA) program offers additional monetary benefits to people who are laid off due to import competition or job offshoring. But this program has not been very effective at compensating people for losses.

Analyzing the Supply Side of the Economy

Supply in the national economy: The production possibility frontier (PPF)

Turn next to the production side of the national economy. How do we determine the capacity of an economy to produce goods (the PPF) and how many goods does it produce in equilibrium?

The first question is: What are the constraints on the supply side of an economy?

1. Supplies ("endowments") of labor, capital and other factors.
2. The technologies available to produce goods (production functions).

If these two items are held fixed, then producing more B requires producing less N. But if factor supplies expand or technology improves, the PPF expands.

We can now define the production possibility frontier: *The PPF shows the maximum amount of N that can be produced for every level of B, with given factor endowments and technologies.*

Characteristics of the PPF:

- It must be downward-sloping, indicating that producing more B requires resources taken from N, so output of N falls.
- The endpoints, which show the maximum amounts of N or B that can be produced if all factors were devoted to N or B, depend on endowments and technologies.
- The slope of the PPF represents the *opportunity cost* of converting N into B. This means the number of N that are not produced in order to free up the resources needed to produce 1 more B.

Define the *marginal rate of transformation (MRT) as the absolute value of the slope of the PPF.* MRT $= |\Delta N / \Delta B|$ for a given set of factor endowments and technologies for producing N and B.

The most familiar PPF is concave, showing **increasing opportunity costs** *at the margin.*

Why is the PPF concave (that is, bowed out away from the origin)? Here is an informal proof that this shape must hold for two goods having CRS production functions.

Consider Figure 2.8 and suppose that nuts are labor-intensive and bikes are capital-intensive. This means B uses a higher ratio of capital to labor in production than N does.

Starting at Max N, suppose the economy attempts to produce more B. Initially, the N sector releases relatively much K and not much L in order to remain efficient (recall that N is labor-intensive). Thus, initially the economy does not lose much N output. But this high K/L ratio generates a large expansion in B output, which is capital-intensive. This means that at a point like A the MRT is small, say $1/2$. This means the economy gives up just $1/2N$ for $1B$ more in production.

But the further along the PPF the smaller the amount of K per L the N sector can release. Thus, at the margin the amount of additional B produced must fall. This means there is a reduced

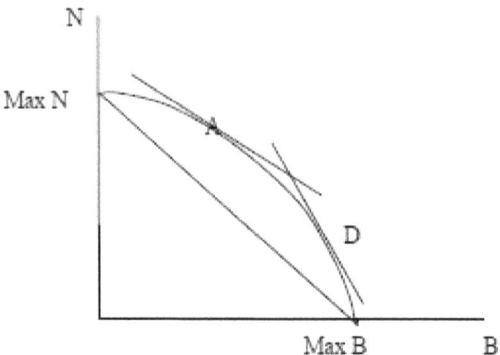

Figure 2.8 The PPF.

Note: Why does the PPF have this concave shape? It depends on features of the production functions for B and N. There are two primary features that matter.

1. *Returns to scale.* We will generally assume constant returns to scale (CRS), which means that if both inputs are doubled then the output of the good is doubled. This holds for both B and N. But later we will consider the implications of having increasing returns to scale (IRS) in at least one good.

2. *Factor intensities.* Let B be *capital-intensive* and N be *labor-intensive*. That means that the production of B always uses a higher capital-labor ratio than does production of N. Conversely, good N has a higher labor-capital ratio than B.

marginal product (lower gain in output) in B for a given fall in N output.

To put it differently, for every 1 unit of higher B the amount of N that must be given up gets larger. At point D this could be an MRT of 2, for example. The economy sacrifices $2N$ for $1B$ in production.

This concavity therefore reflects *rising marginal costs* (or *rising opportunity costs*) of producing B as shown by the higher MRT as the economy moves along the PPF toward more B and less N. This is an *increasing costs* PPF.

And this works in both directions. There are increasing opportunity costs of producing N as you move upward and to the left on the PPF.

Key concept: A concave PPF demonstrates increasing opportunity costs in production. Note that this happens even though each good is produced with constant returns to scale.

We can explain this a little better by imagining in Figure 2.8 that in fact N and B have the same factor intensity, meaning they both use the same capital to labor ratio. In effect, they are the same product as far as production technologies and costs go.

Thus, suppose that the (absolute) slope of the line between Max N and Max B is 1. Then starting at Max N, the economy would lose $1N$ to produce the first B by releasing K and L in exactly the ratio needed by B. This adjustment just linearly reduces N to raise B output. If these intensities never change this linear tradeoff would exist all the way to the Max B point. This situation would involve *constant opportunity costs* in the tradeoff between N and B. This situation is depicted the straight line in the PPF diagram.

But now *if factor intensities are different then we can do better than this tradeoff* because the different intensities permit a more efficient reallocation of K and L from N to B, along the concave PPF.

Summary:

- With identical factor intensities (and CRS) the PPF is a straight line with a constant MRT (constant opportunity costs in production).
- With different factor intensities (and CRS) the PPF is concave ("bowed out") and has a rising MRT as more B is produced (increasing opportunity costs).

Finally, note that to be efficient the economy must produce somewhere along the PPF, which is necessary for full employment.

Study question 2

Which of the following statements about the PPF is false?

A. Endowments of production factors and the state of technologies determine how far the PPF is from the origin.
B. When production functions have constant returns to scale the PPF is a straight line.
C. When production functions have different factor intensities the PPF is concave ("bowed out" from the origin).
D. When the country produces on the PPF it displays full employment of factors.

E. The concave curvature of the PPF reflects increasing opportunity costs.

Discussion of study question 2

The correct (false) answer is B. The concave PPF shown in Figure 2.8 does have CRS production functions. What makes it concave is the difference in factor intensities between goods B and N.

 A is true because the size of endowments and the state of technology determine how large the PPF is. D is also true because the PPF is defined to incorporate full employment.

 C is true as noted above. E is also true because the concavity means a rising OC of producing more of either good.

Bringing Supply and Demand Together

Supply and demand: General equilibrium

Now we bring the two sides of the economy together to determine equilibrium.

 Assume there is perfect competition in the economy. This means there are no price distortions associated with taxes, monopolies, labor unions, and other factors. Stated differently, prices equal marginal costs (MC) of production in each good:

$$p_N = MC_N \quad \text{and} \quad p_B = MC_B. \quad \text{Then} \quad {p_B}/{p_N} = {MC_B}/{MC_N}.$$

Note also that along the PPF it must be that the value of resources released from N must equal the value of resources gained in B (this must be true with full employment):

$$MC_B * \Delta B = -MC_N * \Delta N$$

 Then ${MC_B}/{MC_N} = -({\Delta N}/{\Delta B}) = \text{MRT}.$

 Thus, in an efficient economy with perfect competition, we have ${p_B}/{p_N} = {MC_B}/{MC_N} = \text{MRT}.$ *The slope of the PPF equals the market price ratio.*

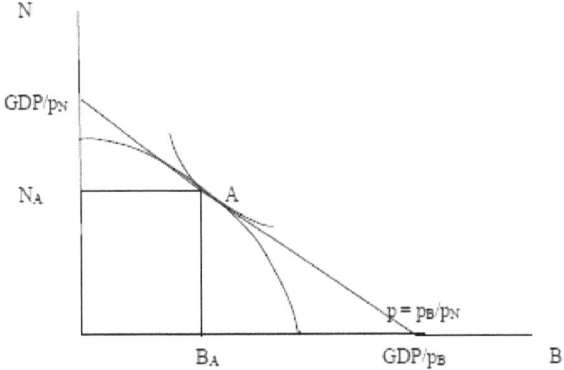

Figure 2.9 Autarky equilibrium and real GDP.

Note: Relative price: $^{p_B}/_{p_N}$ = MRT = MRS at point A. The price ratio equals the slope of both the PPF and CIC in equilibrium. Each market is in equilibrium, because the output in B equals consumption in B, and the same holds for N. These points are B_A and N_A. This equilibrium maximizes real GDP (and real GNI) for the given PPF and preferences. Note that the line with absolute slope p (the relative price in autarky) shows real GDP and is also the economy's budget constraint in autarky.

But we saw earlier that the market price ratio also must equal the slope of a community indifference curve (reflecting demand), which we called the MRS.

This is the meaning of general equilibrium for two goods in a closed economy (autarky). The price ratio equals both the MRS and MRT. The concept corresponds to the idea of supply equals demand at an equilibrium price for a single good (Figure 2.9).

Introducing International Trade in the General Equilibrium

Aggregate demand, the PPF, and international trade

Consider next what happens to output and consumption decisions as the relative price of B rises from the autarky level. From now on we will use p to mean relative price in these general equilibrium diagrams.

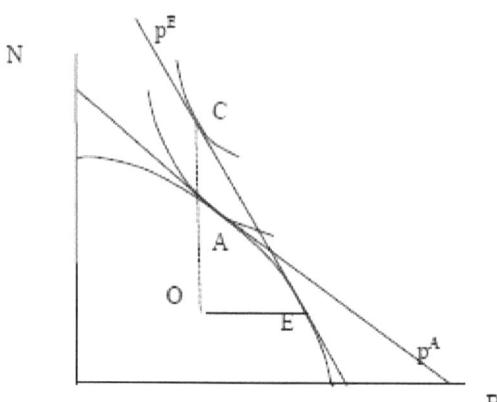

Figure 2.10   The free-trade equilibrium.

In Figure 2.10, let p^A rise to p^E. Again, this is an increase in the relative price of B. We get:

1. The output of B rises (compare A to E along the PPF), so the national supply quantity of B rises. And the national supply quantity of N falls.
2. If the economy can consume along the new price line tangent to production at E, the consumption mix would shift to point C on the higher CIC. Consumption of B (probably) falls compared to autarky. Thus, the national demand quantity of B falls. And the consumption quantity of N rises because it is relatively cheaper.
3. At price ratio p^E the economy consumes outside its PPF, so there is international trade between points E and C. The economy exports OE units of B and imports OC units of N.
    There would be higher national welfare in free trade than in autarky because the economy is on a higher CIC.

The international trade general equilibrium

We want to bring in another country to show trade. But drawing two consistent PPF diagrams is messy, so we turn this thinking into aggregate supply and demand curves with a new pair of general-equilibrium (GE) diagrams. Again, we use the US and Thailand in Figure 2.11.

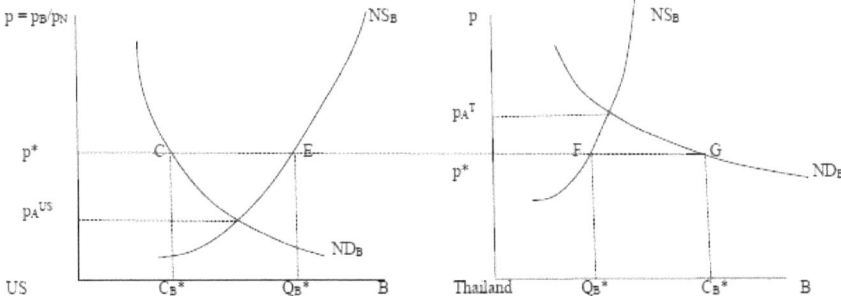

Figure 2.11   Free-trade equilibrium using NS and ND curves.

Note that these curves have the quantity of bikes (B) on the horizontal axis and the *relative price* of B on the vertical axis.

In the PPF diagram above, let the price in US rise from autarky p_A to p_E.

As seen earlier, this price change raises the output of B, so there is an upward-sloping national supply (NS) curve of B in the US.

But it also reduces consumption of B, so there is a downward-sloping national demand (ND) curve in the US.

There is a similar analysis for Thailand for good B.

These national supply and demand curves for good B (bicycles) determine the autarky *relative prices* p_A^{US} and p_A^T in this new diagram.

We see that $p_A^{US} < p_A^T$, so the US has the comparative advantage in B. Also, Thailand has the comparative advantage in N because the relative price of nuts (the reciprocal of these price ratios) would be lower in Thailand.

Now open these economies to trade with each other.

As shown here, the US has a CA in B because its autarky price ratio is below the autarky price ratio in Thailand. Because the US exports bikes, the price of B will rise there. And because it imports nuts the price of N will fall there. The relative price of B rises in the US, because B gets more expensive and N gets cheaper.

Thailand has a CA in N and exports N while importing B. That means the relative price of B will fall in T, because B gets cheaper and N gets more expensive.

Let p^* be the equilibrium price ratio established in free trade. This becomes the equilibrium relative price domestically in both the US and Thailand.

Consumption and production points for the US are shown as C_B^* and Q_B^* on the B axis, and similarly for Thailand. Trade quantities are shown in units of B. Note that US exports of $B(= \text{CE})$ equal Thailand imports of $B(= \text{FG})$.

Question: how do we know that the US and Thailand are better off in free trade than in autarky? They must be because the new relative prices allow both countries to consume on higher CICs than was the case in autarky.

To complete this analysis, note that Thailand has the comparative advantage in nuts and will export N. Let's figure out how to depict the quantity of nuts traded.

To do so, note that in general equilibrium there must be balanced trade for each country in value terms, meaning the dollar value of exports equals the dollar value of imports. For the US we have:

$$\text{EXP}_B p_B^* = \text{IMP}_N p_N^* \text{ which can be rewritten as } \text{IMP}_N = \frac{p_B^*}{p_N^*} \text{EXP}_B$$

The right side of this equation is the product of the price ratio (on the vertical axis of the diagram) and the quantity of exports (on the horizontal axis). Thus, the rectangle coming down from points C and E to the horizontal axis is, in fact, the quantity of US imports (and Thai exports) of N.

We have now come full circle: the diagram above is the general-equilibrium version of the initial supply-and-demand depiction of international trade (for one good) at the beginning of these notes.

Study question 3

In the international trade general equilibrium described above, which statement is true?

A. Free trade maximizes economic welfare and real GDP for each country.
B. Both countries have higher welfare in free trade than in autarky.

C. Both countries have balanced trade in that the value of their exports equals the value of their imports.
D. Both countries consume at a point above their PPFs.
E. All the above.

Discussion of study question 3

The correct answer is E, because A through D are all true statements.

Chapter 3

The Ricardian (Classical) Trade Model

The Foundations of Comparative Advantage

Ricardian model: Introduction

This will be our first theoretical model that explains our basic questions:

- What do countries trade? This is the idea of comparative advantage.
- What are the gains from trade (GFT)?
- Do both (or all) countries gain from trade?

Before starting the model, let's consider three (false) common propositions you may hear about international trade. The first two are as follows:

(1) *Wealthy, high-wage countries cannot afford to trade with low-wage developing countries because their low-wage costs would allow them to produce most goods more cheaply and drive firms in richer countries out of business. Firms and workers in rich nations need protection against imports from low-wage countries to avoid seeing their wages pushed down to those levels.*

(2) *Low-wage developing countries cannot afford to trade with high-wage countries because labor in those countries is so much more productive due to higher skills, capital stocks, and technological*

superiority, suggesting that they would produce most goods more cheaply and drive developing-country firms out of business. Firms and workers in poor nations need protection against imports from more productive nations in order to survive economically.

Which claim should we believe? They can't both be true, even though both are commonly heard in the media and policy circles.

The fallacy with both is that they look at only one component of production costs: wages on the one hand and productivity on the other. But productivity and wages (along with exchange rates, capital costs, and many other factors) combine to determine unit costs of production.

In fact, the US can trade with Mexico or Vietnam to their mutual advantage because American workers are much better at producing some goods (enough better to pay for higher wages) and only somewhat better at producing other goods (in which lower foreign wages are more important).

Another fallacy is to believe that wages, productivity, exchange rates, and other conditions would not adjust as the economy changes. But US trade with poor countries could raise wages in those nations. For example, this adjustment has been happening in China and Mexico for many years.

The classical theory of comparative advantage (CA) is well suited to demonstrating the simple proposition that wealthy and poor countries can trade with each other to their mutual advantage. Further, rich countries can trade beneficially among themselves and poor countries among themselves. All that is required is some *efficiency differences (cost differences) between them that allow countries to specialize in producing the goods at which they are most productive.*

This outcome is no different from the idea that a lawyer and a plumber can profitably specialize and trade. The lawyer may be better at both the law and fixing sinks, but he/she is much better at the law and only a little better at sinks. It follows that if he/she specializes in the law and leaves the plumber to deal with the sinks, both can have higher incomes. This is the essence of comparative advantage and the GFT for countries.

And here is the third false proposition, called **mercantilism, which is essentially the belief that exports are "good" and imports are "bad" for economic welfare.**

(3) 18th- and 19th-century "mercantilism" argued that power and wealth are associated with domestic production and exports. Foreign trade is welfare-increasing only if a country exports (i.e., produces goods) and welfare-decreasing if it imports (for then, production is elsewhere). The policy goal was to maximize the trade surplus through restrictive import barriers, such as the English Corn Laws of the 18th and 19th centuries, which greatly limited agricultural imports into Britain.

The basis for this belief is that a trade surplus implies that people and firms in the domestic economy accumulate greater ownership of foreign assets (which was largely gold in those years), so running a surplus was seen as a means of *appropriating wealth from abroad in a zero-sum way.* (We will study the relationship between trade imbalances and wealth in the notes on international finance.)

Thus, mercantilism was (and is still believed by many) the belief that trade among countries could not be beneficial for all but was instead a competition to accumulate the world's wealth by increasing exports and decreasing imports.

But consider this idea carefully. It makes little sense to think of increasing production as the objective of policy. Rather, it is a means of increasing national utility or well-being. And *utility is a function of how much people can consume,* or what is in their consumption baskets and in how much variety.

That is, *economists see consumption as the true welfare objective,* not output or exports. This implies that imports are beneficial because they are items available for consumption or other use. Exports are goods that must be produced but are not domestically consumed, which does not directly raise welfare. Rather, exports are a means of generating the income needed to import goods to consume.

Taken to the extreme, this idea would claim that a country should maximize the trade deficit because that would mean a country gets to consume a high volume of imports and sacrifice few exports. (In an important way, the US is in a unique position to benefit in this way, for by virtue of its chronically large trade deficits, Americans get cars and food and clothing from imports in exchange for smaller volumes of exports. But the balancing item is that foreigners gain greater claims on dollars as the reserve currency, as we will study later. As long as this situation is sustainable, the US may be said to benefit from its excess of imports for consumption.)

Despite this logic, the idea that exports are beneficial and imports are costly remains popular and drives trade policy in some countries. The policy preference would be for high tariffs to reduce imports and perhaps paying subsidies to firms that increase their exports. This idea was part of the foundation for raising tariffs in the recent Trump Administration.

However, note that if all countries were to act in this mercantilist manner, there would be high barriers to trade all around, which is mutually harmful. Getting countries not to do this is the main reason why there is a WTO.

To economists, mercantilism is a flawed idea, as are claims (1) and (2) above.

The first economist to examine these problems clearly was David Ricardo, in early 1800s England. He pointed out that all countries can specialize production in goods they most efficiently produce and export those goods in return for imports that they do not efficiently produce, to their mutual benefit. The trade balance will take care of itself and should not be an object of policy.

The basic notion is *comparative advantage*: The fact that one country may be more productive at producing most or even all goods compared to another is not important for trade. Rather, what matters is *relative cost advantages* or disadvantages.

For example, if the US produces all goods more efficiently than Mexico, the countries can still trade with each other beneficially so long as the US has *greater advantages in some goods than others*, as it always will. It follows that there are lesser disadvantages for Mexico in other goods and both countries will be better off if they specialize and trade.

Students may still be skeptical. This theory will convince them that trade according to specialization and comparative advantage will benefit all countries.

Analytics of the Model

Ricardian model: Assumptions

Assumptions of the model:

- There is perfect competition in all markets. This means that the price of each good equals its marginal cost of production.
- There are two final (consumption) goods, X and Y, and 1 factor of production (labor).
- Labor is perfectly mobile between sectors within a country, implying there is a single nominal wage w, which is the same in both goods X and Y.
- Importantly, all laborers are identical, meaning that if one worker was shifted from X to Y, he/she would immediately be as productive as anyone already working in Y. This also means that there can be only one wage in the economy, paid to all workers.
- There is full employment of the fixed labor force.
- We have these basic production technologies: $X = L_x/a$ and $Y = L_y/b$, where a and b are laborers per unit of output (or hours of work per unit of output). These parameters are assumed to be fixed, no matter how much X and Y are produced.
    - Note that $1/a$ and $1/b$ then give outputs per labor unit. They are both the constant average products of labor and the constant marginal products of labor. Also, note that there are constant returns to scale (CRS) in both goods.
    - Consumer utility (economic welfare) is represented by indifference curves.
    - Goods X and Y are identical ("homogeneous"), no matter the country in which they are produced. There are no quality differences between X produced in the home country and X produced in the foreign country, and similarly for Y.

The final key assumptions are about what makes countries different. We assume there are two countries that could trade with each other.

There are two possible differences between the countries:

1. They have different supplies of labor (labor forces).
2. The major difference is that labor productivities $1/a$ and $1/b$ vary between countries.

This final assumption means that the *essential difference between countries is that they have different production functions (different technologies).* This is the basis for CA in the Ricardian model.

Ricardian model: Example 1

Here is an example, with these numbers being the labor-per-output ratios:

	US	Mexico
Chemicals (C)	1	10
Radios (R)	3	5

The US has an *absolute advantage* in both C and R because the US is more productive than M in both. *Absolute advantage depends only on whether a country is more productive than the other in a particular good.*

Now, in the US, because perfect competition implies the price of a good equals its marginal cost, we have

$$p_{US}^C = w_{US}*1 \quad \text{and} \quad p_{US}^R = w_{US} * 3$$

Then, the *relative price of chemicals* is $p^{US} = p_{US}^C/p_{US}^R = (w_{US*1}/w_{US*3}) = 1/3$. It means that in the US, a chemical unit is worth $1/3$ of a radio. That must be the case because it takes just 1 worker to produce a C but 3 to produce an R.

This is the relative price ratio in the US before permitting trade, that is, the relative price ratio in US autarky.

Note that the wage rate cancels in these ratios. Here is an important point:

Nominal (market) wages do not matter for relative costs or relative prices within a country in autarky.

We can restate the US price ratio in terms of physical units: $1C = 1/3R$ and $1R = 3C$. These are the *opportunity costs* of C and R in the US in autarky.

For Mexico, $p^M = \left(p_M^C \big/ p_M^R\right) = 10/5 = 2$.

The *opportunity costs* are $1C = 2R$ and $1R = 1/2\,C$ in M in autarky.

Comparing price ratios (or opportunity costs), we see that C is relatively cheap in the US and R is cheap in Mexico. We immediately conclude that the US has the comparative advantage in C and Mexico has the CA in R.

Limits to the international (free-trade) price ratio: Define the free-trade price ratio as $\left(p_C^* \big/ p_R^*\right)$. Then, $\frac{1}{3} \le p^* = \left(p_C^* \big/ p_R^*\right) \le 2$ is the range of free-trade relative prices, within which there would be mutually beneficial trade between the US and Mexico. The following notes explain why this is the case.

Study question 1

Suppose there are two countries, Germany (G) and Egypt (E), and two goods, buses (B) and jewelry (J). The labor-per-output measures are

	Germany	Egypt
Buses	50	300
Jewelry	10	20

Which of the following statements is FALSE?

A. Germany has an absolute advantage in both goods.
B. Egypt has a lower opportunity cost in jewelry.
C. Egypt has a comparative advantage in buses.
D. The limits to the free-trade price ratio (defined as $p^* = {}^{P_B^*}\big/{}_{P_J^*}$) are $5 \le p^* \le 15$.

Discussion of study question 1

C is a false statement, so it is the correct answer. The OC of a bus in Egypt is 300/20 or 15, while the OC of a bus in Germany is 50/10 or 5. Thus, Germany has the CA in buses and Egypt in jewelry.

A is a true statement because it takes fewer workers to make both B and J in Germany. B is true because the OC of J in Egypt is $1/15$ and in Germany, it is $1/5$. D is true because these price ratios equal the autarky OCs of buses in both countries.

Back to example 1

Now, look at this case graphically with PPFs. Let the labor endowments be $L^{US} = 600$ workers and $L^M = 2000$ workers. (Note that with CRS, the units do not really matter. This could be 600 million and 2000 million workers, for example, see Figure 3.1.)

Then, for the US, we have Max $C = 600$, Max $R = 200$. For M Max $C = 200$, Max $R = 400$. Also, the relative autarky prices are fixed: $p^{US} = (p_C/p_R) = 1/3$ and $p^M = (p_C/p_R) = 2$.

Note that the (absolute) slopes of the PPFs show the relative prices, defined as the price of the good on the horizontal axis divided by the price of the good on the vertical axis.

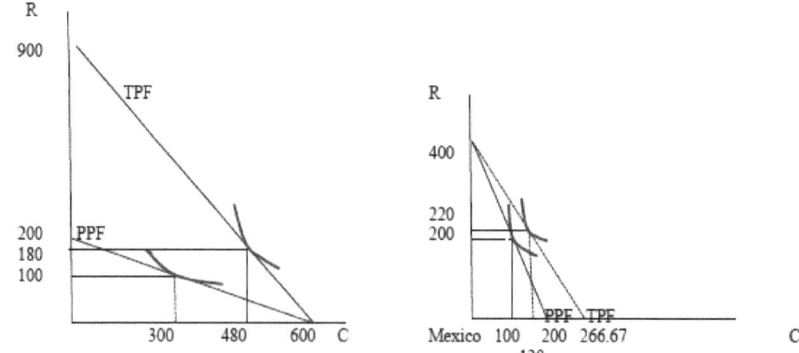

Figure 3.1 Comparative advantage and trade equilibrium in Example 1.

Example 1

Note that these PPFs feature *constant opportunity costs* in production. Due to the unchanging marginal productivities of labor, the PPFs are just straight lines. (Example: To get one more C in the US always costs 1/3R, no matter where the economy is on the PPF.)

Now consider the equilibrium and economic welfare in autarky. We can draw in CICs for both countries. In principle, these could be tangent to PPFs at any point depending on preferences. Let's just suppose that the tangent CICs split the labor force in half in both the US and M. Then we have

	Country	Outputs	Consumption	Trade
Autarky	US	$300C$, $100R$	$300C$, $100R$	NA
	Mexico	$100C$, $200R$	$100C$, $200R$	NA
	World	$400C$, $300R$	$400C$, $300R$	NA

Now, let the countries trade and suppose the world price settles at $p^* = 1.5$. This means that $1C = 1.5R$ in trade and $1R = 1/1.5C$ or $1R = 2/3C$. Then, the US gets $1.5R$ in imports for each $1C$ in exports, a better trade-off than in autarky (where $1C$ was worth $1/3$ R). And Mexico can export $1R$ and get back $1/1.5C = 2/3C$, a better situation than in autarky (where $1R$ was worth $1/2C$).

Both Countries would Gain From Trade:

- That is, US gains because $1C$ buys $1.5R$ ($>1/3R$ in autarky).
- Mexico gains because $1C$ costs 1.5R($<2R$ in autarky). Or we can state that $1R$ buys $2/3C$ ($>1/2R$ in autarky).

Next, translate this outcome into trade possibility frontiers (TPFs). Think of TPFs as national budget constraints in free trade.

Note that *each country would choose to specialize completely.* This is because as a country produces more of either good, the productivity figures never change. *Thus, it makes sense to take full advantage of the productivity advantage by completely specializing.* In Figure 3.1, the US would produce $600C$ and $0R$, while Mexico would produce $400R$ and $0C$.

Suppose in free trade that the US exports $120C$ for $180R$ (which is consistent with $p^* = 1.5$). The equilibrium figures, including the GFT, now become

Free Trade	Outputs	Consumption	Trade	GFT
US	$600C, 0R$	$480C, 180R$	$120C$ for $180R$	$+180C, +80R$
Mexico	$0C, 400R$	$120C, 220R$	$180R$ for $120C$	$+20C, +20R$
World	$600C, 400R$	$600C, 400R$	as noted	$+200C, +100R$

Trade possibility frontiers (TPFs) are the national budget constraints in free trade. They start at complete specialization (US in C, Mexico in R) and extend to the max of the other good if a country were to export all its production. The US *could* (it won't in equilibrium) export $600C$ and get back $900R$ at $p^* = 1.5$, and Mexico *could* export $400R$ and get back $400/1.5 = 266.67C$ in imports. Equilibrium depends on how much the countries demand to consume these goods (preferences).

Note the "trade triangles": US exports $120C$ and imports $180R$; M exports $180R$ and imports $120C$.

Example 1: Notes on the equilibrium

Important points:

- Both the US and M gain from trade, whether you look at higher CICs or the higher consumption bundles. Another way to see this is that the TPFs are above the PPFs so there is an improved budget constraint for both economies (Figure 3.2).
- Trade is balanced. This means two things:
  1. Physical terms: US exports of C = Mexico imports of C; Mexico exports of R = US imports of R.
  2. Value terms (trade is balanced in dollar or peso terms; there are no trade deficits or surpluses).

For the US: $p^* = \frac{p_C^*}{p_R^*} = \frac{IM_R}{EX_C} => p_C^* EX_C = p_R^* IM_R$ (the asterisks $*$ refer to free-trade prices). To illustrate trade balance, using dollars: let $p_C^* = \$200$ and $p_R^* = \$133.3$. Then, the value of

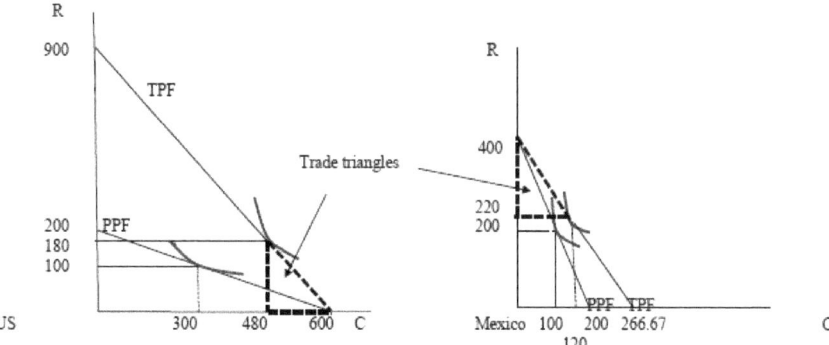

Figure 3.2 Trade equilibrium with complete specialization.

US exports = $200 \times 120C$ = $24,000 and the value of US imports = $133.33 \times 180R$ = $24,000). Students should show that Mexico also has balanced trade in dollars at these prices.

The Gains from Trade

Example 1: Gains from trade

Note an important outcome from the table (in previous page): without any change in labor supplies, there is more consumption and production in the world. How? Think of the GFT.

Where do these GFT come from? There are really two sources.

- Specialization of labor in each country into its most productive use: We can refer to this outcome as the "gain from specialization". This is like a technological improvement, because specialization permits countries to produce more of both goods in total, without any increase in labor forces.
- Consumers and producers in both countries get to exchange goods at better price ratios: We can call this the "gain from exchange". Exporters receive higher prices and consumers face lower import prices.
- None of this is magic. These gains are the result of specialization according to comparative advantage and international trade.

- Comparative advantage is the most fundamental and important characteristic underlying globalization and the GFT. Every student should remember this primary concept.

Distribution of the GFT: Internal

Our example showed that both countries gain from trade. But this raises important additional questions:

- Do all people within each country gain welfare?
- What determines the split of the GFT between the two countries?

    Start with the *internal distribution of a country's* total gains among people within the country. In the Ricardian model, the answer is straightforward: All workers within a country gain the same amount because they are all identical and have the same wage. That is, in the US, each worker (person) gets $1/600$ of the higher consumption basket; in Mexico, each gets $1/2000$.

    Since workers in each country are identical in productivity and income changes, they all share equally in the GFT. One way to see this outcome is that, because they are identical, each person's personal budget constraint must equal the national budget constraint divided by the labor force, both in autarky and free trade. Thus, each person's b.c. in trade lies above his/her b.c. in autarky, just as happens with the national budget lines. Students should reason through this theory and draw the associated diagrams.

Distribution of the GFT: External

Next, the *external distribution* refers to how the GFT are shared between countries. Intuitively, a country stands to gain more, the higher is the relative price of its export good in free trade compared to autarky, for then its exports are capable of purchasing more imports.

In this model, the amount by which each country gains depends on the change in the terms of trade (how much the relative price in free trade differs from the relative price in autarky).

A country's **terms of trade** are the ratio of its export-good price to its import-good price:

T of $T = \frac{P_{EX}}{P_{IM}}$. This is a very important concept.

The more general concept is that the T of T is an index of a country's export prices divided by an index of its import prices.

In Example 1, for the US, the T of $T = \frac{p_C}{p_R}$.

This price ratio went from 1/3 in autarky to 1.5 in free trade (a relative price increase of +350%). This is excellent news because it implies that each unit of C commands 350% more units of R in trade than in autarky.

For M, the T of $T = \frac{p_R}{p_C}$. This price ratio went from 1/2 in autarky to 2/3 in free trade (a price increase of +33%). This is also beneficial because each R can buy 33% more C in trade.

But the increase in Mexico's export price is smaller than that for the US, suggesting that the US gains the greater share of the GFT than does Mexico. That was true in our example, where the US gained +180C and +80R, while Mexico gained +20C and +20R.

Clearly, in free trade, the US would like to see the highest possible price for C and M would like to see the lowest possible price for C. The US would prefer the lowest possible price for R and M would prefer the highest possible price for R. In terms of relative prices, the US wants to see the highest possible p^* and Mexico wants to see the lowest possible p^*.

But recall from the earlier theory that there are limits to the free-trade price ratio, given by each country's autarky price ratio:

$$\frac{1}{3} \le p^* = \left(P_C^* / P_R^*\right) \le 2$$

Our analysis suggests that the US would like p^* to be as close to 2 as possible and Mexico would like it to be as close to 1/3 as possible.

What determines the free-trade price ratio? As we will see shortly, it depends on the world (US plus Mexico) demands for and supplies of the two goods. Thus, the *external (between-country) distribution of the GFT depends on world demand for and supply of C and R.*

In example 1, the demand for C must be quite high in equilibrium because $\frac{p_C^*}{p_R^*}$ is near the high endpoint of its possible range. This means that the US gets the larger share of the GFT though both countries are better off in free trade than in autarky.

Aside: When people or politicians say economic welfare rises as a country's exports get larger, what they really mean is that *welfare rises as export prices go up.* This is also very important to remember.

Important implications of this theory:

1. *Free trade raises both countries' well-being compared to no trade (fundamental concept).*
2. *Once countries are in free trade, a worsening of a country's T of T makes it worse off (but still better than autarky), but a rise in its T of T makes it better off.*

Here are clear examples of how the T of T matter for economic welfare:

(1) Oil-exporting countries want the highest possible international prices for oil, but Japan and Korea (major importers) are better off with low oil prices.
(2) Grain and meat exporters like Australia, Canada, and Brazil benefit when world agricultural prices go up.
(3) The US would like to see high world prices for the advanced machinery and high-technology services it exports.

Distribution of the GFT: Changes in the T of T

What could change a nation's T of T? Since many factors could influence supply and demand for products, there are numerous shifts that could do so. Here are some key examples:

- A rise in the country's labor force would expand its export supply and reduce its T of T by driving down the world price of its exports. Then, each person in that country would be worse off on a "per capita" basis.

- A decline (rise) in the world demand for the country's export good worsens (improves) its T of T. But a decline (rise) in the world demand for the country's import good has the opposite effects.
- A technological improvement in producing the country's export good has two offsetting effects:
  - First, the increase in the productivity of labor raises the wage rate in the economy, improving welfare (see the material later in these notes on productivity and wages).
  - Second, better technology would expand export capacity and worsen the T of T, which should reduce welfare.

It is not clear which effect would dominate in this case. The outcome would depend on the circumstances.

Distribution of the GFT: The small-country case

Here is an important special case. Consider a small economy (Costa Rica) trading with a large economy (US) and let them trade hats (H) and cars (C). Suppose that Costa Rica has a comparative advantage in H.

Now, let them go into free trade. It is reasonable to suppose that Costa Rica is so small that even if it specializes in H, it cannot produce enough to meet the demands for H in both CR and the US. This means that the US must produce both H and C in free trade, just as in autarky.

In this case, the US does not completely specialize, and the free-trade relative price must be the same as the US price ratio in autarky. (This must be true, for at any other relative price the US would specialize.) Here, the US gets NO GFT, but neither is it worse off. It remains at the same level of welfare it had in autarky.

Instead, Costa Rica gets ALL the GFT in this case as it gets to trade at the US relative price rather than at the Costa Rican autarky price. And that implies an improvement in Costa Rica's terms of trade. In fact, it would be the maximum possible improvement in Costa Rica's terms of trade.

Result: In the Ricardian model, small countries get all the GFT because they can specialize and trade at different prices established in the large countries (or the world). Large countries neither gain nor lose from trade with small countries.

Study question 2

In the Ricardian model, both countries are better off in moving from autarky to free trade if:

A. The free-trade price ratio of goods is strictly between the autarky price ratios.
B. Each country fully specializes in its good of comparative advantage and exports that good.
C. One country specializes and the other produces both goods in free trade.
D. Both countries export the same good to each other.
E. Both A and B.

Discussion of study question 2

The correct answer is E because both A and B are true. A is true because if the free-trade price ratio lies strictly inside the autarky limits to the price ratio, both countries completely specialize and trade permits them to consume at points above their PPFs. This explains also why B is true.

In C, the country that produces both goods in trade neither gains nor loses from trade. D is impossible.

Prices and Real Wages

Prices and wages in the Ricardian model: A closer look

So far, the theory has mostly ignored nominal prices, wages, and exchange rates, arguing that only relative prices (which compare goods in real terms) matter. Yet, policymakers argue about low wages abroad all the time. Why are these factors not central to the basic analysis?

The answer is that nominal prices, nominal wages, and exchange rates must adjust to establish balanced trade according to comparative advantage.

It is important to remember that these variables are endogenous, which means they adjust to achieve equilibrium. They do not cause an equilibrium.

Start with an important definition. A country's real wages $=$ $\frac{w}{p_R}$ and $\frac{w}{p_C}$. These figures (nominal wages divided by prices) show the amount of each good the nominal wage can purchase.

Recall in this model that each worker in a country has the same nominal wage, so these ratios indicate how much purchasing power every worker has.

Prices and wages

Now compare real wages in our example between autarky and free trade. If it is right that everyone is better off in trade, it must be that real wages go up in both countries.

Recall our example 1 with these figures for labor (days) per unit of output:

	US	M
C	1	10
R	3	5

The opportunity costs are US $1C = 1/3\text{R}\,(1R = 3C)$; Mexico $1C = 2R\,(1R = 1/2C)$. Now consider real wages in autarky in the US and M.

Recall that in each good, price $=$ average cost (and price $=$ marginal cost, which is the same here) because of perfect competition. But average cost is just the wage times the amount of labor needed per unit of output.

Thus, in the US in autarky, $p_C = w^{US} * 1$ and $p_R = w^{US} * 3$.

Then, $\frac{w^{US}}{p_C} = 1$ and $\frac{w^{US}}{p_R} = {}^1/_3$ are the real wages in terms of C and R in autarky in the US. (Again, this is how many C and R the wage can purchase.) Note that these real wages are equal to average productivity (and marginal productivity) of labor, $1/a$ and $1/b$ in the US.

Important point: A worker's real wages in autarky are equal to the marginal products of labor in each good. Be clear what this means:

All workers (because they have the same nominal wage) have the same *real wages* in terms of buying C and R.

The same theory will show us that real wages in Mexico are 1/10 in C and 1/5 in R.

Note that real wages in autarky are higher in the US than in Mexico because labor is more productive in both goods in the US.

Now consider how wages must adjust in free trade if they are excessively high or low to achieve balanced trade. This is possible by figuring out the limits to the ratio of market wages in the US versus Mexico in free trade.

Note that the US labor is 10 times more productive than M labor in C, which is the biggest productivity advantage for the US. *It follows that if the US wage $> 10x$ Mexican wage, then Mexico would produce both C and R more cheaply.*

How can this be shown? First, note the Mexican wage is in pesos, which we need to convert to dollars.

The Mexican wage in dollars would be $w^{M\$} = w^{MPeso} * E$, where E is the dollar/peso exchange rate. (Example: Let \$1 be worth 15 pesos (pesos/dollars), so $E = 1/15$ (dollar/peso). Suppose $w^{MPeso} = 150$ pesos per day, then $w^{M\$} = 150\,\text{pesos} \times 1/15\,(\text{dollar/peso}) = \$10$ per day). For now, leave the exchange rate aside by setting $E = 1/15$ and keeping it fixed.

Suppose also that the US wage is $w_{US} = \$180$ per day. Note that this is more than 10 times higher than the M wage so it should be a problem. What are the unit costs (and therefore prices) if the US and M traded with each other?

	US	M
C	$1 \times \$180 = \$180$	$10 \times \$10 = \$100$
R	$3 \times \$180 = \$540$	$5 \times \$10 = \$50$

Here, Mexico would export both goods to the US. But this cannot be an equilibrium because M would have a trade surplus and the US a trade deficit. (It would actually mean M produces both goods and the US produces none, which is inconsistent with full employment.)

Thus, the wage would rise in M and fall in the US. This would happen until $w^{US} \leq 10 * w^{M\$}$.

An alternative adjustment would be with the exchange rate. Suppose that nominal wages are "sticky" and cannot change in peso and dollar terms. Then, because M produces both goods more cheaply than the US, the peso would *appreciate* and the dollar would *depreciate*.

But that would raise the M wage in dollar terms, having the same kind of effect. In particular, the exchange rate would adjust until Mexico's wage is sufficiently higher and the US wage sufficiently lower (both expressed in dollars) to establish a wage ratio within the limits.

Thus, suppose the new $w^{US} = \$100$ and the new $w^{M\$} = \$20$ (which would be 300 pesos per day at $\$1 = 15P$). Now, what are average costs?

	US	M
C	\$100	\$200
R	\$300	\$100

These unit costs are consistent with CA and the US will specialize in C and export C and M will specialize in R and export R. (*Note again that this outcome works despite the US having an absolute advantage in both goods.*) And observe that the US wage is now five times the M wage, so this is below the maximum ratio (of 10) noted above.

Now try the other extreme. The US is 5/3 times as productive in R => if $w^{US} < \frac{5}{3}w^{M\$}$, the US would produce both goods more cheaply and export both. This is not possible, so the US wage would rise and the Mexican wage would fall until they are established within the allowable range.

Alternatively, the peso would depreciate relative to the dollar, reducing the peso wage in dollar terms. Students should work on this on their own: Let $w^{US} = \$15$ and $w^{M\$} = \$10$ and show that US produces both goods more cheaply.

Limits on relative wages across countries

What this logic says is that there are limits on the *relative wage* rate between countries in free trade: $5/3 \leq (w^{US}/w^{M\$}) \leq 10$. This would be the expression where both wages are expressed in dollars, which is sufficient for understanding concepts in this model. (That is, ignore the exchange rate E going forward.)

These are the limits that are consistent with balanced trade, and nominal wages must adjust to be inside these limits. Again, where do these limits come from? 10 is the maximum US absolute advantage in productivity (in good C). Any higher wage ratio makes US costs higher in both goods, which can't happen. And $5/3$ is the minimum US absolute advantage (in good R). Any lower relative wage makes US costs lower in both goods, which can't happen.

Here is more perspective: If the US wage is in the numerator, then the maximum wage ratio comes by comparing national productivities in the good in which it has a CA (chemicals) and the minimum wage ratio comes by comparing productivities in the good of comparative disadvantage (radios).

Relative wages must lie between these limits given by labor productivity.

Summary: Since trade must be balanced, nominal wages will adjust to within limits determined by labor productivities. This adjustment could be in exchange rates, wages, or both.

Prices, real wages, and the terms of trade

Recall that there are also free-trade relative price limits: $1/3 \leq (p_C^*/p_R^*) \leq 2$. The theory added free-trade relative wage limits: $5/3 \leq (w^{US*}/w^{M\$*}) \leq 10$. Both statements must be true, and both are consistent with both countries enjoying GFT.

Of course, the ranges are closely related to each other. In free trade, only the US produces C and only Mexico produces R because of specialization. This means we must have these free-trade prices (with wages in dollar terms):

$$p_C^* = w^{US*}x1 \quad \text{and} \quad p_R^* = w^{M\$*}x5$$

$$(p_C^*/p_R^*) = (w^{US*}x1/w^{M\$*}x5) => (w^{US*}/w^{M\$*}) = 5(p_C^*/p_R^*)$$

Therefore, $1/3 \le (p_C^*/p_R^*) \le 2 \Leftrightarrow 5/3 \le (w^{US*}/w^{M\$*}) \le 10$. Note this means that *a rise in the US T of T implies a rise in the US relative wage*.

Again, the US wants both these ratios to be as high as possible and Mexico wants them to be as low as possible. The higher the price ratio (the US terms of trade), the better off the US. In turn, a higher US relative wage means that US workers are better off. But as long as both ratios are inside their limits, both the US and M will gain from trade.

Real wages rise in free trade

This analysis can now show that real wages are higher in free trade than in autarky in both the US and M.

Recall what we already showed:

Autarky $\frac{w^{US}}{p_C} = 1$. This is the *real wage* in terms of C.

$\frac{w^{US}}{p_R} = 1/3$. This is the real wage in terms of R.

And in Mexico, $\frac{w^M}{p_C} = 1/10$ and $\frac{w^M}{p_R} = 1/5$. These are real wages in autarky in M. Again, these real wages are equal to labor productivities in each country.

Note that *real wages are higher in the US*. This is due to higher labor productivity.

In example 1, we had $p^* = 1.5$, implying that the relative wage ratio is $5 \times 1.5 = 7.5$.

Now consider free trade with $w^{US*} = \$150$ and $w^{M\$*} = \$20$. Compare the costs (prices) at these wages if countries had to produce both goods (no trade) and in free trade with specialization. (But note clearly that free-trade nominal wages would be different from autarky nominal wages, so this calculation is only an illustration.)

Costs if No Trade	US	M
C	$150	$200
R	$450	$100
Costs in Free Trade	US	M
C	$150 (produced in US)	$150 (imported from US)
R	$100 (imported from M)	$100 (produced in Mexico)

What are real wages in free trade?

$w^{US*}/_{p^*C} = 1$ (no change from autarky) $w^{US*}/_{p^*R} = 1.5 (>1/3;$ higher than autarky)

$w^{M\$*}/_{p^*C} = 20/150 = 0.133 (>1/10;$ higher) $w^{M\$*}/_{p^*R} = 20/100 = 1/5$ (no change from autarky)

Note what happened. In the US, the real wage remains the same in C as in autarky because the US still produces it and there is no change in marginal labor productivity. But because the price of R is lower through imports (from $450 to $100), the real wage rises from 1/3 to 1.5.

In M, the real wage remains the same in R as in autarky. But M imports C from the US at a lower price ($150 instead of $200) and the real wage in C rises from 0.1 to 0.133.

Summary: Autarky and free-trade real wages are the same in the export good (no change in MPL) but are higher in the import good due to lower import prices.

Since real wages are higher for all workers, all workers gain from trade. But note also that even in free trade US workers have higher real wages than Mexican workers. Again, this is because US workers are more productive than Mexican workers.

Study question 3

Which statement is false?

A. A country wants to see its terms of trade rise as much as possible in free trade.

B. The reason a country GFT in this model is that the price of imports is lower in free trade than the price of the same good in autarky.
C. In free trade, in this model, each country GFT because its labor becomes more productive in free trade than in autarky.
D. A country with higher labor productivity has higher real wages in free trade than the other country.

Discussion of study question 3

The correct (false) answer is C. In the Ricardian model, labor productivity does not change in moving from autarky to free trade.

A is true because countries benefit from higher export prices and lower import prices. B is true. The cheaper import price permits an improvement in each person's budget constraint. D is true because higher labor productivity implies higher real wages.

Study question 4

In comparing each country's real wages in free trade versus autarky, all the following are true except:

A. Real wages are higher in free trade than in autarky in both countries if the international price ratio lies between the limits given by autarky.
B. In each country, the real wage stays the same in its imported good but rises in its exported good.
C. In each country, the real wage rises in its imported good but stays the same in its exported good.
D. A country that is less productive in both goods has lower real wages in both autarky and in free trade than the other country.

Discussion of study question 4

The correct (false) answer is B. The real wage rises in the import good because it has a lower price but does not change in the export good.

This shows that C is true. A is true because an intermediate price ratio permits specialization and raises the real wage in the import good in both countries. D is true as noted in question 3.

A note on labor migration and productivity

In the example, in free trade, the US still has higher real wages in both goods. This equilibrium would establish an incentive for L to migrate from Mexico to the US. In fact, in the Ricardian model, all L in M would move to the US, which suggests the Ricardian model may not capture reality all that well.

An interesting observation: In this model, labor productivity depends on where a worker is located, rather than being a characteristic of the workers. This is an interesting empirical question that will be addressed later in the notes on immigration.

But the primary point here is that high-wage countries in free trade are also the high-productivity countries. They can trade beneficially with low-wage countries (and vice versa) due to the combined influence of wages and productivities.

What determines the marginal productivities of labor in producing goods, which are the key to CA and the reasons there are trade and GFT?

In general, differences in productivity depend on national differences in technology, skills, education, endowments, economic and social organization, infrastructure, government policies, and other factors. The better these are, the higher are labor productivity figures (and capital and land productivity).

These factors can be considered the national sources of international competitiveness.

Key policy implication: To keep the real wages of workers rising over time, countries need to invest in improving such factors.

Implication: "international competitiveness"

The most basic definition of *international economic competitiveness* relates to comparisons of unit labor costs across countries within industries. The Ricardian model offers a deep insight about such comparisons.

If the nominal wage rates in a country's industries get so high that real wages are considerably above labor productivity, then unit labor costs get very high, and an economy loses "competitiveness" in those sectors. Output is likely to fall, and net imports (imports minus exports) are likely to rise.

Over time, various changes will happen to reduce these costs. These changes could be lower nominal and real wages, a depreciating currency, and employment losses where wages are both high and "sticky", meaning that they cannot readily go down in nominal terms due to labor contracts.

In contrast, if nominal wages are low compared to labor productivity, unit labor costs will be low, and output and net exports are likely to rise. In turn, nominal and real wages will rise as a result of trade.

Some famous examples:

- The US and UK steel industries in the 1970s–1980s had high labor costs and old technologies, resulting in large declines in employment and output (and reduced union power as imports went up). Over time, negotiated hourly wages have fallen relative to other parts of the US economy, such as high-technology and knowledge-based services. Employment fell dramatically in steel.
- During the EU financial crisis in 2008–2012, Greece (with relatively low labor productivity) saw large reductions in employment and real wages. This was partly because its currency is the euro, meaning it could not permit depreciation of a national currency relative to its chief trading partners, such as Germany and France. This history will be examined further in the international finance segments.
- East Asian economies that grew rapidly from the 1980s to now, such as South Korea, Malaysia, China, and Vietnam, all entered the period with low wages compared to labor productivity in export goods. Those real wages rose sharply over time due to trade,

along with high rates of investment, education, and technological change.

Summary: Key points of the Ricardian model

1. Real labor productivities in products determine absolute advantage and comparative advantage.
2. Comparative advantage (relative labor costs and therefore relative prices of goods in autarky) determines the trade pattern and the limits to terms of trade.
3. Comparative advantage also is what permits GFT for all countries.
4. The world demands for, and supplies of, goods determine the equilibrium relative price ratio of goods in free trade and therefore the split of the GFT between countries.
5. The international price ratio (terms of trade) and the relative wage ratio are related closely to each other.
6. Absolute advantage determines which country has higher real wages. The country with higher labor productivity rates will have the higher real wages in both autarky and trade.

Finishing example 2

Here is one more example for additional practice. Suppose there are two countries, Vietnam (V) and Germany (G), and two goods, clothing (C) and medicines $(D$ for drugs$)$. And we have the following figures on hours of labor per unit of output:

	G	V
C	3	5
D	3	15

Students should see immediately that drugs are very expensive in V but not expensive in G, in relative terms. But consider answers to our basic questions.

- G is more productive in both goods, so it has the absolute advantage in both. V has the absolute disadvantage in both. Note this means G will have higher real wages than V.
- In V, it takes 15 hours to produce D but just 5 to produce C. Thus, D must be more expensive than C in Vietnam. It is, for $1D = 3C$ in Vietnam. The OC of $1D$ is $3C$ and $p^v = \left(p_D^V / p_C^V\right) = \frac{15}{5} = 3$. The OC of $1C$ is then $1/3D$.

In G, it takes 3 hours to produce either D or C. These goods would have the same cost and $1D = 1C$. The OC of $1D$ is giving up $1C$ in production. And

$$p^G = \left(p_D^G / p_C^G\right) = \frac{3}{3} = 1.$$

It follows that V has a comparative advantage in C and G has a CA in D. The limits to the relative price in free trade would then be $1 \leq \left(p_D^* / p_C^*\right) \leq 3$.

This is the relative price of drugs in free trade. Any free-trade price ratio lying strictly between those limits would imply that both V and G gain from trade.

It also would be the terms of trade for Germany, since G would export drugs. G would like this relative price to be as high as possible, but V would like it to be as low as possible (for then it would import D at a low price).

What are the real wages in autarky? They are the inverses of these figures for hours of labor per output (because the inverses are the marginal products of labor). That means real wages are

	G	V
C	1/3	1/5
D	1/3	1/15

But we can see this also by noting that real wages are nominal wages divided by prices. Prices equal average costs. Thus, for example, in Vietnam, $p_C^V = w^V * 5$ since it takes 5 hours of labor to produce one unit of C and each hour gets paid the wage w^V.

Thus, the real wage in terms of buying C is $(w^V/p_C^V) = 1/5$. The same kind of calculation holds for the other real wages.

What are the limits to the relative wage ratio defined as (w^{G*}/w^{V*})? Look back at the labor output ratios. Germany is five times as productive in D (15/3), so the maximum relative wage is $15/3 = 5$. Any higher wage ratio would permit V to produce both goods cheaper than G, which can't be an equilibrium. To see this, suppose in free trade we have $w^{G*} = 200$ euros and $w^{V*} = 25$ euros (forget about the Vietnamese exchange rate with the euro).

Then, $(w^{G*}/w^{V*}) = 8$, which our theory says is too high. Using these nominal wages to compute the costs of production:

	G	V
C	$200 \times 3 = 600$ euros	$25 \times 5 = 125$ euros
D	$200 \times 3 = 600$ euros	$25 \times 15 = 375$ euros

Thus, both costs (prices) would be lower in V than in G, which is not an equilibrium. This would drive the V wage up and the G wage down until the relative wage ratio is below 5.

But Germany is just 5/3 times as productive in C, so the minimum relative wage is 5/3. Any lower wage ratio would permit G to produce both goods cheaper than V, which can't be an equilibrium.

Thus, these relative price and relative wage limits hold:

$$1 \leq (p_D^*/p_C^*) \leq 3$$

$$5/3 \leq (w^{G*}/w^{V*}) \leq 5$$

Note that the second equation is just 5/3 times the first equation, so

$$(w^{G*}/w^{V*}) = (5/3)(p_D^*/p_C^*)$$

Now, determine the PPFs and the GFT using hours of labor to measure the labor forces. Suppose the labor force in G is 120,000 hours and in V it is 450,000 hours. Then, the PPFs are as follows.

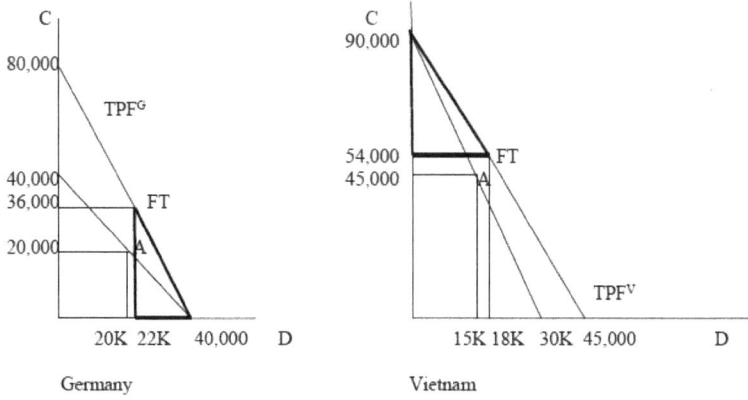

Figure 3.3   Trade in example 2.

Note that in autarky, the relative prices are $p^G = 1$ and $p^V = 3$. Suppose that both G and V split their labor in half. Then, autarky output and consumption are as shown at the two points A. Now, suppose $p^* = 2$ in free trade. This means in trade that $1D = 2C$ ($1C = 0.5D$) and the TPFs are as shown. Let G export $18{,}000D$ and import $36{,}000C$, while V exports $36{,}000C$ and imports $18{,}000D$. The trade triangles and the GFT are shown in Figure 3.3.

In fact, the GFT are $+2000D$ and $+16{,}000C$ for Germany and $+3000D$ and $+9000C$ for Vietnam. Both countries seem to get significant GFT because the world price ratio is in the middle of the possible range, implying they both get notable improvements in the T of T. For G, the percent change in price (from 1 to 2) is $+100\%$. For V, it is (from $1/3$ to $1/2$) $= +50\%$.

How does this translate into real wages in free trade? First, if $\left(p_D^*/p_C^*\right) = 2$, then $\left(w^{G*}/w^{V*}\right) = (5/3) \times 2 = 10/3 = 3.33$. Germany's nominal wage in free trade is $3.33\times$ that in Vietnam.

Real wages in free trade

In Germany

real wage in buying D $= \left(w^{G*}/w^{G*}x3\right) = 1/3$, the same as in autarky;

real wage in buying C $= \left(w^{G*}/w^{V*}x5\right) = (10/3)/5 = 2/3 > 1/3$, higher than in autarky.

In Vietnam

real wage in buying D $= (^{w^{V*}}/_{w^{G*}x3}) = (3/10)/3 = 1/10 > 1/15$, higher than in autarky;

real wage in buying C $= (^{w^{V*}}/_{w^{V*}x5}) = 1/5$, the same as in autarky.

Workers in both countries have a higher real wage in the import good but have the same real wage in the export good, compared to autarky. Germany has higher real wages in buying both goods because its labor is more productive.

Chapter 4

The Factor Proportions (Heckscher–Ohlin) Model of Trade

Why a More Complicated Model is Needed

Problems with the Ricardian model

The Ricardian model of trade is helpful for understanding the nature of comparative advantage and the gains from international trade. It has important insights that are fundamental to how the global economy works.

However, there are obvious problems with the simplifications made in the model. Here are the primary simplifications, which are surely false in the real world.

1. There is only one factor of production with constant marginal products in both goods. But we know there are multiple factors, such as labor, capital, and land.
2. The model predicts that countries completely specialize their production in free trade. But we rarely observe countries being so specialized, except perhaps for major oil exporters.
3. The model predicts that all people gain from trade. Put differently, there is no redistribution of income among people within an economy due to trade. Rather, all individuals gain the same amount. However, as described in Chapter 1, trade makes some groups better off and others worse off.

Approaching a more realistic model

We can relax these restrictions considerably by studying our next model.

Here are the basic ideas:

A. Rather than there being one factor, there are many (the new model assumes two but delivers strong insights). Countries are abundant or scarce in their endowments of particular factors.
B. Products (technologies) make more intensive use of some factors and less intensive use of others.
C. The model predicts that countries export the products that intensively use their abundant factors and import the products that intensively use their scarce factors, which is intuitively sensible. Note this outcome means that trade in goods is implicitly the same as trade in the services of factors. This means that different factor endowments are the real driver of CA and trade.

This is the simple version, but the actual theory is more complicated, as developed in the following notes.

Model assumptions and data

This model was largely worked out by two Swedish economists, Eli Heckscher and Bertil Ohlin, in the early 20th century. In essence, it applies neoclassical producer and consumer theory to international trade, so it is also called the neoclassical trade model.

Supply-side assumptions:

1. There is perfect competition in all markets.
2. There are two countries, say, Japan and China. They have different relative factor endowments: $(\bar{K}_J/\bar{L}_J) > (\bar{K}_C/\bar{L}_C)$.
3. There are two factors, capital (K) and labor (L). They are homogeneous and in fixed supply. These factors are mobile between industries but cannot move between countries. Note this means that the wage rate (w) and price of capital (r) are the same

in all goods within Japan and China, though they can be different between J and C.

4. There are two final goods, say, shoes (S) and autos (A) which differ in relative factor intensity:
   Assume that $K_A/L_A > K_S/L_S$ in both countries. That is, A is $K - intensive$ and S is $L - intensive$ in both J and C.

5. The technologies for producing A and S are CRS and are the same in both Japan and China.

Illustrative data on relative factor intensities and endowments

The next two tables illustrate the concepts of *factor intensities and factor endowments*.

   Table 4.1 lists data in two years for major US manufacturing industries on

1. value added (which is total sales minus purchased inputs and is a measure of size);
2. production labor (which are workers on the factory line, sometimes called "blue-collar" workers);
3. capital expenditures divided by production labor (a rough measure of capital intensity $\frac{K}{L}$ by industry);
4. non-production labor (largely managerial, design, and technical workers, sometimes called "white-collar" workers) divided by production labor (a rough measure of skill intensity by industry).

   The data are ranked by $\frac{K}{L}$ ratios in 2019. The top several industries are capital-intensive and many are also skill-intensive, such as computers and transportation equipment. Further down are industries that are largely skill-intensive. At the bottom are sectors, such as textiles and apparel, that have low capital intensity and skill intensity. These are the most labor-intensive industries.

   It is interesting to note that outputs and employment have shifted over time. Production labor employed in the apparel industry fell from 423,000 in 2000 to just 59,000 in 2019.

Table 4.1   Measures of factor intensities in US manufacturing industries.

	2000				2019				Evident Intensities
	Value Added ($ millions)	Production Labor (PL; 000)	Capital Expend per PL ($)	Non-production Labor per PL	Value Added ($ millions)	Production Labor (PL; 000)	Capital Expend per PL	Non-production Labor per PL	
Petroleum and coal products	45,748	67	74,624	0.51	127,825	71	189,197	0.51	Capital, skill
Chemical products	235,614	508	41,112	0.75	399,796	476	66,456	0.58	Capital, skill
Computer and electronic prods	291,125	848	33,227	0.94	180,471	373	39,946	1.12	Capital, skill
Wood and paper products	114,260	914	12,234	0.24	131,829	578	22,431	0.25	Capital
Transportation equipment	240,989	1,349	12,529	0.36	361,438	1,115	21,271	0.39	Capital, skill
Food, beverages and tobacco	255,245	1,244	11,714	0.35	411,274	1,337	19,192	0.28	Capital
Mineral products	55,722	408	14,820	0.28	74,122	301	16,684	0.31	Capital
Metal products	215,545	1,839	8,729	0.30	291,713	1,339	15,237	0.31	Capital
Plastic and rubber products	92,333	862	10,086	0.26	123,609	605	15,160	0.27	Capital
Electrical equipment and appliances	62,991	431	9,069	0.37	65,763	235	14,064	0.47	Skill
Machinery	148,798	920	10,116	0.52	192,009	686	13,219	0.52	Skill
Miscellaneous products	70,621	501	8,219	0.49	98,452	342	12,254	0.55	Skill
Textile products	35,225	475	5,130	0.27	22,901	150	8,393	0.27	Labor
Printing	63,446	597	7,398	0.39	48,258	287	7,592	0.38	Skill
Furniture and related products	42,267	515	4,011	0.25	42,191	277	5,863	0.30	Labor
Leather products	4,510	55	2,813	0.25	2,115	20	4,600	0.30	Labor
Apparel	28,210	423	2,302	0.24	5,616	59	3,373	0.25	Labor

Source: Compiled by author from US Department of Commerce, *Annual Survey of Manufactures.*

Production labor employment fell in most industries but by relatively different amounts. Overall, this reflects a shift in the US economy away from manufacturing and toward services, as discussed in later notes.

Table 4.2 displays estimated data for several countries on

1. capital stock per worker, which includes all private and public capital divided by the labor force;
2. arable land per worker, in hectares;
3. an index of human capital, which is based on the average years of schooling in the population. The term human capital refers to the total education, skills, and experience of workers in an economy;
4. the number of researchers in R&D activities per million people in the population.

Singapore is the most capital-abundant country in the table, followed by Finland and Germany. The capital-abundant countries all are advanced, rich economies. They also have high levels of human capital and R&D workers. Australia, Canada, and the US also have relatively large stocks of arable land. The final five countries are labor-abundant because they have low ratios, implying relatively large labor forces.

Note that China and India have seen large increases in their capital–labor ratios and human capital indexes. This is due to high rates of investment in capital and education, particularly in China, over the period. This trend indicates that factor endowments change dynamically over time because countries have different rates of national investment, education, and R&D spending. However, in the HO model, we will assume that factor endowments are fixed, permitting them to determine CA in a static equilibrium.

Model assumptions and data

The final assumption in the HO model removes demand differences between countries as a source of comparative advantage, leaving just factor endowments and factor intensities (on the supply side) to determine trade patterns.

Table 4.2 Measures of relative factor endowments.

	2000				2019			2010	
Country	Capital Stock per Worker, US$	Arable Land per Worker, Hectares	Human Capital Index	Researchers in R&D per million people	Capital Stock per Worker, US$	Arable Land per Worker, Hectares	Human Capital Index	Researchers in R&D per million people	Evident Abundance
Singapore	466,841	0.00	2.72	4,128	573,268	0.00	4.35	6,242	Cap, Skill, R&D
Finland	389,052	0.95	3.13	7,822	480,415	0.84	3.50	7,720	Cap, Skill, R&D
Germany	435,355	0.30	3.57	3,168	467,845	0.26	3.68	4,058	Cap, Skill, R&D
United Kingdom	416,458	0.21	3.51	2,895	466,140	0.18	3.77	4,043	Cap, Skill, R&D
Australia	392,882	2.64	3.54	3,475	459,724	2.41	3.55	4,532	Cap, Land, R&D
Canada	349,915	2.74	3.50	3,527	453,805	2.00	3.72	4,646	Cap, Land, R&D
Rep. of Korea	243,700	0.08	3.19	2,287	417,883	0.05	3.77	5,331	Cap, R&D
USA	356,100	1.26	3.58	3,496	410,987	1.00	3.75	3,885	Cap, Land, Skill
Japan	370,720	0.07	3.35	5,078	373,536	0.06	3.59	5,104	Cap, R&D
Mexico	192,274	0.60	2.42	225	198,824	0.43	2.78	337	Labor
South Africa	129,705	1.00	2.09	311	155,171	0.64	2.91	365	Labor
Brazil	136,089	0.67	2.05	295	145,987	0.59	3.09	686	Labor
China	18,768	0.16	2.31	539	127,319	0.15	2.70	885	Labor
India	24,072	0.39	1.78	110	71,186	0.31	2.17	156	Labor

Source: Compiled by the author using data from Penn World Tables, v10; World Bank World Development Indicators; Food and Agricultural Organization FAOSTAT.

Demand-side assumption:
Preferences for goods are identical in both countries and these preferences do not change as countries achieve higher income levels.

This means two things, which are convenient but empirically untrue:

- The community indifference curves are the same in both China and Japan.
- As a country, say Japan, gets richer, consumers continue to spend the same percentage of their incomes on each good. This means that, whether the country is rich or poor, it still spends, say, 15% of income on food, 20% on housing, 10% on clothing, 10% on vehicles, etc.

This last element is unrealistic because there are differences in spending patterns across countries. For example, far greater proportions of income are spent on housing, food, and other basic needs in poor countries, while rich countries spend greater proportions on leisure goods, services, and technology. We will make this assumption for now but study later how demand differences may affect trade.

Study question 1

Which of the following is not an assumption of the factor proportions model?

A. Countries have different relative supplies of factor endowments.
B. Countries have different production functions for producing goods.
C. Consumers in both countries share identical preferences for goods.
D. Industries are different in their capital and labor intensities.

Discussion of study question 1

The correct answer is B. Rather than different production functions, the HO model assumes they are identical, in order to eliminate differences in technologies as sources of CA. The other assumptions all are made by the factor proportions theory.

Model Analytics and Equilibrium

PPFs and equilibrium

Turn next to representing these various assumptions in general equilibrium diagrams, which we use to explain trade patterns.

How are the supply-side assumptions reflected in PPFs? Recall that each country is relatively abundant in one factor (and scarce in the other), while each good is relatively intensive in one factor. Here, Japan is abundant in K and China is abundant in L, while autos are K-intensive and shoes are labor-intensive.

These elements combine in an intuitive way:

Each country's PPF is biased toward the good that intensively uses the country's abundant factor. (This will be explained in more detail a bit later, but it makes sense.) The PPFs for Japan and China are shown in Figure 4.1.

The demand-side assumption is represented by drawing identical CICs in China and Japan. Note that because the PPFs are biased and demand patterns are the same, the Japanese autarky equilibrium at

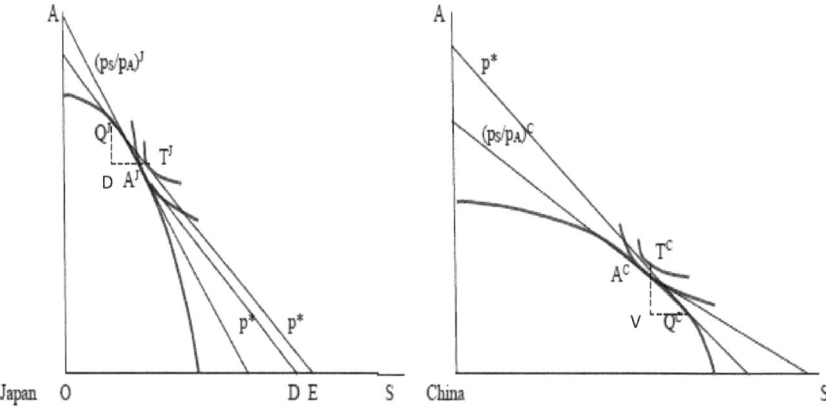

Figure 4.1 Biased PPFs in the factor proportions model. Capital-abundant Japan's PPF is biased toward autos and labor-abundant China's PPF is biased toward shoes.

point A^J lies further up and to the left on its PPF than the Chinese equilibrium A^C lies on its PPF.

This means that the autarky price ratio in Japan is steeper than the one in China, so we have

$$({p_S}/{p_A})^J > ({p_S}/{p_A})^C \text{ due to the biases in the PPFs}$$

But this means that China has the comparative advantage (CA) in S and Japan has the CA in A. For example, we could have $({p_S}/{p_A})^C = \frac{1}{2}\left(1S = \frac{1}{2}A\right)$ *and* $({p_S}/{p_A})^J = 3(1S = 3A)$.

Implication: With our assumptions, the determination of CA is based completely on two supply-side factors:

1. *relative factor endowments of the two countries;*
2. *relative factor intensities of the two industries.*

Trade equilibrium and the Heckscher–Ohlin theorem

For reasons discussed in the Ricardian model, there will be mutually beneficial trade in the price range

$$({p_S}/{p_A})^C < ({p_S}/{p_A})^* < ({p_S}/{p_A})^J$$

In the diagram, the free-trade price ratio is labeled p^*. In free trade, this becomes the price ratio that exists in both countries.

Note carefully that in moving from autarky to trade, the relative price ratio falls in Japan (making A more expensive and S cheaper) and rises in China (making S more expensive and A cheaper). These price changes are related to the trade pattern:

China exports S and imports A. As a result, p_S goes up and p_A goes down in China.

Japan exports A and imports S. As a result, p_S goes down and p_A goes up in Japan.

We can state the HO theorem: *Let two countries have different relative factor endowments and produce two final goods with identical CRS production functions, one of which is labor-intensive and one is capital-intensive. Then, in free trade, each country will export the good that intensively uses its abundant factor and import the good that intensively uses its scarce factor.*

Adjustments to reach the trade equilibrium

Next consider the equilibrium production, consumption, and trade volumes in free trade. With no trade barriers or trade costs, exports and imports achieve equilibrium at an intermediate p^*, where trade balances for both countries.

To understand the equilibrium, consider the adjustments that happen in the two countries. The next two charts, shown in Figure 4.2, "blow up" the relevant parts of the earlier diagram.

Outputs:
In China, output of S rises and output of A falls because of the higher price of S and the lower price of A. In Japan, output of S falls and output of A rises.

Thus, there is a *tendency toward specialization* but only until the ratio of prices equals the slopes of the PPFs at points Q^C and Q^J. These are the new equilibrium production points. In equilibrium, in this model, there is *incomplete specialization*, meaning that both countries produce both goods in free trade.

Note the importance of concave PPFs. This means there are rising marginal costs (or rising opportunity costs) along the PPFs. Recall from earlier notes that the (absolute value of) the slope of a PPF is the marginal rate of transformation (MRT).

Thus, in China, the relative cost of S rises until (the absolute value of) the slope of PPF = $\text{MRT}_C = p^*$ at point Q^C.

In Japan, the relative cost of A rises until $\text{MRT}_J = p^*$ at point Q^J.

Equilibrium adjustments

Consumption:
Since the price of S rises and the price of A falls in China, Chinese consumers will buy more autos and (probably) fewer shoes (Figure 4.2). The consumption point is T^C. Note that it is on a higher CIC than the one in autarky. Again, trade permits consumption above the PPF. Thus, free trade raises economic welfare in China.

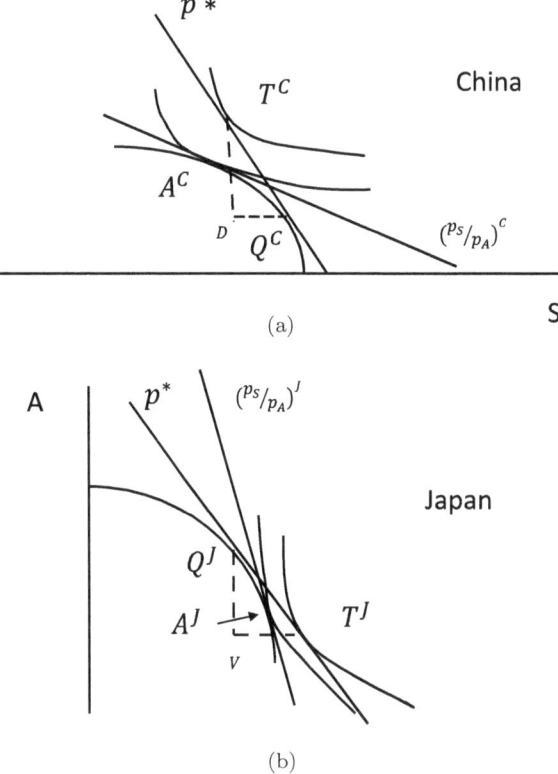

Figure 4.2 (a) Expanded view of the Chinese trade equilibrium; (b) expanded view of the Japanese trade equilibrium.

For similar reason, Japanese consumers will purchase more shoes and (probably) fewer autos. Its consumption point is T^J. Japan also gains from trade.

Trade pattern:
Now, consider the trade triangles. Japan exports A and imports S, with its trade triangle being $Q^J V T^J$. China exports S and imports S, with trade triangle $Q^C D T^C$. Trade is balanced in physical terms (equal trade triangles).

And trade is balanced in value terms (value of exports = value of imports). To see this, note the (absolute value of) the slope of the hypotenuse of China's trade triangle is p^*. But that also equals the rise over run, or $^{IM^C_A}/_{EX^C_S}$. That is, for China, $IM^C_A = EX^C_S \left(\frac{p_S}{p_A}\right)^*$, which implies that $p^*_A IM^C_A = p^*_S EX^C_S$. And that also implies that $p^*_A EX^J_A = p^*_S IM^J_S$.

Gains from trade

There are multiple ways of describing the gains from trade in this model.

1. Both Japan and China are on higher indifference curves (CICs) than in autarky.
2. Both economies consume outside their PPFs, which was not possible in autarky.
3. Real GDP is higher in free trade than in autarky, as shown in the following diagram.

Real GDP rises

Recall from the earlier notes (Chapter 2) that real GDP can be measured as the endpoints of the price lines tangent to the PPF in any equilibrium.

However, to compare real GDP levels at two different equilibrium points requires using the same relative prices to value output. If different prices were used, it would be impossible to sort the effects on GDP from price variations versus quantity changes.

The appropriate comparison is to use relative world prices, not autarky prices. The reason is that free-trade prices are not distorted by limits on trade, while autarky prices are distorted by barriers that eliminate trade and are inefficient.

Recall the situation in Japan (shown again Figure 4.3):

- Free-trade output is at Q^J, generating real GDP of OE (in units of S) at world prices p^*.
- Autarky output is at A^J, generating real GDP of OD (in units of S) at world prices p^*.

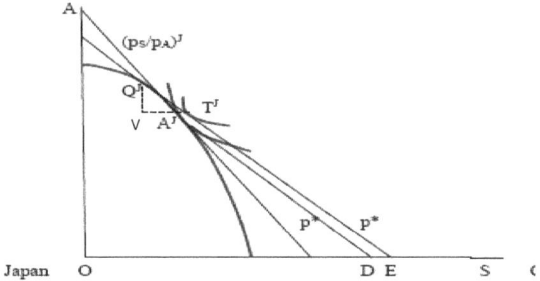

Figure 4.3   Evaluating real GDP in autarky and free trade.

Implication: Free trade permits partial specialization toward Japan's more efficient good (the one in which it has the CA), which raises real GDP. In turn, we could invoke the compensation principle, so Japan has higher welfare.

The same would be true for China. Students should show that China also has a higher real GDP when measured in shoes at price ratio p^*.

Equilibrium with national supply and demand curves

It is useful to develop an easier way to represent this international trade equilibrium. This may be done with *national supply and demand curves*. These are derived from the PPF and CIC diagrams. In the following diagram, put one good (shoes) on the horizontal axis and p^* (the relative price of shoes) on the vertical axis.

Looking back at the PPF/CIC diagram for Japan, note that as the relative price line gets flatter (the price of shoes falls and the price of autos rises), Japan moves along its PPF toward producing more A and less S. That means the Japanese national supply (NS) curve of shoes is upward-sloping because a lower price generates lower output.

Next, as the relative price of shoes falls, Japan's economy consumes more shoes. This means that the Japanese national demand (ND) curve for shoes is downward-sloping.

As the relative price falls below the autarky level, Japan's quantity demanded of imports (the horizontal difference between NS and ND) goes up (Figure 4.4).

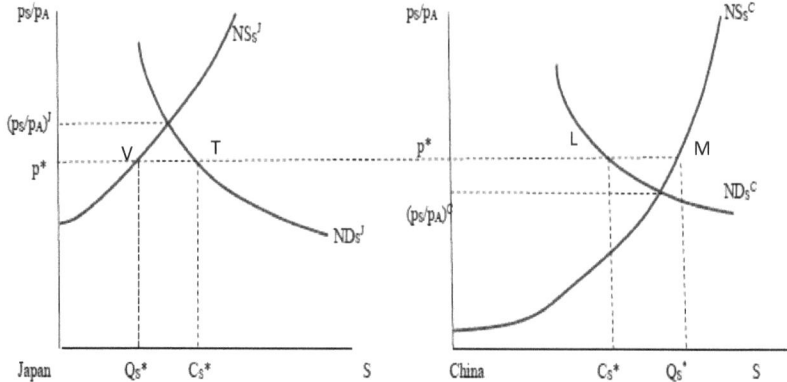

Figure 4.4   Trade equilibrium with NS and ND curves.

Similar analysis shows that China exports more as the relative price of shoes rises above its autarky level. Exports are the horizontal difference between ND and NS.

Notes on this trade equilibrium

Japan imports shoes and China exports shoes at the free-trade price ratio p^*. Trade is balanced, as was shown with the PPF curves and trade triangles earlier. Specifically:

- What Japan imports in units of S (horizontal distance $Q_S^* C_S^* = VT$) equals what China exports in units of $S (= LM)$.
- Trade is balanced in value terms. As before for Japan, $p_A^* EX_A^J = p_S^* IM_S^J$.
- But this means it is possible to figure out what the quantity of trade in autos is because $EX_A^J = (p_S^*/p_A^*)IM_S^J$. Thus, Japan's exports of A (and China's imports of A) are the box made by the horizontal trade quantity in S and the relative price line in free trade. The box is $VQ_s^* C_S^* T$ using the Japanese part of the diagram.

Both countries are better off in free trade than in autarky. We know this because moving to a price ratio different from the autarky price ratio permits both to consume on higher CICs.

Study question 2

Which of the following statements is false in the HO (factor proportions) model?

A. In free trade, countries implicitly export the services of their abundant factors.
B. Free trade will cause the price of the imported good to fall.
C. Each country has a higher real GDP in free trade than in autarky.
D. Both countries completely specialize in the good in which they have a comparative advantage.
E. Free trade permits countries to consume outside their PPFs.

Discussion of study question 2

The correct (false) answer is D. Countries only partially specialize in the HO model, meaning that they continue to produce both goods in free trade.

A is true because each country exports the good that is intensive in its abundant factor. B is true because imports come from a cheaper source and reduce the domestic price.

C is true because trade generates efficient partial specialization, raising real GPD. And E is true because trade establishes new prices, permitting consumption outside the PPF.

Brief model comparison: Ricardian and HO

It is useful to compare the two models we have so far.

Ricardian (classical)	*HO (factor proportions)*
Constant opportunity costs	Rising opportunity costs
Different technologies	Identical technologies
CA depends on labor productivity	CA depends on factor endowments and factor intensities
Complete specialization in trade	Partial specialization in trade
Trade allows consumption outside PPF	Same

Both models provide important insights and help explain some aspects of actual trade flows.

The Interactions of Factor Endowments, Trade, and the Real Incomes of Capital and Labor

Factor endowments, trade, and factor prices

This model offers important insights about how opening an economy to trade affects wages and prices of capital.

A note on terminology. We use the variable r to indicate the *rental rate on capital*. This reflects the cost of buying an hour (or day or year) of the use of a unit of capital, not the purchase cost of a machine or a building. This approach is consistent with the concept of a wage, which is the cost of an hour (or day or year) of labor.

We also refer to r as the *price of capital* or the *return to capital* because it is the income earned by capital owners on a unit of capital. It is closely related to the familiar concept of an interest rate, which is the payment received by an investor lending her funds to the capital market.

A key point: The HO model states that each country exports the good that intensively uses its abundant factor and imports the good that intensively uses its scarce factor. Another way of stating this result is that *countries implicitly export the services of their abundant factor and import the services of their scarce factor.*

This means that free trade generates higher demand for the abundant factor in each country, so its price rises. And it generates lower demand for the scarce factor, so its price must fall. This insight already indicates that income distribution changes when a country opens to trade.

But there is a deeper question: Is it just nominal or also *real* factor prices that change?

This is an issue because if trade (exports) drives up the price of autos *and* the price of capital in Japan, how do we know what happens to the real price of capital, which is r/p_A? And if trade (imports) drives down the price of shoes *and* the wage rate in Japan, how do we know what happens to the real wage, w/p_S?

To answer this, return to the basic theory. First, recall that in autarky, shoes are expensive (and autos cheap) in Japan compared to China:

$$\left(^{p_S}/_{p_A}\right)^J > \left(^{p_S}/_{p_A}\right)^C$$

Now suppose, hypothetically, that Japan and China both faced the same relative price ratio as China's autarky ratio, $\left(^{p_S}/_{p_A}\right)^C$. Looking at the NS and ND curves (Figure 4.5), at this price ratio, Japan would produce fewer shoes (and therefore more autos) than it does at its own autarky price ratio. To see that, compare point A (Japan's autarky) to point G (what Japan would produce if it faced China's autarky price ratio) in Japan's diagram. Thus, in autarky (where the NS and ND curves intersect at point A), Japan produces more shoes (and fewer autos) than it would if it faced China's autarky price ratio.

But S is labor-intensive, and A is capital-intensive, so this logic must mean that in Japan's autarky, there is a higher demand for labor and a lower demand for capital compared to what the situation would be in Japan with China's price ratio.

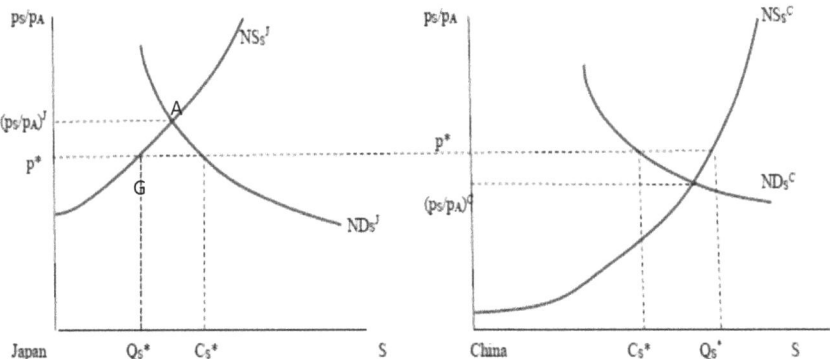

Figure 4.5   Proof that Japan has higher real wages than China in autarky. In autarky, Japan produces more S and fewer A than it would if its economy faced China's autarky relative prices. This implies that Japan has a higher price of labor relative to capital than China does in autarky.

We therefore get this important result in autarky:

$$\left(\frac{w}{r}\right)^J > \left(\frac{w}{r}\right)^C$$

This result is not surprising. It simply reflects relative factor abundance. Labor is scarce in Japan, so it has a high price. Capital is abundant so it has a low price. The opposite is true for China, where labor is cheap and capital is expensive.

It is useful to put all this together in a statement of autarky relationships:

$$\left(\frac{\bar{K}}{\bar{L}}\right)^J > \left(\frac{\bar{K}}{\bar{L}}\right)^C \Rightarrow \left(\frac{w}{r}\right)^J > \left(\frac{w}{r}\right)^C \quad \Leftrightarrow \quad \left(p_S/p_A\right)^J > \left(p_S/p_A\right)^C$$

In words, Japan is relatively capital-abundant and labor-scarce, implying that it has a higher ratio of wage to rental rate. In turn, shoes are relatively expensive in Japan in autarky. China is labor-abundant and capital-scarce, meaning it has a lower wage-rental ratio and a lower relative price of shoes in autarky.

Factor intensities and real factor prices

To complete this analysis requires some additional and important economic theory. Remember the meaning of *factor intensities*. Autos are capital-intensive and shoes are labor-intensive if $K_A/L_A > K_S/L_S$.

But what do these capital–labor ratios depend on? They depend on several things in the actual economy. But we will focus on the most essential one: the ratio of the price of labor to the price of capital, w/r.

The basic idea is that if w/r goes up, labor gets more expensive relative to capital. Then, firms in *both* industries (autos and shoes) will *substitute capital for labor* and the capital–labor ratio rises in both. That is,

$$(w/r) \uparrow \Rightarrow K_A/L_A \uparrow \text{ and } K_S/L_S \uparrow \text{ (and, in turn, } L_A/K_A \downarrow \text{ and } L_S/K_S \downarrow)$$

In words, if labor becomes more expensive, both A and S use relatively more K and less L (but A continues to have a higher ratio than S).

These relationships hold in both Japan and China. Why? Remember that the production functions for A and S are the same in both countries, by assumption.

Now, recall the ranking in autarky: $(\frac{\bar{K}}{\bar{L}})^J > (\frac{\bar{K}}{\bar{L}})^C \Rightarrow (\frac{w}{r})^J > (\frac{w}{r})^C$

That is, because capital is relatively abundant and labor is relatively scarce in Japan, it must be that labor is expensive in Japan (and capital is cheap) and labor is cheap in China (and capital is expensive).

It follows that in autarky, the capital–labor ratios in both A and S are higher in Japan than in China:

$$\left(\frac{w}{r}\right)^J > \left(\frac{w}{r}\right)^C \Rightarrow \left(K_A/L_A\right)^J > \left(K_A/L_A\right)^C \text{ and } \left(K_S/L_S\right)^J > \left(K_S/L_S\right)^C$$

Again, this makes sense. If Japan is capital-abundant and labor-scarce compared to China, we should observe Japan producing both goods with relatively more capital and less labor in autarky.

To summarize the analysis at this point, here are the important comparisons of Japan and China in autarky:

1. Japan is capital-abundant, and China is labor-abundant. This means that the PPFs are biased, with Japan's tilted toward the A axis and China's toward the S axis. In turn, this explains why in autarky, shoes are relatively expensive in Japan and relatively cheap in China, and why autos are relatively cheap in Japan and expensive in China.
2. It also means that, in Japan, labor is relatively expensive and capital is relatively cheap. The opposite is true in China.
3. As a result, *both autos and shoes use higher capital–labor ratios in Japan than they do in China.*

Study question 3

Suppose France (F) is capital-abundant, and Egypt (E) is labor-abundant. Machines (M) are capital-intensive, and carpets (C) are labor-intensive. Then, in comparing the autarky equilibriums for France and Egypt, we can conclude that the following:

A. Egypt has a relatively higher $(\frac{w}{r})$ ratio than France.
B. France produces both M and C with a higher capital–labor ratio than does Egypt.
C. Machines are relatively more expensive in France than in Egypt.
D. France has a higher capital stock and more labor than Egypt.

Discussion of study question 3

The correct answer is B. Since France is capital-abundant and labor-scarce it has a higher ratio of wage to capital price in autarky. Thus, it will use more capital-intensive techniques in both goods.

This means that A is false. C is also false because capital is relatively cheaper in France, making machines relatively cheaper.

Finally, this model is about relative endowments, not absolute endowments. It is possible that France has more of both K and L than Egypt does, but that does not matter. What matters is that the ratio of the capital stock to the labor force is higher in France.

Marginal productivities and real factor prices

Recall from the Ricardian model that the real wages of labor depended on the marginal products of labor. The factor proportions model extends that insight considerably and will complete the analysis of trade and real factor incomes.

What determines the productivity of labor and capital in this model?

In the real world, many things matter, such as returns to scale, market competition, infrastructure, government policies, and human capital. But in the essential model, here it is just the capital–labor ratio in the production of A and S.

Here is the basic idea: If the K/L ratio rises in the production of autos, it means that each unit of labor has more units of capital to work with. That will raise the marginal product of labor in autos.

A simple example: Initially, let there be 5 units of K per L. Now, raise K to 7 per L, holding the amount of L fixed. The fact that each L now has $7K$ instead of $5K$ to work with makes labor more productive. On the other hand, if the K/l ratio falls, the MPL falls also.

This process works in both directions. A higher K/L ratio makes capital less productive but a lower K/L ratio (that is, more L per K) makes K more productive. In the simple example above, each unit of K initially had $1/5$ L using it but now it has $1/7$ L using it, making that unit of capital less productive. This logic is at the core of income-distribution analysis in neoclassical economics.

Here is the simplified theory about marginal products in the factor proportions model, coming from neoclassical production theory. The theory assumes *diminishing marginal productivity of labor and capital* (Figure 4.6).

What that means is that if a firm holds the amount of capital fixed in producing a good but increases its use of labor, the *additional output* generated goes down, as in this basic diagram for production functions in autos, A (the vertical axis is output of A):

For a given capital stock, K_A^0, say 5 units of capital, the first unit of L produces 10A, the second L generates 15A, and the third L produces 17A. So, the MPL of the first L is 10, that of the second L is 5, and that of the third L is 2.

But if there is a higher capital stock, K_A^1, the output function is higher and so are the MPLs. For example, with 8 units of capital,

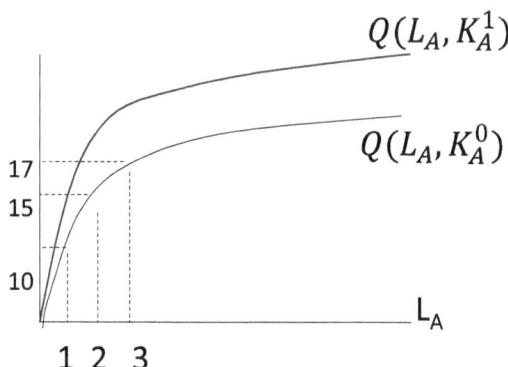

Figure 4.6   Diminishing MPL in autos.

Table 4.3 Example of diminishing marginal productivity of labor in autos.

K_A^0	L_A	Q_A	MPL_A
5	1	10	10
5	2	15	5
5	3	17	2

K_A^1	L_A	Q_A	MPL_A
8	1	14	14
8	2	22	8
8	3	25	3

outputs could be 14, 22, and 25 as L expands. These figures are listed in Table 4.3.

The diagram assumed a fixed capital stock for each curve. We could draw a similar diagram showing a diminishing MPK_A as autos use more capital for a given labor employment.

But this general statement applies as follows:

As $(K_A/L_A)^J$ rises, the MPL_A^J goes up and the MPK_A^J falls. The same is true for shoes.

Putting this all together establishes:

- As $(\frac{w}{r})^J$ goes up, both $(K_A/L_A)^J$ and $(K_S/L_S)^J$ also rise. That means that both MPL_A^J and MPL_S^J go up and both MPK_A^J and MPK_S^J go down.
- As $(\frac{w}{r})^J$ goes down, both $(K_A/L_A)^J$ and $(K_S/L_S)^J$ also go down. That means both MPL_A^J and MPL_S^J fall and MPK_A^J and MPK_S^J rise.

These relationships also hold in China.

To summarize this situation in autarky, where Japan uses more capital-intensive ratios in both goods than China, we have

- MPL_A and MPL_S are both higher in Japan than in China in autarky.
- MPK_A and MPK_S are both higher in China than in Japan in autarky.

In words, labor is more productive at the margin in Japan, while capital is more productive at the margin in China in autarky.

Now, just extend our logic from the Ricardian model (which had only labor):

Real wages equal the marginal products of labor and real returns to capital equal the marginal products of capital.

That outcome is intuitive but can be demonstrated more formally. To see this in the HO model, think about the nature of equilibrium in the labor and capital markets.

An important definition: The *value of marginal product of labor* in a good (e.g., A) is $\text{VMPL}_A = p_A \text{MPL}_A$. This formula shows how much revenue an additional worker generates in production, which is the additional output gained (MPL) times the price of that output.

In fact, the VMPL_A curve is the demand curve for labor in autos, shown in Figure 4.7. This is because it depicts the extra revenue earned from hiring more labor, which determines how much labor to employ.

Equilibrium is determined by the fact that firms would be willing to hire more workers until the additional cost of hiring (which is the wage rate) equals this additional revenue earned by the firm.

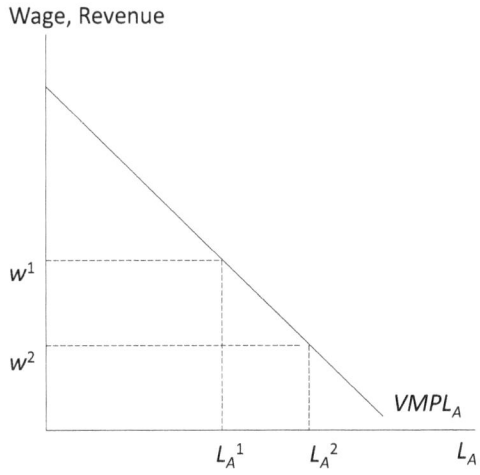

Figure 4.7   The VMPL curve.

$\text{VMPL}_A = p_A * \text{MPL}_A$. Any particular VMPL_A curve is defined for a given (fixed) price of good A and a given (fixed) capital stock used in A. The curve is downward-sloping because of the diminishing marginal product of labor, meaning that MPL_A goes down as more labor is hired in autos.

Suppose (for now) that firms in the auto industry face a market wage rate of w^1. It would not maximize profits to hire fewer workers than L_A^1 because the wage would be less than the marginal revenue earned by hiring more workers. And firms would not hire more than that because the gain in revenue would be less than the additional wage cost. Thus, the equilibrium requires wage $= \text{VMPL}_A$, which determines how many workers are hired. If the wage gets lower, the auto firms hire more workers. The VMPL curve really is the demand for labor in autos.

A similar analysis holds for the S industry and both S and A would hire labor where $w = \text{VMPL}$. But this diagram only shows a partial equilibrium in autos.

State this equilibrium condition as $w = \text{VMPL}_A = p_A \text{MPL}_A$.

But that means in equilibrium the *real wage in terms of buying good A* is $w/p_A = \text{MPL}_A$.

The same logic for capital would say that the *real return to capital in terms of buying good A* is $r/p_A = \text{MPK}_A$.

For our two countries:

- In Japan, the real wage in $A = \text{MPL}_A^J$ and the real wage in $S = \text{MPL}_S^J$.
- In China, the real wage in $A = \text{MPL}_A^C$ and the real wage in $S = \text{MPL}_S^C$.
- In Japan, the real capital return in $A = \text{MPK}_A^J$ and the real capital return in $S = \text{MPK}_S^J$.
- In China, the real capital return in $A = \text{MPK}_A^C$ and the real capital return in $S = \text{MPK}_S^C$.

Keep in mind that these are statements about the ability of all workers and all capital owners to purchase A and S. It does not mean there are different wage rates or rental rates on capital in A and S.

Recall that in autarky, the MPLs are higher in Japan. Thus, it immediately follows that *real wages in terms of buying both goods are higher in Japan than in China in autarky. And real returns to capital are higher in China than in Japan. Again, this reflects factor endowment abundance and scarcity.*

Note this means that if we permitted labor and capital to migrate across borders, L would move to Japan and K would move to China. In principle, this would happen until the wage would fall in J and would rise in C until they became equal, and the return to capital would rise in J and fall in C until they became equal. But in this model, we do not permit L and K migration.

Summary of this key point: In autarky, the real wages are higher where labor is scarce and lower where labor is abundant. The real returns to capital are higher where capital is scarce and lower where capital is abundant.

Study question 4

Which of the following is true in comparing autarky in capital-abundant Japan and labor-abundant China?

A. Shoes are relatively cheap in Japan.
B. China has higher real wages than Japan.
C. Japan produces both goods with higher capital–labor ratios than China does.
D. If it were possible, capital would move from Japan to China and labor from China to Japan.
E. Both C and D.

Discussion of study question 4

The correct answer is E because both C and D are true. A is false because shoes would be expensive in Japan. B is false because the marginal products of labor are lower in China than in Japan in autarky. C is true because Japan is capital-abundant and has a higher wage-rental ratio than China. D is true because real wages are higher in Japan and real prices of capital are higher in China in autarky.

How International Trade Redistributes Income

The effects of trade on real factor prices

Effects of moving from autarky to free trade in goods

Now, consider how international trade in goods affects all this. Consider the result in Japan of moving from autarky to free trade with China.

In Japan, $(^{p_S}/_{p_A})^J$ falls to the equalized free-trade price ratio p^*. But that means output of S falls and output of A rises in Japan. *There is a tendency toward specialization in the good of CA and exports. But it is incomplete specialization and both countries continue to produce both goods.*

During this adjustment, the output shift generates an excess demand for capital and an excess supply of labor in Japan. This is because labor-intensive shoes release a lower ratio of K to L than the capital-intensive autos industry wants to employ. In turn, this means that w falls and r rises until we reach a new output equilibrium with more A produced, less S produced, and both K and L are fully employed.

Result: Free trade raises the nominal price of the abundant factor and reduces the nominal price of the scarce factor.

Trade and factor price equalization

By the same analysis in China, $(^{p_S}/_{p_A})^C$ rises, so the nominal wage rises and the nominal r falls. What we have then is that as $(^{p_S}/_{p_A})^J$ falls, so does $(\frac{w}{r})^J$. And as $(^{p_S}/_{p_A})^C$ rises, so does $(\frac{w}{r})^C$.

This happens due to adjustments in output along the PPFs: Japan produces more autos (fewer shoes) and China produces more shoes (fewer autos).

But more can be concluded. Free trade generates equalized relative goods prices because p^* becomes the new price ratio in both C and J. And that means that relative factor prices must be driven together also

$$({}^{p_S}/_{p_A})^{J*} = p^* = ({}^{p_S}/_{p_A})^{C*} \qquad \Leftrightarrow \qquad (\tfrac{w}{r})^{J*} = (\tfrac{w}{r})^* = (\tfrac{w}{r})^{C*} \text{ in free trade}$$

That is, free trade in goods generates equalized goods prices. This result then generates *relative factor price equalization*. This is true so long as both countries produce both goods (that is, there is partial or incomplete specialization).

Trade and relative FPE

The reason this happens is our assumption that *Japan and China have the same production technologies for A and S*. This means that they share the same technological relationships between relative goods prices and relative factor prices, as long as both goods are produced in both countries. Thus, when goods prices are equal, so are factor prices.

Let's state this as a theorem:

Factor Price Equalization Theorem: Let two countries have identical CRS production functions in two goods. Then, free trade in goods establishes equalized relative factor prices between the countries so long as both countries remain incompletely specialized.

Trade and changes in real factor prices

But there is a remaining puzzle to work out, which is what happens to the real factor prices themselves. At this point, the following is known in the movement to free trade.

In Japan, the nominal wage falls, and the price of autos (exported) rises, so $({}^{w}/_{p_A})^J$ must fall. Japan therefore has a lower real wage in buying autos. But because the price of shoes also falls, the effect of the real wage in shoes $({}^{w}/_{p_S})^J$ may seem unclear.

Further, the price of capital rises in Japan, so $(^r/_{p_S})^J$ rises. Thus, there is a higher real capital income in buying shoes.

But the price of autos rises so what can we conclude about $(^r/_{p_A})^J$?

Similar questions exist for China. What may be concluded about whether labor and capital are better off or worse off?

Trade and absolute FPE

To answer that the theory says something much stronger in this model. Take it in steps:

1. Free trade equalizes the prices of goods: $p_A^{J*} = p_A^{C*} = p_A^*$ and $p_S^{J*} = p_S^{C*} = p_S^*$.
2. This means that free trade establishes relative FPE: $(\frac{w}{r})^{J*} = (\frac{w}{r})^* = (\frac{w}{r})^{C*}$.
3. But because the ratio of factor prices determines the capital–labor ratios in production these are also equalized, if both countries produce both S and A:

$$(^{K_A}/_{L_A})^{J*} = (^{K_A}/_{L_A})^{C*} \quad \text{and} \quad (^{K_S}/_{L_S})^{J*} = (^{K_S}/_{L_S})^{C*}$$

4. But this means the marginal products are equal in free trade:

$$\text{MPL}_A^{J*} = \text{MPL}_A^{C*}; \text{MPL}_S^{J*} = \text{MPL}_S^{C*}; \text{MPK}_A^{J*}$$
$$= \text{MPK}_A^{C*}; \quad \text{and} \quad \text{MPK}_S^{J*} = \text{MPK}_S^{C*}$$

5. Finally, because the marginal products give us real factor prices, it follows that

$$(^w/_{p_A})^{J*} = \text{MPL}_A^{J*} = \text{MPL}_A^{C*} = (^w/_{p_A})^{C*};$$
$$(^w/_{p_S})^{J*} = \text{MPL}_S^{J*} = \text{MPL}_S^{C*} = (^w/_{p_S})^{C*}$$
$$(^r/_{p_A})^{J*} = \text{MPK}_A^{J*} = \text{MPK}_A^{C*} = (^r/_{p_A})^{C*};$$
$$(^r/_{p_S})^{J*} = \text{MPK}_S^{J*} = \text{MPK}_S^{C*} = (^r/_{p_S})^{C*}$$

What this remarkable outcome means is that *free trade generates identical real factor prices, or the same real living standards for both factors in both countries, if both countries produce both goods.*

This is called the **absolute FPE theorem**.

Note that if this outcome actually happened, it would remove all incentives for labor and capital to migrate across borders.

The Stolper–Samuelson theorem: Trade and income distribution

To answer the earlier questions, it can be seen now that the MPL in Japan falls in both goods because both S and A have lower capital–labor ratios (both goods become less capital-intensive).

Therefore, both $(^w/_{p_A})^J$ and $(^w/_{p_S})^J$ fall in moving from autarky to free trade. Similarly, the MPK in Japan rises in both goods, so both $(^r/_{p_A})^J$ and $(^r/_{p_S})^J$ rise.

In China, the MPL rises in both goods so both $(^w/_{p_A})^C$ and $(^w/_{p_S})^C$ are higher, while the MPK falls in both goods so both $(^r/_{p_A})^C$ and $(^r/_{p_S})^C$ go down.

Recall that in autarky, Japan had higher real wages in buying both goods and China had higher real returns to capital in buying both goods. Now, they are equalized in free trade.

This must mean that the real wages of labor in terms of both goods fall in Japan and real returns to capital in terms of both goods fall in China as a result of free trade. Also, real wages of labor rise in China and real returns to capital rise in Japan. Put differently, free trade reduces the real income of the scarce factor and raises the real income of the abundant factor in both countries.

This outcome is summarized in the following theorem, named for two trade theorists in the mid-20th century named Wolfgang Stolper and Paul Samuelson.

The Stolper–Samuelson theorem: Let free trade equalize goods prices and let both countries produce both goods, with identical, CRS production functions. Then, free trade reduces the real income of the scarce factor and raises the real income of the abundant factor in terms of both goods, in both countries.

Note clearly what this means: we now have an explanation for trade in which opening to trade redistributes income and creates winners (abundant factors) and losers (scarce factors).

Thus, trade in goods implicitly arbitrages differences in factor endowments, effectively equalizing them by trading their services as embodied in goods.

Does this income redistribution mean economies lose from trade? No, for we already saw that trade raises real GDP. Thus, the income gains to the abundant factors exceed the income losses to the scarce factors and compensation could be paid in principle.

Context and comments

Relative FPE and absolute FPE are powerful results. They claim that if countries export goods that intensively use their abundant factors and import the goods intensively using their scarce factors, there will be a global tendency toward convergence or even equalization of real labor and capital incomes.

And the Stolper–Samuelson theorem is a critically important prediction. It says that scarce factors lose from trade and abundant factors gain from trade.

We can put even more context into this analysis. Implicitly there is a *substitution principle: trade-in goods substitutes for trade-in factors.* This is because countries export implicitly their abundant factors and import implicitly their scarce factors through trade in goods. *Thus, free trade in goods tends to drive factor prices in different countries together, just as would direct labor migration and international capital flows.*

Study question 5

In the factor proportions (or HO) model, which of the following statements is false?

A. Countries export the good that intensively uses their abundant factor.
B. Free trade in goods effectively substitutes for international labor and capital movements.

C. In each country, the scarce factor gains higher real income, and the abundant factor suffers lower real income, in the movement to free trade.
D. If both countries produce both goods in free trade, both relative and absolute factor prices will be equalized between countries.
E. In autarky, the real wages of labor are higher in the capital-abundant country than in the labor-abundant country.

Discussion of study question 5

The correct (false) answer is C. In this model, the scarce factor is made worse off by trade liberalization and the abundant factor is made better off.

A is the HO theorem and B is true because countries export the good that is intensive in their abundant factor. D is true because of FPE. E is true because capital-abundant countries have higher real wages in autarky.

Brief comment on trade and migration policy

A critical implication of this analysis is that blocking international labor and capital migration is not enough to protect the incomes of scarce factors. Free trade in goods will also reduce those incomes.

But if countries raise barriers to imports of goods (e.g., tariffs), that will prevent factor prices from moving together and therefore set up incentives for factors to migrate. *Thus, if policymakers are worried about the distributional effects of cheap imports. they would need both trade and migration barriers.*

Example: Consider the joint effects of US barriers to labor immigration from Mexico and trade barriers on imports of labor-intensive goods from Mexico. The tariffs on goods would reduce export prices in Mexico, lowering the real income of workers there (note this assumes that Mexico is labor-abundant). This would raise the incentives those workers have to migrate to the US.

A good example came from the early 2000s. There were strict US import quotas on tomatoes from Mexico, which seemed to reduce Mexican agricultural wages and induce more illegal migration.

Most trade economists think NAFTA has raised real labor incomes in Mexico and reduced real wages of low-skilled workers in the US, though there remains a debate. This tendency helps explain why illegal immigration from Mexico has fallen over time, as Mexican real wages moved up toward US levels in low-skill jobs. We will have more to say about this when we study immigration policy.

More context on FPE and Stolper–Samuelson

There is considerable evidence to support these ideas, particularly when we consider trade among rich, skill-abundant countries. Trade is largely free among these nations, which have similar real wages and real capital incomes and therefore little need to protect incomes of scarce factors. But import barriers are higher in rich countries against labor-intensive imports from poor countries.

There is also evidence of a tendency toward convergence in real wages between emerging economies (e.g., China and Mexico) and real low-skilled wages in rich countries since the 1990s.

But these theorems are based on very strong assumptions. *All the following are necessary conditions for FPE and SS to hold*:

- There are perfectly competitive goods and factor markets, meaning no monopolies or labor unions, no market distortions, and no taxes on labor or capital.
- K and L are homogeneous and can move without cost between industries within each country.
- Free trade in goods fully equalizes prices of goods across countries. But goods could be differentiated and monopolized, and there could be transport costs and tariffs.
- Technologies must be identical and CRS. If they were not CRS, we could get different results. Briefly, suppose there are good with strong IRS, such as software, films, and airplanes. Then, bigger countries with more human capital would produce more goods with IRS and therefore would have higher labor productivity and higher real wages.

Further, the following key condition must also be true. There is incomplete specialization and both countries produce both goods in free trade.

What if this were not true? Suppose that in our example, Japan ends up producing only autos and not shoes in free trade. That is, it produces at the autos endpoint of its PPF in free trade. Let China produce both goods. In this situation (follow this carefully):

1. All of Japan's K and L go to produce autos. But Japan's K/L endowment ratio is higher than China's because it is capital-abundant. This means that autos production in Japan is more capital-intensive than both autos and shoes production in China, even in free trade.
2. In turn, in free trade, labor is more productive in Japan than in China and the real wages are higher in Japan than in China. Further, the real returns to capital are lower in Japan.

Critical point:

Even in free trade, complete specialization in capital-intensive goods keeps the real wages of labor in Japan higher than they would be with FPE. Only if a capital-abundant country continues to produce the labor-intensive good in free trade is there pressure on real wages to fall to the world level.

How does a country achieve such specialization in capital-intensive goods? It does so by being so heavily abundant in capital that it makes no sense to produce the labor-intensive goods if they can be imported. The efficient outcome is to produce only the capital-intensive goods. And that means having exceptionally high investment rates in capital. *Thus, if a country wishes to sustain high real wages, it should invest in sufficient capital to avoid producing unskilled labor-intensive goods.*

Similar statements hold for investments in education (skills), R&D (technologies), and communications infrastructure. High endowments of these factors will sustain high real wages by preventing domestic production of low-wage goods.

In fact, several countries have exceptionally high wages in part because they produce almost no labor-intensive, low-wage goods. (And the textiles and apparel they do produce are design-intensive and appeal to high-wage consumers.) Examples are Switzerland, Sweden, Finland, and Singapore.

What do they produce primarily? Financial services, design, technology, consulting, precision machinery, and other high-technology, skill-intensive goods and services.

Trade and Income Distribution in the Short Run

The specific factors model: Introduction

The Stolper–Samuelson (SS) theorem predicts that, under the assumptions of the HO model, opening to trade reduces the real income of the scarce factor and raises the real income of the abundant factor. And the idea holds more generally: With multiple productive factors, the most abundant factors gain from trade liberalization and the scarcest factors lose real income.

This important and powerful insight explains a great deal about whether people (as unskilled workers, skilled workers, or capital owners) are in favor of open trade or opposed to it. The following chapter looks deeply at issues of trade and income inequality.

At this point, it is important to stress that the SS theorem is a result pertaining only in the long run, after capital and labor move from the contracting (import-competing) sector to the expanding (export) sector and a new equilibrium wage and capital price are established. That is, SS assumes that labor and capital are fully mobile between industries and that they are homogeneous in their characteristics.

Again, that is a strong assumption that does not hold in shorter time periods. Instead, workers in one sector may have skills that are useful in the production of that sector's good but not very useful or efficient in the production of the other good. The same may be said of capital, where machines designed for use in one industry cannot readily be refitted to work well in the other.

In our primary HO example, when Japan entered free trade with China, the effect was to expand auto production but reduce shoe production, which reduced the real wage of all workers in Japan as they moved from shoes to autos, reducing their productivity. The real returns to capital rose as all units of capital became more productive.

Imagine instead that workers have been trained and capital inputs have been designed to be used only in a particular industry. In that case, workers and capital are what economists call "specific factors" in that for a period of time, they can only be used in a particular activity, either shoes or autos.

Over time, shoe workers can be retrained as auto workers, taking on those skills, while capital in the shoe industry can be depreciated and sold off, with the proceeds used to invest capital in the auto sector. These adjustments are assumed to happen in the HO and SS models, but they take time.

There is an important difference between what happens to incomes when factors are specific and what happens to them when they are mobile. To analyze this issue, economists distinguish two adjustment periods:

1. In the *short run*, at least one factor is specific and at least one is mobile.
2. In the *long run*, all factors are mobile between industries.

In this context, HO and SS are *long-run theories*. The following notes consider impacts on factor incomes of trade liberalization in the short run.

Analysis of the specific factors model

This model is most useful for understanding income distribution effects. It does not change the essential concept of the HO model that comparative advantage is determined by relative factor endowments in the long run. Thus, in free trade, Japan will export autos and import shoes, while China will export shoes and import autos, even in the short run.

These notes consider impacts of trade in Japan in the short run. The analysis in China will be similar and students should work through it.

The key relationship in analyzing factor incomes was defined earlier in the notes, which is that in equilibrium, each nominal factor price equals the value of that factor's marginal product. Thus, in any long-run equilibrium, it must be that

$$w = \text{VMPL}_A = p_A\text{MPL}_A \quad \text{and} \quad w = \text{VMPL}_S = p_S\text{MPL}_S$$

$$r = \text{VMPK}_A = p_A\text{MPK}_A \quad \text{and} \quad r = \text{VMPK}_S = p_S\text{MPK}_S$$

These equations reflect the fact that in the long run, with mobile labor and capital, there is just a single nominal wage and a single nominal price of capital in Japan.

Recall from earlier in these notes that the VMPL functions are the demand curves for labor in goods A and S. Further, the VMPK functions are the demand curves for capital in these goods.

In the short run, suppose that labor is mobile, but capital is sector-specific. This means that there are actually two types of capital, which are labeled $\overline{K_A}$ (specific to autos) and $\overline{K_S}$ (specific to shoes). (This model is also called the "three-factor model" because it has one mobile factor and two specific factors.)

Then, there would be a single nominal wage in both S and A but different nominal capital prices. For example, in the short run, these equations would be

$$w = \text{VMPL}_A = p_A\text{MPL}_A \quad \text{and} \quad w = \text{VMPL}_S = p_S\text{MPL}_S$$

$$r_A = \text{VMP}\overline{K}_A = p_A\text{MP}\overline{K}_A \quad \text{and} \quad r_S = \text{VMP}\overline{K}_S = p_S\text{MP}\overline{K}_S$$

The second pair of equations emphasizes that the capital stocks are fixed, though their marginal products can change if they are combined with different amounts of labor.

The effects of trade opening on labor

Consider the short-run effects of Japan entering free trade with China. Japan has the comparative advantage in autos and would export autos and import shoes. As discussed earlier, this implies that the price of autos would rise in Japan and the price of shoes would fall.

Also, the autos sector would expand output and the shoes sector would reduce output. This would raise the demand for labor in A and reduce it in S, causing labor to move from S to A as the nominal wage goes up.

At this point, in the short run, price changes are $p_A \uparrow$, $p_S \downarrow$, and $w \uparrow$. One may conclude immediately that $(w/p_S) \uparrow$. Thus, workers have a higher real wage in terms of buying shoes.

What about (w/p_A)? To answer that, note that labor entered autos but the capital stock in autos is fixed. Thus, in the short run, there is a higher ratio of labor to capital in A, implying a lower MPL_A. From the theory, it follows that $w/p_A \downarrow$. Workers have a lower real wage in terms of buying autos in the short run. (For completeness, note that labor left the S industry, and its capital is also fixed, implying a lower L/K ratio and a higher real wage.)

Thus, there is a different result in the short run than in the long run. In the short run, whether workers are better off or worse off depends on whether they prefer to consume autos or shoes. *Their ability to buy A falls but their ability to buy S rises. The impact on real wages overall is ambiguous.*

Compare that to the long-run (SS) result: All workers end up with lower real wages in both goods in Japan as a result of greater trade competition.

The effects of trade opening on specific capital stocks

It is straightforward to analyze the impacts on the specific capital stocks in A and S. In autos, labor flows into the industry, implying that the fixed K stock has more labor to work with, which raises $\overline{\text{MPK}_A}$. Capital in autos becomes more productive and that raises the real return to capital specific to autos: $r_A/p_A \uparrow$. It immediately follows that $r_A/p_S \uparrow$ rises also. *Real returns to the capital specific to the automobile sector go up in terms of buying both goods.*

Similar analysis shows that the ratio of L to K in shoes goes down, reducing the marginal product of capital in shoes. Thus, $r_S/p_S \downarrow$ and immediately it follows that $r_S/p_A \downarrow$ also. *Real returns to the capital specific to the shoes sector go down in terms of buying both goods.*

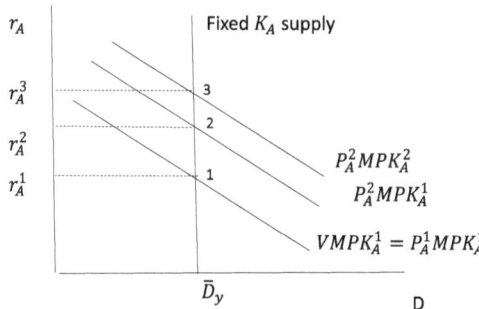

Figure 4.8 Graphical view of specific factor effects.

Figure 4.8 offers a graphical explanation for this outcome in the auto industry. It shows the VMPK_A curve, which is the demand for A capital. The vertical line is the fixed short-run supply of A capital. The initial capital price is r_A^1 and equilibrium in the A sector is point 1.

Now, let Japan go to free trade, which raises the price of autos. As a result, the demand for A capital rises by the amount of the rise in the auto price. On that basis, the nominal capital price also rises by that amount to r_A^2 at point 2.

But because labor flows into autos, the MPK rises in autos and that shifts the demand for capital up even further. Thus, in the short run, the new nominal capital price, r_A^3, goes up by more than the price of automobiles, indicating a higher real return to capital. Equilibrium is at point 3. Thus, there are two reasons the real capital price rises: (1) a higher price of A and (2) more L employed in A.

Summary of short-run effects

With fixed capital stocks and mobile labor, the model makes the following predictions:

1. Trade liberalization has an ambiguous effect on the real wages of labor, which is the mobile factor. The real wage rises in shoes, the declining industry with the lower price, and falls in autos, the expanding industry with the higher price.

2. The real returns to specific capital in autos rise in terms of both goods but those in shoes fall in terms of both goods.

The impacts on specific capital stocks are not surprising. In the expanding sector, there is an increase in demand for capital but no way to increase the supply of capital, driving its price up considerably. In the declining sector, the specific capital stock sees a large fall in its price.

It should be understood that the impact on labor is due to it being the mobile factor. If labor were specific and capital were mobile, then labor in the autos sector would gain real income and labor in shoes would lose real income while the capital effects would be ambiguous. What determines income effects in the short run is not factor intensities but factor mobility versus specificity.

Finally, note the contrast with the long-run SS predictions. In Japan, in the long run, all capital gains higher real income and all labor suffers lower real wages.

Study question 6

In the short-run, specific factors model, let labor be the mobile factor and let there be specific capital stocks in goods X and Y. Suppose an economy goes from autarky to free trade, in which case it imports good Y, which is capital-intensive in the long run. Then, we may conclude that

A. Workers are worse off in the short run but better off in the long run.
B. Owners of capital in the Y sector are worse off in both the short run and the long run.
C. The real wage falls in good Y but rises in good X in the short run.
D. Owners of capital in the X sector are better off in both the short run and the long run.

Discussion of study question 6

The correct answer is B. Importing good Y implies a lower price and output of good Y. In the long run (SS model), owners of all capital have lower real returns because Y is capital-intensive. In the short run, owners of capital in Y (the declining industry) have lower real returns.

A is incorrect because the effects on real wages in the short run are ambiguous: higher in Y but lower in X. C is incorrect because the real wage rises in Y but falls in X. D is incorrect because X-capital owners gain real income in the short run but lose real income in the long run.

Practical implication

An important consequence of these differences in short-run and long-run income distribution effects is that whether workers and capital owners support or oppose free trade depends on whether they consider the short run or the long run.

In the Japanese example, workers would support free trade in the short run if they prefer to consume shoes but would oppose it if they prefer to consume autos. They would oppose trade if they take a long-run view.

Capital owners in shoes would oppose trade in the short run but should favor it in the long run. Capital owners in autos should prefer it no matter their time perspective.

It follows that lobbying for or against trade may be based more along industry lines in the short run, in which both workers and capital take the same view, than in the long run where they would have different interests. Both shoe workers and shoe capital might lobby strongly against opening to trade in Japan, for example.

This would especially be the case if workers were also specific factors over some time period. Then, both workers and capital owners in shoes (the import sector) would suffer short-term losses in real income, while both those factors in autos (the export sector) would benefit from trade.

This analysis describes how complex the welfare trade-offs can be when authorities make trade policy. Much depends on the time horizons of both factor owners and politicians, who make decisions based on election prospects.

Changes in Factor Endowments

A final point in the factor proportions model

What if countries experience changes in factor endowments over time? How does it affect production? This may be analyzed with another basic theorem developed by a British economist in the 1950s.

Rybczynski theorem: Let goods and factor prices be held constant and suppose a country always produces both goods. Then, a rise in one factor endowment will cause the country to produce more of the good intensive in that factor and less of the other good.

This theorem implies that there will be changes in the outputs of goods as a result of the new factor endowment.

Basic proof: Consider a rise in the K endowment in Japan, holding the L endowment fixed. If factor prices were constant, then firms would continue to produce goods with unchanged K/L ratios. That is, A and S would remain equally capital-intensive or labor-intensive as the K endowment rises. The rise in the K endowment must favor more output of A (autos), but for it to expand, Japan must see the S (shoes) sector contract to free up the needed labor. Overall, the output of A rises and the output of S falls.

This means that as capital accumulates for a given labor force, the economy shifts its output toward K-intensive goods and away from L-intensive goods (the PPF shifts toward that bias).

In fact, this is why Japan's PPF was biased toward A and China's was biased toward S in the initial diagrams earlier in these notes. Japan has a higher K/L endowment ratio, so its PPF favors A and China's favors S.

A key insight: Growth in factor endowments matters over time. Countries with high capital investment rates will move production into more K-intensive goods. The same is true for investments in skills (human capital), which will expand outputs of high-technology goods. Comparative advantage can change from L-intensive to K-intensive and skill-intensive goods over time.

This logic offers real insight into why China has seen its production move from labor-intensive, low-wage manufacturing to more capital-intensive and R&D-intensive goods from the 1990s to now. The same dynamics happened in Japan and South Korea in earlier decades.

Chapter 5

Globalization, Technology, and Inequality

Understanding Globalization Better

Introduction: More observations on globalization

In the first chapter, there was an initial primer on globalization and its primary effects. But there is much more to understand before discussing trade, technology, and inequality.

Among the most important economic and political forces of the current era is the growth and continuation of globalization of production, trade, and investment. Politics are driven in part by the need to manage economic and social pressures that arise from globalization.

One of the great intellectual challenges for economists, international relations specialists, international legal scholars, and policymakers is to devise sustainable international rules and norms for promoting the benefits of globalization and ensuring that those benefits are widespread, while trying to minimize its costs.

These complex issues do not lend themselves to easy solutions, and students should be skeptical of anyone (scholars, politicians, columnists, news commentators, neighbors, relatives, and anyone on social media) who claim to know how to resolve them without deep thought and sustained policy effort.

A deeper look at globalization

To define the basic term, *globalization is the reduction in natural barriers and policy restrictions that segment national and regional markets, leading to market integration across borders.* In economic terms, these markets include those for goods and services, productive factors (capital and labor), knowledge, and technological information.

By integrating commercial markets, globalization tends to move prices and qualities of goods, factors, and technologies together in different countries. It facilitates *economic arbitrage* by moving goods, factors, and knowledge from where they are cheap to where they are expensive, pushing prices together.

Moreover, there are implicit markets for *national policies*, in which governments choose trade and regulatory policies. Typically, these are the key policy objectives:

1. to compete in bringing business investment from abroad, potentially raising local employment;
2. to protect domestic economic, social, and public interests in some way; and
3. to promote societal goals through domestic regulations that may affect trade and FDI.

In this context, globalization can also be a force for reducing (arbitraging away) differences in policies across countries.

For example, think of the 2017 US tax reform law. Among other things, it drastically cut the rate of taxation on corporate income to be more in line with other advanced economies. This idea was justified as a way to make US taxes more competitive and to reduce the incentives of US firms to invest abroad.

Here is another example. If a country wished to attract more FDI and technology to its economy, it would need to establish a strong domestic "business climate". This refers to a socioeconomic environment with low corruption, strong governance, an emphasis on the rule of law, efficient infrastructure, reliable communications systems, more rigorous intellectual property rights, strong educational

Table 5.1 2019 Global Competitiveness Index 4.0. The index measures national competitiveness — defined as the set of institutions, policies and factors that determine the level of productivity.

Country	Index (0–100)	Rank	Country	Index (0–100)	Rank
Singapore	84.8	1	Israel	76.7	20
United States	83.7	2	China	73.9	28
Hong Kong SAR	83.1	3	Chile	73.5	33
Netherlands	82.4	4	Russian Federation	66.7	43
Switzerland	82.3	5	Mexico	64.9	48
Japan	82.3	6	South Africa	62.4	60
Germany	81.8	7	India	61.4	68
Sweden	81.2	8	Brazil	60.9	71
United Kingdom	81.2	9	Botswana	55.5	91
Denmark	81.2	10	Pakistan	51.4	110
Republic of Korea	79.6	13	Chad	35.1	141
Canada	79.6	14			

Source: World Economic Forum, http://reports.weforum.org/global-competitiveness-report-2019/competitiveness-rankings/.

systems, support systems for innovation, and other factors that increase confidence that foreign firms can be profitable operating in such economies.

Globalization raises pressures on national and local governments to realign their regulations, taxes, property rights, and other factors in order to be competitive with other economies in attracting and creating businesses.

To illustrate, Table 5.1 shows the ranking of several countries (among 141 in total) in the 2019 "Global Competitiveness Index 4.0", compiled by the World Economic Forum. These rankings are based on over 100 sub-indexes covering institutions, governance, property rights, infrastructure, macroeconomic stability, human capital and education, openness to trade, labor market flexibility, financial markets, and innovation capabilities. Governments pay attention to such rankings.

A few observations are in order about this index.

First, richer and more developed economies dominate the top of these competitiveness rankings. Such countries have stronger institutions, better infrastructure, greater innovation profiles, and so on. Many argue that these are the reasons they are richer and more developed, and that the proper avenue to greater economic development is for countries to invest in such factors.

While it is difficult for poor countries to move up these rankings, it does happen. For example, China was ranked 48th in the 2005 index. It is also possible to move down; India was ranked 45th in 2005. Students may recognize that the intellectual basis for such rankings is the Ricardian view that productivity is a feature of countries, not inherently a characteristic of workers.

The barriers to globalization

It is useful first to understand the impediments to expanding trade and investment. *Natural barriers* to international market integration include geographical distance, transport costs, communication costs, cultural and language differences, and so on. These costs can be internal as well as external. In many Sub-Saharan African countries, it costs more to ship a good from the interior of the country to the port than from the port to the US or Europe.

As noted earlier, there have been major reductions in transportation costs over time, due to improvements in railways, highways, ports, containerization, airports, cargo jets, the logistics of shipping, and so on. These have dramatically cut the costs of both internal and external trade.

And there have been significant improvements in communication technologies, promoting international diffusion of production, especially through vertical supply chains that spread across borders. More will be said about supply chains in later notes. Importantly, lower information and communication costs have made many services, along with knowledge and technologies, far more tradable than ever before.

There are also *policy barriers* that can slow down globalization. Some major ones include the following, though there is an enormous variety of such policies:

- Taxes on trade (e.g., import tariffs) and limits on the amount of trade (e.g., quotas).
- Restrictions on inward FDI and the activities of multinational enterprises (MNEs).
- Many types of non-tariff barriers (NTBs) to trade and investment, such as product safety regulations, "buy domestic" laws, "minimum domestic content" rules, and various taxes. The main issue is whether such domestic taxes and regulations discriminate against foreign competitors. These restrictions apply to goods but even more so to trade and investment in services.
- Technology and information flows may be blocked by various policies limiting investment, joint ventures, and licensing.
- A major current policy debate has to do with digital trade: Should there be limits on trade in consumer data? Should concerns over data privacy lead to restrictions on whether information-based firms can transmit consumer data across borders?

Eliminating such barriers

In the decades before the Trump Administration, there were significant and sustained reductions in policy barriers to trade in goods, services, and investment.

This happened unilaterally as many developing countries chose to deregulate and liberalize their economies. This was largely an outcome of the so-called "Washington Consensus" in the 1980s through the 2000s. This position held that more open economies with strongly pro-business environments and commitment to transparency and the rule of law should experience faster growth. It was advocated by the International Monetary Fund, the World Bank, and major national governments to induce policy changes in emerging and developing economies. It also happened regionally through various free trade agreements, like NAFTA and the EU.

And it happened, most importantly, at the multilateral level through the negotiation of freer global trade and investment through the World Trade Organization (WTO) and other organizations. These processes will be the subject of notes later in the course.

How Do Countries Gain from Trade Liberalization and Globalization?

Gains from trade opening and globalization

Earlier notes described basic gains from trade through specialization and trade. But economists have identified many sources of GFT, which are worth describing here. They will be analyzed more fully in later sections.

Efficiency gains in production
Segmented or isolated markets (such as autarky) are highly inefficient in economic terms. Thus, trade and globalization generate efficiency gains of various forms. These effects all raise total output capacity in an economy and raise GDP.

Here are several forms of improved efficiency associated with the opportunity to trade.

1. There are *allocative efficiency improvements or gains from specialization*, meaning movements along the PPF toward producing more goods of comparative advantage and less of other goods. This generates exports and permits other consumption needs to be met through imports. This adjustment is the source of the specialization GFT in the Ricardian and HO models.
2. There are gains from improvements in *total factor productivity* (TFP), resulting from higher productivity of all factors jointly producing GDP, as the economy reduces trade barriers, gaining greater access to advanced technologies, new management techniques, and more competition from abroad. Trade can also induce more innovation by domestic firms, leading to dynamic gains in total economic productivity. A few comments:

   • This idea refers to both movements up toward the existing PPF and increases over time in the PPF due to technological improvements.
   • Gains in TFP help explain how China could grow so rapidly for so long after reforming and (partially) opening its economy from the 1980s through the 2000s. There were large TFP

gains in Singapore, Japan, South Korea, and other East Asian economies in recent decades.

- This process inevitably runs into diminishing returns at some point, causing TFP growth to slow down. Using labor and capital more efficiently and investing in new capital and labor skills generate large gains in output in inefficient economies with lagging levels of technology. But once a country approaches the global technology frontier, it becomes increasingly difficult to push its growth forward based mainly on increases in capital and labor. Instead, economies must become increasingly innovative and develop new technologies and products to sustain rapid growth.
- Japan essentially hit this barrier in the 1990s, while China seems to be experiencing slower growth now compared to the prior 20 years.

3. Next, economists refer to *scale efficiency*, which refers to lower costs as firms take advantage of greater economies of scale when cutting trade barriers gives them more access to wider global markets. This subject will be discussed in more detail in the next set of notes.

4. There is also *rationalization efficiency*, the idea that international competition forces uncompetitive domestic firms to shut down and leave the market, while competitive new firms (or firms that efficiently reorganize themselves, perhaps through being taken over by foreign investors) come to life and enter the market. The next set of notes will explain how trade liberalization favors larger and more competitive domestic firms over smaller and less efficient firms. By transferring economic resources from inefficient firms to efficient firms, overall productivity rises.

5. Finally, there are *network efficiencies*, as multinational firms (that is, international corporations) build international production networks and supply chains. This process involves investing in facilities internationally and outsourcing (or "offshoring") jobs and activities that can be produced more cheaply somewhere else. Offshoring will be addressed in later notes on multinational firms.

All these outcomes are important and widely studied empirically by economists. There is considerable evidence that many countries have experienced these efficiency improvements after opening to trade and investment. However, the extent to which they happen after a country opens its markets depends on particular country characteristics, implying that these gains are not uniformly felt across nations.

Gains in consumption

It was shown in earlier notes that consumers gain from open trade due to lower prices. There are really two sources of consumption gains from trade, and both are critically important.

1. Lower import prices both directly benefit consumers and generate greater competition for domestic firms, lowering domestic prices. In this context, it is important to learn that cutting tariffs (taxes on imports) is a *progressive tax policy*, in that the benefits of lower import prices are disproportionately gained by low-income households. This is because consumption of goods (including imports) takes up a larger share of incomes for poorer households. In turn, raising tariffs on consumer goods disproportionately harms lower-income households. See Figure 5.1 for the US, which

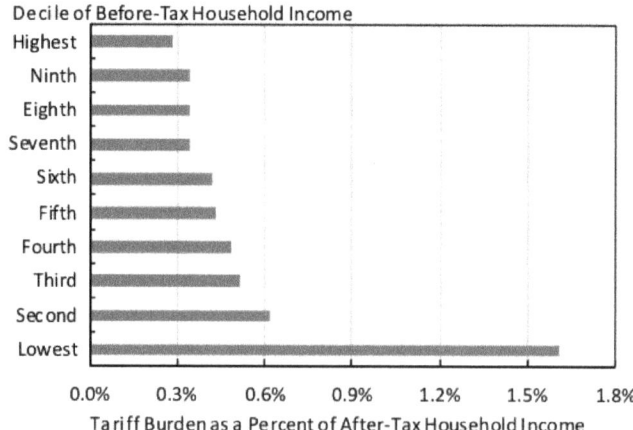

Figure 5.1   Tariff costs broken down by household income decile.

Source: Jason Furman, Katheryn N. Russ, and Jay Shambaugh, "US Tariffs are an Arbitrary and Regressive Tax, https://voxeu.org/article/us-tariffs-are-arbitrary-and-regressive-tax.

shows that US households with the lowest 10% of income pay over 1.5% of their disposable income on tariffs, while the richest group pays less than 0.3%.

2. Greater access to international supply sources generates a larger variety of goods and services available for consumption. Imports raise the available varieties of autos, wines, food products, and nearly all other goods and services. These *variety gains from trade* are important and will be the primary subject of the next trade model.

How Might Countries be Made Worse Off by Trade Liberalization and Globalization?

The possibility of losses from trade due to market and policy distortions

These various concepts indicate that in the aggregate, countries are made better off through engaging in open trade. Trade liberalization raises real GDP, implying higher average incomes and living standards.

But openness to trade and investment remains a controversial idea in many countries, where many people oppose more tariff cuts. Further, as noted earlier, much of the world is experiencing a backlash against globalization.

There are essentially two reasons for this opposition. First, open trade does make certain individuals and groups worse off, even if total GDP rises. Moreover, technological change may combine with globalization to accentuate this income redistribution. These issues are the subject of the balance of these notes after a brief aside.

Second, the various gains discussed above may be limited by the fact that opening an economy to more trade when domestic markets are distorted, or when regulatory policies are poorly designed, can make the effects of such problems worse, as discussed next.

In brief, producing more goods for export is efficient if that production does not generate other economic and social costs. But if, for example, it makes pollution worse, the economy's gains can be reduced or even become negative, an important lesson to learn.

The possibility of losses from trade due to market distortions and policy failures

To state this idea clearly, if free trade occurs in the presence of significant *economic distortions*, such as monopoly power or inefficient taxes and subsidies, or *market failures*, such as air and water pollution, and regulatory policy does not account for those problems, then, in principle, openness to trade can worsen overall economic welfare. The important trade-off is the following:

- Openness to trade generates the standard gains from trade discussed above.
- But additional production or consumption may worsen the welfare losses of the distortions or market failures.
- Whether an economy is made better off or worse off depends on which of these effects dominates.
- One obvious recent example is China's massive increase in manufacturing exports since the 1990s, which worsened air quality in the cities through more coal burning and transportation based on burning fossil fuels. Over time, the export-led growth also raised congestion costs, housing costs, and similar problems. Until recently, few in China would argue that these problems outweighed the country's economic benefits, but now there is considerable concern about the environment.
- Note clearly that the real problem here is not trade but the inability or unwillingness of governments to optimally deal with the market failures. If governments effectively regulate air pollution and enforce rules reducing monopoly power, and so on, the benefits of trade would dominate.
- This issue is important to understand and will be the subject of later notes on trade and the environment.

Understanding Sources of Inequality

Globalization and wage and income inequality

Turn now to the main social problem that people in many countries, including the US and those in the EU, associate with globalization.

This is rising income (or wage) inequality, evidenced by a growing gap between those with high and rising salaries and wages and those with low and possibly falling wages.

In richer countries, this gap has increased steadily between capital owners and high-skilled workers, on one side, and low-skilled or low-educated workers, on the other. There has been a corresponding rise in wealth inequality as rising capital incomes (e.g., stock prices) favor those who own capital.

There has been a considerable increase in measured inequality in the US since 1980, with the (pre-tax and pre-transfer) Gini coefficient of income distribution rising from 35 in the mid-1980 to just over 41 in 2016, as shown in Figure 5.2. This diagram shows that the largest increase in inequality happened in the 1980s and 1990s, a period of rapidly growing trade.

For students who are unfamiliar with it, the Gini coefficient for any country ranges between 0 and 100. A coefficient of zero means

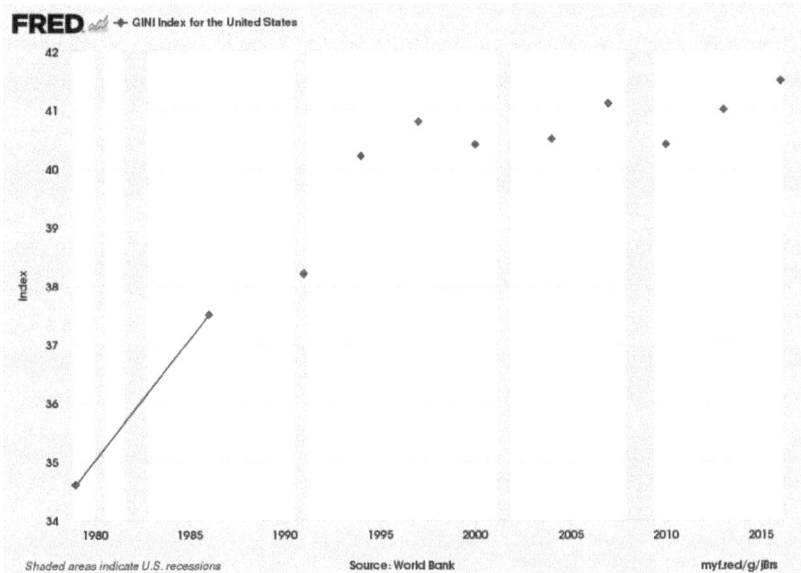

Figure 5.2   US pre-tax and pre-transfer Gini coefficient.

Source: Federal Reserve Bank of St. Louis FRED database, https://fred. stlouisfed.org/series/SIPOVGINIUSA.

that income is equally distributed across all households, while the higher is this coefficient, the less equally distributed is income. The coefficients shown in Figure 5.2 are based on income distribution figures before taxes were paid and any social transfers were made, though these policies make little difference in the US.

Another indication of growing inequality is that between 1980 and 2019 the share of pre-tax income received by the top 1% of households in the US rose from 10.5% to 19%. At the same time, the share of the bottom 50% of households fell from 19.1% to 13.3%. Incomes include wages, salaries, profits, dividends, and capital gains.[1]

Yet another measure is that the ratio of the top 10% of weekly wages to the bottom 10% went from 2.7 in 1979 to 5.0 in 2021, according to data from the US Bureau of Labor Statistics.[2]

Further, the real (inflation-adjusted) median income of a family of four in the US fell from $62,512 in 2000 to $56,912 in 2014, though it has increased since then.[3]

Finally, the lifetime discounted real difference in incomes between those with a four-year college degree and those with a high-school degree rose from about 15% in 1980 to over 50% today, suggesting that the returns to investing in skills have grown sharply in the globalization era.[4]

Inequality in international settings

The situation is similar (but less extreme) in the UK, Canada, and Japan. The problem is somewhat different in Western Europe, where long-term unemployment rates among unskilled workers have risen to high levels, while relatively more generous social transfer programs have sustained lower disparities in after-tax wages and incomes.

---

[1] World Inequality Database, https://wid.world/country/usa/.

[2] https://www.bls.gov/webapps/legacy/cpswktab5.htm.

[3] Federal Reserve Bank of St. Louis FRED database, at https://fred.stlouisfed.org/series/MEHOINUSA672N.

[4] Major decisions: What graduates earn over their lifetimes, https://www.brookings.edu/blog/up-front/2020/10/08/major-decisions-what-graduates-earn-over-their-lifetimes/. Note that these figures do not account for the costs of attending college.

In many developing countries, inequality rose considerably after significant trade liberalization episodes. Mexico, Brazil, Argentina, Indonesia, and China are good examples. In all these cases, there was a marked rise in demand for skilled workers (most prominently medium-skilled workers in manufacturing) and a relative fall in demand for low-skilled workers.

This outcome seems surprising in light of the Stolper–Samuelson theorem: Trade liberalization in labor-abundant countries should raise the real wages of low-skilled labor. And those wages have risen over time but by less than the real incomes of medium-skilled workers. This puzzle will also be addressed in later notes on multinational firms and offshoring.

Globalization and inequality

These changes in income distributions took place during and after the great increases in market integration in the 1980s and 1990s. Thus, many people tend to attribute them to increasing international competition from imports, outsourcing of jobs by MNEs, and other channels of globalization.

Growing inequality is an issue of the first importance and has attracted much research by economists, political scientists, and sociologists, among others. High or extreme economic and social inequality can support political polarization, resentment, and extremist violence, outcomes that have happened many times in world history.

These notes report on the evidence raised by economists, who tend to take a more model-based approach to analyzing wage disparity and trade. In short, the evidence about the sources and extent of inequality is mixed but something very important has been going on for some time and continues today.

Sources of inequality

Before looking at the US evidence, consider first the many possible sources of rising wage inequality in high-income economies. These can be grouped as follows:

Globalization effects

1. International trade in goods and services should redistribute income from scarce to abundant factors (Stolpe–Samuelson effects).
2. Globalization has spurred rapid technology diffusion from rich nations to emerging countries through multinational enterprises (MNEs) investing abroad and transferring technological knowledge to their affiliates. This transfer facilitates productivity gains in the recipient countries and may spur increases in innovation in affiliates and domestic firms there. However, it also reduces demand for lower-skilled workers in the rich countries by inducing MNEs to focus their efforts on R&D, management, and other activities requiring skilled workers, as discussed in the following chapter of notes.
3. Similarly, MNEs may shift employment to lower-wage areas through offshoring and production networks.
4. If globalization encourages migration of low-skilled labor from poor to rich countries, it may reduce the wages of poorly educated native workers in the destination countries, as explained in later notes on migration.

Skill-biased technological change

1. This is technological change that replaces lower-skilled and medium-skilled workers with automated processes and robots. Many believe that the development of artificial intelligence will accelerate this process.
2. Technological change also raises the demand for skilled (managerial, technical, and creative) workers. These changes are mainly due to improving software and information technologies, which permit the most talented workers to sell services to broad groups of clients, including those abroad.

Agglomeration effects

1. "Agglomeration" refers to the concentration of economic activity in particular locations, associated with local increasing returns to scale. These increasing returns are called "external economies

of scale" because they do not happen within firms but rather the collection of many firms lowers all their costs. The primary reasons are that skilled workers in close proximity to one another can share ideas and information, collaborate on innovation, and learn from each other, reducing costs. These economies generally arise in cities that have features, such as universities, infrastructure, and cultural amenities, that encourage high-technology industries to locate there. Since this process involves increasing returns, it can support significant concentrations of firms in many high-technology manufacturing and service industries, which supports high wages of skilled workers.

Clear examples are Seattle (Microsoft, Boeing, and Amazon), San Jose (Google, eBay, and others in Silicon Valley), Los Angeles (entertainment, design, and financial firms), and New York (financial firms). Similar comments apply to London, Paris, Milan, Tokyo, Shanghai, and other major cities.

The contribution of technology-based agglomeration to inequality is that it attracts skilled and younger workers to the cities, tending to raise the income and employment gaps between cities and rural areas. While this is largely a story about technological change, illustrated by software and communications sectors, globalization plays a role to the extent that these increasing-returns industries find larger markets through exports and foreign investment, while sharing technological information with foreign agglomeration centers. There is much evidence that these links to globalization matter.

Market-power effects

1. In rich countries, there has been a considerable decline in wage-setting power on the part of labor unions since the 1980s, associated mainly with the shift of employment from manufacturing to service industries. However, competition from both globalization and technological change has contributed to this falling ability of workers to bargain for wage increases. One effect has been an increase in the shares of national income going to capital owners and a decrease in the shares going to workers in many nations.

2. Since the 1990s, we have seen rapidly growing market power, or economic concentration, among the largest firms across nearly all producing industries and many services. This has raised the shares of profits (and share prices) relative to the share of wages in value added. This trend is obvious in major technology and social-media firms, which have grown enormous and face few rivals. But it's true in nearly all other industries, which seems to be due to economies of scale: The biggest firms invest more and get more productive, permitting them to attract the greatest talent. A consequence of this process is growing wage disparities between those working in larger and more innovative firms and those doing similar jobs in smaller and less innovative firms.

Tax and transfer policies

1. Tax policies, especially in more developed economies, have shifted tax burdens to the lower and middle-income classes while reducing the share of taxes paid by higher-income groups and the wealthy. In part, this is due to the greater international mobility of capital and skilled workers, making them harder to tax. It also reflects their relatively greater political lobbying power.
2. The share of transfer payments made in the US has fallen for programs supporting low incomes and childhood development, while rising for medical care and senior benefits. Seniors tend to be wealthier than average.

Educational inadequacies

1. Many scholars argue that, at least in the US, young people from lower-income and middle-income backgrounds have suffered from attending underfunded schools that make relatively poor educational efforts and fail to produce enough skills to meet growing demands for skilled workers. (See Goldin and Katz, *The Race between Education and Technology*, 2008.)

   The last point is important. Put differently, over time there has been a rise in demand for skills that has not been met by an increase in the domestic supply of needed skills. This is reflected in the large differences in earning power between high-school educated and those with college degrees or greater. Numerous studies show that people in the highest earnings brackets are overwhelmingly made up of those with higher education. For example, US census data reveal that in 2010, 78% of those individuals earning more than $200,000 had a bachelor's degree (with four years of higher education completed) or higher. However, just 9% of those in that income bracket had only a high school degree or less.

Sources of inequality: Observations

This long list of 12 factors underlying growing inequality points out what a complex situation this is. How is it possible even to sort out the relative contributions of these factors?

In fact, they are all interrelated in various ways, and it is quite difficult to separate their effects through data research. As a simple example, should the growing disparities in income between urban and rural communities be attributed to skill-biased technological changes, urban amenities, better schools, or the expansion of export markets? They all matter and interact with each other.

This means in turn that any simple, one-channel policy focus is likely to result in misleading or even damaging policies. For example, the Trump Administration argued that raising barriers to trade would protect the incomes of lower-skilled workers in manufacturing. Instead, as discussed in the later notes on tariffs, the tariffs it raised likely have diminished manufacturing employment overall.

The Role of Trade and Globalization in Inequality

Trade openness and inequality

Now consider more closely the impacts of globalization. To begin, recall our theory of factor price equalization (FPE). The primary conditions for FPE include the following: (1) free trade (and/or free international factor mobility); (2) factors are homogeneous; (3) identical, constant-returns-to-scale (CRS) technologies in all countries; (4) perfect competition and the absence of market distortions; and (5) countries must produce the same (or similar) goods. The last point means that countries are not specialized and the products they make are perfect, or at least quite close, substitutes.

Then, the absolute FPE theorem claims that the real incomes of factors will be the same everywhere. That idea is clearly false. But a weaker version surely has a strong influence on world factor markets: *Free trade and open investment should establish a tendency toward the convergence of real returns to factors across countries. That is, workers of identical (or similar) skill characteristics in countries like China, Malaysia, India, or Brazil will, as a result of globalization, see their real wages moving toward levels that exist in the United States.*

As noted earlier, there is much evidence of this convergence between wages of medium-skilled workers in emerging countries and lower-wage workers in advanced economies. (For further evidence, see Richard Baldwin, *The Great Convergence: Information Technology and the New Globalization*, 2016.)

The fear felt by lower-skilled workers in rich countries is expressed by the question: "Are your wages set in Beijing?" (This was the title of a famous economics paper on the subject.)

The basic answer is that if a high-wage country produces low-skilled labor-intensive goods that are relatively freely imported, it will certainly feel downward pressure on real wages, especially of low-skilled labor.

As noted in later notes, imports of many labor-intensive goods, such as textiles and apparel, are restricted by high tariffs in the US and Europe. However, those countries still import the great majority of such goods they consume. Electronics, shoes, toys, furniture, and many others are other examples of such goods, which are also protected by tariffs.

The way that trade affects real wages is worth revisiting. Trade and globalization effectively have increased global labor supplies at the low-skill end, which reduces global prices for labor-intensive goods. This is good for consumers but bad for low-skilled workers in high-wage economies. If these imports compete directly with domestic products, the falling goods prices translate into lower real wages (and employment) for low-skilled workers. In turn, because these workers could move into other low-skilled jobs, the lower wages spill over into services and other sectors.

On the other hand, capital owners and highly skilled workers in richer nations find their services in greater demand as a result of trade, raising their real incomes.

Evidence: The "China Shock"

Economists have studied these questions for a long time, but their findings did not enter the political debate very much until the publication in 2013 of a famous paper titled "The China Syndrome: Local Labor Market Effects of Import Competition in the US" (*American Economic Review*, written by David Autor, David Dorn and Gordon Hanson, or ADH).

ADH pointed out that the rise of Chinese imports corresponded closely with a dramatic drop in manufacturing employment in the US, beginning in the 1980s. See Figure 5.3, showing that jobs in manufacturing fell from a peak of 19.5 million in 1979 to a low of 11.6 million in 2010.

The bulk of this loss came in the 2000s, especially during the major financial crisis of 2008–2011. It is interesting that about 1.3 million additional manufacturing jobs emerged between 2010 and 2020 before collapsing due to COVID-19.

ADH did not claim that all this was due to Chinese imports. By their calculations, perhaps 1.2 million jobs were lost to such imports between 1990 and 2007.

The reason this was a credible claim is the careful nature of their analysis. They classified US "commuting zones" (CZs) in terms of their exposure in 1990 to Chinese imports. This means that some

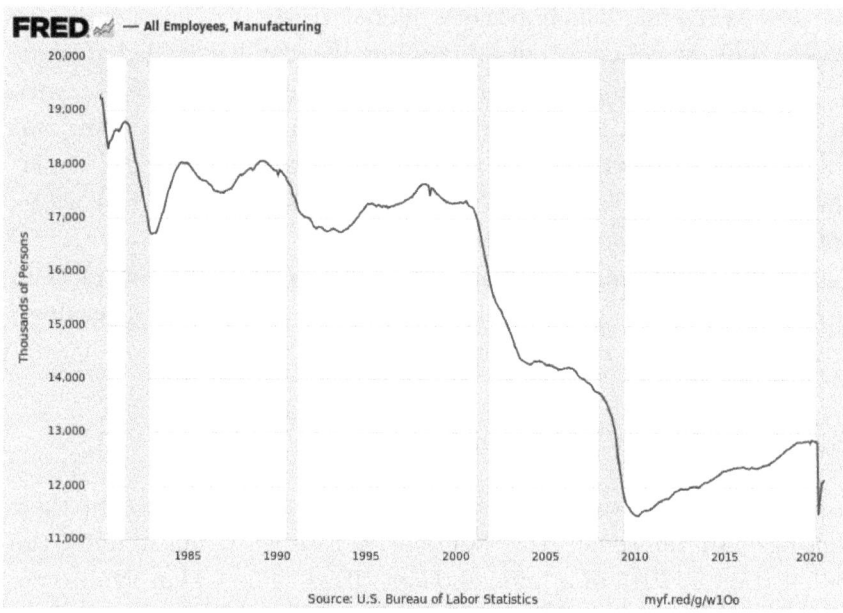

Figure 5.3 Trends in US manufacturing employment.
Source: Federal Reserve Bank of St. Louis FRED database, https://fred.stlouisfed.org/series/MANEMP.

CZs had relatively more production in textiles, toys, and other goods heavily imported from China, while others had production structures more focused on other goods, including exported goods. Then, they analyzed what happened to local employment and other variables as Chinese imports mounted. The surprising result — the "China Shock" — is that the effects were strongly negative in multiple ways in the CZs more exposed to import competition.

 To summarize, in their empirical analysis, ADH found the following results, among others:

1. Manufacturing employment was reduced significantly in more exposed CZs.
2. Displaced workers largely moved into unemployment or left the labor force. There was a significant rise in unemployment

insurance (SSDI payments) to those regions. Surprisingly, however, there was not much reduction in the populations of CZs.
3. Wages fell sharply in the more exposed areas, even for college-educated workers.

There have been many other studies since then, extending this analysis of impacts of Chinese imports on CZs. They found that in the most exposed regions, there have been long-term increases in opioid addiction and suicides, reductions in educational attainment, and increases in disability payments.

The primary lesson of this work is that the local impacts of import competition can be powerful and long-lasting. A second is that workers in these exposed areas seem far less able and willing to move. That is an important issue: Why don't lower-skilled workers in declining areas move as much as one would expect?

ADH is one of the most influential papers ever written by economists. There is one major criticism by other trade economists: ADH only considered the effects of Chinese imports on US labor markets. Studies find that the employment effects of growing US exports to China and elsewhere in this period came close to creating the same number of jobs that were lost due to imports from China. However, those export-oriented jobs were mostly created in high-wage services in less exposed CZs.

Adding Technological Change

The role of technological change

Next, consider the role of technological change, which in recent decades overwhelmingly has been the rising use of rapidly advancing information technologies (software, communications, information, robotics, and so on) in economic activities. In the view of many historians of technology, this is the most fundamental technical change in history because of its potential for raising productivity, developing new products, and solving complex problems.

More than that, there appears to be no limit to computing power, so it is not clear when there will be diminishing returns to investing in software and machines. It seems that the world is entering the next great phase of this evolution, involving driverless vehicles, the Internet of things, machine learning, and artificial intelligence (AI).

It is evident that these changes involve intensive inputs of highly skilled programmers, while the innovations they produce mostly raise demands for workers who are sufficiently skilled to use them efficiently. Economists refer to this trend as *skill-biased technological change* (SBTC).

These changes have had (and continue to have) impacts on factor demands that are not yet entirely understood. Whether they are a source of greater wage inequality or equality depends on how the technologies are used.

On the one hand, digital processors can "dumb down" complicated tasks, like operating cash registers, raising the demand for lower-skilled workers. On the other hand, they allow people with talents and skills to serve a wider audience. Consider what a single architect can do with computer-aided design programs or a movie director can do with special effects. Television and recorded music are disseminated far wider than ever before. Further, the ability to develop software is in great demand, generating large income gains for those who can establish software standards that become widely accepted. Examples include Microsoft, Amazon, Apple, and Facebook.

This perspective suggests that the effects of new information technologies on incomes are non-monotonic:

- Some technologies raise wages somewhat at low-skill levels.
- Others greatly raise wages at high-skill levels and the salaries of those who can use advanced technologies.
- But effects may be negative for middle-skill workers and medium-technology jobs. These "medium-tech" or "routine" jobs are the ones that are most easily replaced by software, robots, and AI. In

fact, recent evidence suggests that these demand shifts and "wage polarization" are exactly what is happening in the US right now.

These trends indicate that skill-biased technical change is a significant source of rising wage and income inequality.

Here are two other interesting observations about technological change and incomes.

1. Computer-facilitated technologies have a very strong tendency to concentrate (or agglomerate) business and high-skilled employment in urban areas. Thus, SBTC contributes to growing urban–rural divergence in jobs and incomes.
2. As machine learning and robotics become increasingly common, the advantages of producing goods in low-wage locations abroad will erode over time because robots can replace workers. In turn, this suggests the following:

   - Employment will move back toward high-income economies over time as labor-intensive parts of supply chains erode. This is one reason why manufacturing jobs are growing again in the US.
   - The poorest countries may find it increasingly difficult to link themselves to global production networks. It is not clear whether using exports as the spur to economic development will work as well for them in the future as it has worked for Korea, Malaysia, China, and similar countries.

Empirical Evidence and Policy Implications

Empirical evidence

What does the empirical evidence say about the impacts of trade, technology, and other factors on wage and income inequality?

Again, this is a difficult question to answer because all these factors are interrelated. For example, it is somewhat misleading to think of trade and technology separately because trade liberalization can spur technical change, while technical change also affects international prices and trade. Economists have not been very successful at sorting all this out, so there is an active ongoing debate.

However, there is a large literature on this subject (including the papers by ADH on the China Shock and its many effects).

Interested students could read the influential analysis by Baldwin in his book *The Great Convergence*, mentioned earlier. Baldwin emphasized these factors:

- Information technologies have encouraged massive increases in outsourcing of labor-intensive assembly operations and service tasks from high-wage countries to developing countries.
- Outsourcing and trade in intermediate goods are significant contributors to wage inequality within the US and other advanced economies.

Those results make sense. But there is a puzzle in the data for the US. Manufacturing employment fell considerably in the 1980s through the 2000s, as shown in Figure 5.3.

Surprisingly, however, the real dollar volume of manufacturing output is nearly as high as ever (except for the effects of the pandemic). See Figure 5.4. How can that be, given the drop in employment?

It must be that technological change has driven manufacturing productivity up, even as employment fell, reflecting two trends:

- First, there have been large increases in the demand for skilled labor in high-wage services and the R&D, management, and design areas of manufacturing.
- Second, there have been significant investments in productivity-enhancing inputs, such as software, robotics, and computer-driven machines, that reduced the demand for lower-skilled labor and medium-skilled labor. The workers who remain in manufacturing have considerably higher productivity than those laid off.

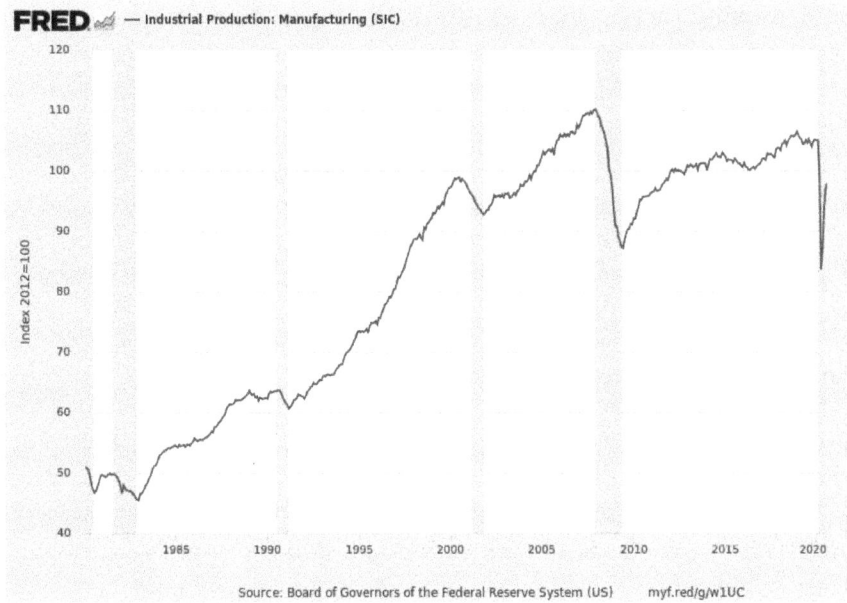

Figure 5.4   Industrial production in US manufacturing.

Source: Federal Reserve Bank of St. Louis FRED database, at https://fred. stlouisfed.org/series/IPMAN.

Some observations on policy to address inequality

Suppose policymakers believed that import competition is an important source of rising inequality and wanted to do something about it. What policies are suggested?

The obvious idea is to erect greater protection from imports through tariffs and quotas. The difficulty (as studied later) is that this policy costs more than it gains, sacrifices the consumer gains from lower prices, and is basically a strategy of trying to fight off inevitable global change. It is a short-run solution at best and does not get at the real problem of limited skills.

A second choice is to try to limit international technology diffusion through preventing multinational firms from investing abroad and offshoring jobs. Or policy could raise barriers to foreign firms seeking to acquire domestic technologies through taking over domestic firms. However, the same comments apply.

Policy could consider trying to slow down domestic technological change, perhaps through taxes on innovation or investments in R&D. But this would be damaging to a country's growth prospects and is politically unpopular.

Finally, it is possible to clamp down on unskilled immigration. As will be seen in the notes on that subject, doing so would have virtually no effect on low-skilled wages of domestic workers in the US.

Some observations on policy

What would be appropriate approaches to the goal of reducing inequality?

The key to making good policy is to figure out what the underlying problems really are and to aim policies directly at solving those problems.

First, it really does not matter much whether workers are laid off because of technical change or international trade. What matters is that they suffer costs of adjusting into new employment and may end up with lower wages. Most economists would argue that the appropriate policies for managing income-distribution and adjustment problems include the following:

1. Have an active social-safety net of supplemental unemployment compensation, wage insurance, opportunities for retraining, relocation assistance, and tax relief for low-income workers.
2. Pay more attention to why workers are so immobile and do not move much from declining areas to expanding areas. One major problem is that housing is often unaffordable in growing urban areas, such as San Francisco and Boston. Reducing such costs by expanding housing supply is a critical solution to this problem.
3. Federal and local governments should invest in rural infrastructure and offer localized economic development incentives.
4. Finally, recall why incomplete specialization is important for FPE. A country or region that does not produce low-skill,

labor-intensive goods does not face low-wage import competition, meaning that lower-priced imports represent a benefit to all consumers.

How do countries achieve this outcome? By being sure to endow their workers with adequate skills through providing technical education and higher education. If the workforce is dominated by high-skill workers, the local economy will specialize toward more skill-intensive goods, which would sustain higher wages.

In this case, trade liberalization provides virtually an unambiguous benefit.

Chapter 6

Intra-industry Trade and the Product Cycle Model

Expanding Trade Theory to More Realistic Cases

Problems with basic trade theories

To this point, the notes have studied the two primary, "benchmark" theories of what explains international trade and its effects.

1. The Ricardian (classical) model is useful for understanding how productivity or technology differences determine comparative advantage and drive trade, and for studying the basic gains from trade.

2. The factor proportions (HO) model is useful for understanding how national economic characteristics (factor endowments) interact with industry variables (factor intensities) to determine comparative advantage and trade. It is also important for studying how trade and globalization affect income distribution between scarce and abundant factors.

Economists more recently have developed a third central theory, which focuses on individual firms and how they engage in trade. This concept will be treated briefly when we discuss multinational enterprises and international investment later.

There remain obvious problems with the two primary theories:

First, they rely on highly restrictive assumptions. In economics, this approach is necessary in order to build basic logical frameworks that give us clear theoretical predictions. But it ignores all kinds of interesting issues that clearly are important for trade, such as the following:

- Products are not "homogeneous" (identical in quality). A Japanese car is different from an American car and a German car. Products are *differentiated.*
- Often firms have *increasing returns to scale* rather than constant returns to scale.
- There may not be perfect competition. Instead, there may be firms with market power.
- Technologies may be different across countries rather than identical. More than that, technologies are *dynamic* and subject to change over time in important ways, including innovation of new goods.

Second, the models study the movement from autarky (no trade) to free trade, meaning no barriers to international commerce. But governments do interfere with trade through tariffs, quotas, and regulations.

Third, beyond trade in goods and services, there is also trade in productive factors. Labor, capital, and technologies may be mobile across borders.

This chapter of notes will focus on the main elements in the first point. Trade policy and factor mobility will be addressed later.

Differentiated Products and the Variety Gains from Trade

Taking demand seriously: The demand for variety and intra-industry trade

The Ricardian and HO theories are based only on supply-side differences between countries. But demand-side differences matter as well, as these empirical points should make clear.

First, the greatest amounts of international trade are among rich countries with similar technologies and factor endowments, not between rich and poor countries with different technologies and endowments. The US trades far more with Canada and the EU than it does with India and even with China and Mexico when country size is controlled for.

Here are some simple data on this point, taken from the US Census Bureau. The top three developed countries that the US trades with (exports plus imports of goods, 2019 data) are, in order, Canada, Japan, and Germany. Total US trade in goods with them was $1,018 billion. The top three developing countries are, in order, Mexico, China, and Brazil. (To clarify, in terms of total trade with the US, Mexico is number 1 and China is number 3). Total US trade with them was $1,265 billion. But if we divide these trade amounts by the populations of those three countries, we get (in 2019) the following:

- Total US trade per person with Canada, Japan, and Germany = $4,121.
- Total US trade per person with China, Mexico, and Brazil = $434.

Thus, trade is considerably higher in proportional terms among the rich countries.

This difference would be even larger if the calculations included trade in services, which is heavily dominated by commerce among developed economies.

Product differentiation and varieties

It is important to understand that these high trade volumes among developed countries are dominated by *differentiated products*. These are similar versions of particular goods (e.g., cars, wines, machines, chemicals, medicines, cosmetics, computers, even bottled water, and so on) that are differentiated in some ways.

How are products differentiated?

1. By quality, characterized by the design, style, and performance of goods and services. Think of "typical" cars by country or "typical" furniture styles by country. What explains those differences?

2. By brand loyalty, because firms advertise to build brands and trademarks that attach (at least in the consumers' minds) various desirable characteristics to their goods and services.

   Sometimes, these differences are mostly perceived rather than real. It is difficult to believe that there are truly 45 different qualities of soft drinks or that brands of bottled water are inherently different. Shampoos seem highly differentiated by brand but use primarily the same ingredients.

3. By timing. It is difficult to get fresh fruits and vegetables from domestic sources during the US winter. But imports of produce from Chile, Argentina, and Central America increase considerably because the US winter is their summer growing season. Another interesting example: Young ski-resort workers during the US ski season often come from Australia and Chile, while American resort workers go there during the US summer.

All this suggests that consumer demands are more complex and interesting than simply thinking they consume corn and wheat or autos and shoes. Instead, consumers have a clear *taste for variety.* They like to be able to choose from among multiple versions of types of goods, which may differ in quality, whether real or perceived.

Here is a simple way to think of such tastes. Suppose a person has a $20 candy budget. If she has a taste for variety, she is better off buying 10 different candy bars (at a price of $2 per bar) than 10 of the same candy bar.

And, while it may be less obvious, producing firms can gain more efficiency, permitting them to produce at lower costs or increase the quality of their own products, if they have access to a greater variety of intermediate inputs. For example, a furniture producer would like to choose from multiple fabrics and materials. Thus, as regards intermediate inputs they buy, firms also have a taste for variety.

These preferences for wider choices of varieties strongly correlate with the idea of product differentiation and branding. Two varieties of bran flakes may be quite similar but if each variety is somewhat differentiated, it can command a higher price in the market.

The gains from variety in trade

What is the role of international trade? It is reasonable to assume that other countries produce varieties of similar goods because firms in all countries face consumers that prefer a variety of choices. At the same time, the varieties produced in country A may be rather different from those in country B because of different national characteristics. Here is an example to help explain this idea.

Consider the automobile industry. Broadly stated, US passenger cars are bigger sedans with comfortable seating, German cars are highly engineered for performance, and South Korean cars are smaller, with better gas mileage. Obvious reasons for this development are that the US has long travel distances, German cars navigate the high-speed Autobahn, and distances are short and gasoline prices are high in South Korea.

But then, opening to trade benefits consumers and firms from a variety gain because international trade offers more choices than a closed economy does. In both these examples, trade is beneficial because there are Germans who prefer American cars (and vice-versa) and Americans who prefer South Korean cars (and vice-versa).

Here are some obvious examples, but this idea extends across a broad range of industries:

- Wine and beer; clothing of different quality levels; automobiles; furniture; high-tech precision machinery; medicines; specialized industrial chemicals; movies and recorded music; ski resorts; and hotels.

Intra-industry trade (IIT)

This logic indicates that countries are likely to trade more with other nations that produce varieties of products similar to those at home. It is evident (but more will be said later) that developed, high-income economies are likely to have the greatest volumes of trade in similar products because they produce differentiated varieties of similar goods. Such countries all have similar per-capita incomes, meaning their consumers share closely related taste patterns. And their firms have similar technologies, encouraging them to import closely related intermediate inputs.

If countries trade heavily with each other in similar goods and inputs, there would be considerable amounts of *intra-industry trade (IIT)*. This is the phrase economists use to describe the fact that countries trade back and forth high volumes and many differentiated versions of similar products within broader industries.

Note clearly that this form of trade is distinct from the *inter-industry trade* analyzed by the Ricardian and HO models. There, countries trade wheat for clothing or radios for shoes. Trade was across industries. Here, however, countries trade cars for cars, wines for wines, and so on. Trade is within industries.

Measuring IIT

Think of IIT as *two-way trade in similar goods within industries*. Here is a standard formula for computing an index of IIT for a country (EX is exports; IM is imports):

$$\text{IIT} = 100 * \left(1 - \frac{\sum_{j=1}^{n} |\text{EX}_j - \text{IM}_j|}{\sum_{j=1}^{n} (\text{EX}_j + \text{IM}_j)} \right)$$

Here, subscript j indicates particular goods or industries, which are groupings of similar goods. There are n industries in the country. This calculation of IIT ranges between 0 and 100.

If $\text{IIT} = 0$, it means that in any good j, there are only exports or imports, and therefore no trade in similar goods. This would be pure inter-industry trade, which is what the Ricardian and HO models are about.

If $\text{IIT} = 100$, it means that for every good j, exports exactly equal imports and all trade is in similar goods. This would be pure IIT, driven by tastes for variety.

Following are some illustrative examples, using actual trade data (Tables 6.1 and 6.2).

Table 6.1 IIT calculation for the US with Canada, 2019.

SITC	2019 Trade with Canada (billion $)	US Exports	US Imports	Abs(EX − IM)	(EX + IM)	IIT
04	Cereals and Cereal Preparation	3.02	5.18	2.16	8.21	73.64
33	Petroleum, Petroleum Products	20.90	75.30	54.40	96.19	43.45
51	Organic Chemicals	3.48	3.00	0.48	6.48	92.57
69	Manufactures of Metals	8.32	5.41	2.91	13.73	78.80
75	Office Machines and ADP Equipment	8.14	0.83	7.31	8.98	18.56
78	Motor Vehicles	50.82	53.03	2.21	103.86	97.87
84	Articles of Apparel and Clothing	2.17	0.82	1.35	2.99	54.86
87	Professional Scientific Instruments	6.47	3.36	3.38	10.10	66.52
00-49	All Primary Goods	56.19	123.00	66.81	179.19	62.71
51-89	All Manufactured Goods	206.20	162.93	43.27	369.13	88.28

Source: Computed by the author using data from US Census Bureau, Foreign Trade Statistics.

These computations use highly aggregated production sectors, which hides the fact that there are many varieties within each sector, such as motor vehicles and scientific instruments. (Note: The acronym SITC refers to the "Standard International Trade Classification" of goods. It is used widely by international organizations.)

Even so, there is a great deal of trade in both directions between the US and Canada. For example, 92.6% of trade in organic chemicals is IIT. Generally, US IIT with Canada exceeds that with Mexico.

In North America, an interesting example is the motor vehicles (mainly automobile) industry, which exhibits considerable IIT among all three nations. Cars produced within a firm (e.g., Ford, GM, or Toyota) may be designed in the US. These designs and high-technology inputs and parts are sent to Mexico, where they are combined with other intermediate parts and processed into more advanced parts and then exported back to the US and Canada, where final cars are assembled.

All this kind of trade tends to get counted in the IIT figures because it all occurs within the broad sector. Even at the stage of final

Table 6.2   IIT calculation for the US with Mexico, 2019.

SITC	2019 Trade with Mexico (billion $)	US Exports	US Imports	Abs(EX − IM)	(EX + IM)	IIT
04	Cereals and Cereal Preparation	4.77	1.54	3.23	6.30	48.72
33	Petroleum, Petroleum Products	28.08	13.12	14.96	41.20	63.68
51	Organic Chemicals	5.56	0.90	4.67	6.46	27.72
69	Manufactures of Metals	8.16	7.26	0.90	15.41	94.15
75	Office Machines and ADP Equipment	16.50	28.90	12.40	45.40	72.68
78	Motor Vehicles	21.28	101.25	79.97	122.53	34.73
84	Articles of Apparel and Clothing	1.01	3.58	2.57	4.59	44.04
87	Professional Scientific Instruments	6.47	13.90	7.44	20.37	63.48
00-49	All Primary Goods	58.20	45.76	12.44	103.96	88.04
51-89	All Manufactured Goods	190.83	300.23	109.40	491.07	77.72

Source: Computed by the author using data from US Census Bureau, Foreign Trade Statistics.

cars, the US exports some models to Canada and Mexico and imports other models from Canada and Mexico. These are extremely intricate *supply chains*, which exist in many manufacturing industries.

Table 6.3 presents IIT calculations for selected countries in their total trade in goods with the world. Belgium and France have exceptionally high IIT percentages, nearly across the board. Both are small- or medium-sized rich countries that export and import large ranges of varieties. Much of that trade is with other EU members. Developing countries generally have considerably lower IIT, with their trade reflecting greater tendencies to trade according to factor endowment differences, as specified in the HO model.

Here are some important characteristics of IIT suggested by the Canadian and Mexican IIT numbers and by the IIT figures for other countries.

1. Developed economies tend to have higher IIT percentages than developing countries, especially in manufacturing goods.

Table 6.3 IIT calculations for selected countries in their trade with the world, 2019.

SITC		Argentina	Australia	Belgium	China	France	Japan	Kenya	Philippines	USA
04	Cereals and Cereal Preparation	1.4	53.2	95.5	53.1	57.3	15.8	8.2	12.5	70.9
33	Petroleum and Petroleum Products	94.6	35.9	87.1	26.4	31.8	26.8	25.1	9.1	89.2
51	Organic Chemicals	19.1	17.4	99.6	92.3	74.6	94.5	11.9	38.4	85.4
69	Manufactures of Metals	27.4	25.8	97.4	26.8	76.7	95.4	29.3	43.7	66.5
781	Passenger MVS	20.6	3.5	98.4	31.0	76.0	22.0	1.9	0.2	47.7
84	Apparel and Clothing	12.7	7.0	98.0	11.1	68.3	4.7	64.2	85.9	11.8
87	Professional Scientific Instruments	10.6	66.0	94.4	85.1	95.8	79.5	17.4	77.5	99.7

Source: Computed by the author using data from United Nations Comtrade Trade Statistics.

2. IIT is more common among developed countries than between developed and developing countries.
3. IIT is generally higher in manufacturing than in primary goods, which are agricultural products and natural resources. This is because manufactured goods are much more differentiated and so there are stronger reasons for two-way trade between countries.

Study question 1

Which of the following statements is true about intra-industry trade (IIT)?

A. IIT tends to be higher among developed economies than between developed and developing economies.
B. Countries with very different capital and labor endowments are likely to engage in a high volume of IIT.
C. There is no IIT in manufactured intermediate inputs.
D. IIT is not possible in industries where services are traded internationally.

Discussion of study question 1

The correct answer is A. The others are false statements. The fact that there can be IIT in services (part D) is clear from the earlier discussion of hotels, tourism, skiing, and other services.

Why is IIT important? What explains it?

The first to write about this phenomenon was Staffan Linder, a Swedish economist who explained it in terms of the *demand similarity hypothesis* (or Linder hypothesis).

Countries at similar levels of income have similar tastes for differentiated goods. Firms produce varieties for their home market and then trade permits firms to export their varieties, which are in greatest demand in other countries with similar incomes. This results in IIT among similar countries of differentiated products.

A simple example: Suppose one were asked to explain why the United States exports furniture to Sweden but also imports furniture from Sweden. It seems unlikely that we can find the answer in differences in capital intensity or labor intensity of the furniture industry between the countries.

A more likely explanation is that US furniture is different from Swedish furniture in design and consumers care about this. Traditional US furniture is large, heavy, and complex in design, reflecting the larger homes and buildings there. Traditional Scandinavian furniture is small, sleek, and simple in design, reflecting the smaller homes and buildings and the need to economize on space. IIT emerges because there are US consumers who like sleek and simple furniture, while there are Swedish consumers who prefer the American style.

Gains from trade with differentiated goods

International trade in differentiated products generates another source of GFT. Compared to autarky, trade substantially raises the number of varieties available to consume and differentiated inputs to use in production.

Are the gains from greater variety through trade significant? Empirical evidence suggests that it is. Two economists in 2006 estimated these gains to be 2.6% of the US GDP from 1972 to 2001, which is likely an underestimate. (See Broda and Weinstein, *Quarterly Journal of Economics*, 2006.)

In addition, such gains are far larger in percentage terms for small economies that cannot produce many domestic varieties. This is one reason that volumes of IIT per person are quite large among smaller economies in Western Europe, for example.

In fact, that insight is worth stating as a fourth empirical characteristic of IIT:

IIT is the highest among smaller developed economies because the limited size of their own markets implies that there are few domestic varieties. In turn, a large number of varieties are imported from similar countries.

The fact that small economies cannot produce many varieties leads us to the next important subject helping to explain IIT: increasing returns to scale.

Increasing Returns to Scale and IIT

Bringing in economies of scale

Another important factor underlying international trade is *increasing returns to scale or economies of scale* (IRS), which to this point have not been much discussed.

A production function has IRS if doubling the inputs more than doubles output. More generally, any X% increase in all inputs generates more than X% in additional output.

What does this mean in economic terms? The more a firm produces, the greater is the gain in additional output. Put simply, *with IRS, the average cost of producing a good falls as the firm expands output.*

In the standard thinking, at some point, firms may see rising average costs once production gets above some high level of output because the firm may run into physical limits on its machinery capacity, or it may have to pay higher wages to attract more workers, may find it too costly to manage large facilities, and so on.

But that may not happen in "super increasing returns" industries, such as software, pharmaceuticals, and designing and building passenger jets for airlines. Firms in these sectors tend to produce goods with extremely high fixed costs (for design and R&D) but low marginal costs. The MC of a unit of software, for example, is virtually zero. Firms in such sectors sometimes grow to immense size if the market is large enough.

IRS and international trade: Basic concepts

There are several theories about how economies of scale interact with trade. (The analysis beginning in the next section is the most important idea and requires the most attention.)

Rather than try to develop those ideas analytically, here are some important results, which are intuitive:

1. Countries with larger domestic markets will be better able to take advantage of IRS, meaning they will have a comparative

advantage in producing such goods. This outcome is even stronger if goods with IRS are capital-intensive and large economies are capital-abundant. Think of the US and its productivity advantages in major software platforms, commercial aircraft, and digital entertainment, among other industries.

2. Even if a large country and a small country have similar capital-to-labor ratios (endowments), the large country will have lower costs in autarky in IRS goods. Thus, it will export them to the small country and import other (CRS) goods from the small country. It is possible for this competition to drive the IRS industries out of business in the small country, making it difficult for smaller countries to have an "industrial policy" to support the development of IRS goods.

3. Countries that become mostly specialized in producing IRS goods will have higher real wages in free trade than other countries because producing at a high scale raises labor productivity.

The combined effects of product differentiation and IRS in IIT

Return to the idea that consumers love variety and trade makes them better off because of it. If that were the whole story, people should be consuming (and trading) very small quantities of a very large number of varieties. But this outcome is generally not observed, whether in autarky or free trade. Instead, there are limits to the number of varieties available in markets.

To explain, keep in mind that *differentiated manufacturing goods (and many services) are generally subject to IRS*, at least up to some level of output. This means that, within a country, it only makes sense to manufacture a limited range of varieties but to produce each at some relatively high scale to keep costs low. Think of automobiles, refrigerators, and furniture. There may be many models, but the numbers are clearly finite.

How many varieties are produced in equilibrium? It depends on the size of the market in which firms operate. In autarky, small countries would produce very few varieties and at a high cost because their markets do not provide enough demand to achieve economies of scale. However, large countries would produce more varieties at low costs.

With IRS, the number of varieties that can be produced in each country is limited by the size of the market. Thus, we might have three car producers in Italy, two in France, four in Germany, six in the US, four in Japan, and so on. The industry in each country produces a limited set of models in autarky.

Now, suppose countries open to trade with each other. What are the key impacts?

International trade expands the size of the market facing producers by permitting them to export their varieties. It also means consumers have more varieties to choose from than in autarky, where they can only consume domestic varieties.

Thus, opening to trade has these effects:

1. It expands the number of varieties available. These "variety gains from trade" are a welfare benefit.
2. It permits firms to produce more of each variety, getting larger economies of scale and lower average costs. This makes output more efficient and reduces prices, also a welfare gain on the efficiency side.

These are important **gains from trade** beyond the standard gains from specialization (comparative advantage) and lower import prices for consumers.

An important caveat is that the growing imports of foreign varieties raise competition for domestic firms and their varieties. This competition does place competitive pressure on domestic firms in each country. But put this issue into perspective:

IIT is a "two-way trade", so as more varieties come in through imports, firms in the home country also have opportunities to sell in new export markets.

At least some domestic firms will end up producing more of their varieties for the integrated market at higher volumes, taking advantage of economies of scale. But that raises a big question. Which firms are likely to prosper and grow in the integrated market after trade liberalization?

Intuitively, the successful firms are likely to be those that were already the most productive and innovative. It is also likely that some firms (and varieties) will lose out in this competition and reduce output or even go out of business. These are likely to be the least productive and least innovative firms.

This means that trade competition forces resources to move from lower-productivity firms to higher-productivity firms. Economists think of this "rationalization efficiency" as a third source of gains from trade with differentiated products and IRS because it raises average productivity and wages in the economy. (To reiterate, the first two sources are greater varieties and lower costs of production.)

This rationalization may not be seen as good news in towns where firms shut down, generating short-term unemployment. But economists see it as beneficial due to the better allocation of resources between firms.

There seems to be a trade-off here. There are more varieties due to imports but fewer varieties as some domestic firms go out of business. How do we know which effect dominates?

It turns out that if consumers prefer variety, the new equilibrium must involve a higher total number of varieties available in each market after opening to trade.

Here is an example. Imagine that there are three countries in autarky, each producing 10 varieties of a good. Thus, consumers in each country have 10 varieties initially. Now, let the countries trade with each other and suppose four unproductive firms close down in each country. Despite that, consumers now have $6 \times 3 = 18$ varieties to choose from.

Trade economists see these trade-offs (more varieties and greater economic efficiency) as significantly beneficial for countries that trade. Again, these gains come from IIT, involving *within-industry specialization in varieties.*

IIT: Summary

1. Variety gains in combination with IRS, which achieves lower costs, mean that international trade generates additional gains from trade beyond the perfectly competitive models, such as Ricardo and HO.

2. IIT is the highest among similar developed countries because they have similar preferences for differentiated goods and tend to have larger domestic markets that support firms with IRS.

3. This suggests that IIT in differentiated goods is fundamentally different from inter-industry trade based on differences in factor endowments and intensities (HO model). In HO trade, countries export goods produced in industries that intensively use lots of capital or lots of labor (or land). In contrast, trade in differentiated goods exists within industries. Both types of trade exist, of course. For example, the US exports wheat and imports clothing (inter-industry) while it both imports and exports cars and wine (intra-industry).

4. International trade with product varieties and IRS generates three new types of gains from trade: (1) variety gains; (2) greater economies of scale, producing higher labor productivity; and (3) rationalization efficiency as less productive firms close down while more productive firms expand.

5. And there is an important observation to make about trade policy. With HO (inter-industry) trade, opening to trade makes the scarce factors (unskilled labor in the US) worse off and the abundant factors (skilled labor and capital in the US) better off, so there is a redistribution of factor income. But with IIT, trade is not generated by differences in factor scarcity and factor abundance. Instead, IIT happens to meet the demands for variety among countries. In doing so, efficient firms expand and benefit from IRS. And that means (in principle) that workers who lose their jobs in failing firms should already have the skills to work in similar firms that are expanding in the same industry. In fact, workers could see higher wages as they move to expanding firms.

The adjustment of workers to new jobs is less costly in IIT than in factor proportions trade and they may gain higher incomes in the adjustment.

6. In turn, the political opposition to imports of differentiated goods (IIT) from other developed economies is much less than is opposition to imports of labor-intensive goods from developing economies. This is certainly true. For example, the US, Japan, and the EU retain high tariffs against textiles and apparel from low-wage developing economies but have low or even zero tariffs on most manufactured goods and inputs from other developed economies.

Study question 2

Which of the following statements is NOT true about intra-industry trade (IIT)?

A. IIT generates additional gains from trade due to increases in product variety.
B. International trade in differentiated products generally permits more productive firms to produce larger amounts of each variety, generating economies of scale.
C. IIT is the largest among developed countries with similar income levels.
D. IIT tends to reduce the real incomes of scarce factors and raise the real incomes of abundant factors.

Discussion of study question 2

The correct answer is D. IIT involves considerably lower adjustment costs for workers and capital in moving from declining firms to expanding firms within an industry. Workers may end up being more productive and having higher wages. A, B, and C are all true statements.

Trade in Technologies and Dynamic Elements of Trade and Innovation

Product cycles in trade and foreign direct investment

A current and interesting area of research in international trade is about the *dynamics* of international trade. The prior models are *static*, assuming no changes in endowments, technology, or preferences. The following notes introduce and summarize an important dynamic theory of trade, involving innovation, trade, and technology transfer between countries.

The *product cycle model* is a simple idea but with important implications. The theory is that each product goes through a typical life cycle from newly innovated to fully standardized. Along the way, it changes from being highly skill-intensive and engineering-intensive to unskilled labor-intensive, making it cheaper to produce in emerging countries. This happens through forms of technology transfer, such as reverse engineering to copy a product or FDI as firms choose to shift production overseas.

This dynamic means that the *location of comparative advantage changes over time.*

But since there is always innovation going on, there are always new product cycles starting in new goods.

The product cycle model

Consider a product such as a laptop, a tablet computer, automobile brakes, or an advanced machine tool (a machine used to produce other goods in a factory). Each can be expected to go through the following stages of the product cycle (PC). This is a simplified theory, and the details would be different for each type of good.

Stage 1 (Innovative good): The product is innovated in one of the skill-abundant, engineering-abundant economies, such as the US, Germany, the UK, or Japan. This is because of the skills and engineering there and also because those countries generally have high incomes and demands for new goods. During this time, the new good must go through testing and initial production and it makes sense to locate production in the place where it was innovated or close by, e.g., in Canada for a US innovation. Suppose that this country is the US.

Trade and FDI flows in the innovative stage: Probably there is very little trade or FDI as the good is sold only or primarily to home consumers or industrial users. In this stage, the good is very new, is uncertain in demand, and still needs engineering and testing.

Note that because it is new, there are likely to be some consumers willing to pay a high price for it, meaning that this initial demand is inelastic. At this stage, the innovative firm charges a high price relative to its production costs in order to make profits used to pay its R&D costs. A good example is that some consumers are willing to pay a high price for the newest versions of the iPhone.

Stage 2 (New good): Consumers and users in other developed countries learn about the good and demand to buy it, so the innovator firm starts to export.

Trade and FDI flows in this stage: Expect exports to go to Canada, Japan, EU, and other developed countries (DCs). And, after some time, US MNEs are likely to invest in local facilities or acquire affiliates in those countries in order to sell in those markets more cheaply. Thus, production starts moving to these DCs through foreign direct investment.

In this stage, the good remains skill-intensive and capital-intensive. Demand in DCs is established and is still relatively inelastic, with the innovator still making profits.

Stage 3 (Maturing good): After another period of time, it becomes better understood how to produce the good. It is increasingly advantageous to move production abroad through FDI or licensing the rights to produce. Nevertheless, in this stage, a firm likely would locate production in economies that also have high skill and capital supplies since the good remains somewhat skill-intensive in production.

Firms would also make these investments to make it cheaper to supply the good to local markets (e.g., in Europe or Asia) without having to pay tariffs and transport costs. In this period, demand for the good arises in emerging countries like China, Brazil, and Mexico.

Trade and FDI flows in this stage: Expect FDI to other DCs which produce it in rising quantities and can even export back to the US. They would also export to emerging countries (ECs). At this stage, DCs would export the good to ECs and back to the innovator nation.

In this stage, the good remains skill-intensive and capital-intensive, though by less than at the innovative and new stages. No more engineering is needed as production technologies and know-how are well understood.

Stage 4 (Standardized good): The good eventually becomes fully standardized and increasingly labor-intensive as low-cost labor can be used to replace high-cost skilled labor in production. It becomes cheapest to produce in the ECs (and maybe even poorer developing countries). This would happen through even further FDI (and outsourcing or offshoring). Note that FDI involves *technology transfer*, in that the means and know-how for producing these goods are transferred to ECs.

It is also possible that firms in those countries might try to imitate the good through reverse engineering and to develop and produce their own versions, rather than pay licensing fees to the foreign innovators. This is an uncompensated form of technology transfer. Meanwhile, the US and perhaps other DCs have moved on to innovating a new version of the good.

Trade and FDI flows in this stage: Production shifts to ECs, which then begin to export it and continue to export it as long as there is demand for the good. The US and other DCs are net importers of this good.

Table 6.4 summarizes the various stages of a product going through a typical product cycle. An interesting observation is that because different versions of products (innovative, maturing, and standardized) are being traded throughout the PC, this model is consistent with IIT in similar products of different quality levels.

Table 6.4 Simplified description of stages in the typical product cycle.

Country Type	Initial Innovation Stage	New Product Stage	Maturing Product Stage	Standardized Product Stage
Innovator (e.g., US)	Initial innovation; production only in innovator; no trade	Production rises then falls in innovator; FDI in other developed; net exports rise and then fall	Production falls further in innovator; innovator becomes net importer	Production ceases in innovator; net imports continue to rise; innovative firms invent newer products
Other developed countries (DCs)		Net imports from innovator; inward FDI from innovator to transfer production	Production rises in other DCs; net exports back to the innovator and to other DCs	Net exports diminish and become net imports; production falls
Emerging countries (ECs)			Inward FDI from innovator and other DCs	Production increases and ECs become net exporters

Product cycle: Important observations

1. Not all goods are like this. The PC really refers to industries where firms engage in continuous innovation and technology transfer.
2. Since within an industry different versions of a good (e.g., a tablet versus a hand calculator or software-driven precision machine tool versus an older hand-driven machine tool) will exist. Thus, IIT happens, even between rich and poor countries.

3. Generally, innovative goods and new goods offer high profits to firms because they are new and the firms have temporary monopolies on producing them. They can charge prices above marginal costs ("monopoly markups") due to inelastic demand. But over time, as goods mature and become labor-intensive, profits would fall.

4. This means there is an important economic trade-off to consider:

   - First, the rate of innovation in advanced countries determines how high their profits are in the early stages of a good. High rates of innovation sustain high wages (paid out of profits) in advanced economies.
   - Second, the rate of diffusion or imitation of new technologies and goods to emerging countries determines how quickly firms in those countries gain comparative advantage and produce and export the goods. This process raises wages in ECs (like China) but tends to reduce wages in the US and other developed economies. It is a major source of wage convergence across countries, as discussed in earlier notes.

Point 4 implies that there is a dynamic *race* of sorts. The higher is the rate of innovation, the higher are profits and real wages in richer and more innovative countries. The higher is the rate of diffusion and imitation, the lower are profits and real wages in developed countries but the higher are real wages in ECs.

Generally, firms in the richer "North" want high innovation but limited imitation. This is the main reason we see firms in the "North" push for stronger patent and trademark protection in the ECs of the "South".

If ECs improve their protection of intellectual property rights (IPRs), innovative multinational firms get two benefits:

1. These firms can enforce their patents, generating higher and longer monopoly profits.

2. If stronger IPRs make multinational firms more confident about investing in ECs, they also will transfer technologies through FDI and offshoring to take advantage of lower wages.

At the same time, the "South" countries generally would oppose strong IPRs because that policy would make it more costly to imitate foreign goods while raising the licensing fees their firms must pay to multinational firms. This is an extremely interesting and important area of research in trade and development economics.

Chapter 7

Import Tariffs and Export Subsidies

If Trade is Beneficial, Why Do Governments Interfere with It?

Introduction

The prior chapters studied the primary theories of what determines comparative advantage and which products are exported and imported by countries of different types. Students should now have solid exposure to why and how countries trade with one another.

Further, the notes analyzed the numerous gains from trade of various types. These gains suggest that countries are made better off by engaging in trade, even if there are some people and regions who lose real income inside each country.

If countries are made better off by free trade, an obvious question arises from the fact that there are policies that restrict international trade. *Why do countries limit trade with import tariffs and other barriers?*

At the same time, some governments attempt to expand exports by paying subsidies to exporters, thereby encouraging them to ship more goods abroad. These notes will analyze such subsidies, which are costly and inefficient. *Why do countries expand trade with such policies?*

Start with the important observation that countries are virtually never in autarky nor do countries pursue fully free trade, except rarely. Thus, it is important to understand how *partial restrictions or barriers on trade affect the economy and welfare*. Put differently, if an economy erects policies to restrict or expand trade, is there a possibility of welfare gain?

These notes therefore compare free trade with artificially restricted or subsidized trade, focusing on welfare effects. This chapter also discusses important aspects of the so-called *political economy of trade barriers*, explaining why governments might interfere with trade to protect narrow interests, at the expense of losses.

Basic Concepts

Commercial policy

Commercial Policy is the general term for *official government discrimination in favor of domestic interests over foreign interests.* Typically, this discrimination is enacted on behalf of domestic producers and tends to harm domestic consumers.

There are many kinds of commercial policy, and these notes cover a few of them. Here is a partial list:

Direct limitations of or subsidies to trade:

- import taxes (called tariffs), export taxes, and import and export subsidies (these are "price-based" interventions because they directly change prices);
- quotas and other limits on the volume of imports or exports (these are called "quantity-based" interventions).

Regulations directly affecting trade:

- domestic preference laws, which give domestic firms advantageous access to government purchasing programs;
- domestic content requirements, which mandate that firms must hire or buy a minimum percentage of inputs from domestic sources to qualify for any advantageous policies;
- technical production standards imposed on imports that are more costly than those on domestic goods, such as higher sanitation standards.

Regulations indirectly affecting trade:

- restrictions on inward investments, such as maximum foreign ownership levels in banking, agriculture, airlines, and so-called "strategic industries";
- higher taxes or more onerous regulations placed on the domestic operations of foreign firms than on domestic firms;
- failure to protect the intellectual property of foreign firms as well as that of domestic firms;
- many others.

For something to be commercial policy, it must discriminate in favor of domestic interests. The immediate question is why would countries do this.

Underpinnings of commercial policy

As noted earlier, it is easy to believe that free trade offers higher welfare than no trade (autarky). Countries in isolation deprive themselves of opportunities to specialize, import new varieties, and have access to global technologies.

But does free trade guarantee higher economic welfare than a situation where trade is partially limited by trade barriers or regulations? International economists overwhelmingly think so. But for others, it depends on underlying views of international competition.

Globalist approach: Free trade is the opportunity for foreign producers and consumers to compete on equal terms with domestic producers and consumers. Thus, supply and demand operate on a global basis and competition should ensure that each good seeks out its location of comparative advantage and resources should be allocated efficiently.

A globalist might also argue that policies of open trade and investment expand opportunities for technological progress in emerging and developing countries and, therefore, are pro-development. An important version of this argument based on international relations is that strong trade and investment relations among nations should reduce the likelihood of military conflict. Thus, globalists largely take the view that governments should interfere with international markets as little as possible.

Nationalist approach: It may be that what is best for the world is not the best outcome for a country. Students should not confuse this idea with more political definitions of nationalism and patriotism. The concept here refers to reasons why restricting trade may improve domestic economic welfare, even if it might reduce world welfare.

The notes will show how this is possible in some cases but here are a few initial examples placed into three categories.

Arguments based on economic efficiency:

1. Suppose a country is "large" in that it has sufficient buying or selling power to influence world prices of a good with taxes or quotas. Should it not do so to turn the terms of trade in its favor?
2. Small, developing countries may need to put taxes on trade just to raise government revenues. Many poor countries find it difficult to collect income or property taxes, but it is straightforward to collect tariff revenues at the border.
3. Foreign firms may "dump" their goods in your market, which means selling below the price in their own markets or selling at prices below their costs of production. Dumping puts pressure on your own firms. Importing countries may have reasons to offset this behavior by imposing tariffs on such imports.

Arguments based on preferences to achieve non-market objectives:

1. A country may believe that having some minimum level of domestic production in a declining industry is important for national security reasons, if the output of that industry matters for military or cybersecurity purposes. Then, perhaps it should restrict import competition to sustain higher domestic production.
2. A country may place limits on imports of goods produced under weaker environmental or labor regulations abroad, either to avoid cost disadvantages imposed on its domestic firms or to express its opposition to such practices.

In such cases, economists would ask whether trade barriers are the most effective way of achieving the objectives, an issue studied in later notes.

Arguments based on interests in protecting domestic groups:

1. Students have seen in the HO model that free trade worsens the incomes of scarce factors. They would likely argue for protection from imports in order to avoid this fate. Policymakers might respond to such pressure and restrict imports or perhaps provide domestic employment or output subsidies.
2. It may be that specific firms or industries have sufficient lobbying power to convince policymakers to limit imports. Good examples in the US include sugar and apparel, which are protected by tariffs and quotas, and the shipping industry, insulated by a ban on foreign shippers competing on routes between domestic ports.

Again, such policies raise the question of whether it makes economic sense to use tariffs for this purpose.

It is interesting to note that globalist and nationalist interests in policy restrictions sometimes may be aligned. For example, suppose international trade worsens environmental quality by encouraging the production of polluting goods or by raising emissions through global shipping. In that case, it can be appropriate for countries to develop a global set of rules governing the conditions under which countries can limit trade to offset such costs.

These are complex and interesting questions, which will be addressed in the following two sets of notes. But first, students need to understand how tariffs, subsidies, and other interferences with trade operate and what effects they have.

How Tariffs Work

Import tariffs: Types

Start with basic definitions. *An import tariff is a tax on imports.* It is levied at the port and must be paid before a good can be released by the port authorities to the importer. (Here is an interesting question in this context: How could a government put a tariff on cross-border digital trade on the Internet?)

A tariff operates much like a sales tax in that the consumer ends up paying it in addition to the basic price. But it is different because it is discriminatory: It is not levied on goods produced and sold at home. (It is also different because consumers do not see an entry for "tariff" on their purchase receipts, making it difficult to know how high tariffs are.)

Definitions of types of tariffs.

- A *specific tariff* refers to some dollar amount levied per physical unit of a good imported. Thus, it is a tax amount per car, per pound of cheese, and so on.
- An *ad valorem (AV) tariff* refers to a tariff that is some percentage of the value (or price) of the imported good.
- A *compound tariff* is a combination of these.
- A *tariff-rate quota* is a low *ad valorem* tariff rate up to some specified level of imports and then a very high *ad valorem* tariff after that. In essence, a TRQ uses the tax system to establish an effective quota on the amount of imports because the higher tariff rate deters further imports.

The two main types of tariffs are specific and AV. Clearly, they can be equated. For example, let the price of an imported good be $50. If a specific tariff of $20 is imposed, its AV equivalent tariff per unit imported is $100 * (20/50) = 40\%$.

There is at least one important economic difference between them. The protective power of a specific tariff falls with the inflation of prices because a given tax amount falls as a percentage of the rising import price. But an AV tariff retains its strength because a given percentage tax means that more taxes are collected as the import price rises. When import prices are falling, the protective power of the specific tariff gets larger, but the AV tariff retains the same strength.

Import tariffs: Objectives

Tariffs may be levied for several purposes:

- A *revenue tariff* is enacted to generate revenues for the central government.
- A *protective tariff* has as its main objective the protection of a domestic industry from import competition. The extreme version

of this is a *prohibitive tariff*, which is so high it cuts imports to
zero.

- Protective tariffs may attempt to redistribute income. For example, if tariffs are generally high on labor-intensive imports, they would tend to raise real wages and reduce real capital incomes. The reason is simply that by reducing imports, they reverse some of the effects of import competition on low-skill wages. Often labor-scarce countries such as the US or EU have tariffs that are higher in labor-intensive goods to protect the real incomes of scarce factors.
- Similarly, Japan and Korea are land-scarce and heavily protect domestic agriculture from import competition. Indeed, import restrictions against agricultural goods generally exist to protect the value of farm assets (land and livestock) by keeping domestic crop prices high.

Tariff Analysis in a Small Country

Economic effects of a tariff in a small country

In international economics, a *small country* is a nation that imports a good at a constant world price. Its decisions on how much to import have no impact on that price. A similar definition exists for a small exporter. The concept is exactly like an individual consumer or firm that buys or sells a good at a given market price and has no influence on that price. Such agents are called "price takers" and it applies also to small countries in trade.

Price impacts: Assume there is perfect competition. Then, tariffs have the following price effects, where p_D is the domestic price and p^* is the fixed international price of a good that a small country imports:

$$\text{Specific tariff of } \$T\text{:} \quad p_D = p^* + T$$

$$\textit{Ad valorem} \text{ tariff at rate } t\text{:} \quad p_D = p^* + tp^* = (1+t)p^*$$

The reason the domestic price of imported sweatshirts rises by the full amount of the tariff is that the importers (e.g., Walmart in the US) must pass the cost of the tariff on to consumers. But this

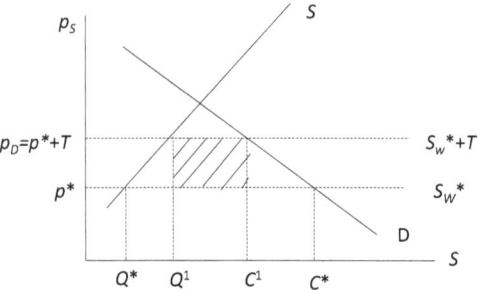

Figure 7.1   Graphical analysis of a specific tariff in a small importer.

Note: This small economy faces a *perfectly* elastic world supply curve of S_w^*, meaning the world will sell as much to this economy as it wishes to import at price p^*. Imports in free trade (before the tariff) were the distance Q^*C^*. With the import tax of $T, we see that p_D is the higher domestic price. This price goes up by the full amount of the tariff (this must be the case for a small economy). For example, if $p^* = \$20$ and $T = \$5$, then the domestic price is \$25.

permits them to raise the price of domestically produced sweatshirts by the same amount. Note that these relationships make the strong assumption that domestic goods and imports are *perfect substitutes*. This means they would have the same price if the tariff did not exist, and the domestic price must equal the tariff-inclusive price if there is an import tariff.

Most of the subsequent analysis will use partial-equilibrium analysis of a tariff on a single good, unlike the earlier general-equilibrium analysis. This is fine because the primary concern here is seeing what goes on with a tariff in a particular imported good. Following is a graphical analysis. Consider a specific tariff of $T per unit on imported sweatshirts (S), in Figure 7.1.

Production and consumption effects

Production rises to Q^1 (production effect), consumption falls to C^1 (consumption effect), and imports (now equal to distance Q^1C^1) are lower. That imports fall is not surprising, for if you tax something, you should expect less of it to happen.

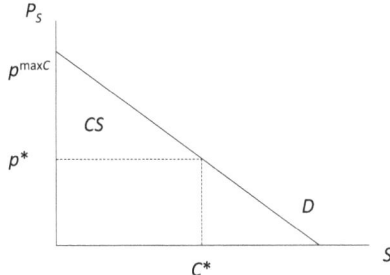

Figure 7.2 Consumer surplus.

Tariff-revenue effect

The government gets tax revenue equal to the shaded box, which is the import quantity times the tariff per unit. Using our example, if the new import quantity is equal to 10 million sweatshirts and the tax is $5 per sweatshirt, the total tariff revenue is $50 million. Tariff revenue is considered a benefit to the economy.

Welfare basics: Consumer surplus

Rather than focus on labor and capital incomes, it is more direct to think of three agents: consumers, producers, and the government. Start with effects on consumers, including a welfare measure (Figure 7.2).

Behind the demand curve: consumer surplus

For this domestic demand curve, in free trade, everybody pays p^* and total quantity is C^*. But the consumers to the left of the marginal buyer would be willing to pay more than p^* for the units of the good they get. The first would be willing to pay p^{maxC} and then each succeeding consumer (or group of consumers) would be willing to pay less as you go down the demand curve. The height of the curve shows the true valuation (or utility) that consumers get from the good. However, the price for all units is p^*. The area above this price but below the demand curve captures the excess utility above the costs of consumption. This area is "consumer surplus" (CS).

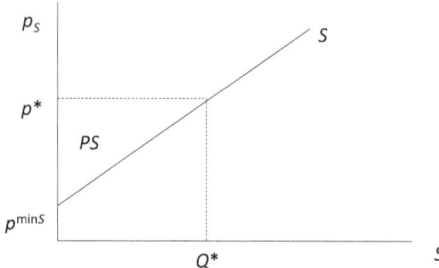

Figure 7.3   Producer surplus.

Consumer surplus is the excess of consumer benefits realized above the costs of consumption. It is a real benefit and counted as a *welfare* gain to the economy.

Next consider domestic producers and a welfare measure.

Behind the supply curve: Producer surplus

This is the domestic supply curve. Producers in free-trade equilibrium get paid p^* per unit of output. yet some producers were willing to supply the good along the supply curve at lower prices. That is, the first unit would be supplied if the price is p^{minS} (for "min" supply price). As the economy moves up the supply curve at higher prices, additional units are offered in the market. Thus, sellers receive *more* than is necessary to get them to sell the good. The difference is called producer surplus (PS) and is measured by the area above the supply curve up to equilibrium (Figure 7.3).

Producer surplus is the excess of producer benefits (measured by payments they receive) over what they would have to receive in order to supply a given amount of the product. This is also a benefit to the economy.

Welfare analysis of a tariff

Draw these concepts together to consider the full benefits and costs of a tariff in Figure 7.4.

Let the small economy impose a tariff of T on imports. Then, the domestic price rises to $p_S^D = p_S^* + T$. As a result, domestic output

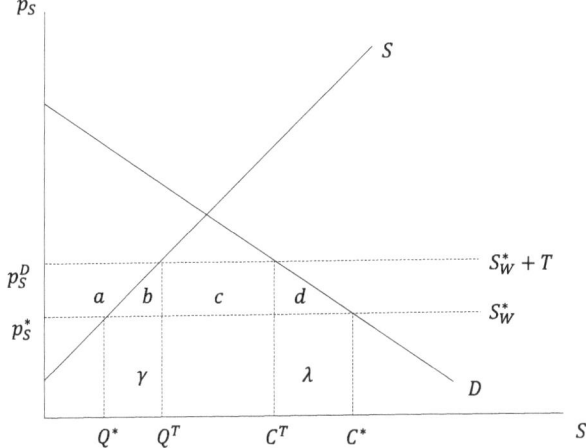

Figure 7.4   Welfare effects of a tariff in a small country.

rises to Q^T and domestic consumption falls to C^T. The impacts on welfare (small letters denote areas) are as follows:

1. Loss in consumer surplus $= -(a + b + c + d)$.
2. Gain in producer surplus $= +a$. This is an income transfer from consumers to producers.
3. Gain in tariff revenue $= +c$. This is an income transfer from consumers to the government.

Adding all these effects we find that the net welfare loss $= -b - d$. This is called the "deadweight loss" of the tariff.

Study question 1

An import tariff imposed by a small country will

A. raise the domestic price and reduce domestic output of the protected good;
B. reduce the international price of the good on which the tariff is placed;
C. make domestic consumers of the good worse off and domestic producers of the good better off;
D. generate tariff revenues that exceed the consumer surplus loss.

Discussion of study question 1

The correct answer is C. By raising the domestic price, the tariff worsens CS but raises PS. A is incorrect because domestic output rises. B is incorrect because a small country has no effect on world prices. D is incorrect because tariff revenues will be smaller than the CS loss.

An empirical illustration

Table 7.1 lists basic estimates of these various impacts of certain tariffs imposed by the United States in the late 1980s. (*Source*: Hufbauer and Elliott, *Measuring the Costs of Protection in the United States*, Institute for International Economics, 1994.) The dollar figures have been updated to 2020 prices using changes in the US GDP deflator over the period in order to place them into current context.

Here are some important observations about these data:

1. These high tariff rates existed on primary commodities (orange juice) and labor-intensive industries, as suggested by our trade models. Trade agreements have reduced these rates considerably over time, but they remain among the highest US tariffs.
2. As the theory predicts, consumer costs (lost CS) considerably exceed producer gains (higher PS).
3. These tariffs generated notable amounts of real tariff revenue.
4. Overall, the deadweight losses were small in each case. This is the common outcome of such estimates. For the US, the static DWLs of trade protection are rarely estimated to be more than 1–1.5% of GDP.
5. However, as the final column shows, *tariffs are a highly expensive means of protecting jobs*. Estimates of the consumer loss per job (CS divided by an estimate of the number of jobs saved by the tariffs) ranged from $194,100 to $1,877,200. In contrast, the average manufacturing employee in the US shoe and leather industry in 2020 earned around $31,000 (*Source*: Statista.com). It would be far cheaper simply to tax US citizens and transfer the

Table 7.1 Estimated gains and losses from certain US tariffs in the 1980s.

Industry	Rate%	Consumer Loss $m	Producer Gain $m	Tariff Revenue $m	Deadweight Loss $m	Consumer Loss per job Saved $th
Frozen orange juice concentrate	30.0	565.0	203.1	291.5	70.3	927.8
Rubber footwear	20.0	418.3	110.6	283.5	24.2	245.9
Ceramic tiles	19.1	279.4	90.5	185.0	4.0	805.6
Luggage	16.3	424.2	32.2	339.8	52.2	1877.2
Women's purses	13.5	297.6	32.2	239.3	26.1	385.1
Glass and glassware	11.0	534.8	325.7	191.1	18.1	362.1
Women's shoes	10.0	756.1	140.8	593.2	22.1	204.3
Costume jewelry	9.0	207.0	92.5	104.5	10.0	194.1

Source: Adapted by the author to 2020 US dollars from data in Hufbauer and Elliott, *Measuring the Costs of Protection in the United States* Institute for International Economics, 1994.

lower wage amount to workers who might lose their jobs to import competition.

6. The industries that were protected by high tariffs are also small. Employment in the leather and leather products industry (including leather shoes) in 1989 was around 138,000, or 0.7% of the 19.4 million jobs in manufacturing that year (US Bureau of Labor Statistics). As a general rule, smaller industries find it easier to organize themselves and lobby for protection from imports. See the following for more perspective on this point.

7. Despite the tariff, employment in these labor-intensive sectors fell considerably after the 1980s. By 2020, it was 11,450 in shoes and leather.

More on deadweight losses

In Figure 7.4, area $-b$ is the "production efficiency loss" from expanding output at higher costs than would be incurred just by buying the good from abroad at price p_S^*. That is, to raise output from Q^* to Q^T costs $(b + \gamma)$ in economic resources but those extra goods would only cost γ if the goods were imported.

Area $-d$ is the "consumption efficiency loss" from forcing consumers to cut consumption and pay a higher price than the import price. That is, the full loss to consumers is $-(d+\lambda)$ but the cost saving from not importing is λ.

The meaning of deadweight losses (DWL): These are *net welfare losses not compensated by any transfer from anywhere else in the economy.* They are lost GDP (or resources) that simply disappear as a result of the tariff. If these effects were added up across all sectors with tariffs and the total deadweight losses summed to 3% of GDP, then GDP would be 3% less than it would be without the tariffs. One primary conclusion of this analysis is that a *small economy makes itself worse off by imposing a tariff on imports.*

Qualifications and extensions

1. The welfare criterion using CS, PS, and tax revenues is a dollar for dollar trade-off among groups, which is the standard economists' utilitarian approach. It is defensible on two grounds:
   (a) The idea is politically neutral; it does not assign a higher weight to one group over the others in considering welfare changes.
   (b) There *are* net losses to the economy, so it is not possible for the gainers to compensate the losers from the tariff and have net gains left over, even in principle.

   But it is important to understand that these trade-offs among groups are the economists' answer to the political question of how to assign such welfare weights. As a matter of policy, perhaps the government would prefer to protect domestic producers of a good while discounting the harm to domestic consumers.

2. Students may wonder about the decision to count tariff revenues as a welfare gain for the economy. The logic is that these revenues would be used by the government to improve the economy in some other way. The government could simply give these revenues back to consumers, say through cutting other taxes. Or it could invest in public infrastructure or some other beneficial public service.

The primary point is that the government is a domestic agent and the revenues it receives from domestic consumers are simply a transfer of income. However, that income is still available for positive uses. Thus, the revenue box is both a loss to consumers and a gain in government revenues.

3. However, political calculations are rarely this neutral. Here is a powerful point to understand about the *political economy of trade protection*. Suppose an industry, such as sugar, clothing, or steel, already has a protective tariff in place. These industries have relatively few domestic producers and workers. For example, in 2021, there were 294 iron and steel manufacturing firms in the US, employing around 81,000 manufacturing workers (IBISWorld Industry Statistics). Further, steel production is concentrated in just a few states.

   Implication: If the country removes the tariff, the losses would be concentrated among the firms and workers in the protected industry and the cities where plants are located. Those groups would have a strong incentive to oppose removing it (or to lobby for an even higher tariff).

   In contrast, there are hundreds of millions of consumers who would benefit from the tariff cut. However, the gain to any consumer or household is small compared to their income or expenditure, meaning their incentive to lobby for the cut is small.

   Thus, the gains from the lower price when a tariff is cut are spread out among millions of consumers. It is nearly impossible to organize them into a lobbying group in favor of cutting the tariff. This means we should expect a political bias in favor of seeing countries protect domestic industries with tariffs.

4. Another effect of the tariff is on income distribution within the country:

   a. The losers are consumers and (in the long run) the economy's abundant factors.

   b. The winners are workers and capital in the protected industry and (in the long run) scarce factors.

Note that these points assume that trade is driven by factor endowments and intensities, as in the HO model. They may not hold for intra-industry trade, as discussed earlier.

But this logic generates another important insight from the political economy of tariffs:

A major reason why tariffs exist, and one explanation of how they vary across industries, comes from the HO model and the Stolper–Samuelson theorem. In many cases, *import tariffs are policies used to protect scarce factor incomes by limiting imports.*

While important for understanding policy, the notes above pointed out that tariffs are an inefficient means of protecting incomes compared to explicit income-redistribution programs, based on income taxes and transfers from those who gain from trade to those who lose from trade.

5. There are further important impacts of tariffs that are not shown in the simple diagram:

   a. By raising domestic output of protected industries, tariffs draw resources away from competitive export sectors and from non-traded goods like services. Thus, there are welfare losses in general equilibrium. This insight is important: Protecting imports is likely to draw resources away from the production of exports, implying that placing higher tariffs on imports can be expected to reduce exports.

   b. Tariffs on inputs raise costs of producing final goods, an issue the notes will consider later.

   c. There are important dynamic effects. Tariffs distort investment and skills into inefficient sectors so that over time a country with extensive trade protection likely suffers lower growth and lower labor productivity. Many economists argue that these dynamic distortions generate the largest costs of trade restrictions.

There is considerable evidence that this was a large economic problem in relatively closed developing countries from the 1950s through the 1990s. It continues to be a problem today in more closed economies in such regions as sub-Saharan Africa and Latin America.

Study question 2

Economic logic suggests that in a country where unskilled labor is relatively scarce, tariff rates would likely be highest in industries that are

A. Labor-intensive with small amounts of employment.
B. Capital-intensive with large amounts of employment.
C. Highly innovative and profitable.

Discussion of study question 2

The correct answer is A. Workers in labor-intensive sectors see greater downward pressure on their real wages from imports and will lobby for tariffs. This is easiest if the industry is relatively small.

Tariff Analysis in a Large Country

Effects of a tariff in a large-country importer

Next, consider the analysis of a tariff imposed by a *large country*. A country is large if its decision to reduce imports with tariffs forces foreign exporters to reduce their prices in order to continue to sell in the large country's market. Such a country has *monopsony power* in international trade, in that it can change world prices by restricting trade.

To analyze this case, consider trade between two large countries. This means that each nation's decisions on trade taxes affect prices in the other country.

Take as an example the US and China, with the US importing footwear (F) from China. Figure 7.5 shows their partial-equilibrium supply and demand curves, linked together. Note again that this approach assumes that US and Chinese footwear are perfect substitutes for each other.

Free trade occurs at price p^*, where the quantity of US imports $(Q_{US}^* C_{US}^*)$ equals the quantity of Chinese exports $(C_C^* Q_C^*)$.

From free trade at a price of p^*, we see that the US tariff of T per unit of footwear pushes up the US price as expected. *But now because this reduction in demand matters in China, we see that Chinese exporters are forced to cut their price as well.*

The price relationship becomes $p_{US}^D = p_C^D + T$. There is a lower volume of trade.

Following the graph are welfare calculations in both countries.

Welfare analysis: US

Impacts in the US:

- There is a loss in consumer surplus $= -(a + b + c + d)$.
- There is a gain in producer surplus $= +a$.
- There is a gain in tariff revenue $= +c + e$.
- The net welfare effect $= +e - b - d$.

As before, $-b$ and $-d$ are the deadweight losses. The new element here is the area e, which is the *income transfer from Chinese exporters to US tariff revenues*. This is a new gain for the US, associated with its ability to use a tariff to force down the price it pays for the import good. We refer to this area as the *"terms of trade gain"* from the tariff. Since the US faces a lower import price, its T of T is improved.

Is the US better off or worse off? It depends on whether the T of T gain is larger or smaller than the sum of the deadweight losses.

The concept of the "optimal tariff"

Define the *optimal tariff* for a large country as the one that maximizes net welfare gains or maximizes $e - b - d$.

What determines how big the optimal tariff is? Intuitively, these factors matter most:

1. How big the importing country is as a share of world demand for a good. The greater is its share in demand, the higher is the optimal tariff because it has larger market power to force down foreign prices by cutting imports.

Corollary: *The optimal tariff for a small country is zero.* A small country cannot gain welfare from imposing a tariff. The tariff makes it worse off.

2. The extent to which the exporting country cannot find other export markets to sell the good. If it is difficult to find or expand into other markets, the exporter must cut its price to the importer by relatively more, meaning a higher optimal tariff for the importer.

   In practical terms, this second issue refers to whether China in the example can readily divert its exports away from the US and toward Europe, Japan, or other markets. The more difficult that is and the longer it takes, the more China must accept a lower price for its exports to the US.

Other key points:

1. If a large country imported many goods from multiple sources, it would have a menu of optimal tariffs, which would vary by product and exporter. Trying to figure out and implement that menu would be extremely difficult and likely lead to arbitrary and inefficient tariff rates, which is one reason that trade economists argue against such "fine-tuning".
2. As discussed next, these tariffs harm the exporting countries, which would be expected to retaliate with their own tariffs on the exports of the original country. This would offset the benefits of the tariffs for the importer.

Welfare analysis: China

China is the exporter facing this tariff in the example. What happens there? Refer again to Figure 7.5 for this analysis.

- The domestic price of footwear in China goes down because it must fall by the same amount as the price of the footwear China exports falls. As a result, output falls and consumption rises.
- There is a gain in consumer surplus $= +f + g$.
- There is a loss in producer surplus $= -(f + g + h + i + j)$.

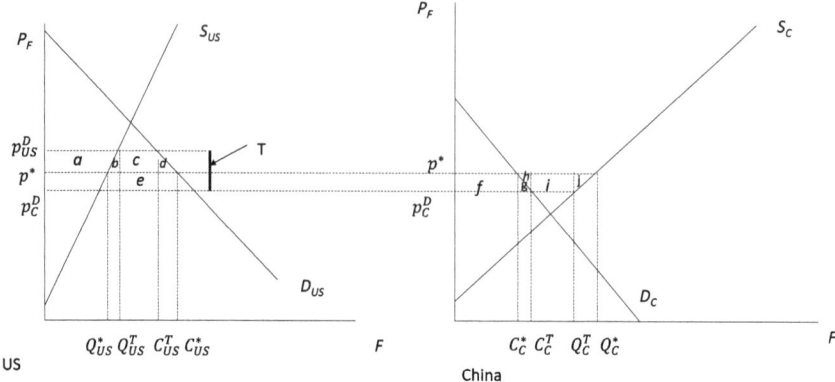

Figure 7.5 Effects of an import tariff when both countries are large.

- No tax revenues are generated (the tax is levied by the US and revenues go to the US government).
- Thus, the net welfare impact is a loss of $-h - i - j$.

Areas $-h$ and $-j$ are the deadweight losses imposed on China by the US tariff. Why are these efficiency losses to China?

First, Chinese consumption is expanded artificially by the lower price in China. Those additional goods consumed would have been worth more if exported at the original free trade price. That is, their true economic value is the area $(f + g + h)$, which is sacrificed. Compared to the CS gain of $+f + g$, the consumption efficiency loss of $-h$ is left over. Note that $-h = -g$, showing that the part of the CS gain is due to inefficiently higher consumption.

Second, output in China falls. This saves resources under the supply curve, which is beneficial, but that lost output was worth more at the free-trade price. The difference between the resource savings and the true output loss is the production efficiency loss of $-j$.

Finally, area $-i$ is a transfer of income from China's producers to US taxpayers and is a welfare loss from China's perspective. We call this the *terms of trade loss* for the exporting country because the country earns a lower price for its export.

Note that area i equals area e, so the Chinese T of T loss just equals the US T of T gain. It is an exact transfer of income from

Chinese footwear firms to the US government caused by the US tariff pushing China's footwear price down.

Study question 3

A tariff imposed by a large importing country has all the following effects except:

A. Raises the domestic price of the protected good.
B. Generates government tax revenue in the importing country.
C. Increases output of the good in the foreign country facing the tariff.
D. Raises consumption of the good in the foreign country facing the tariff.
E. Transfers economic welfare from the exporting country to the importing country.

Discussion of study question 3

The correct answer is C because the tariff causes foreign production to fall, not rise. The other answers are all true effects of the tariff.

Comments on tariff retaliation

Since the exporting country is made worse off, it might choose to retaliate with a tariff imposed on the good(s) it imports from the other nation.

Here, suppose China retaliates with a tariff on imports of a different good, say corn, from the US. (The graphs are not shown here.) What would happen?

- China would get a terms-of-trade gain (like the one above) from a lower US export price for corn. Tax revenues would be transferred from US corn producers to China. The US would be made worse off in this second round.
- One might then expect the US to retaliate with a higher tariff in a third round, then China responds, and so on.
- In the end, after multiple retaliation rounds, the situation would be the following:

A. The offsetting tariffs virtually eliminate the possibility for either country to generate terms of trade improvements.
B. Tariff revenues (transfers) move in both directions, basically offsetting each other.
C. Trade volumes in both footwear and corn would be much lower than in free trade. And this cut in trade volumes would also limit the tariff revenues generated in both countries.
D. In principle, the retaliation rounds would end up only with increasingly larger deadweight losses in both the US and China.

There are clearly instances of tariff retaliation in the real world.

First, such retaliation has happened numerous times in history. The most famous example emerged in the Great Depression of the 1930s. The US moved first to raise tariffs to high levels, averaging almost 60% across most imported goods, in the Tariff Act of 1930, the so-called Smoot–Hawley tariffs. The goal was largely to increase domestic employment at the expense of jobs in other countries. But more than 40 other major countries quickly raised their own tariffs in retaliation and the volume of world trade fell from around \$3 billion in 1929 to \$1.9 billion in 1933.

Second, major countries routinely impose so-called antidumping tariffs in current trade policy, which often is undertaken in retaliatory rounds. Anti-dumping will be discussed in later notes.

Third, the United States and China engaged in a retaliatory "trade war" from 2018 to 2020, with each side raising its tariffs on goods from the other several times. A truce was reached in January 2020, but the higher tariffs imposed largely remain in place.

These possibilities raise an obvious and important question: How do countries mutually agree not to establish high optimal tariffs and to retaliate? Avoiding such a fate is globally beneficial, even if individual countries think they might gain from tariffs. The answer is to have a global trading system that sets rules discouraging such episodes.

In large part, the WTO exists to remove pressures for such tariff-setting and retaliation possibilities. The notes will discuss this issue in detail later.

Effects of an Export Tax

Export taxes: Introduction

A tariff is a tax on imports. It is also possible to place a tax, or tariff, on exports.

Countries rarely impose export taxes, largely because such taxes would diminish exports, reducing output and employment in export sectors.

Such taxes are banned by the US Constitution, in Article 1, Section 9, which states that "No tax or duty shall be levied on articles exported from any state".

However, some commodity exporters on occasion place taxes or quotas on exports of certain agricultural goods or mineral exports. The primary reasons for such limits include the following:

1. Attempting to keep domestic prices of such goods low at a time when world commodity prices are rising. For example, many countries engaged in such export bans on rice, wheat, corn, and other goods when world prices rose quickly in 2007 and 2008.
2. Using export taxes to increase government revenue. Argentina imposes such taxes on agricultural exports periodically to support its tax base.
3. Improving the country's terms of trade to the extent that it has monopoly power to drive up world prices of its export goods through such taxes.

Effects of an export tax in a small country

A small exporter cannot affect the world prices of its export goods but can sell all it wants at a given world price. It is a *price-taker*.

Since the world price is fixed, if the country imposes an export tax, it can only export the good if its domestic price falls by the amount of the tax, making the tax-inclusive price competitive with the world price. The price relationship is then

$$p^D = p^* - V$$

where V is the \$ amount of the tax per unit of exports.

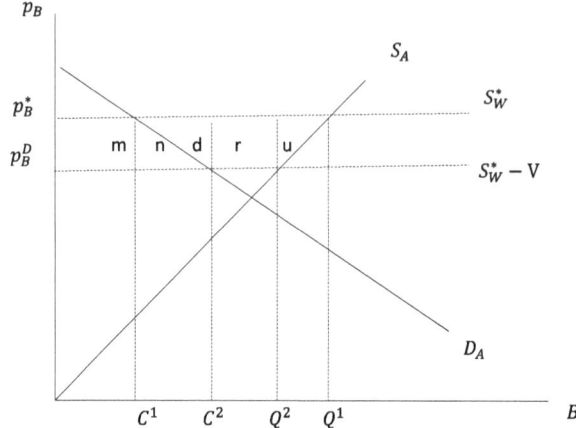

Figure 7.6 Welfare effects of an export tax in a small country.

The graphical analysis is in Figure 7.6. Let the country be Argentina (A) and the export good be beef (B). Argentina's domestic supply and demand curves are as shown. It faces a *perfectly elastic world demand curve* given by S_W^*. Argentina is an exporter because its supply curve is to the right of its demand curve at the world price.

In free trade, Argentina exports quantity C^1Q^1 at price p_B^*. When it taxes exports, the domestic price must fall by the full amount of the tax, so the price falls to p_B^D.

We see these effects immediately:

- Consumption rises to C^2 and production falls to Q^2.
- As a result, exports are lower in the quantity C^2Q^2.

Again, taxing exports reduces their quantity.

Here are the welfare effects in Argentina:

Since the domestic price is lower, there is a CS gain of $+m+n$ and a PS loss of $-(m+n+d+r+u)$. Area $m+n$ is an income transfer from beef producers to consumers.

Tax revenues are generated in the amount $+r$. This is a transfer of income from beef producers to the government.

The net welfare impact is $-d - u$. This is the DWL of the tax, made up of the efficiency loss from artificially expanding consumption and the efficiency loss from cutting domestic production.

As this analysis shows, export taxes are harmful for producers of export goods. The other earlier extended comments about tariffs apply here also. In particular, such taxes push resources and investment out of efficient export sectors into inefficient import-competing industries, generating dynamic distortions that slow productivity growth over time.

An export tax in a large country

It is possible that the taxing country is large in the sense that an export tax would change the world price of its export good. This would happen because the tax would make the country's exports scarcer on world markets, driving up the world price.

Here, there would be two price effects: The domestic price would fall, and the world price (domestic price plus the tax) would rise. As in the case of an import tax for a large country, we would have these impacts:

1. domestic DWLs by expanding consumption and cutting production artificially;
2. terms of trade gain by forcing the world to pay a higher price (including the tax) to the importing country.

Thus, again there is the possibility of a welfare gain and there would be an "optimal export tax", depending on how important the exporter is in the world market. However, this tax would make the importing country or countries worse off, and one might expect them to retaliate, either with their own export taxes or, more likely, with tariffs on other goods imported from the taxing country. Students would find it useful to draw the appropriate diagram for this case.

Subsidies on Exports

Trade subsidies: Introduction

To this point, the notes have addressed taxes on imports (tariffs) and on exports. The first policy is common, while the second is rare. Both reduce trade. Both are welfare-reducing in a small economy but could raise welfare in a large economy, though only by making foreign trade partners worse off.

The opposite of a tax on trade is a subsidy, which is a payment made to importers or exporters to encourage them to increase trade volumes. Import subsidies are rare because they raise the quantity of imports and thereby reduce domestic prices received by firms producing goods that compete with imports. As such, they are politically unpopular.

On occasion, however, developing countries that import agricultural goods and food products choose to pay subsidies to such imports in order to have more supply in the domestic market, driving down consumer prices. This may help reduce hunger in times of domestic food scarcity.

More common are export subsidies, which are government payments to firms that export particular products, often agricultural goods, primary commodities, or strategically important industrial products. The remainder of these notes analyze the effects of an export subsidy and the potential for retaliation by importing countries.

Analysis of an export subsidy

Sometimes, countries think that artificially expanding exports would be a beneficial policy. In part, this idea reflects the mercantilist concepts discussed in the notes on the Ricardian model. An export subsidy might also be viewed as a means of raising employment in a sector or expanding output seen as important for strategic or political reasons. However, it should be evident that artificially increasing trade with subsidies is likely to generate costly outcomes, just as does artificially decreasing trade with taxes.

First, what is an **export subsidy**? It is a policy by which the government of the exporting country pays domestic exporters of a good a subsidy tied to the amount of exports. Sometimes, an export subsidy is paid directly to foreign importers to buy the country's export good. Again, the subsidy can be *specific*, meaning a given dollar amount per unit exported, or *ad valorem*, which is a percentage of the export price or the value of exports.

The major example is the EU's long-standing policy of subsidizing exports of certain agricultural goods in order to ship abroad the surpluses created by the Common Agricultural Policy (CAP). Under the CAP, farmers are guaranteed a minimum price for their output, often in excess of production costs, inducing them to overproduce wheat and other grains, dairy products, and even wine. The US also had a common policy of subsidizing wheat exports in order to dispose of surplus domestic production.

The EU and the US largely ended agricultural export subsidies in the 1990s because of agreements reached at the WTO to discourage such policies. The WTO's role will be discussed later.

Analysis of an export subsidy: Small country

To understand the impact of an export subsidy, suppose a small economy, Thailand (T), decides to increase its exports of rice (R) through paying a subsidy. Figure 7.7 shows T as a small economy because it can sell as much rice as it wishes at the world price p_R^*. The world demand for Thai rice is *perfectly elastic* at that price, meaning Thailand is a price taker. The free-trade quantity of exports is C^1Q^1.

This means that the world price Thai exporters get for their R is fixed. But under the policy, for every unit of rice exported, these exporters receive an additional subsidy of $\$S$. Thus, farmers receive a total price of $p_R^D = p_R^* + S$. For example, if the world price is $\$100$ per kilogram and the subsidy is $\$5$, then rice exporters receive a price of $\$105$ per kilogram.

In turn, the rice producers will not accept a price below $\$105$ for sales in the domestic market because they could export all their output at that price. It follows that *despite the subsidy being paid only on exports, the domestic price rises by the full amount of the*

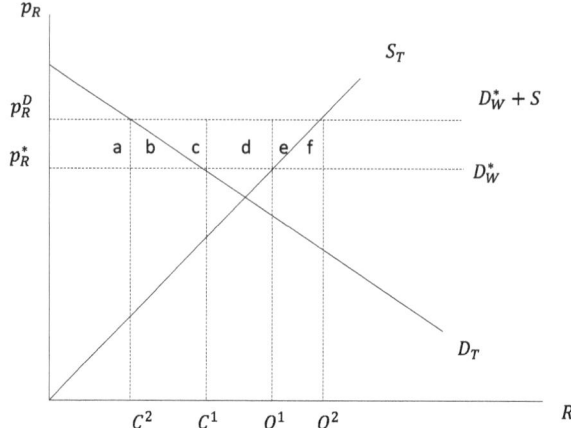

Figure 7.7   Welfare effects of an export subsidy in a small country.

subsidy. The important point is that the subsidy encourages farmers to export rice, which makes rice scarcer in the domestic market, pushing up its price and harming consumers.

The quantity of exports rises to C^2Q^2. As expected, paying farmers to export produces more exports.

The welfare effects are by now familiar with one new insight. The loss in CS $= -(a + b)$. Consumers are worse off.

The gain in PS $= +a+b+c+d+e$. Note that $a+b$ is an income transfer from Thai rice consumers to producers.

The new insight is that the subsidy does not generate revenues for the government. Instead, it results in a *fiscal cost of the subsidy,* which is the total dollar paid out to exporters. It is a welfare loss because these funds could have been used for other beneficial purposes in the economy.

The amount of the fiscal cost is the box $-(b + c + d + e + f)$, or the new export quantity times the per-unit subsidy. (Again, the negative sign indicates it is a welfare loss.) If the export quantity is 100 million tons and the subsidy is \$5 per ton, the fiscal cost (paid to exporters) is \$500 million.

Bringing all the effects together shows that the net welfare effect of the export subsidy is $-b-f$. Area $-b$ is the deadweight loss from artificially reducing domestic consumption of rice, while area $-f$ is the deadweight loss from artificially expanding domestic production of rice. Thailand (the small economy) cannot improve its welfare with an export subsidy. Rather, the tax reduces Thai welfare.

Study question 4

This question asks students to compare an export tax with an export subsidy for a small country. In comparing these two policies, which answer is correct?

A. The export tax raises the domestic price of the exportable good, while the export subsidy reduces the domestic price.
B. The export tax raises producer surplus, while the export subsidy increases consumer surplus.
C. Both policies generate government revenues.
D. Both policies make the small country worse off.

Discussion of study question 4

The correct answer is D. A small country cannot improve its welfare by imposing a tax or subsidy on either imports or exports.

   A is incorrect because the policies have the opposite price effects to those listed. B is incorrect because the tax harms producers and the subsidy harms consumers. C is incorrect because the subsidy forces the government to spend money (the "fiscal cost") rather than raising revenues.

Analysis of an export subsidy: Large country

In the case of the optimal tariff, we found that a large country could improve its welfare with an import tariff. Is the same conclusion warranted for an export subsidy?

   To analyze this possibility, consider a situation where the EU exports wheat to North Africa (NA). The EU pays NA importers a specific subsidy of S euros per unit of wheat the EU exports there. (The economic effects are the same whether the payment is to NA importers or EU exporters.)

First, consider the price relationship: Since the EU pays NA to buy its wheat, the NA price must be lower than the EU price:

$$P_{EU}^S - S = P_{NA}^S \quad \text{or} \quad p_{EU}^S = p_{NA}^S + S$$

Note that this price relationship is similar to the one for the small exporter but here there are two price effects: the NA price falls (because the EU is a large exporter) and the EU domestic price rises (by engineering scarcity on the EU market).

For example, if the domestic EU price is 1000 euros per metric ton exported and the subsidy is 100 euros per metric ton, the NA price would have to be 900 euros. The EU pays NA importers a check of 100 euros per ton.

But note again that the subsidy would change two prices. It would raise the EU price (because the subsidy ships some of the good out of the market) and reduce the NA price.

In Figure 7.8, the initial free-trade price of wheat (W) is p^* without the subsidy. The EU exports quantity $C_{EU}^* Q_{EU}^*$ to NA.

The export subsidy causes a rise in the EU price and a fall in the NA price. There is a rise in exports to $C_{EU}^S Q_{EU}^S$.

In effect, the EU chooses to reduce its export price in order to export a higher quantity. This implies that the EU decides to worsen its terms of trade by paying NA to buy its exported wheat.

Outcomes in the EU:

- The higher EU price implies reduced consumption and a loss in consumer surplus, which is $-(a + b)$.
- The higher price also implies higher domestic wheat production and a gain in producer surplus, which is $+a + b + c$.
- The higher output and lower consumption imply a higher volume of exports $(C_{EU}^S Q_{EU}^S)$.
- There are no tax revenues generated. Instead, there is a fiscal cost of the subsidy, which is the subsidy S times the volume of exports, given by area $-(b - c - d - e - f - g - h - i)$. (To clarify, this is the heavily outlined box.) This area is a welfare loss for the EU.
- Recall that this subsidy must be paid on the entire volume of exports, not just the additional exports the subsidy creates.

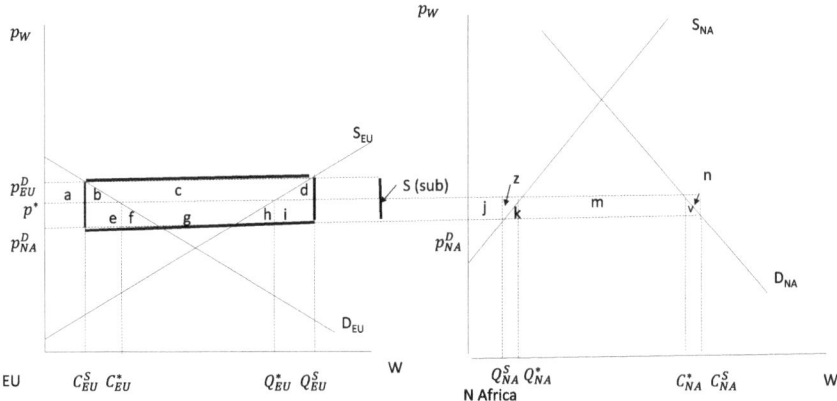

Figure 7.8 Effect of an export subsidy paid by a large exporting country.

The EU net welfare loss $= -b - d - (e + f + g + h + i)$. The areas $-b$ and $-d$ are the deadweight efficiency losses of the subsidy from artificially cutting consumption and raising production, respectively. Area $-(e + f + g + h + i)$ represents an income transfer from the EU to NA. This transfer exists because the EU has paid NA to accept its wheat at a lower price than in free trade. In essence, the EU is writing a check from its treasury to North Africa.

Area $-(e + f + g + h + i)$ is therefore the *terms-of-trade loss for the EU*. By artificially expanding its export supply, the EU has driven down the price it receives for its wheat exports.

Next, consider the welfare outcomes in NA:

- There is a lower price in NA, which implies expanded consumption and a gain in consumer surplus, which is $+j + z + k + m + v$. Consumers of wheat are the beneficiaries of this policy.
- The lower price in NA implies reduced wheat production and a loss in producer surplus, which is $-(j + z)$.
- No tax revenues are generated, and no fiscal costs are paid in NA.
- Thus, the net welfare effect $= +k + m + v$. NA actually gains welfare from the EU's export subsidy.

And note the following for completeness. The lower price of EU wheat in NA implies a *terms-of-trade gain* for *NA* of $+z + k + m + v + n$. It is exactly equal to the EU terms of trade loss, which shows the income transfer from EU to NA. But $-k$ and $-v$ are the deadweight efficiency losses from artificially cutting production and raising consumption, respectively. Thus, in NA, the net welfare gain is $+k + m + v$.

Export subsidy: Comments

There is more to say about impact on EU citizens. They are both consumers and taxpayers, meaning they suffer a "double hit" in that they both pay the subsidy fiscal cost and also pay a higher domestic price for wheat (and wheat products, like baguettes).

The subsidy makes the EU worse off, despite the higher level of exports. Policymakers should never make the mistake of believing that using public resources to subsidize a higher volume of trade is likely to raise welfare. It is just the opposite. Put differently, more trade is not beneficial if it exists because of a policy distortion.

Why would the EU consciously make itself worse off with the subsidy?

The answer may be taken from the political economy of trade policy. The EU farming lobby (like those in the US, Japan, Korea, and many other countries) is very powerful and lobbied for both the CAP and the ensuing subsidies to export excess domestic production.

There is another important implication to understand. Agricultural land is a fixed asset and often forms the bulk of a farming family's wealth. By raising the domestic prices of agricultural goods, export subsidies help keep up the price of agricultural land in the EU, sustaining the wealth of the farming sector.

Analysis of an export subsidy: The importing country's response

What might North Africa be expected to do in response? The EU subsidy is a good thing for them in terms of having access to cheaper food (better terms of trade), so we might expect NA to write a big thank-you note.

But there is a losing group, which is NA farmers. If they are also a powerful political lobby, they would ask their governments to oppose the subsidy. The policy that such governments might impose as a result would be a *countervailing tariff*, which would mean a tariff placed on imported wheat from the EU. This tariff would offset the effects of the EU subsidy. (This is called a *countervailing duty* in actual trade policy.)

Then, we would find ourselves in a situation where the EU subsidizes higher exports, but NA puts a tariff on those imports, which would essentially push the prices and trade quantity back toward the original equilibrium. Interestingly, however, NA would gain welfare both from the subsidy paid by the EU and from the import tariff revenue. Both these outcomes are harmful to the EU, which might be expected to remove the subsidy, restoring free trade. More generally, it might deter the EU from paying the subsidy in the first place.

In this sense, the CV tariff can actually be globally efficient because it both helps restore the original equilibrium and penalizes the export subsidizer.

Countervailing duties are a major issue in global trade policy and are permitted by WTO rules, as later notes will describe. The point here is that their use can be globally welfare-enhancing by stopping large countries from using export subsidies in the first place.

Study question 5

If a large country decides to subsidize an export good, we can conclude that

A. The foreign price of the good will fall and the domestic price in the subsidizing country will also fall.
B. The foreign (importing) country will be worse off and the domestic (exporting) country will be better off.
C. The fiscal cost of the subsidy in the exporting country will be greater than the producer surplus gains.
D. Consumers in both countries are better off.

Discussion of study question 5

The correct answer is C, as shown in Figure 7.8. A is incorrect because the domestic price rises. B is incorrect because the importer is better off and the exporter worse off. D is incorrect because consumers in the exporter are made worse off.

Chapter 8

Import Quotas and Other Non-tariff Barriers

What are Non-tariff Barriers to Trade?

Introduction

A *non-tariff barrier (NTB)* is a policy that restricts trade but is not a tax on trade or a subsidy paid to engage in trade. There are many examples, starting with the familiar import quota, which is the primary policy considered in these notes.

An import quota is a limit on the quantity or value of imports. Most frequently, it specifies the maximum quantity of a good that may be imported into a country. But there are also value quotas, meaning limits on the monetary value of a good that may be imported.

Import quotas in developed countries remain reasonably common in certain agricultural goods. For example, the US constrains imports of dairy goods, sugar, meats, some produce, and other crops. The EU has similar policies. However, developed economies rarely place such limits on industrial or consumer products, reflecting agreements reached largely at the WTO. Quotas are considerably more common in developing countries, both in agriculture and industrial and final goods.

As these notes emphasize, import quotas generally have worse impacts on domestic and world welfare than do tariffs, which is why the WTO rules attempt to limit or eliminate their use. Beyond import quotas, there are also export quotas, which are also uncommon.

Economists also label as NTBs a large range of non-tax policies that restrict trade and foreign direct investment. These include limits on FDI, restraints on the ability of foreign firms to acquire domestic technologies, domestic content requirements, discriminatory product standards, and many other policies. Such policies are important but beyond the scope of these notes.

Effects of an Import Quota in a Small Importer

Quota analysis for a small country

Consider first how an import quota works, analyzing a small importing nation that imports soybeans (S). In Figure 8.1, the quota is set to equal distance $Q_S^1 C_S^1 = AB$. Once AB units have been imported into the economy, no more imports of soybeans are permitted.

An initial important point is that the standard welfare effects are much like a tariff: Domestic price rises to make the amount of the quota equal to the difference in domestic supply and demand, which is necessary to establish a new equilibrium. *The quota has engineered a shortage on the market, requiring the price to rise.*

There is a loss in consumer surplus of $-(a+b+c+d)$. There is a gain in producer surplus of $+a$. The quota offers the same protection as the tariff to domestic producers, who get to raise the price of the domestic good by the same amount that the price of the imported good goes up.

The area c is what are called "quota rents". In economics, a *"rent" is the payment to owners of a scarce asset in excess of what is required to supply the good.*

Here, the amount imported under the quota could be imported at the world price p_S^* but those goods command a higher domestic price p_S^D. These rents are a form of income that goes to whoever

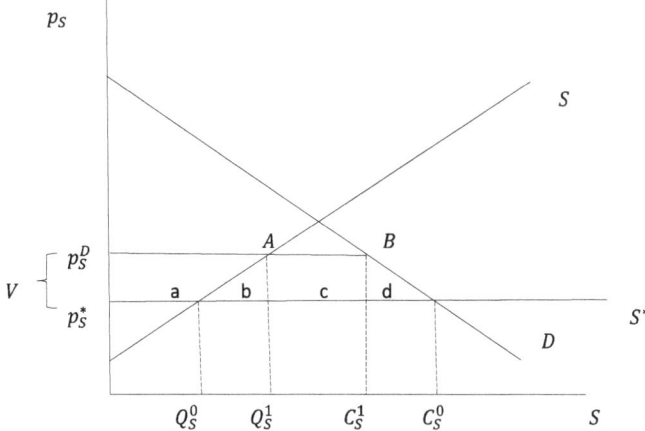

Figure 8.1 Effects of an import quota in a small economy.

owns the rights (licenses) to import the soybeans and sell them domestically.

Discussion of quota rents: Are they an economic benefit?

To understand the welfare effects of the quota, an important question is how are these quota rents allocated by the government. They could be allocated in many ways, but here are the main possibilities:

1. The government could sell the quota rights in an efficient (competitive) auction to anyone willing to bid for them. In this context, "competitive" means that there is free entry into the auction and no single buyer has the market power to dictate the price of these rights to the government.

   If the auction were truly competitive, bidders would bid up the price of the rights to import each unit of the quota to $V = p_S^* p_S^D$. If the price were below that, bids would go up to capture any remaining rents. Thus, the area c becomes *quota auction revenues* to the government.

   This situation is fully analogous to the case where the government receives tax revenues with a tariff. Again, the net welfare effect is $-b - d$, as with a tariff. Under these circumstances, the *tariff and the quota (set at the same level of imports) are equivalent policies.*

2. The government could simply give the licenses away to domestic interests, most likely to domestic producing or importing firms in the same industry. Then, these firms would receive the quota rents because they can import the good at the world price and sell it at the domestic price.

   But since these firms are domestic agents, economists think of the rents (area c) as just a transfer from consumers to the recipients of these domestic quota rights. Then, area c is again properly considered a welfare gain for the economy and the net welfare effect is $-b - d$ again.

Discussion of quota rents and rent-seeking

The problem with case 2 is that because the quota rights are valuable, it is unlikely that the government would just give them away without incurring any costs. Instead, domestic firms are likely to engage in *rent-seeking behavior* to gain the rights to import.

Rent-seeking is the act of spending real resources (labor, capital, real estate, and so on) to gain ownership of the scarce quota rents.

It is important to understand that these resources are wasted in economic terms because they would not be invested in this way if there were no quota. That is, rent-seeking emerges only because of the quota, which encourages this behavior artificially.

Here are prominent examples of costly rent-seeking:

- A firm or industry may build a lobbying office and hire lawyers and consultants to convince the government to give the quota rights to them. They may also engage in public advertising to strengthen their case.
- Firms may invest in additional and unneeded production capacity to convince the government that they are larger than they really are and therefore should be given a higher share of the quota licenses. This behavior is common because governments find it

natural to hand out quotas to firms based on their market shares. It is inefficient investment, however, and a waste of the capital used.

How much rent-seeking might be expected? *In principle, enough wasteful rent-seeking would occur to fully account for the quota rents, in which case area c becomes an economic loss.*

That is, area c is taken away from consumers by the quota, but no offsetting income is generated because resources are lost in acquiring the rights to these rents. In essence, area c is dumped into inefficient resource waste, reducing GDP and welfare. In that case, the net welfare effect of the quota becomes $-b - d - c$. There are two types of efficiency losses: the standard deadweight losses plus a resource waste due to rent-seeking. Both reduce real GDP.

Students should understand that rent-seeking is not the same thing as bribery or simply making direct payments to government officials to get the quota rights. Bribery is more like case 2 above, just in a different way. That is, if there is free entry into bribing officials, it will be done without the associated rent-seeking. In this sense, bribery is not necessarily inefficient.

However, this sanguine outcome is highly unlikely in the real world, where bribery happens behind the scenes and contributes to public corruption. In this context, policymakers in economies where rents exist are likely to demand extensive payments, which in turn gives them incentives to establish even more quotas, charge applicants for licenses, and so on. The possibility of corruption encourages people to become policymakers who sell quota rights, rather than to invest in human capital or other resources beneficial to the economy. Empirical evidence clearly shows that corruption is a major impediment to economic growth.

In a corrupt environment, it is likely that rent-seeking and corruption are highly correlated. Again, evidence finds that there is a considerable amount of wasteful rent-seeking in the world.

For example, estimates in the 1960s suggest that rent-seeking costs were more than 7.3% of GNP in India and more than 15% of

GNP in Turkey. The calculation for India was not just for quotas on trade but also included several kinds of domestic licensing rights (*Source*: Krueger, *The Political Economy of the Rent-Seeking Society, American Economic Review* 1974.)

More recently, economists estimated that the United States may have suffered a loss of 22% of GNP in 1985 to all forms of rent-seeking (*Source*: Laband and Sophocleus, *The Social Costs of Rent-Seeking: First Estimates, Public Choice* 1988.) Such estimates may be overly broad, but they point to the high social costs of rent-seeking.

In this regard, one significant benefit for economies that have cut their tariffs, eliminated quotas, and reduced other so-called "red tape" costs that deter efficient investments and competition has been a marked reduction in rent-seeking. Trade economists see such outcomes as important forms of the gains from trade liberalization and of reforms of costly regulations.

Discussion of quota rents: They may go to foreign exporters under VERs

A final possibility is that the importing-country government might prefer to establish a *voluntary export restraint* (VER), in which it tells the exporting country's government to limit exports to the importer's market to the distance AB in Figure 8.1. This would have the same effect on price in the domestic economy and therefore the same effects on producer surplus and consumer surplus.

But in this case, the scarcity values (quota rents) go to the foreign country because their exporters now recognize that they can simply raise their export price to the importing economy up to p_S^D. They can do so because they are the ones now limiting trade, as required by the exporting government.

Again, questions arise about how the exporting government allocates the export licensing rights. These could be auctioned, handed out according to some rule, or could disappear in rent-seeking.

The main point for our analysis is that because area c now goes to someone overseas, it is no longer a gain in terms of revenues or rents for the home country. The net welfare effect of the VER for the home (importing) country is then $-b - d - c$, equivalent to the case where there is full and wasteful rent-seeking.

Study question 1

An import quota imposed by a small country has all these effects except:

A. It raises the domestic price of the imported good.
B. It generates quota rents in the importing country.
C. It reduces the importing country's welfare by more than a tariff would if there is rent-seeking.
D. It improves economic welfare in the importing country.

Discussion of study question 1

It should be obvious that the correct answer is D.

Effects of a Quota in a Large Importer

Quota analysis for a large country

Figure 8.2 depicts the corresponding analysis for a large importer. Suppose the US imports sugar from Brazil and imposes a quota of horizontal distance AB on imports from Brazil.

US welfare impacts

Again, the US domestic price rises to p_S^U because the quota makes imports scarcer. But because the US is large, the Brazilian price falls to p_S^B in order to reduce Brazilian exports to match the lower import quota.

The quota rents in the US are areas $+c +e$. Using analysis similar to that above (and thinking back to the large-country tariff) one can see the following impacts. Students should think through the

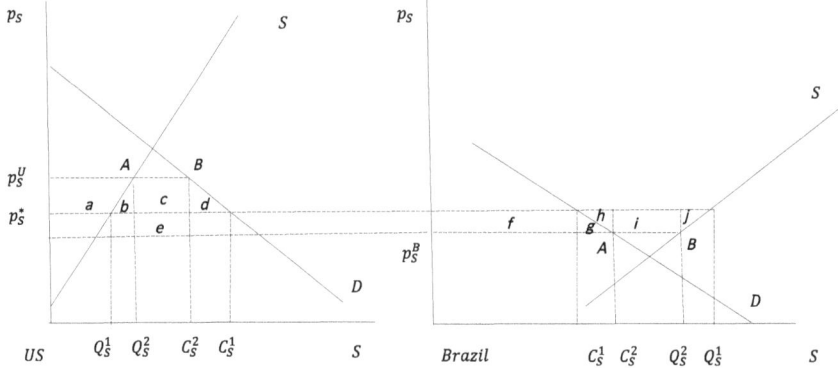

Figure 8.2   Import quota in a large country.

consumer surplus and producer surplus changes to get the complete answers:

- The US overall gain or loss $= -b - d + e$. Here, area e ($=$ area i) is the transfer from Brazilian exporters to the US associated with the lower import price. This is a terms-of-trade change that favors the US and is bad for Brazil. But this welfare outcome assumes the US government or other domestic quota recipients acquire the rents efficiently, i.e., there is no rent-seeking.
- Again, we can see the idea of an "optimal quota" based on the possible improvement in the US terms of trade.
- But if there is full rent-seeking, areas c and e disappear into wasted resources. In this case the US welfare effect is $-b - d + e - (c + e) = -b - d - c$. This is an overall welfare loss because both the terms of trade gain e and the domestic rents c disappear into rent-seeking.

Brazilian welfare impacts

From Brazil's standpoint the US quota is shown again as the horizontal distance AB. Students should think through the impacts on producer surplus and consumer surplus.

If the US policy is implemented as an import quota, then (as before with the tariff) Brazil loses area $-h - i - j$. Area i (equal to area e) is the transfer from Brazilian exporters to US recipients of the quota rents. *But if it's a VER, in which the US asks Brazil to limit its exports, then Brazilian exporters (or the Brazilian government) would receive the VER rents.*

In this case, Brazil's gain or loss $= -h - i - j + (c + e) = -h - j + c$ if there is no rent-seeking in Brazil. In this case, area c is ceded to Brazil by the US; in effect the US policy is to "give" the quota rents to Brazil, perhaps in order to make their exporters choose not to lobby their government to protest the US policy.

Finally, if there is full rent-seeking in Brazil then Brazil's VER rents would disappear into resource wastes. Then, the overall Brazil loss $= -h - i - j + (c + e) - (c + e) = -h - i - j$. Here, $-h$ and $-j$ are deadweight efficiency losses and $-i$ is the loss to Brazilian sugar producers that disappears into rent-seeking in Brazil.

How Tariffs and Quotas Differ

Differences between tariffs and quotas

Here is a summary of the analysis to this point:

- In the simplest analysis, import tariffs and import quotas have identical effects on the home country. This is the case of no rent-seeking for quotas. Both policies generate deadweight losses offset by either tariff revenues or quota rents.
- But if there is rent-seeking, the scarcity rents of import quotas disappear into inefficient resource wastes and/or bribery. *The conclusion is that quotas are worse than tariffs in this case.*
- If the policy is to "ask" foreign exporters to limit their exports with a VER, the quota rents go to the foreign governments or exporters. This means that VERs clearly are worse than import quotas for the home country.

Thus, we can rank these NTB policies in terms of home welfare losses as follows: Tariffs are least costly, quotas are more costly, and VERs are most costly.

In fact, for these reasons, countries in the global trading system have largely eliminated VERs and quotas through WTO rules.

However, there still are quotas and VERs are occasionally imposed. The simple answer for why VERs are used is that they are a way of "managing trade" and paying off exporters who lose sales in the home country by granting them the rents. Further, foreign government may choose not to oppose the VERs or to retaliate because their firms get the rents. This is another example of the *political economy of trade protection.*

To illustrate, the Trump Administration imposed high tariffs on steel imports against most foreign suppliers in 2018. However, some of these restraints actually were VERs. A more relevant example were the VERs imposed by President Reagan in the 1980s on Japanese automobile exporters, discussed a bit more later.

Thus, rent-seeking and VERs are important differences between NTBs and tariffs. But there are further important differences between tariffs and quotas. Following is a list of such differences:

1. Rent-seeking under quotas and VERs, which does not happen with tariffs. These notes have already analyzed this case.

2. Domestic market responses to shifts in supply and demand vary between tariffs and quotas. Recall the basic diagram for a small importer of soybeans, reflected in Figure 8.3.
   - The higher domestic price arises under either a tariff or an *import-equivalent quota*. Tariff: $P_S^{D,T} = P_S^* + T$. Quota: Government selects the quota amount AB, which equals the lower import quantity under the tariff. The result is the same higher domestic price.
   - But now imagine there is an increase in domestic demand (D shifts to the right, to D'). What happens?
   - Under the tariff there is no limit on the quantity of imports, so the adjustment is that imports rise at a constant price

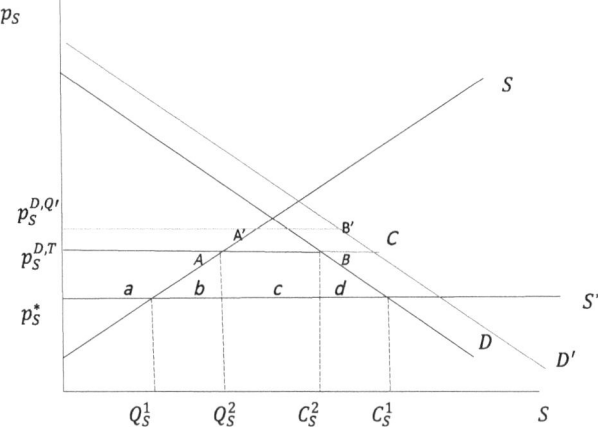

Figure 8.3 Market responses to shifts in demand under a tariff and an import-equivalent quota.

(see point C). Domestic price remains at $p_S^{D,T}$. Consumption rises and production is unchanged.

- However, under the quota the quantity of imports is fixed at AB units. The market adjusts through a higher domestic price $p_S^{D,Q'}$ for the fixed level of imports, now shown as $A'B'$. Production is higher and consumption is less than under the tariff when demand shifts upward.

This result raises another important point about *political economy*: Domestic producers would rather be protected by a quota when markets are expanding because that policy raises the price they receive. Consumers would prefer a tariff, though they may be unaware that any trade restriction exists.

Students should work through this analysis in cases where domestic demand falls, domestic supply rises, and domestic supply falls. In each case, characterize what happens to the quantity of imports, domestic price, and domestic production and consumption under the tariff versus the quota.

3. Domestic effects are different between a tariff and quota when there is a *domestic monopoly*. This means there is just one domestic producer of the good being imported. The graphical proof

is complicated and beyond the scope of these notes. However, following is an intuitive explanation:

- With a tariff, the monopolist cannot raise the price it charges above the domestic price (world price plus the tariff) for if it did, no one would buy from the monopolist. Thus, the monopolist must behave as a perfectly competitive firm when protected by a tariff.
- With a quota, once the amount AB is imported, no more can come in from abroad. The *monopolist then is the only seller on the domestic sales volume above the fixed imports of AB*. This permits the firm to act monopolistically by cutting its output and raising its price and gaining profits. Thus, we expect a higher domestic price under a quota than under a tariff.

Again, from a welfare perspective, we find that the tariff is better than the quota. Understanding this analysis, it is not surprising to learn that in many countries, a domestic monopoly (or an industry with few domestic firms that have market power) is often protected by import quotas instead of tariffs, despite this cost imposed on consumers. These powerful domestic producers lobby the government for protection through import limits, giving them room to act as monopolists. This is yet another reason why the WTO rules attempt to convince governments to avoid using quotas rather than tariffs as protection policies.

4. The possibility of *quality upgrading* with an import quota (and especially with a VER).

   Suppose a foreign firm is restricted in terms of the number of units it can sell in the importers' market because of an import quota. But the quota lets that firm choose which versions of the product (e.g., cars, wines, cheeses, clothing, footwear) it will export. It will be more profitable to fill the quota with high-value, high-quality versions of the good. Or we can think of this as the choice the domestic importer makes in ordering versions of the good from abroad. It will order high-quality versions of such goods from foreign suppliers.

   The reason is that the higher-quality goods command a higher price but both versions have about the same transport costs per unit, meaning there will be higher quota rents earned per unit for higher-quality goods. The outcome is that quota-constrained imports shift into higher-quality and higher-priced varieties after the quota is imposed.

Some prominent examples from US history include the following:

(1) the dramatic increase in the quality of Japanese cars in the US market during and after the 1980s VER;
(2) imported cheeses in the US are generally higher quality (and more expensive) than similar versions in their home markets;
(3) apples grown in Washington state and exported to Japan are gorgeous, tasty, and expensive compared to the qualities and prices of apples sold in the United States.

Indeed, economists refer to this quality-upgrading phenomenon as "shipping the good apples out". It explains why shoppers typically encounter only high-quality versions of imported consumer products protected by quotas.

Study question 2

Which of the following statements is true regarding differences between a tariff and a quota that limits imports by the same amount as a tariff?

A. When domestic demand for the good increases, the domestic price rises under the quota but remains unchanged under the tariff.
B. A tariff permits a domestic monopolist to cut its output for the home market, but a quota does not.
C. The quality of imports will be upgraded the same under the tariff as under the quota.
D. Rent-seeking is more likely with a tariff than with a quota.

Discussion of study question 2

The correct answer is A because the price rises with a demand increase under the quota but not under the tariff. B is incorrect because the quota permits monopoly behavior, not the tariff. C is incorrect because the tariff does not incentivize quality upgrading.

D is incorrect because the quota encourages rent-seeking, not the tariff.

Using Trade Policy for Other Purposes

Trade policy to achieve non-economic goals and address market failures

A final subject to address: Are trade taxes (or quotas) effective means of achieving *non-economic goals or dealing with market failures?*

A non-economic goal is a policy preference that emphasizes achieving some social or political objective that may not be achievable by relying on private markets alone. Some examples (among many) include the following:

- Raising domestic production of products or technologies seen as essential for national security. Policymakers may believe that the private market generates too much imports and too little domestic output of such goods.
- Supporting minimum levels of agricultural output, perhaps to sustain farming incomes.
- Providing health care to the poor, which may not be available in private medical markets.
- Achieving an equitable income distribution if the market generates inequality.
- Establishing minimum and sustainable levels of crop biodiversity. Biodiversity is important for avoiding diseases that may reduce outputs of major single crops.

Closely related is the idea of a market failure. Left alone, the market may generate undesirable side effects (often called "externalities").

Economists define an externality as a situation in which actions taken by one set of individuals or firms impose costs on others (negative externality) or provide benefits to others (positive externality).

The key policy question is whether policy should be used to make those who generate external costs pay for those costs (through, for example, a tax), in which case, the policy is said to *internalize the negative externality.* Or policy could internalize a positive externality by encouraging the activity through, for example, a subsidy.

Here are prominent examples of market failures (among others):

- Excessive levels of air and water pollution. For example, a chemical firm may dump waste matter into streams, causing higher costs of cleaning drinking water.
- An unwillingness to get vaccinated, which increases the likelihood that an infectious disease will spread widely.
- A failure of the market to protect innovation and knowledge creation from copying by others. This problem would reduce economic growth, productivity, and incomes.
- Excessive risk-taking by banks and financial institutions, especially if macroeconomic policy may absorb their losses. This is an example of "moral hazard", which could increase macroeconomic instability and cause taxpayers to pay for private risky behavior.
- The private provision of education may not be sufficient to educate all citizens. There is a positive externality from education by developing more involved citizens and voters.

Countries sometimes use trade policy to try to deal with such problems. This raises a fundamental and critical question: Does it make sense to use tariffs or trade subsidies to deal with market failures?

The general answer is no because trade interventions are an indirect approach and may achieve these goals (if at all) only by imposing higher welfare costs than would happen using a directly aimed policy.

In economics, the directly aimed policy is called the "first-best" policy. Tariffs, quotas, and trade subsidies are "second-best" policies. What that means is that a trade barrier might fix the problem, but in doing so, it imposes additional costs and may make the situation worse overall.

Here is an important qualification: What if the problem is a global or cross-border externality? Market failures that cause problems to spill over across countries are called *international externalities* and their solutions are called *global public goods (GPGs)*. Key examples of GPGs include the following:

- climate change mitigation to reduce global warming;
- financial regulations to limit international financial contagion (international spread of economic crises);
- provision of global public health (such as access to vaccines in a pandemic).

When costs cross borders, there may be a good argument for trade barriers to deal with them.

Simplest case: A national security goal

Consider the non-economic goal of raising domestic production of a good (aluminum, A) seen as important for national security. Use the example of a small importer.

Suppose the goal is to raise domestic output to Q_A^1 in Figure 8.4. If the country imposed a tariff of $\$T$ per unit, home price would rise to P_A^D and output would increase to the desired level, meaning the policy would work. The standard welfare cost would be $-b-d$. Thus, the economy would achieve the goal but suffer both the usual DWLs.

An alternative policy would be to pay an *output subsidy* directly to domestic aluminum producers. Let the subsidy $\$Z = \$T$ per unit of output, meaning home firms would be paid that amount for every unit of aluminum they produce. This would expand the supply curve from S to S', where the vertical distance between these curves equals the subsidy.

What would the new equilibrium be with this production subsidy?

Consider consumption first. There is no tax on imports and so no increase in the market price of either imported or domestic aluminum. Thus, p_A^* is still paid by consumers, who remain at C_A^0 *There is no loss in consumer surplus and no consumption DWL.*

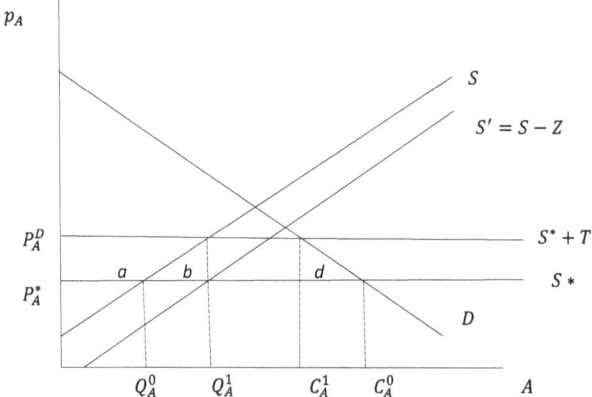

Figure 8.4 Using a production subsidy to expand domestic output of an industry.

On the production side, firms get a total price of $p_A^* + Z$ per unit, expanding output to Q_A^1. This policy also works to achieve the objective.

To see this effect, note that at Q_A^1 producers face a marginal cost of p_A^D along their supply curve but the market price they get remains p_A^*. Thus, the output subsidy of Z compensates them for the additional cost and they would respond by raising output.

Note that imports would fall to $Q_A^1 C_A^0$. But this decline is smaller than that under the tariff.

The private producer surplus gain would be $+a$. But the subsidy fiscal cost would be $-(a + b)$, which is the subsidy times the total production. *Thus, the overall welfare loss would be $-b$. The economy would suffer the production DWL only.*

The main point is that the *output subsidy is the direct policy* to raise output and therefore would generate lower costs than the tariff, which is indirect. The subsidy would not cause secondary distortion on the consumption side, as there would be with the tariff.

This is an example of the principle stated earlier. The direct policy achieves the goal without additional costs. The indirect policy achieves the goal but at the expense of an additional cost imposed on consumers.

Some other non-economic goals

Here are a few other types of "non-economic goals" for which trade policy has been commonly used. We can ask what the direct (and best) policy is.

Goal	Direct Policy
Expand or cut production	Output subsidy or tax
Expand or cut consumption	Consumption subsidy or tax
Smooth farming incomes when prices are volatile	Crop insurance
Redistribute income	Redistribution policies (e.g., progressive income tax, tax credits for low incomes, wage insurance, relocation assistance)

All this analysis raises a simple question. When would a tariff be the direct (and first-best) policy? *This would be the case when the policy goal is to limit imports.*

For example, as analyzed in the last set of notes, a large country seeking to gain welfare by forcing down the world price of an import would do so with a tariff. But recall that this policy would harm foreign countries and they likely would retaliate with tariffs on the original country's exports.

Simplest example of a market failure: Pollution

Again, are tariffs or quotas the best way to address market externalities? Generally, they are not because they are indirect (second-best) policies. Authorities should use the most direct policy that aims at the source of the problem.

Example: Suppose domestic consumption of gasoline (G) pollutes the air in an economy that imports gasoline. This pollution causes health problems, raises the costs of cleaning buildings, makes costs of agriculture higher, and so on. It also contributes to climate change. But these external costs are not paid for by domestic drivers in the private market.

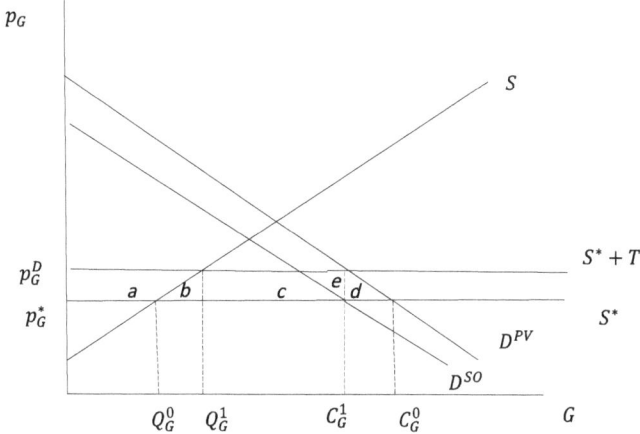

Figure 8.5 Using a consumption tax to eliminate a negative consumption externality.

We depict this idea in Figure 8.5 by showing the private demand curve D^{PV} lying above the "socially optimal" demand curve D^{SO}. The social demand curve embodies the externality costs, for if drivers had to pay them, they would demand less gasoline, effectively shifting the private demand curve downward to the social D curve.

Note that at the world price p_G^*, the socially optimal level of consumption is C_G^1, which is below the market level C_G^0. The policy challenge is to find the cheapest way to force drivers to consume gasoline along the social demand curve at level C_G^1.

Again, the policy must "internalize" this externality. One possibility is an import tariff, which would raise the domestic price to p_G^D, reducing consumption to C_G^1, as desired. Again, the tariff would work.

But this higher price would raise domestic output to Q_G^1, which is an undesired side effect. The welfare loss would be $-b - d$, the usual DWLs of a tariff. Here, $-b$ is the secondary distortion on the production side, which policy should avoid.

The better policy would be to tax consumption directly by establishing a gasoline tax of $\$T_G = \$T$, rather than imposing a tariff. Then, consumers would pay $p_G^* + T_G$ as the full price. This would reduce the demand curve effectively to D^{SO}. Consumption would fall to C_G^1 as desired. But there would be no rise in production because there is no impact on the price producers and retailers of gasoline receive. Imports would fall to $Q_G^0 C_G^1$, less than the decline under the tariff.

With the consumption tax, the loss in consumer surplus $= -(a + b + c + d + e)$. The gain in tax revenues $= +(a + b + c + e)$, which is the tax times the quantity consumed. Thus, the net welfare loss $= -d$, which is simply the consumption DWL. Again, we see that the direct policy (consumption tax) is less costly to the economy than the indirect policy (tariff).

In fact, environmental economists would argue that area $-d$ isn't really a net loss. The tax just pushes consumption to the optimal level by making consumers pay for the externality of consuming gasoline. Thus, drivers are worse off in private terms but society is better off by the same amount due to lower pollution. This is what is really meant by "internalizing the externality".

Market failures

Here are some other such externalities from domestic market failures and the direct policies that would address them.

Market Failure	Direct Policy
Pollution due to consumption	Consumption tax
Pollution due to production	Production tax
Too little domestic R&D	Patents and subsidies or tax credits for R&D spending
Unsafe products	Safety regulation, taxes, or fines

Study question 3

The *primary* reason that economists are skeptical about using tariffs or quotas to achieve domestic non-economic goals or fix market externalities is:

A. Tariffs and quotas cannot achieve such goals or fix such problems.
B. Tariffs and quotas may attract retaliation from countries that have seen their exports fall.
C. Tariffs and quotas are not the most direct policy to achieve such goals or fix such problems.
D. Direct interventions such as taxes or subsidies can achieve such goals or fix such problems at lower welfare costs than tariffs and quotas.
E. Both C and D.

Discussion of study question 3

The correct answer is E, for both C and D offer similar explanations for the superiority of direct policies over indirect trade policies. A is false because tariffs and quotas can achieve the desired outcome, albeit at higher cost. B is a true statement but not the primary reason economists oppose using trade policy to achieve other objectives.

International market failures

A final important question is when might we use trade policy for regulating cross-border market failures?

The answer is that where distortions and externalities cross borders through trade in goods and services, limiting trade will directly internalize the costs in principle. Here are some examples:

- If there are large foreign firms that operate as monopolies in an export market through exporting at high prices, the importing nation can benefit by imposing tariffs on those goods. By cutting domestic quantity demanded, the tariff would force the foreign monopolies to reduce their prices. It would also generate tax revenues for the importing government.
- If products from abroad are unsafe for consumption, it is appropriate to reduce their imports. However, a better policy would be to require those imports to meet domestic quality and safety standards without putting on a tariff.

- There may be human and animal health problems that cross borders through travel and trade. This situation would call for temporary bans on imports and travel until the health issues are over.
- Transporting goods across borders may generate environmental problems, such as fossil-fuel emissions through shipping. In such cases, tariffs would reduce the volume of trade and emissions.

While that principle is sound, implementing trade restrictions to address foreign externalities is an exceptionally difficult problem, raising many additional issues. Here is one example.

Consider the problem of child labor use in poor countries. This problem exists because of desperate poverty, poor schools, the high costs of going to school, and similar issues, which are not directly related to trade.

But citizens in rich countries may not want to consume goods produced in this way and therefore might wish to impose tariffs on such imports. What would this accomplish?

Assuming that the importers (such as the US and the EU) are large countries, these tariffs would cause foreign prices and outputs to fall. This would significantly reduce demand for these goods in the targeted countries, pushing down local prices and output and forcing children into (probably) worse kinds of work. This is another example of "second-best" economics: imposing the tariff could worsen the situation it tries to address.

It is worth asking in what sense the child labor problem is really a cross-border externality. It is, but only through the discomfort felt by consumers in the rich world. In that context, the best (direct) policy would be to "tax" consumers in the importers (which would get those people to pay for this discomfort) and transfer the resources generated to programs directly targeted at reducing child labor in poor countries.

A related problem is that it may be difficult to distinguish imports made with child labor and those not made in that way. One way to accomplish this would be to create effective labeling and monitoring programs, which is not easy. Other direct policies would be foreign aid grants, support for education, direct income support to poor families, and so on.

The primary international externality: Climate change

Most economists would argue that an important means of combating global warming is for countries to impose a significant cost on burning fossil fuels through a carbon tax or a system of limited permits to use fossil fuels (pollute by emitting greenhouse gases). Those permits could be traded at a price.

But suppose that a major political impediment in rich countries to enacting domestic carbon pricing is that it would raise the costs of production in the energy-intensive sectors (coal, oil, construction, housing, metals manufacturing, driving, some agriculture, and others). This would expand imports of cheaper foreign goods and reduce output and employment as some of those activities move overseas.

Policymakers might prefer to permit countries that do enact carbon pricing to offset these losses with taxes on carbon-intensive imports. Such taxes, called "border carbon adjustments" or BCAs, are under consideration by the EU and the United States.

The idea is that technical experts would compute the "carbon content" of imported goods. Then, BCAs would be imposed, depending on these calculations. For example, if the US had a 25% carbon tax on production, its BCA would be 25% on imports from countries without carbon prices. It is a sound argument, and many policy analysts are trying to work out how to make these computations.

But here are some problems that would arise with BCAs:

- Policy should understand the likely effect on global fossil fuel (FF) prices. If the (tax-inclusive) prices of energy-intensive goods are increased in the regulating countries, it would reduce FF demands there. Energy suppliers could shift their sales to non-regulating countries, driving down prices and raising emissions there.
- The BCAs (tariffs) could generate significant terms-of-trade losses for countries against which they are levied.
- They also could reduce GDP growth in those countries and delay the time at which local citizens demand cleaner air.

- The rules of the WTO at present forbid import taxes imposed on the basis of how a good is produced. This roadblock would need to be removed through negotiations.

Now here are some additional arguments for permitting BCAs:

- The importing countries could use the tariff revenues generated to pay for programs that reduce emissions worldwide. If they could commit to this idea, it could accelerate progress in developing countries in fighting climate change.
- Having this "relief valve" to prevent increases in import competition should help generate the political will to enact carbon taxes in the rich countries.

Study question 4

Economists argue that it is sensible to restrict trade with tariffs in cases where a market failure operates across borders. Which of the following is not a case where a tariff is the direct policy?

A. Shipping goods across oceans produce emissions through burning fossil fuels.
B. International trade reduces the real wages of unskilled workers.
C. Implementation of a domestic carbon tax raises imports of cheaper foreign carbon-intensive goods.
D. A foreign monopolist exports a good to an importing country and charges a high monopoly price for it.

Discussion of study question 4

The correct answer is B. In this case, imports do cause an income distribution problem but the most direct approach to solving that is through domestic redistribution policies. In each of the other cases, the problem is associated with trade flows, suggesting that limiting trade is the most direct policy approach.

The Effective Rate of Protection

The idea of "effective protection"

So far, tariffs and quotas have been discussed in these notes as affecting only the prices, outputs, and consumption levels of a *final good*. A final good is a product that goes directly into consumption.

But approximately 2/3 of global trade in merchandise is in *intermediate goods*, such as chemicals, glass, rubber, metals, and machinery, which are inputs used to produce other intermediate goods and final goods and services. Another form of intermediate input is a license paid by one firm to use another firm's technology or to gain local production rights.

The use of traded intermediate goods means that a tariff (or quota or other restriction) on imports of key intermediate inputs (such as steel and aluminum) can raise the production costs of downstream industries and products, causing output and employment to fall there. Thus, while steel may be protected directly by its own tariff, steel-using industries, such as metal products, construction, machinery, and automobiles, would have higher costs because of that tariff. The logic of the *effective rate of protection* (ERP) is that one must account for all tariffs (and other restrictions and subsidies that change prices) in computing the total amount of protection that is really provided to both outputs and inputs.

Effective protection and value added

Following is the simple theory of ERP, which is based on the concept of *value added*. Unit VA is the difference between a good's sales price and the cost of all produced intermediate inputs needed to produce one unit of the good. For a firm or industry, total VA is total dollar sales revenue minus the total dollar costs of purchasing intermediates in a year.

Importantly, VA measures the amount of revenues the firm has left over to pay its *primary factors*, such as labor, capital, and land. These are the factors that, in fact, matter for employment and incomes, making VA the right concept for analyzing how the whole set of tariffs on inputs and outputs change jobs, wages, investment, and so on.

It is also important to understand that VA, also called "net output", is the firm or industry's contribution to an economy's *gross domestic product* (GDP). Total sales would vastly overcount true outputs (and incomes of factors) in a country because it would count the value of inputs both when they are produced and when they are used. Thus, GDP is the total of VA produced in an economy.

An example of the ERP

Following is an example of how to compute the ERP on a final good. This analysis assumes the importing country is small and, therefore, the prices of imported intermediate inputs are fixed.

Suppose that autos (A) use steel (S) as an input, along with other intermediates. Then the *domestic value added* (DVA) in producing one car is $p_A - \theta_S p_S - \sum \theta_j p_j$ where θ_S is the share of steel needed to produce an automobile (e.g., tons of steel per car). The summation term is the share of all other inputs j in the automobile. For simplicity, assume that there are no tariffs or subsidies on these other inputs. *The prices in DVA are measured with domestic prices, inclusive of tariffs.*

Example before tariffs (free trade): let $P_A = \$40,000$, $P_S = \$20,000$, $\theta = 0.4$, and the cost of other intermediate inputs per car $= \sum \theta_j p_j = \$24,000$. Then in free trade $DVA = \$40,000 - \$8,000 - \$24,000 = \$8,000$. This is the per-car net revenue used to pay wages, returns to shareholders, rents to land, and so on in the domestic automobile industry.

Now suppose an *ad valorem* tariff of 25% is placed on imported steel. Then the cost of steel per automobile rises to $\theta_S p_S (1 + t) = (0.4 * \$20,000) * (1.25) = \$10,000$.

Now DVA per auto $= \$40,000 - \$10,000 - \$24,000 = \$6,000$. DVA per car has fallen from \$8,000 to \$6,000, or by -25%. Because of that, autos will employ less labor and capital unless they can pass this higher steel cost onto consumers through a higher price. But even then, the number of domestic cars purchased would go down, reducing domestic employment.

Again, the ERP of a particular good accounts for how all tariffs and other trade restrictions and subsidies, on both the good itself and on intermediate inputs, change value added in that good.

ERP is then defined as the *percentage difference between domestic value added (including all tariffs) and world value added.* WVA is what value added would be in the industry if there were completely free trade, that is, no tariffs on the final good or on any intermediate inputs.

Here is the general formula for the ERP in autos (A) for a small economy.

$$\text{ERP}^A = 100 * \left(\frac{\text{DVA}^A - \text{WVA}^A}{\text{WVA}^A} \right),$$

where

$$\text{DVA}^A = P_A^*(1 + t^A) - \theta_S p_S^*(1 + t^S) - \sum \theta_j p_j^*(1 + t^j)$$

$$\text{WVA}^A = P_A^* - \theta_S p_S^* - \sum \theta_j p_j^*.$$

Here, the asterisks $(*)$ refer to world prices.

Notes on the ERP

From this formula, we find the following intuitive outcomes. The size of the ERP in automobiles depends on the following:

(1) The size of the importing country's tariff on autos, which is what directly protects autos from imports. A higher tariff on autos raises DVA and expands employment and output in the sector.
(2) The price of the intermediate good (steel), the tariff on the intermediate good, and the importance of steel in the costs of production (θ_S). An increase in any of these would make it more costly to produce cars, lowering the ERP in autos.

- For example, if the world price of steel rose or there were a higher tariff on steel, DVA in automobiles would be reduced.
- *This implies that the ERP in autos would be lower than the actual tariff rate on autos. These factors would shrink output and employment in cars.*

(3) The prices, tariffs, and input shares of other intermediates. Recall that in our example, we assumed these tariffs were zero in order to focus on the steel tariff.

Study question 5

The ERP shows that

A. The actual tariff rate on the final good may be a misleading measure of protection when there are also tariffs on intermediate inputs.
B. High tariffs on intermediate inputs tend to raise value added in the final good.
C. High tariff rates on intermediate inputs reduce the effective protection and employment in the final good.
D. Both A and C.

Discussion of study question 5

The correct answer is D. Both A and C are true statements. B is false because tariffs on intermediates reduce value added in the final good.

An important example from actual policy: The impacts of recent US steel tariffs

On March 1, 2018, the Trump Administration imposed tariffs on imported steel (25%) and aluminum (10%) from nearly all sources, hoping to raise DVA and jobs in the US steel industry. Economists often use ERP analysis to make basic computations of the costs of steel tariffs. Rather than go through the detailed analysis, here are highlights of one illustrative calculation, done by the author of these notes using readily available data.

As background, steel employment had been falling in the US for many years. Figure 8.6 shows primary metals, which include both steel and aluminum (and a few other metals). Steel is the largest employer in the group.

To analyze the potential effects of the steel tariff, begin with the basic market data in Table 8.1

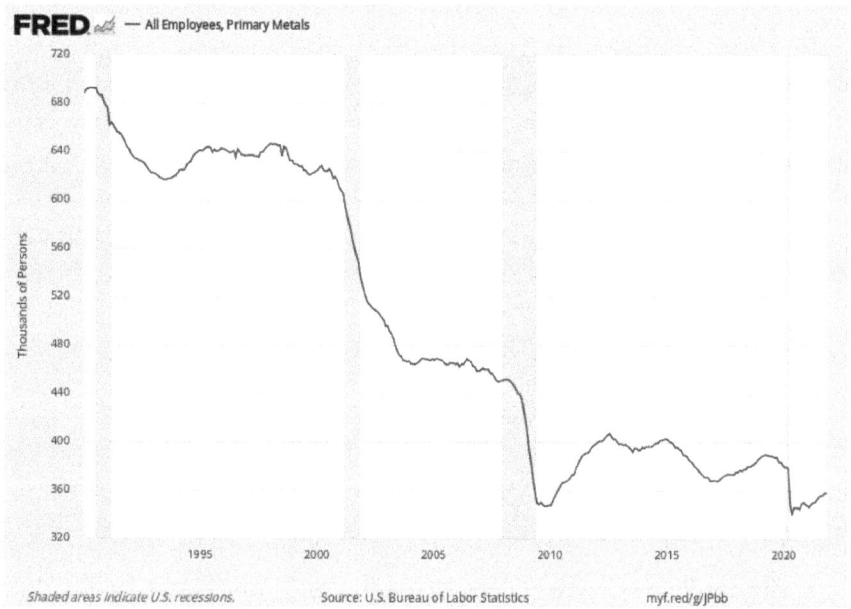

Figure 8.6   US annual employment in primary metals.

Source: Federal Reserve Bank of St. Louis FRED database, at https://fred.stlouisfed.org/series/CES3133100001.

Table 8.1   Market data for US steel industry, 2017 (MT = metric tons).

US steel production, 2017	81.6 million MT
US steel imports, 2017	34.9 million MT
Average steel import price	$839.5 per MT
Average steel domestic price	$869.5 per MT

Source: US Bureau of Economic Analysis.

Computation of the effects of the steel tariff

The following notes apply basic economic and international trade theories to "predict" the job impacts in steel versus those in the steel-using (downstream) industries. This analysis is not meant to be precise. Rather, it illustrates how to use the ERP concept in a simple model based on real data.

To do that requires some additional information:

1. How much would the US steel price rise and the foreign steel price fall due to the US tariff? It is likely that the US is a large importer, implying that the foreign price would fall, unlike our small-country assumption above.

   One estimate, based on reasonable values of the elasticities of US import demand (elasticity $= -2$) and foreign export supply (elasticity $= 4$), would be that the new US price $= \$981$ (up 15.4%) and the new world price $= \$785$ (down 7.6%). Note that there is a 25% difference between these prices because of the tariff.

2. How much would steel imports fall? Using the same import elasticity, the corresponding estimate would be that the new level of steel imports $= 24.4$ mmt (down 30.4%). (*Note*: The US Commerce Department predicted a slightly larger fall in its comparable model.)

   - Actual 2019 US steel imports were 26.3 mmt, so imports did not fall as much as expected.

3. How much would US steel output rise? A related estimate (based on a domestic supply elasticity of 1) would be that new home output $= 94.2$ mmt (up 15.4%). (US DOC predicted new output $= 90$ mmt.)

   - Actual 2019 US steel production was 88 mmt, so output did not rise as much as expected.

4. How many jobs would be "created" in the steel industry by the tariff? Assume that employment rises in proportion with output (this is very unlikely). Then, this basic model would predict that

there would ultimately be 30,253 more jobs in steel. Of those, 23,776 would be production-line or "blue-collar" jobs.

This is likely to be an overestimate if steel firms invested some of their higher profits in automation or other activities that do not directly employ labor. Steel firms could also choose to limit their output growth and act as oligopolists or firms with market power to raise prices above costs.

- The actual gain in primary metals employment from 2017 to 2019 was 4,500 or about 1.2% of 2017 jobs. This was far less than expected, suggesting that relatively little of the higher profits were used to raise hiring.

Here are some important steel-using industries and their employment levels in 2017, and the primary metals θ coefficients (how much steel in dollar they need per dollar of output).

5. Next, use the concept of effective protection to compute the implied cost increases in each of the seven downstream industries listed in Table 8.2. The last column shows the input coefficients θ expressed in value terms (dollars of steel per dollar of output in each industry).

These cost increases would be the higher steel price (15.4%) multiplied by the steel-input coefficients. The model finds that these steel-price increases would range from 0.4% in construction to 1.8% in electrical equipment. However, to some extent, these

Table 8.2   Downstream steel-using industries and the importance of steel.

	Employment	Steel Input Share θ
Fabricated metal products	1,450,000	0.30
Electrical equipment	256,000	0.21
Machinery	700,000	0.15
Motor vehicles and parts	1,140,000	0.11
Furniture	287,000	0.08
Miscellaneous manufacturing	376,000	0.08
Construction	5,300,000	0.05

Source: Computed by author using data from US Bureau of Economic Analysis.

impacts would be offset by the ability of these firms to partially pass these cost increases to consumers. Taking these factors into account, the model estimates that DVA would fall by between 0.3% in construction and 0.9% in electrical equipment.

Assume (again, this is unlikely) that employment would fall by the same percentages. Doing these calculations predicts that there would be an overall job loss of 66,433 (of which 48,078 would be blue-collar jobs) in those industries. Compare this to the predicted jobs gain in steel of 30,253 (of which 23,776 would be blue-collar).

6. It is worth noting that the average production worker wage in steel in 2016 was $62,179. In the downstream industries, the weighted-average production worker wage was about $47,000.

To summarize, the steel tariffs seemed likely to reduce employment in downstream sectors by much more than the job gain in steel itself in order to protect a small number of higher-paying jobs. This is a practical example of how to use the ERP idea. And it again shows the inefficiency of using tariffs for protecting jobs.

Chapter 9

US Trade Policy and the World Trade Organization

How US Trade Policy Works

A brief history of US trade policy

In the years from the founding of the United States as a federated nation until the mid-19th century, tariffs were used largely as the primary source of revenue for the federal government, though several industries were protected by trade taxes also. From the mid-19th century through the early 20th century, the primary motivation for high tariffs was to protect domestic industrialization. (This was an example of "infant-industry protection" in which new industries could grow behind high tariff walls.)

- High industrial tariffs were a significant contributor to North-South tensions leading up to the Civil War.
- By 1913 and the introduction of the federal income tax, reliance on tariffs for revenue became unimportant.

In the early 1930s, the US enacted the Smoot–Hawley tariff, dramatically raising tariffs in an attempt to fight the oncoming Great Depression. Other major countries retaliated, and global trade fell a great deal. This history led to a strategy in the late 1930s of negotiating bilateral trade agreements built on countries offering each other "most favored nation" tariffs, as described later in these notes.

In the 1940s–1950s, major countries built the post-WWII global development policy and international institutions:

- The US Marshall Plan and renewed fixed exchange rates under the "Bretton Woods system".
- Emergence of international economic institutions: the World Bank and International Monetary Fund.
- The General Agreement on Tariffs and Trade (GATT, 1947–1995) was the precursor to the World Trade Organization (WTO). It was designed to reduce tariffs among major countries through multilateral negotiations.

Major elements of US trade law today

1. The Trade Expansion Act of 1962 was enacted to approve the tariff cuts negotiated in the "Kennedy Round" of the GATT. It also established the Trade Adjustment Assistance (TAA) Program.

   The main provision of this act was Section 232, which is the US legal authority for imposing tariffs for *national security reasons*:

   - It permits unilateral imposition of tariffs (or other trade limits) by the President to protect industries seen as important for defense if imports threaten national security.
   - An investigation is done by the US Department of Commerce (DOC). The President can accept, reject, or modify the DOC Secretary's recommendations for trade protection.
   - Tariffs imposed under Section 232 could last until the concern over national security dissipates; in principle, they could be permanent.

Most WTO members have such national security provisions in their laws. However, there is a high potential that they could be abused by governments declaring almost any politically powerful industry as important for national security.

Thus, a major focus in the negotiation of the WTO rules in the 1990s was to limit this kind of trade barrier. Under WTO rules, imposing national security trade protection requires extensive investigation and demonstration of the following: (1) the importance of the good for defense; (2) the potential that foreign supply sources could be disrupted; and (3) a sufficiently reduced domestic production capacity associated with high imports. With these rules, national security tariffs were rarely used after the WTO was founded in 1995. Member countries informally agreed not to use them.

However, as the last chapter discussed, the US imposed steel and aluminum tariffs in 2018. Without question, these policies, which are mostly still in place, fail these WTO tests.

An interesting note about the steel and aluminum tariffs is that Section 232 investigations are done by the Department of Commerce, but the process requires consultation with the Department of Defense (DoD). The US DoD in this case said the tariffs were unnecessary for military security and could be counterproductive because they could cause a rift in relations with US allies.

2. The Trade Act of 1974 was enacted to approve the tariff cuts in the "Tokyo Round" of the GATT. It has two major provisions:

First is *Section 201 "safeguards" tariffs* or the "escape clause", which offers temporary tariffs to protect a domestic industry suffering from import competition. It is called an escape clause because safeguards actions can raise tariffs on products above the "bound" levels agreed in the GATT/WTO, as described later.

In Section 201, tariffs or other import limits could be imposed temporarily if both these conditions can be demonstrated:

- Imports cause or threaten to cause "serious injury" to a domestic industry producing similar products.
- Imports must be a "substantial cause" of serious injury, which means they must be important and not less significant than any other factor.

Safeguards tariffs are legal under WTO rules. Specifically, they are permitted under GATT Article XIX.

- Here is an interesting question: Why would parties who have agreed to tariff cuts need the ability to temporarily restrict imports by raising those tariffs?
- In essence, this policy acts as "insurance" against unexpected surges in imports after tariffs have been cut.

Section 201 does not require a finding that foreign trade practices are "unfair".

Under Section 201, Investigations and recommendations are done by the US International Trade Commission (USITC). Again, the President can accept or reject the Commission's recommendations and impose whatever barriers seem appropriate.

The US has not used Section 201 safeguards tariffs often because the legal criteria are hard to satisfy. But here are some interesting examples:

- Tariffs on motorcycles were raised from 5% to 50% in 1983 for five years (declining over time) to protect the Harley-Davidson Company.
- Tariffs on steel were raised from around 0.5% to 8−30% in March 2002, scheduled for five years. The EU, Japan, and others threatened to retaliate and filed a WTO dispute. The WTO ruled against the US because the USITC failed to demonstrate serious injury. The WTO authorized the EU and Japan to impose retaliation tariffs on $2 billion of US exports. The US withdrew the tariffs in December 2003. It was a huge political controversy.
- The US imposed 30% tariffs on solar panels from China in January 2018, using Section 201.

The second major provision of the 1974 Act was *Section 301, authorizing trade barriers against unfair foreign trade* or trade-distorting practices. It permits the President to take any trade interventions (tariffs, quotas, filing WTO disputes, and others) against a foreign policy that violates a trade agreement with the US or is seen as unjustified or unreasonable and is a burden to US commerce.

There is a narrower provision, called "Special 301", which permits similar actions to be taken against countries that are unfair in their treatment of US intellectual property rights.

Here are some comments:

- What is "unjustified or unreasonable"? That is for the US Trade Representative (USTR) and the President to decide. USTR performs an investigation of the foreign practice, recommends some action, and the President can accept it or do anything else.
- The US trade war against China, which began in 2018, is based on a Section 301 investigation and a finding of unfair practices regarding technology transfer, investment restrictions, and IPR violations.

The approach used in Section 301 demonstrates "unilateralism" by the US in dealing with foreign trade barriers. It was enacted at a time of increasing trade deficits, concern about a rising economic power (Japan), and dissatisfaction with the weakness of the GATT in settling trade disputes between nations. The GATT system was seen by US policymakers as ineffective in disciplining foreign trade practices.

Many cases under Section 301 were launched in the 1970s and 1980s, especially in an attempt to force foreign governments to improve protection of US intellectual property. However, foreign countries hated this unilateral approach and filed numerous GATT complaints against the US. This tension was a primary reason why the US and other countries negotiated the WTO, which replaced the GATT. A big part of the "grand bargain" was that the US essentially agreed to stop using Section 301 in return for establishing stronger dispute settlement procedures at the WTO. This understanding held until the Trump Administration revived the use of Section 301 and put US trade policy back onto a unilateralist track.

US trade law: Anti-dumping tariffs and countervailing duties

A final major part of legislation regarding trade barriers is made up of various US laws permitting use of anti-dumping (AD) and countervailing duty (CVD) tariffs against foreign unfair dumping and export subsidies. These laws go back to 1919 but were considerably strengthened in the 1974 Trade Act and in later updates. It is worth understanding AD procedures a bit, starting with the concept of dumping.

Dumping is the practice of a foreign firm to sell its products in an importing market at a price that is either (1) lower than its home price or (2) lower than its average costs of production.

Why might dumping exist?

- Foreign firms may try to get rid of (temporary) excess production associated with a recession or lower demand at home.
- Foreign firms may try to act monopolistically by charging low prices in import markets to drive firms there out of the market. Later, they would raise prices there as monopolists. This is called "predatory dumping" and is unlikely to succeed except perhaps in small markets with little domestic competition.
- "Equilibrium dumping" is associated with firms having some market power to set different prices in different countries. Such firms tend to charge lower prices in the markets they export to than in their own markets. This happens because demand abroad for their goods is more elastic (consumers are more sensitive to prices) and firms have limited pricing power there. But they face more inelastic demand in their own markets, supporting higher prices.

Under US AD policy, the USITC must find that dumping exists and there is "material injury" to domestic firms. This is a much weaker legal standard than is "serious injury" under safeguards tariffs. If both conditions are true, then we have the following:

- AD tariffs are levied against *specific firms* to cover the "dumping margin", which is the percentage difference between the lower price in the US and the higher price in the exporter's market.

- These tariffs remain in place until the dumping stops or domestic and foreign firms agree to a settlement in which foreign firms agree to raise their prices in the US. Many AD cases result in such settlements, which economists have shown to be means of permitting both foreign and domestic firms to collude in setting higher prices in the US market.

The processes are similar in CVD, but the tariffs are imposed against firms that received an export subsidy from their government. Recalling the analysis in Chapter 7 of the effects of an export subsidy paid by a foreign government, the imposition of a CVD may deter or end the subsidy, resulting in higher welfare and efficiency. This is why WTO rules permit CVD actions.

The World Trade Organization

The WTO is physically located in Geneva, where there is a Secretariat with two primary functions. The WTO

- sponsors multilateral negotiations over tariffs and other trade-related regulations; and
- manages legal disputes between countries about such policies.

More broadly, the WTO is an agreement among member countries to abide by a set of mutually negotiated rules and to engage in recognized dispute settlement procedures, rather than to set their own trade policies unilaterally and without consultations with other members.

The WTO was founded in 1995. Its rules and procedures are built on the foundations of the GATT but added agreements on rules governing foreign investment, trade in services, protection of intellectual property rights, and other areas.

Since 1995, many countries have joined, most notably China in 2001. The WTO membership now is 164 countries. (The EU as a collective is one member and each EU country is also a member on its own.)

The logic of the WTO

Why do we need a WTO? What are its essential roles?

1. The WTO serves as a *barter market for exchanging market-access commitments*. It is politically difficult for countries on their own to cut tariffs and eliminate trade barriers. Doing so concentrates the pain on specific industries and workers but the gainers (consumers) are more diffuse. This means that acquiring foreign market access for exporters is essential for a country in agreeing to cut its own tariffs.
2. The WTO can be seen as a "code of conduct" among countries. It is a *rules-based system*, rather than a power-based unilateralist system.
3. WTO rules try to *discipline (prevent or punish) the use of beggar-your-neighbor policies*. That is, they try to prevent abuses of trading power. One primary example is that smaller countries can use the dispute settlement system to try to force larger countries to remove their trade restrictions.
4. WTO consultations and dispute resolution cases discourage the tendencies of countries to mutually raise tariffs and engage in retaliation. Without a WTO system, countries could readily end up in a "Prisoner's Dilemma" situation with high tariffs all around.

The WTO: Six basic principles

1. The system relies on *full consensus* of the members to change important rules. Major new negotiations or agreements must be agreed by all members (with some exceptions).
2. WTO rules are *disciplines* against government policies, not against private business actions (except AD).
3. The WTO is founded on the concept of non-discrimination. This has two components:

   (a) *The Most-Favored-Nation (MFN) Principle*: If a member cuts its tariffs or makes its regulations less restrictive, all WTO members should receive those benefits. This rule should

(1) enhance global economic efficiency; (2) prevent abuse through powerful partners offering each other better market access than offered to weaker nations; and (3) make it easier to negotiate tariff cuts multilaterally because countries do not have to decide on different tariff cuts for different trading partners.

(b) *The National Treatment (NT) Principle*: A WTO member must offer the same tax and regulatory advantages to foreign firms as it provides domestic firms. This rule should (1) also raise economic efficiency and (2) help avoid regulatory policies that are disguised barriers to trade and investment.

It is useful to think of MFN as non-discrimination across external partners and NT as non-discrimination between the domestic economy and the rest of the world.

There are major exceptions to these non-discrimination principles:

1. Subsets of countries may enter into free-trade areas (FTAs), such as the US-Mexico-Canada Agreement (USMCA, which replaced the earlier North American Free Trade Agreement or NAFTA). This is an exception because it permits countries within the FTA to offer lower or zero tariffs to other members but not to non-members.
2. Lower tariffs levied against poor countries, called the Generalized System of Preferences (GSP), than against middle-income or rich countries. Most developed economies have a GSP system in place.
3. Certain domestic regulatory actions taken to protect the environment and public safety may treat foreign goods and firms less favorably if importing their goods raises regulatory risks.
4. Members of the WTO *negotiate reciprocal concessions in market access*:

   - Countries negotiate to reduce their MFN tariff rates to "bound" levels above which they cannot later rise. (Again, there are temporary exceptions: The use of "safeguards" tariffs and AD and countervailing duties means going above these rates under certain circumstances.) Bound tariff rates may actually be higher than the actual tariff rates a country applies.

- The WTO agreements include market access commitments in certain regulatory areas:

  ○ intellectual property rights (the "TRIPS" agreement);
  ○ foreign direct investment (the "TRIMS" agreement);
  ○ trade in services (the "GATS" agreement).

- There are also several agreements among subsets of countries on such issues as government purchasing rules, regulating international trade in digital goods, and some elements of environmental protection and labor rights. These so-called "plurilateral agreements" are becoming more common.

5. Member countries recognize the importance of *making markets more open and contestable* through imports and FDI:

- Countries should eliminate quantitative restrictions (quotas and VERs) on trade.
- Countries should avoid protecting domestic firms with market power (monopolists and state-owned enterprises) from foreign competition.

6. Members should *sustain their commitments to negotiated market access through dispute settlement procedures*:

- The WTO's dispute settlement system (DSS) involves country-versus-country lawsuits alleging "nullification and impairment" of the access benefits its firms have gained abroad, due to some foreign policy that reduces or overturns that access. The policies that attract the most lawsuits are AD tariffs and regulations that violate national treatment.
- There is an appeals procedure that usually decides contentious cases.
- If the defendant country loses the case, it is ordered to remove or modify the policy.
- DSS panels may award damages by authorizing retaliation through trade restrictions or other measures.

A few important comments on dispute settlement:

1. The great majority of disputes involve a major country (e.g., the US, EU, China, and India) as either a plaintiff or defendant. This is simply because their markets are big and their trade policies really matter, so their policies attract many complaints.
2. About 2/3 of cases are settled before reaching a judiciary panel or appeals court.
3. The US has won nearly every case it has brought to the WTO as plaintiff (91% of adjudicated issues). That's because governments file cases when they are sure they can win.
4. That means the US also loses most cases brought against it (about 80%). Most of these are complaints about US AD procedures. As of 2021, there were 17 disputes filed about the steel and aluminum tariffs imposed in 2018.

   But there have been major lawsuits on other issues. The biggest and longest-standing conflict is between the US and European Union over subsidies to their major aircraft producers (Boeing in the US and Airbus in the EU).

The WTO: Existential threats

In recent years, the WTO has come under severe threat, and it remains to be seen if it can survive. It does need fundamental reforms. Here are the major threats to its effectiveness and even existence:

1. With so many members requiring consensus, it became increasingly hard to reach further rules on difficult trade and regulatory questions. This is the primary reason why preferential trade agreements have become so common in recent years.
2. The binding nature of WTO disputes is seen by some as limits on national policy sovereignty. Some major examples are as follows:

   - The tuna-dolphin dispute between the US and Mexico in the 1980s and 1990s, which eventually reached a sound outcome.

- The EU ban on importing beef treated with growth hormones, which is still an unresolved issue.
- The US implemented a rule in the 2000s requiring origin labels on imported beef. The US lost that dispute.
- Australia and Thailand require tobacco companies to label their goods essentially as poisons. The WTO upheld these rules.

3. There has been growing US opposition to the WTO under recent US presidents. WTO rules are increasingly seen as limits on domestic legal sovereignty. For example, the US often sees adverse WTO legal rulings as going beyond the authority of the WTO system.

   One major outcome of this concern is that the US has refused for several years to approve any new judges for the WTO appeals court. There now are not enough judges for the system to continue and it will end if that situation does not change.

4. One of the biggest challenges to the WTO's legitimacy arises from China (though similar issues could be raised about India, Brazil, and some other major emerging countries):

   - Chinese labor-intensive exports have caused distress in the US and other developed countries, fueling anti-trade populism.
   - China engages in extensive industrial policy, involving limits on foreign competition, subsidies to domestic firms, and other elements that expand exports artificially and keep prices low around the world. Steel is the best example. Another is their heavy subsidies of solar panels.
   - China has policies that effectively force foreign firms to surrender their technological information to domestic joint-venture partners.

   As noted above, US frustration with such policies led to its trade war with China, based on a Section 301 case. The European Union and other major countries are also concerned about China's industrial and technology policies.

5. Finally, there is the whole question of whether the trading system makes it more difficult for countries to combat climate change. For example, as discussed in Chapter 8, major developed economies

are increasingly interested in imposing border carbon adjustment taxes on imports of carbon-intensive goods. But this may not be permissible under current WTO rules.

More broadly, can the WTO rules be changed so that the system is based somewhat less on encouraging free trade and investment and somewhat more on sustainable development? This issue is highly complex and the subject of ongoing debates.

Chapter 10

Preferential Trade Agreements (PTAs)

Preferential Trade Agreements: Introduction and Basic Data

Introduction

One of the most important elements of trade policy in the world is the rapid growth of various forms of Free Trade Agreements (FTAs), more generally referred to as Preferential Trade Agreements (PTAs) or Regional Trade Agreements (RTAs). Rich nations often negotiate Trade Partnership Agreements (TPAs) with developing countries, and these involve less extensive trade liberalization.

These accords involve a small number of countries (often just two) agreeing to cut their tariffs and other barriers on trade among them but not to do so for countries outside the agreements. Such agreements have been in existence for many centuries in various forms, such as the Hanseatic League among northern German principalities and parts of Scandinavia in the 13th–17th centuries and various trade agreements among Italian republics during the Renaissance.

The first major PTA after World War II was the European Coal and Steel Community (ECSC), which eventually became the European Community and now the European Union. The first major agreement involving the United States was the North American Free

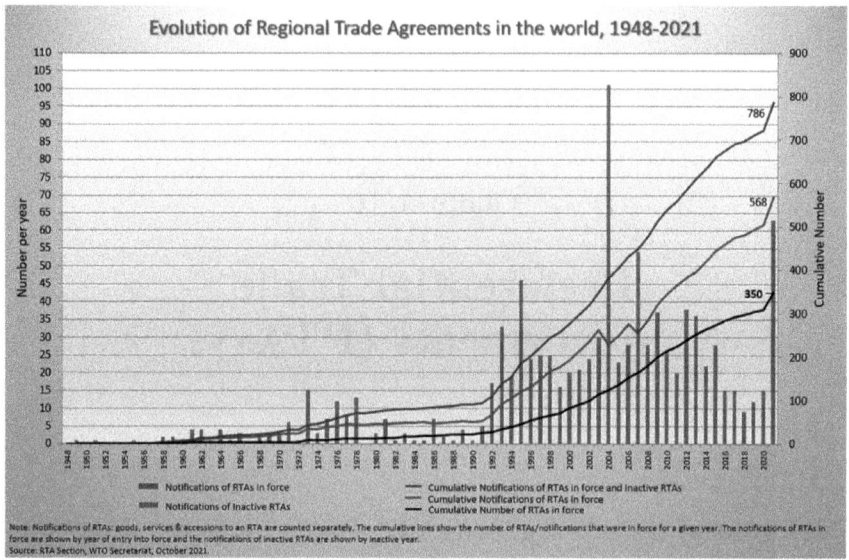

Figure 10.1   Growth of regional trade agreements.
Source: WTO   Secretariat,   https://www.wto.org/english/tratop_e/region_e/region_e.htm.

Trade Agreement (NAFTA) with Canada and Mexico in 1994, which succeeded the Canada-US FTA. NAFTA was renegotiated as the US–Mexico–Canada Agreement (USMCA) in 2019.

PTAs really began to grow in number and scope after NAFTA. As of October 2021, there were 568 such agreements in place involving nearly all countries in the WTO, as shown in Figure 10.1.

US PTAs

In recent decades, PTAs have become the primary way that the US and the EU try to manage their trade relations with specific countries or groups of countries. In addition to the USMCA, the US has the following agreements, involving 18 partner countries in total:

- There are bilateral FTAs with Australia, South Korea, Israel, and Singapore among rich countries.
- The Central American Free Trade Agreement (CAFTA) has six partners.

- There is a bilateral FTA with Chile and bilateral Trade Promotion Agreements with Peru, Colombia, and Panama.
- In the Middle East, there are bilateral FTAs with Jordan, Bahrain, and Morocco.
- Most recently, the Trump Administration negotiated a modest PTA with Japan, in which Japan offered some access to its agricultural markets and US lowered tariffs on some industrial goods. And there is a bilateral agreement on rules covering trade in digital products and data.

Other PTAs

The European Union itself is a massive PTA with 27 current members. It is actually a customs union, as explained later in these notes.

- The EU also has a PTA with the members of the European Free Trade Agreement (EFTA, which involves Switzerland, Norway, Liechtenstein, and Iceland) and a customs union with Turkey and some smaller countries.
- The EU recently concluded major PTAs with Mexico and Canada (separately) and Japan.
- The EU also developed TPAs with countries in Eastern Europe, Central Asia, the Middle East, and North Africa.
- The Comprehensive and Progressive Agreement for Trans-Pacific Partnership (CPTPP) involves 11 countries in the Asia-Pacific, including Canada, Mexico, and Japan.
- The Regional Comprehensive Economic Partnership (RCEP) is a major PTA involving China, India, Japan, South Korea, Australia, New Zealand, and the 10 ASEAN countries.
- Other prominent agreements are MERCOSUR (five countries in South America), CARICOM (20 Caribbean nations), and COMESA (19 countries in eastern and southern Africa).

Other attempts worth knowing about

The earlier Trans-Pacific Partnership (TPP) was signed in 2016 but fell apart when the US Trump Administration pulled out in January 2017. The other 11 countries later formed the CPTPP.

The Trans-Atlantic Trade and Investment Partnership (T-TIP) involved negotiations between the US and the EU over free trade and deep regulatory cooperation. It never progressed much and is no longer under negotiation.

Comments on "mega-regional PTAs"

Since some PTAs cover many countries, they are often called "mega-trade deals" or "mega-regionals". These would include USMCA, the EU, RCEP, CPTPP, and MERCOSUR.

Such agreements are less about cutting tariffs and removing quotas and more about reaching agreements on many regulatory issues that go beyond trade. Major examples include the following:

- trade and FDI in services;
- rules on investment;
- "rules of origin" regarding what constitutes within-PTA production;
- intellectual property rights (IPRs);
- state-owned enterprises (SOEs);
- standards for recognizing product safety and quality;
- data flows, privacy, and e-commerce;
- labor rights and environmental protection.

These are important and interesting issues that generally lie beyond the scope of international trade policy. They will be covered in these notes only in passing. And they can be controversial, such as provisions that expand patent protection for medicines in developing countries.

Categories of PTAs

Types of PTAs (Depth of integration)

1. A *Partial Free Trade Agreement* involves two or more countries offering each other lower (or zero) tariffs on a range of goods but not all goods.

2. A *Free Trade Agreement* (FTA) involves two or more countries offering each other zero tariffs and no quotas on all goods (though there are exceptions, usually in agriculture).

A key point is that in a PFTA or an FTA, each country keeps its own trade policy against non-member countries. In USMCA, for example, Canada, Mexico, and the US all have different tariff schedules against countries outside the agreement.

That situation raises the obvious problem that firms from other countries would choose to ship their goods to countries where the import tariffs are lowest and then transship them freely between member countries without paying additional trade taxes.

To offset this, all FTAs have in place complex *rules of origin* (ROOs). To qualify for zero-tariff transshipment around Canada, the US, and Mexico, for example, products must have been produced with at least a minimum percentage of their value coming from one or more of those three countries. The percentage varies by product but ranges from 25% to 80%; the average is around 55%.

The treatment of US domestic content in automobiles was a central element of the renegotiation of NAFTA into the USMCA. It raises the percentage of minimum regional content to 67% and has a minimum US content and a minimum labor content produced for at least $16 per hour.

3. A *Customs Union* (CU) is an FTA in which members give each other zero tariffs and agree to have the same trade policy against non-members. This situation is called having a "common external tariff".

The EU is a customs union. Tariff rates are set in Brussels and shared by all countries in the EU. This reduces the ROO's problem quite a bit.

Some countries in a CU may become annoyed that they cannot set their own trade tariffs. This was a big reason many in the UK voted in 2016 to leave the EU, a decision called "Brexit". (In fact, the bigger trade issue was that the UK had to conform to various standards set by the EU in how products are made, safety regulations, and so on.) The EU countries negotiate as a group at the WTO or in any other trade agreements.

4. A *Common Market* is a CU in which labor and capital are permitted to move freely among member countries.

The EU is actually a common market in that most restrictions on capital and labor migration are removed, implying that workers can move freely among countries to work and live. This free labor migration policy was probably the biggest reason for Brexit because it meant that the UK had no independent immigration controls.

5. An *Economic Union* is a Common Market in which there is also a single centralized fiscal and monetary policy. There would be just one central government permitted to set federal taxes and expenditures, one central bank, and one centralized system for regulating financial markets.

The ultimate EU goal is to become an economic union but is a long way from it. Later notes will consider this issue in terms of how the European Union reacted to the fiscal crisis of 2008–2012.

It is important to understand that *the United States is an economic union*. Capital and labor are free to move among states. Moreover, there is a centralized fiscal policy and the Federal Reserve manages monetary policy. The EU ultimately wants to achieve the same kinds of macroeconomic policy integration.

Study question 1

The primary difference between a free trade agreement (FTA) and a customs union (CU) is:

A. Members of an FTA retain their own tariff schedules against non-members but there is a common external tariff schedule in a CU.
B. A CU requires extensive rules of origin, but an FTA does not.
C. An FTA is discriminatory against non-members, but a CU is not discriminatory against non-members.
D. A CU permits full internal labor and capital mobility, but an FTA permits each country to have its own policies on capital flows and immigration.

Discussion of study question 1

The correct answer is A, which defines the main difference between an FTA and a CU. B is incorrect because the nationally different tariff policies among FTA members are what force countries to adopt ROOs, which is unnecessary under a CU. C is wrong because both policies discriminate against non-members. D is wrong because neither an FTA nor a CU involves free labor and capital migration. That is what characterizes a common market.

Economic Analysis of PTAs

General comments on the economics of PTAs

Since they involve two or more countries giving each other policy preferences that they do not give to non-members, PTAs are explicitly *discriminatory*. This means that they violate the basic GATT and WTO principles of non-discrimination (most favored nation (MFN) and national treatment (NT)). But the GATT and the WTO have rarely tried to intervene and stop the formation of any such agreement.

PTAs are permitted under GATT Article 24.3, which states that such agreements are OK if

(1) they cover the substantial majority of trade among members; and
(2) the PTA members do not raise their tariffs against other WTO members.

Basic economic analysis of PTAs: Do they increase welfare and efficiency?

In principle, PTAs have offsetting effects on economic efficiency. First, because they cut tariffs among members, they seem to be a movement toward freer trade and more efficiency. But second, because they do so in a discriminatory way, they could be a movement toward more restrictive trade and less efficiency.

Thus, the basic economic question is as follows: Does a PTA generate more welfare gains through *trade creation* or more welfare losses through *trade diversion*?

First, some definitions:

Trade creation (TC) exists when a policy change (such as a PTA) causes output to move from a higher-cost location to a lower-cost location within the region. It is usually associated with an expansion of trade volumes within the PTA. This is an efficient change and generally raises welfare within the PTA.

Trade diversion (TD) exists when a policy change (such as a PTA) causes output to move from a lower-cost location outside the region to a higher-cost location within the region. It is usually associated with a reduction in trade volume with non-member countries. This is an inefficient change and generally reduces welfare within the PTA. It also can make non-PTA members worse off because they lose an export market.

Simple examples

In any PTA, both these outcomes are possible, so member countries (and the world, if the PTA is large enough) could gain or lose welfare from forming a PTA. To understand TC and TD, consider the formation of the European Union in the early 1970 when the agreement was called the Common Market.

Trade Creation: When the UK joined in 1973, its domestic steel and automobile producers suddenly faced lower-cost competition from other members of the EU (e.g., Germany, the Netherlands, and France) and imports of such goods rose substantially. This was efficient trade creation, even though it placed competitive pressure on UK steel and auto producers, resulting in lower output and employment.

However, the UK also exported things it made more efficiently to the rest of the EU, such as financial services. This was also TC, which operates on both the import and export sides for a member country.

Trade Diversion: The European Union also had a high-cost set of agricultural price and output supports, called the Common Agricultural Policy (CAP). By reducing trade barriers within the EU on agricultural trade, there was more farming output generated in France, Belgium, Spain, and other locations, much of it exported to the UK, Germany, and other EU members.

But this extra output and trade came at the cost of excluding cheaper wheat, corn, and so on from North America, South America, and Australia. This was an inefficient trade diversion.

Basic graphical analysis

Following is a simple graphical example of TC, TD, efficiency, and welfare effects of an FTA.

Let countries A and B be small relative to the rest of the world (which will be called the world in this analysis). In Figure 10.2, country A is a high-cost producer of good X, as indicated by the high price at which its domestic supply and demand curves intersect.

Thus, A imports good X and can choose between buying it from the world at price p^* or from B at a higher price p^B. Since the price from B is higher, it is a less efficient producer than the world.

Suppose initially that A imposes the same ("most favored nation" or MFN) tariff of $T against X coming from both B and the world.

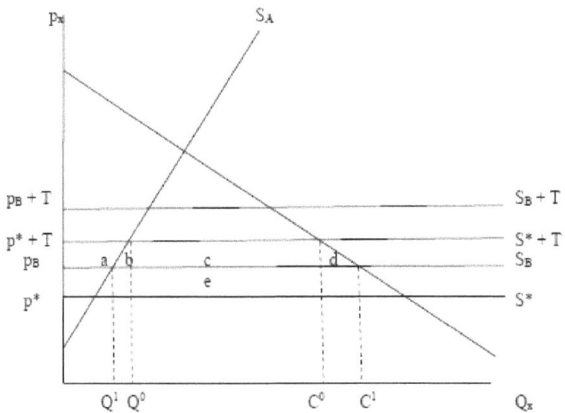

Figure 10.2   Analysis of an FTA involving two small countries.

In that case, the lowest available price to the market in A is $p^* + T$. That would be the initial domestic price in A. Domestic output in A would be Q^0 and domestic consumption would be C^0 with this MFN tariff in place. As a result, the initial import volume is $Q^0 C^0$ *and all those imports come from the world* (none from B).

Now, let A and B form an FTA, eliminating tariffs between them. But country A maintains the tariff against good X from the world.

This means that good X now would be available in A's market at price p^B rather than $p^* + T$. Since the price would be lower, the domestic price in A would fall to p^B. The consequences are the following:

- Domestic output in A would fall to Q^1 and domestic consumption would rise to C^1.
- Imports would be $Q^1 C^1$ *and all these imports would come from B* (none from the world).

Note that there are two kinds of changes in imports here:

- First, there would be an expansion of imports of X into A in the amounts $Q^1 Q^0 + C^0 C^1$. This is new trade that did not exist before and is associated with trade creation.
- Second, the initial volume of imports $Q^0 C^0$ would still exist, but its source has changed from the more efficient world to the less efficient partner B. This change is associated with trade diversion because the imports have been diverted from one source to another.

Welfare analysis

Here are the welfare calculations in country A:

- Loss in producer surplus $= -a$.
- Gain in consumer surplus $= +a + b + c + d$.
- Loss in tariff revenues $= -(c + e)$.

It is important to understand why there would be this loss in tariff revenues. Before, the FTA country A received the tax amount $\$T$ on each unit of imports from the world and in total that amounted to revenues given by the boxes $(c + e)$. *Now, all that revenue has disappeared because there is no tax on imports from B.*

The net welfare gain or loss in $A = +b + d - e$. The areas $+b + d$ are the efficiency gains (the opposite of the usual deadweight losses) from having country A bring in imports from B, which are produced more cheaply than they would be at home in A. *These are the welfare gains from trade creation.*

The area $-e$ exists because country A now buys those imports from B at a higher price than the country had been paying to the world. In essence, this is a decision by A to worsen its own terms of trade by buying from a higher-cost source within the PTA. *This is the welfare loss from trade diversion.*

As for country B, a similar analysis would be performed on the good it imports to see if it has net trade creation or trade diversion.

In general, there are thousands of goods that FTA partners trade and the full analysis would add up TC and TD effects across all of them in all partner countries to see what the overall effects might be.

As for the World, since by assumptions A and B are small, this FTA does not really matter in welfare terms. But if it were a large FTA, such as the USMCA, the EU, or the CPTPP, the world would care about the implied welfare effects. If A and B together made up a large FTA, then their trade partnership would materially reduce demand for many goods exported to them by the world, *even if A and B did not raise their individual tariffs against the world.* This outcome likely would make the world worse off, though again it would require careful accounting across many thousands of goods.

Trying to make such comprehensive calculations for particular FTAs is a major job for trade economists around the world. They use sophisticated statistical and theoretical models of how entire economies work to estimate the likely welfare effects of FTAs.

What factors affect TC and TD?

This analysis raises an obvious question: What are the characteristics of FTAs or PTAs that would make their formation more likely to generate more trade creation than trade diversion?

1. *There is likely to be more TC than TD the larger the economic size of the PTA.* This is because larger PTAs imply that less of the world is left out to suffer from TD. In the extreme, if the entire world had free trade among all countries, there would be just TC in this sense.

2. *There is likely to be more TC than TD the more the member countries in the PTA differ in their comparative advantage (relative cost differences).* Where this is true, the price adjustments within the PTA would be larger, as would the TC triangles (efficiency gains).

   To see this in the diagram above, if p^B were substantially lower than the initial domestic price in A, the expansion of trade within the FTA would be larger and the efficiency gains from TC (areas +b +d) would be correspondingly larger. However, the TD loss (area $-e$) would be smaller.

3. *TC is likely to exceed TD where the pre-FTA tariffs that get removed are high.* This simply means that the FTA partners would eliminate what were high tariffs, likely generating a large volume of within-FTA trade.

NAFTA and TC versus TD

Given these factors, consider whether NAFTA (the older North American FTA) was likely to have generated more TC or more TD. NAFTA was a very large agreement (any FTA with the US as a member would be large, almost by definition, but NAFTA had three big countries). This suggests that there was significant net TC (Factor 1).

Although the US and Canada are similar in their cost structures, Mexico has quite different relative costs from the US and Canada. In fact, NAFTA encouraged Mexico to specialize more in labor-intensive and assembly operations. Mostly, this supported net TC and has done so in an extreme way with the emergence of supply chains in autos, textiles, and electronics. This difference suggests there was considerable net TC (Factor 2).

Pre-NAFTA tariffs were high in Mexico but were quite low in the US and Canada. So, this outcome is not as clear (Factor 3).

Available estimates, from about 10 studies done by economists, suggest that NAFTA has generated considerably more TC than TD when measured using concepts similar to this analysis.

Study question 2

When a set of countries join together in an FTA, there is likely to be more trade creation than trade diversion where:

A. All the countries are small and have low tariffs against each other.
B. Together, the countries make up a large area and have high tariffs against each other.
C. Countries are physically far apart from each other.
D. Countries have very different cost structures in producing various goods.
E. Both B and D.

Discussion of study question 2

The correct answer is E because the elements in both B and D should create significant TC and little TD. A is incorrect because small countries do not have enough market size to generate much TC, while if their initial tariffs were low, cutting them to zero would have little impact. C is incorrect because countries that are far apart from each other would not end up trading much after the tariff cuts due to high transport costs. This explains why FTAs almost always happen among countries that are in close geographical proximity to each other.

Other economic effects of PTAs

This analysis of TC and TD is important, but it misses a number of arguments made about PTAs. The remaining notes describe other important impacts that PTAs may have.

1. *Lock-in effects*: One reason Mexico joined NAFTA was to commit itself to maintaining the required tariff cuts and other liberalizing policies. Due to that, future Mexican administrations (and Canadian and US ones) would be very unlikely to go back on these commitments and raise tariffs. The main reason is that firms (domestic and multinational) make large investments based on the rules of NAFTA and become effective lobbyists against changing the rules later.

   This force is powerful. For example, it was possible for countries to pull out of NAFTA but doing so was never seriously considered before the Trump Administration, which threatened to withdraw in order to encourage the renegotiations that led to USMCA.

2. *Larger joint size and the terms of trade*: Individual countries may be too small to have much impact on world trade flows and the terms of trade. But by joining together, a grouping of such countries might have more influence on prices and global trade policies.

   This is one reason why MERCOSUR (Brazil, Argentina, Venezuela, Paraguay, and Uruguay) was formed. Clearly, the EU as a bloc is a huge customs union with considerable ability to affect world trade.

3. *Greater economies of scale due to larger market size*: Smaller countries face the problem that their markets are not large enough for firms to modernize, grow, and take advantage of lower costs through increasing returns to scale.

   Such countries could just unilaterally cut tariffs. Being open to global trade can help make exporters in such countries more efficient by selling into large world markets. But then, domestic firms would also face formidable global competition.

   A useful mid-step could be to form PTAs with preferential market access inside the regions. Then, surviving firms from smaller countries may gain considerably in terms of economies of scale in the larger joint market.

   Evidence suggests that many Canadian and Mexican manufacturing industries became more productive and grew larger as a result of NAFTA and the need to compete in the large three-country market. At the same time, several other sectors became less competitive and shrank.

4. *Dynamic effects*: The larger markets and greater policy certainty of PTAs should attract more foreign direct investment (FDI) by multinational enterprises.

   The amounts of FDI into Mexico from the US, Canada, and non-member countries have been far larger than was originally anticipated. This was especially the case for FDI from Japan and the EU to take advantage of producing cars and other goods for the North American market.

   Available estimates consistently suggest that there was considerably more FDI in the EU as a result of the single-market (free trade) program there. A collateral dynamic gain is that FDI brings with it new technologies that help make domestic economies more productive.

   It is worth noting that we could also study the concepts of *investment creation* (IC) and *investment diversion* (ID) in PTAs. IC would refer to additional FDI from within the region, such as US companies investing in Mexico to take advantage of lower wage costs as a result of NAFTA. ID would refer to reduced FDI from outside the region, which might happen if, say, EU companies felt disadvantaged in operating in Mexico. But there is not much evidence of this negative outcome in major trade agreements.

5. *An easier path toward regulatory harmonization*: One major reason that the US and the EU have increasingly turned to PTAs is that they find it easier to negotiate with a few countries than with many countries on convincing member nations to "harmonize" (make more equal) their regulatory approaches.

   Thus, recent PTAs involving the EU and the US have focused on IPRs, investment policies, services regulations, labor rights, digital trade, environmental protection, and other complex issues that cannot be successfully negotiated at the WTO with so many countries involved.

Basic PTA analysis: Summary

In theory, PTAs can be a source of welfare gain or loss, which depends on the circumstances. Whether they move the world closer or further away from global free trade is not altogether clear. However, the larger and more successful ones seem to generate more TC than TD.

PTAs establish larger joint markets for achieving economies of scale and dynamic gains in investment and technology transfer. PTAs also facilitate negotiation of regulatory harmonization. For these reasons, trade economists generally support the formation of PTAs, the larger the better.

Chapter 11

International Labor Migration

Introduction to International Factor Movements

International factor mobility: General comments

The following concepts make up what economists consider "international factor flows", meaning the movement of production factors across borders.

1. Portfolio investment capital flows: These are financial investments seeking high returns and risk diversification. Examples are stocks, bonds, government bonds, bank deposits and loans, and various more complex instruments. These amounts are enormous, amounting to trillions of dollars per day, and have grown rapidly as emerging countries have opened their financial markets in the last few decades.

   What motivates these flows? Anything that changes the expected risks and returns on foreign investments relative to domestic investments. Major examples are changes in interest rates, asset prices, exchange rates, and riskiness across countries. These issues will be studied in the following part of the course, but a couple of comments are useful to understand at this point:

   - First, highly risky countries attract relatively little capital and may see outward "capital flight" even if their interest rates are higher than those in safer locations. This is a common problem in sub-Saharan Africa, South Asia, and parts of Latin America.

- Second, sudden changes in expected asset returns can cause major outflows and inflows of capital, potentially destabilizing financial markets and exchange rates. This process often characterizes international financial crises.

2. Foreign aid and multilateral assistance and lending in response to development needs and crises in poor countries: Much of this assistance is provided by the World Bank, International Monetary Fund, and other international financial organizations.

3. Foreign direct investment (FDI) within multinational enterprises (MNEs): FDI involves building or purchasing production or distribution subsidiaries abroad. These flows depend partly on financial factors but much more on structural issues, including market size, growth rates, taxes, labor costs, transport costs, and so on. FDI flows are far more stable than portfolio capital flows, which are more "footloose".

4. Flows of technology, called international technology transfers: A critical component of economic development is the spread of productive knowledge around the world. Here are the main channels through which technologies are transferred across borders:

   - International trade in high-technology goods and services, especially machinery and inputs that are used in production technologies in recipient countries.
   - FDI and outsourcing through MNEs because these firms tend to deploy more advanced technologies in foreign subsidiaries.
   - Licensing of new technologies for use by firms abroad.
   - Temporary international flows of skilled labor. An interesting example occurs where graduate students earn engineering and science degrees abroad and return home to apply technical skills.

5. Labor migration, which is by far the most limited factor flow due to immigration restrictions: This is an extremely complex issue and is subject to more political argument and debate than almost anything else in international economics. These notes focus on the primary economic issues, but migration also involves politics, sociology, culture, and many more areas.

GDP versus GNI

Before undertaking an analysis of factor migration, we need to remember an important difference from national income accounting. Gross Domestic Product (GDP) is the total of all final output produced in a country, regardless of whether it is produced by domestic factors (labor and capital) or by foreign factors (inflows of labor and capital). Gross National Income (GNI, which used to be called Gross National Product or GNP) is the total of all income earned by domestic factors (labor and capital) whether it is earned at home or abroad.

If there are no factor movements across borders, then GDP = GNI. But if a country has many of its people working abroad, it should have GNI > GDP because the income those workers earn is in the country's GNI but not its GDP. Some examples are El Salvador, the Philippines, and Romania from which many laborers work temporarily abroad.

The US owns more capital working abroad than foreign investors own capital working in its economy, so GNI > GDP due to these K flows. But it also has more foreign workers here than US workers abroad, meaning that GDP > GNI due to L flows. Overall, these closely balance, and GDP is very close to GNI. The difference between GDP and GNI is important in understanding the economic effects of labor migration and capital flows.

Economic Analysis of Labor Migration

The basic economics of labor movements

Assume that we have only two factors (L and K) and that they combine to produce a single "good" called GDP. Initially, the main concern is not how immigration affects specific products but how it changes total production and consumption. Sectoral output effects are studied later in these notes.

In each country, the L and K stocks are fixed but we permit labor to move across borders. To keep the analysis straightforward, assume for now that capital cannot move internationally.

Importantly, assume also that any migrant to a foreign country is as productive as the workers already there. Thus, *productivity is a feature of countries, not people.* The truth of this assumption is an interesting question discussed in the following. Technically, immigrants and domestic workers are *perfect substitutes.*

Define the national demand curve for labor as VMPL = P*MPL, where P is a national price index for GDP and MPL is the real GDP produced by an additional worker. Thus, VMPL stands for the *value of the marginal product of labor.*

Why is this the demand for labor? Since the *VMPL is the value of additional GDP produced by employing one more worker.* If that VMPL is higher than the wage, the worker will be hired. If not, a worker will be laid off.

The country's (single) wage rate is the price of labor. Thus, equilibrium in the national labor market requires that wage = VMPL.

Figure 11.1 illustrates this simple analysis, using two countries, the US and Mexico. In the diagram, in each country, the VMPL (labor demand) curve is defined for a given price index. VMPL slopes downward because as the economy employs more labor, the marginal product of labor goes down. This assumes that the total capital stock is fixed so that labor has diminishing marginal productivity in producing GDP.

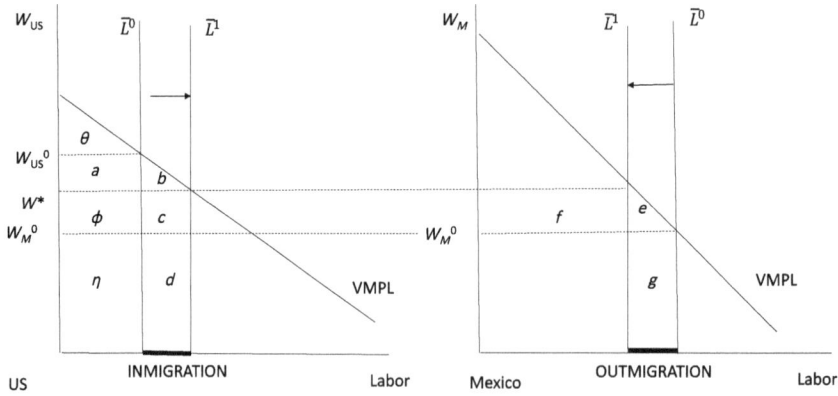

Figure 11.1   Welfare analysis of wage-equalizing labor migration.

Pre-migration equilibrium

The fixed labor forces (labor supplies) are given by the vertical lines. The initial (pre-migration) equilibrium points are where VMPL curves intersect the labor supply curves, generating the national wage rates before there is any migration. For example, the initial US wage rate was W_{US}^0, established by where the VMPL curve intersects the labor supply curve, L^0.

It is important to understand that in each diagram, as the economy employs more labor, the value of GDP rises. The increase in GDP is given by the area under the labor demand curve. This is because the height of VMPL is given by the extra (marginal) output. (Technically, GDP is the integral of the VMPL curve.)

Thus, at the US equilibrium wage W_{US}^0, initial total GDP was given by the area $\theta + a + \phi + \eta$. Next, observe that the wage rate times the labor force is total labor income. In the US, this amounts to area $a + \phi + \eta$. This was the amount of GDP paid in wages.

It follows that the triangle above that is capital income, amounting to θ. This was the amount of GDP paid to capital owners. (From now on, it will be possible to ignore the Greek letters.)

In the same way, students should work out what the initial labor and capital incomes were in Mexico. To complete the pre-migration analysis, suppose that Mexico had a relatively large amount of labor, so its initial wage was lower than the US wage.

Note that for this wage difference to exist, there must have been something preventing factor-price equalization (FPE), a concept studied in the HO model. In practical terms, many things could prevent equalized wages, such as transport costs, tariff barriers, and different technologies of production.

Post-migration equilibrium

Now, let workers migrate from Mexico to the US, which would continue until wages were equalized at W^*. Note that the horizontal outmigration (or emigration) from Mexico is the same as the immigration into the US. What would be the effects?

Regarding total welfare, remember that the earlier trade models considered whether countries could consume outside their PPFs due to free trade. But in this macroeconomic model, there is not a PPF between goods because GDP is the single good. GDP (production) is not the right measure of welfare. Rather, GNI is the correct welfare indicator because income is what matters for a country's ability to increase consumption.

Welfare effects of labor movements

In terms of who gains or loses income, there are five groups to consider: income changes of L and K in the US, the same in Mexico, and those of the migrants.

In the US:

- The wage rate would fall to W^* as workers move in. The existing US workers would lose area $-a$. *Immigration causes the wages (income) of native workers to fall.*
- Capital owners in the US gain areas $+a + b$ in income. *Capital is more productive due to having more labor in the economy.*

The net welfare impact in the US would be $+b$, which is the efficiency gain from having more workers. It is also the increase in US GNI, so this efficiency gain refers to higher GNI. Note that the increase in US GDP is $+b + c + d$, but only $+b$ is the GNI gain. We will analyze the difference in upcoming notes.

In Mexico:

- The wage would rise to W^* as workers leave. Thus, the workers who remain in Mexico would gain area $+f$ in income. *Outmigration makes the remaining workers better off.*
- Capital owners in Mexico would lose areas $-f - e$ because capital is now less productive. *Capital is less productive because there are fewer workers after the outmigration.*

At this point, the net welfare impact (change in income) is $-e$, the domestic efficiency loss from having fewer workers. But that is not the whole story because we need to account for what happens to the migrants. They are Mexican factors so their incomes must count in Mexico's GNI.

Consider the income changes for the migrating workers:

- In the US, they would earn income $+c + d$.
- But they would give up the former income they were earning in Mexico, which is area $-g$.
- Note that $-g$ is the same size as $+d$, so that part is just the lost income at home they replace in the US. The net gain in income for the migrants is then $+c$.

Migrant workers would gain income by earning the post-migration wage in the United States, which is higher than the pre-migration wage in Mexico.

The total effect on Mexico's GNI would be $-e + c$. However, because $c = 2e$, Mexico's GNI overall would rise by $+e$.

These changes can be added up to figure out the "world" (US plus Mexico) welfare impact:

The total world welfare change would be $+b + e$. The 1st term is the GNI gain in the US and the 2nd term is the GNI gain in Mexico (including the higher income of migrants).

Both countries are better off from the migration. We find that there is higher income in the world after the labor migration. That is no surprise because workers have moved from where they were less productive to where they are more productive.

Comparing GDP and GNI effects

This analysis in terms of GNI is the correct way to consider welfare impacts of migration. But public opinion and politicians often are confused about this and think about GDP changes. Some possible reasons for this misunderstanding could be the following:

(1) Higher GDP seems to correlate with more employment of domestic workers (but it does not in this analysis).
(2) If migrants spend their incomes in the US, it seems like the income is "kept" there. But if the incomes are sent back to Mexico, somehow that may be viewed as a negative.

To analyze this, break the model down a bit more by looking at the GDP effects. In the US, output (GDP) would go up by the areas $+ b + c + d$. In Mexico, output (GDP) would fall by the areas $-e - g$. The gain in US output would be bigger than the loss in Mexican output, which again makes sense because the migrants are now producing in a more productive location.

The net impact on the world GDP is $+(b + c + d) - e - g = +b + e$. *The gain in world output is the same as the gain in world income, as it must be.*

Labor remittances

Thus, in terms of effects on GDP, migration is negative for countries losing labor and positive for countries gaining labor. While not the right welfare measure, there is a lot of political power in that claim.

Further, there is another practical issue to consider that may affect views about how migration affects the distribution of welfare gains between the US and Mexico. How much of the incomes they earn do migrants send back to Mexico? Such payments, which typically are paid to family members remaining in Mexico, are called *labor remittances.*

In this context, there are three natural possibilities to consider:

Case 1: The migrants spend all their income in the US and send none home to Mexico. US politicians and the media could argue that because this expenditure stays in the US, it is beneficial. Is this true?

In this case, the US efficiency gain plus the migrant income spent in the US would be $+b + c + d$, which is simply the GDP increase. Those who think that the GDP increase raises welfare presumably should make this a political argument in favor of immigration. *Again, however, recall carefully that migrant spending should not be considered a welfare gain in the US because the migrants are foreign citizens.*

In Mexico, the efficiency loss plus the income no longer spent in Mexico $= -e - g$, equal to the GDP loss. The same logic would suggest Mexico is worse off, though it is not. But it could be a political argument in that country for restricting outmigration.

Case 2: The migrants send all their income earned in the US back to Mexico as remittances.

In this case, the US GDP gain minus the remittances would be $+b$, the actual GNI change. The Mexican US GDP loss plus remittances $= +c + d - e - g = +c - e = +e$. This is actually the primary case considered above using GNI effects. *Here, both countries gain from migration.*

Case 3: The migrants just send back their additional income, area c, earned in the US.

Then, the US GDP gain minus remittances would be $+b + d$ and the Mexican GDP loss plus remittances would be $+c - e - g$. This is likely to be seen as somewhat better in Mexico than in Case 1.

All this points out that it is important to account for migrant income remittances. It is important for calculating changes in GDP versus GNI, though only GNI changes matter for welfare impacts. But remittances also have some political relevance.

Study question 1

In this basic analysis, migration of workers from low-wage to high-wage countries tends to:

A. Raise capital incomes in the source country (from where migrants leave).
B. Raise GDP in the destination country (to where migrants go) and reduce GDP in the source country.
C. Raise wages in the destination country.
D. Raise welfare in both countries.
E. Both B and D.

Discussion of study question 1

The correct answer is E because both B and D are true statements. B is true because the movement of labor removes a production factor from the source country, reducing its GDP, and raises it in the destination country, raising its GDP. D is correct because GNI rises in both countries, accounting for migrant incomes as part of the source country's GNI. A is false because with a lower labor force, capital loses income in the source country. C is false because the inflow of labor reduces the wage in the destination country.

Data and Evidence on Immigration Flows and Effects

Facts and figures: Recent US data

Moving from economic theory to the real world, consider the facts about immigration using basic US data. Under US law, there are two categories of legal immigrants into the United States:

1. Those who get a "green card" (long-term permanent residency or LPR). There have been about 1 million recipients per year since 2000. Here are the categories under which someone gets a green card:

   - "New arrivals" who are approved by US authorities for immigration from their home nations. These are mostly immediate family members of US citizens. They amount to about 45%–50% of new LPR approvals each year.
   - "Adjustments" in status are people already in the US, typically on work visas, who shift to LPR status. This status amounts to around 50%–55% of LPR approvals.
   - There are certain preferences, permitting some applicants to be ranked higher, that could apply to either category: (1) more distant family members (subject to limits), sometimes referred to as "chain migration", and (2) preferences for professionals, special workers, and "investment immigrants". The last group must invest a minimum amount of dollars in the US economy.

2. Those who are admitted as refugees, seeking to migrate due to wars or persecution at home. Over three million refugees in total have been admitted since the original legislation was passed in 1980. There is an annual cap on the number of refugees, which the President can decide to change.

The shifting origins of refugees to the U.S. over time

Number of refugees admitted to the U.S., by region of origin of principal applicant and fiscal year

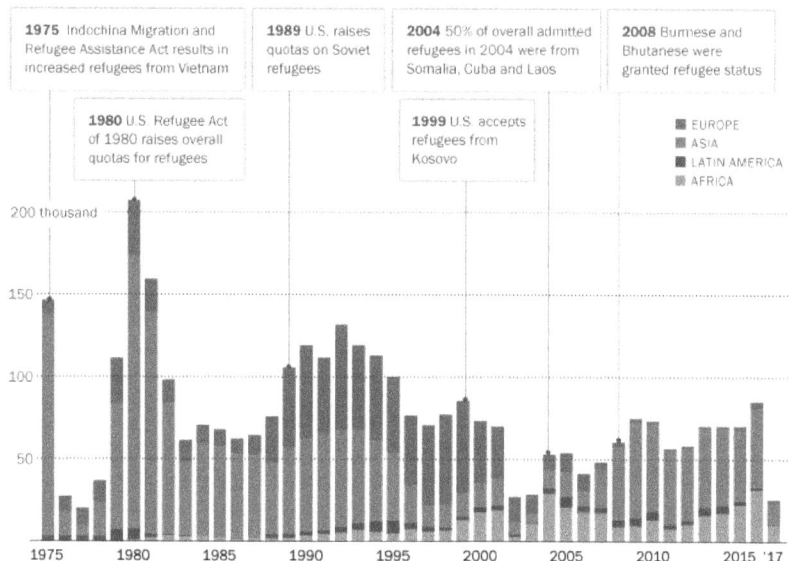

Source: Refugee Processing Center, 1975-2016.
Note: Data do not include special immigrant visas and certain humanitarian parole entrants. Does not include refugees admitted under the Private Sector Initiative. Europe includes former Soviet Union states. Asia includes Middle Eastern and North African countries. Africa includes sub-Saharan Africa, but also Sudan and South Sudan. Latin America includes Caribbean. Data for fiscal 2017 are through Dec. 31, 2016; fiscal 2017 began Oct. 1, 2016.

PEW RESEARCH CENTER

Figure 11.2   Sources of US refugees 1975–2017.
Source: https://www.pewresearch.org/fact-tank/2017/02/03/where-refugees-to-the-u-s-come-from/.

Data showing annual refugee inflows are in Figure 11.2. The Trump Administration cut the maximum refugee cap from 110,000 in 2017 to 18,000 by FY 2020. "The Biden Administration raised the cap back to 125,000 by 2022, reflecting the need to accommodate a large inflow of refugees from Afghanistan and Iraq.

Statistics on illegal immigration

A person is "illegal" or "undocumented" or "unauthorized" if she or he overstays a visa or enters the country without a visa. It is difficult

U.S. unauthorized immigrant total rises, then falls

In millions

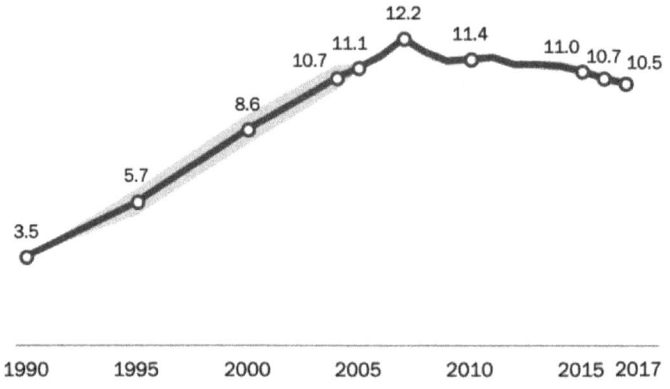

Note: Shading shows range of estimated 90% confidence interval.
Source: Pew Research Center estimates based on augmented U.S. Census Bureau data.

PEW RESEARCH CENTER

Figure 11.3   Estimated number of unauthorized immigrants in the US.

Source: Pew Research Foundation, https://www.pewresearch.org/short-reads/ 2019/07/12/how-pew-research-center-counts-unauthorized-immigrants-in-us/.

to estimate the annual net entrants of undocumented persons into the US. But Figure 11.3 shows that the estimated stock of undocumented migrants leveled off at 12.2 million around 2007 and declined to 10.5 million in 2017. This represents around 25% of the foreign-born population in the country. What this decline suggests is that *net* illegal immigration flows (the addition to the stock each year) are small and negative now in the US, though this may have changed after 2019.

The most important factors behind this drop are likely the following:

(1) There has been relatively faster economic growth in Mexico than in the US since the 2000s, making wages in the US relatively less attractive than before.

(2) The US significantly increased its border enforcement, beginning around 2008.

(3) Recent demographic changes in Mexico, where birth rates have fallen sharply since the 1970s, reducing the number of young adults wishing to migrate illegally.

Figure 11.4 shows the number of encounters (apprehensions plus expulsions) of undocumented immigrants by month from 2000 to 2021, along the US border with Mexico. Ordinarily, these people are placed into a legal process to determine whether and when they will be deported. Here are some comments:

1. There is a seasonal element to such immigration because the migrants often work in agricultural sectors. Indeed, many undocumented migrants cross the border more than once per year, depending on the season.

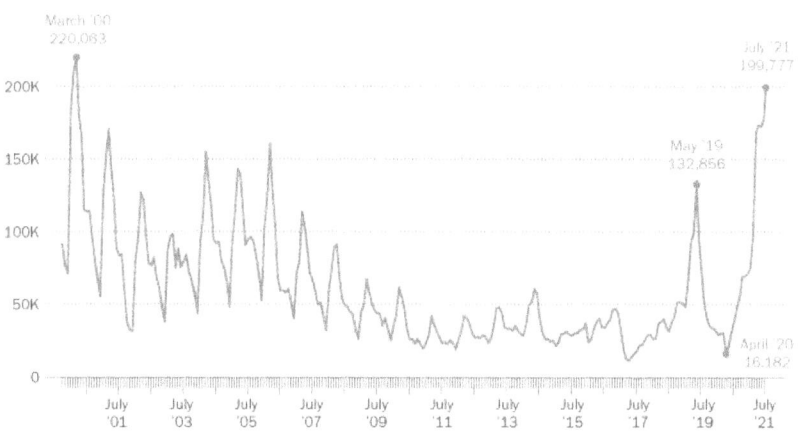

Migrant encounters at southwestern border have soared in recent months

Migrant encounters at U.S.-Mexico border, by month

Note: Beginning in March 2020, monthly totals combine apprehensions and expulsions into a new category known as encounters. Monthly totals before March 2020 include apprehensions only.
Source: U.S. Customs and Border Protection.

PEW RESEARCH CENTER

Figure 11.4   Changes in encounters of the US Customs and Border Patrol with undocumented migrants.

Source: Pew Research Center, https://www.pewresearch.org/fact-tank/2021/08/13/migrant-encounters-at-u-s-mexico-border-are-at-a-21-year-high/.

2. After reaching a peak of 220,000 in March 2000, there was a sharp decline in monthly encounters at the border through 2017. This figure went up sharply to over 133,000 in May 2019 and returned to 200,000 in July 2021 and has continued to rise.

3. The sharp decline to a low of just over 16,000 in April 2020 was due to a policy of the Trump Administration seeking to prevent migrants from entering at all in order to limit entry of those who might carry the COVID virus. These people were sent immediately back to their last country of transit (Mexico) or country of origin without entering immigration processing.

4. The source countries of such immigration have changed from Mexico (the net flow now often is back to Mexico) to primarily Central America, from where people seek to escape difficult economic conditions and physical dangers.

5. Illegal immigration from Central America and Venezuela has risen sharply in recent years, including in 2021 after the COVID-based eliminations were relaxed by the Biden Administration. The large increases in 2019 and 2021 were due primarily to rapid increases in illegal crossings by family units and unaccompanied minors.

Economic Impacts of Immigration

The big economic questions about immigration

Turn now to some major questions about immigration and available economic evidence about them.

Question 1: What would the global income gains be if the world allowed free labor mobility?

Imagine that there were completely free migration of workers from poor countries to high-wage countries and this happened until wages were equalized. Then, economic models that simulate the world economy find staggeringly large potential gains in world output.

For example, the gains in output would be from 67% to 150% of world GDP (see Clemens, *Journal of Economic Perspectives*, 2011 for a review). Current world GDP is estimated to be $85 trillion. The reason for this massive increase is that labor would move from where it is less productive to where it is more productive.

In contrast, similar simulation models of the effects of completing another major round of trade negotiations (tariff cuts) at the WTO forecast that there would be welfare gains of less than 2% of world GDP. In Clemens' words, we are "leaving trillion-dollar bills on the sidewalk" by preventing significant migration flows. As a political matter, such large flows are highly unlikely because voters in the destination countries fear immigration for many economic and cultural reasons; some of them are discussed in the following.

Characteristics of migrants in the US

Question 2: What are the characteristics of adult immigrants in the US?

A highly informative recent source on this question is National Academies of Sciences, Engineering, and Medicine, 2017. *The Economic and Fiscal Consequences of Immigration*. Washington, DC: The National Academies Press.

Define immigrants as adults born abroad who are living in the United States, whether legally or illegally. This definition refers to the stock of foreign-born people in the US, whether citizens or not. It is different from thinking of immigrants as a new inflow each year.

As of the 2010 census, approximately 10% of these people were born in Europe, 30% in Mexico, 19% in Central America or Caribbean, 28% in Asia, and 12% in Africa and South America. In terms of education, about 40% of immigrants did not finish high school (compared to 17% of US natives); 24% finished HS (39% natives); 29% had some college or a four-year degree (40% natives); 7% had advanced degrees (4% natives). Thus, the immigrant pool is certainly heavily tilted toward the less educated, though slightly more focused on advanced degrees than natives. These percentages vary greatly across source regions.

Regarding demographic differences, immigrants tend to be younger and to have a higher ratio of males to females than do

US natives in each educational group. This is due primarily to the preponderance of male migration over female migration, though that has changed in recent years.

Impacts of immigration on US (native) wages

Question 3: How do immigrants affect the wages of US workers?
This is a much harder question to analyze than one might think. One promising idea is to use cities (or local labor markets) to compare the effects. But here are some problems that would arise:

- Suppose, for example, that El Paso gets many more immigrants per capita than Denver. Intuitively, one would expect the wage impact on El Paso to be larger. But if native workers responded by leaving El Paso, then the impact measured there on wages might be small.
- Moreover, the natives remaining in El Paso could be higher skilled (and have higher wages) than those who move out. Then, the estimated impact on local wages could be strongly positive but that would tell us nothing about the impacts on low-skilled native wages.
- Or suppose in general that immigrants tend to move mostly to cities where wages are higher. Then, we would get a spurious positive correlation because high local wages attract immigrants, rather than immigrants changing local wages.

Immigration and US wages

The following notes summarize how economists have tackled these problems. The basic approach is to assume that migrants and natives in similar skill classes are *highly substitutable within cities* and look only at what happens to wages within similar skill groups. Economists also see if the arrival of more migrants causes natives to leave the city-level labor market.

Figure 11.5 offers interesting insight from a comprehensive study of cities, skill groups, and wages. It shows that having a higher

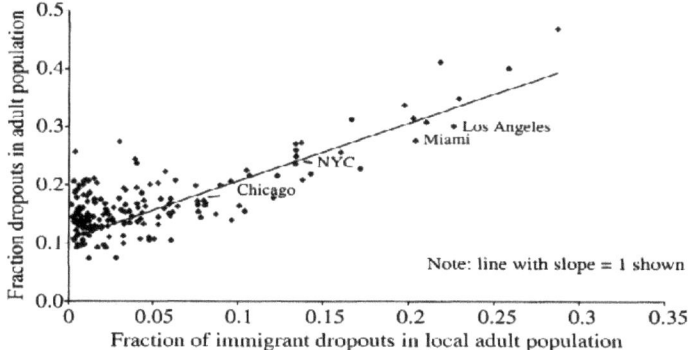

Figure 11.5 Cities with more immigrant high-school dropouts do not see lower shares of dropouts overall.

Source: David Card, Is the new immigration really so bad? *Economic Journal*, November 2005.

percentage of immigrant high-school dropouts in a city does not reduce the fraction of native high-school dropouts. This suggests that migration into cities expands the low-skilled labor supply, rather than pushing local low-skilled workers to move elsewhere. One may infer from this that cities effectively are local labor markets and if immigration generates noticeable wage effects, they should be found in city-level data. How could these effects be measured?

Note that it is unlikely that high-school dropout immigrants would compete with US natives who have a high-school education or better. That is, dropouts are not close substitutes for those with a secondary education or better.

In that case, one would expect the gap between the wages of native high-school educated workers and native dropouts to get bigger as more high-school dropout immigrants arrive. Alternatively, the ratio of native skilled (high-school graduates) to unskilled (dropouts) employment should rise. But this is not true, as shown in Figure 11.6 from the same study.

A similar result (not shown) holds for employment: The ratio of high-school graduates employed to the employment of high-school dropouts across cities is not related to the immigration of low-skilled workers.

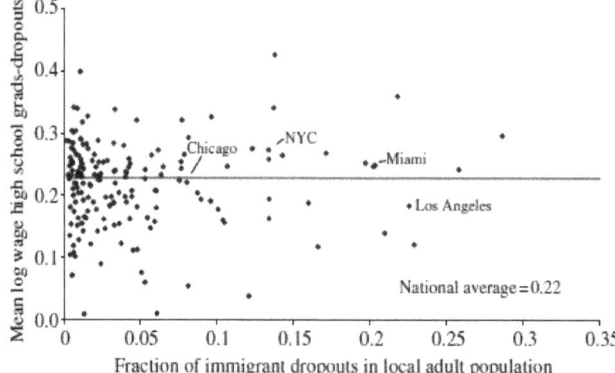

Figure 11.6   There is no relationship between the presence of immigrant high-school dropouts and education-based wage differentials.

Source: David Card, Is the new immigration really so bad? *Economic Journal*, November 2005.

Direct data evidence from econometric studies

There are many deep econometric studies of immigration and wages. The great majority find essentially no relationship between the city-level low-skilled immigration population and low-skilled native wages in the US across cities and over time. Some find modest negative impacts, but as David Card, a Nobel Prize-winning economist noted: the "worst-case scenario" is that low-skilled immigration reduced wages of natives without a high-school education by 5% over 20 years.

This lack of impact is a puzzle, not least to labor economists. What might be some explanations?

A. Unskilled immigration could generate as much local demand for goods and services (raising labor demand) as supply of labor, keeping wages from falling. The immigrants would be absorbed into existing industries (e.g., manufacturing, agriculture, construction, restaurants, and hotels), each of which would grow bigger without diminishing the demand for native workers. There is strong evidence supporting this hypothesis.

An interesting historical example was the "Mariel boatlift" of workers from Cuba and Haiti to the US in 1980. The Castro government in Cuba announced in early 1980 that anyone who wanted to emigrate could do so. Most emigrants were actually released prisoners. The Carter Administration decided to permit a large increase in refugees and about 150,000 arrived over seven months. Most of these settled in Miami (aided by Cuban Americans). But several studies found almost no effect on low-skilled wages in the Miami area after a year or two. This is because output expanded in labor-intensive goods and services, absorbing these workers without reducing local wages. Students should recognize this as a practical example of the Rybczynski theorem from Chapter 4.

B. Illegal immigrants may compete mostly with other illegal immigrants, and therefore compete less with legal immigrants, and very little with natives. Evidence of this is from a study by the Pew Foundation in 2009, which found that undocumented aliens residing in the US for less than 10 years earned 18% less than legal migrants, while those in the US for more than 10 years earned 42% less on average. Both groups of illegal immigrants earned considerably less than US natives with similar skills and employment.

C. An important possibility is that immigrants and natives in fact are not highly substitutable. Rather, in important sectors, immigrants and natives seem to be complements. *This means that the more migrants there are, the higher is demand for native workers.*

This idea and detailed evidence supporting it are largely due to economists Peri and Sparber (*American Economic Journal: Applied Economics*, 2009).

The logic is that more low-skilled immigration permits native workers, who speak English better and understand local culture better, to specialize in higher-value and more complex tasks (e.g., signing contracts with homeowners) while the migrants do the lower-skilled work that does not require such interaction. Indeed, native workers may form new businesses within which they set contract terms and negotiate with customers, earning higher wages.

This impact holds true also using data from Western European countries, as found in related studies. Thus, the best evidence suggests that increasing amounts of low-skilled immigration in the

US and Europe induce natives to take on more complex and higher-valued jobs.

The implication is that more low-skilled immigration *raises* the wages modestly of native workers but *reduces* the wages of recent immigrants. A later paper by these authors found that such immigration from 1990 to 2006 in the US reduced the wages of prior immigrants by around 7%. A practical political implication is that recent immigrants who become voting citizens may be more opposed to increasing low-skilled immigration than native workers.

Study question 2

Economic evidence suggests that in the US and Western Europe, immigration of low-skilled workers does not seem to reduce wages of domestic workers. Potential reasons for this include the following except:

A. The influx of labor expanded employment in labor-intensive goods without reducing demand for local workers.
B. Domestic workers tend to move away from areas where immigrants locate.
C. Domestic workers and immigrants may be complements.
D. Immigrants compete more with other recent immigrants than with domestic workers.

Discussion of study question 2

The correct answer is B. Evidence shows that low-skilled native workers do not tend to move to other cities in response to an influx of immigration. A, C, and D are all valid additional reasons for the absence of wage impacts from low-skilled immigration.

How quickly do immigrants assimilate in the US?

Question 4: How many generations does it take for migrant families to catch up to natives in terms of education and incomes? For further perspective, consult the National Academy of Sciences study mentioned earlier.

Studies find that recent (two years or less) male legal migrants make around 67%–75% of male natives in similar jobs, which is mostly attributable to their lower education and limited wage bargaining power. This proportion rises to 90% or so not long after. The figures are similar for females.

What about their children, who are more likely to stay permanently in the US? Second-generation migrants currently make up about 15% of US teenagers. Nearly all will stay in the US and pay taxes like anyone else. Statistical analysis finds that

- 2nd-generation immigrants generally have more education (0.4−0.5 years on average) than kids born to US natives.
- 2nd-generation immigrant males are considerably more likely to work than lower-skilled native males. This situation exists also for 3rd-generation immigrant females.
- 2nd-generation immigrants make somewhat higher wages than similar natives, attributable to their greater educational status. This difference tends to be even larger at the 3rd-generation. After that, there is full assimilation and wage differences disappear.

It is interesting that these general patterns have existed for many waves of legal immigrants from different locations over many years. It is also true for Hispanic immigrants today.

Immigrant claims on public services

Question 5: Do immigrants use up large amounts of public services? It is generally believed that immigrants use up more public services, such as health care, education, and the criminal justice system, than they pay in taxes. But is it true? First, consider some basic observations.

1. Immigrants are younger and more likely to work on average than natives. Those who work do pay taxes, even if here illegally, unless they are in the informal economy.
2. Since immigrants are considerably younger on average, they tend to use fewer health resources.

3. Unskilled and illegal immigrants are disproportionately males traveling alone (except quite recently) so they have fewer demands on K-12 education.
4. Immigrants are statistically not more likely to commit violent crimes than are natives.
5. Immigrants generally do not move in disproportionate numbers to locations (states and cities) where welfare support is the highest. The most careful statistical evidence finds that they go where the job opportunities are greatest. Often, these cities pay higher benefits, so the correlation is largely spurious.

Immigrants and taxes

Question 6: Do immigrants pay taxes?
The first question to address is whether immigrants are required to pay income taxes to their home or host nations. The laws on this vary a lot across countries.

The United States taxes the incomes of even temporary immigrants, including illegal immigrants, to the extent they work in the formal sector. (The Internal Revenue Service operates independently of the immigration control authorities.)

Overall, surveys show that immigrants are net contributors to the social welfare system, meaning overall they pay more taxes than they cost in public services. This may not be true in smaller towns near the Mexican border, which may bear a high public-cost burden until migrants move on. It is often the case that the greater fiscal costs are incurred by immigrant-source countries, which find it difficult to tax incomes earned abroad and may not even tax incoming remittances.

Migration and remittances

Question 7: Are remittances a major feature of the global economy?
Labor remittances are large and important income transfers. In current dollar terms, total migrant remittances to developing countries rose from around $60 billion in 1990 to around $550 billion in 2019.

Table 11.1   Net worker remittances for selected countries.

2015: Inflows and Outflows of Labor Remittances (Current US$ millions)

Source: World Bank, Migration and Remittances Data

Country	Inflows	Outflows	Net	GNI Current US$	Net/GNI%
El Salvador	$4,288	$74	$4,214	$24,962	16.88
Jamaica	$2,361	$287	$2,074	$13,747	15.09
Philippines	$29,799	$153	$29,646	$354,144	8.37
Yemen	$3,351	$333	$3,018	$36,380	8.30
Egypt	$18,325	$623	$17,702	$326,997	5.41
Mexico	$26,233	$811	$25,422	$1,143,815	2.22
Romania	$3,085	$526	$2,559	$173,768	1.47
Germany	$16,133	$19,170	−$3,037	$3,437,869	−0.09
US	$6,562	$62,501	−$55,939	$18,581,144	−0.30

Source: World Bank, *World Development Indicators* databank.

(Such data for every country are available on the World Bank World Development Indicators website.)

In contrast, total foreign assistance from all rich-country donors to developing countries was about $155 billion in 2015 (OECD data). This is a notable figure, but it is swamped by remittances.

Table 11.1 shows remittances for selected countries in 2015. It shows that small countries with significant workers abroad may receive remittances amounting to 15% or more of gross national income.

Brain drain versus brain gain

Question 8: Does out-migration from poor countries reduce human capital there?

"Brain drain" refers to the idea that it is the most skilled, educated, and entrepreneurial among workers who leave poor countries to migrate to rich countries. This is often true, in part because of immigration preferences in rich countries for high-skilled workers.

The obvious concern about brain drain is the potential loss of human capital at home, which is a direct loss in productive capacity, if not GNI. But there are other concerns:

- BD may have negative spillover effects in reducing the productivity of those who remain at home.
- Emigration of health professionals could lower source-country health status by reducing the supply of doctors and nurses.

These impacts are often assumed to be pervasive in poor countries and support calls for limiting outward skilled-labor mobility. Many policymakers in source countries call for rich-country governments to compensate them for these transferred skills.

Economists have often called for a "brain tax" to help pay these costs. This would be a special tax on the incomes of higher-skilled professional, managerial, and engineering workers, with the proceeds sent back to source countries.

But here is one big qualification. More recent thinking and analysis suggest that a "brain gain" is perhaps more likely in the source nations.

The opportunity of educated professionals to move abroad for higher wages and better working conditions can induce more young people to invest in schooling, resulting in a higher home stock of educated labor on net. Microeconomic evidence suggests that this impact is large enough to offset, with a time lag, the direct impacts of out-movements on human capital (see Docquier and Rapoport, *Journal of Economic Literature*, 2012). Thus, the costs and benefits of brain drain remain a wide-open issue in economics.

Further notes on skilled immigration

There is ample evidence that technically skilled immigrants (scientists, engineers, managers, PhD students, and so on) contribute disproportionately to the creation of knowledge and innovation in the countries where they settle. For example, such immigrants are important in creating basic knowledge. Since 2000, 39% of US-resident Nobel Prize winners in chemistry, medicine, and physics were foreign-born.

The foreign-born in the US achieve patents (innovation) and start businesses at rates at least as high as similarly skilled US natives (Hunt and Gauthier-Loiselle, *American Economic Journal: Macroeconomics*, 2010). Interestingly, in this area, more high-skilled immigration does seem to reduce wage growth marginally for natives also engaged in high-skilled and technical activities (Borjas, *American Economic Review*, 2005). Overall, most economists see significant net benefits from this kind of immigration and argue for a more open visa policy for highly skilled workers.

Chapter 12

Foreign Direct Investment, Offshoring, and Global Supply Chains

Introduction

Characteristics of foreign direct investment

An international investment is called foreign direct investment (FDI) if the investor acquires a substantial controlling interest in a foreign firm or builds a subsidiary in a foreign country. Most FDI involves mergers with or acquisitions of (M&A) existing facilities. Since FDI results in a parent firm, say in the United States, owning production facilities in foreign countries, such firms are called *multinational enterprises* (MNEs). The essential difference between FDI and portfolio investment is that FDI involves acquiring an ability to control foreign management, while portfolio investment does not.

An interesting initial question is "How much ownership confers management control?" Countries have different standards on this issue. The US standard is that FDI must procure ownership of at least 10% of a foreign affiliate by a domestic enterprise or at least 10% ownership of a domestic facility by a foreign enterprise. This means that a US firm could be both an affiliate of a foreign MNE and an MNE itself, with affiliates in foreign countries.

In practice, significant equity is usually purchased in a takeover, averaging 80% for US FDI abroad and foreign FDI in the US.

However, this depends on government regulations. For example, the US only allows foreign firms to own up to a 25% voting interest in any US air carrier without special authorization. There are complex restrictions on the operations of foreign firms in the US banking and financial markets. It is still common in developing and emerging countries to limit foreign equity in many sectors to 49%.

It is important to note that most financing for building and expanding affiliates abroad is raised on local capital markets. The implication is that FDI does not really constitute a transfer of financial capital abroad. Rather, FDI involves ownership and management decisions.

This means that FDI is based on strategic and structural factors, discussed later in these notes. FDI flows rarely come into a country and then leave quickly. Rather, MNEs tend to retain their local operations for a long time once they have been located. Thus, FDI is different from portfolio investment, which can move in and out of a country quickly.

The extent of FDI differs markedly by industry. It is greatest in banking, finance, tourism, mining, and manufacturing sectors in which *knowledge capital*, which refers to innovations, product quality, and technology, is important. The last fact supports the view that, in large part, *MNEs are channels for transferring knowledge and technologies abroad.* They do so by implementing their proprietary technologies into the production processes of foreign subsidiaries and affiliates.

There is also much FDI in consumer products in which consistent quality is important and consumers know what to expect when they buy a service or product. This feature explains why major American MNEs include McDonald's, Kentucky Fried Chicken, Starbucks, Disney, and Nike.

A final characteristic to emphasize is that most MNEs are very large corporations, with global sales in the hundreds of billions of dollars. Some of the biggest MNEs are General Electric, Siemens, Royal Dutch Shell, Ford Motor, Exxon, General Motors, Google, Microsoft, Apple, IBM, Toyota, Volkswagen, Mitsubishi, Mobil, and Nestle. And major international banks, such as JP Morgan, Citigroup, HSBC, and Mitsubishi, are top MNEs.

Intra-firm Economic Integration

Types of international integration within firms

An MNE is a firm with productive activities located in at least two different nations. These activities could include management, R&D, technical services, resource extraction, production, distribution, and wholesale or retail sales.

Thus, *MNEs are firms that integrate activities across borders but within the enterprise.* Broadly, MNEs may be integrated horizontally, vertically, or both.

Horizontal integration means that an MNE produces similar goods, such as cars, at different locations. In principle, it is no different from doing so within a single country, such as General Motors producing cars at many US plants. The differences are that (1) global production may be more efficient due to cost differences and expanded markets; and (2) there are more regulations and uncertainty facing transborder production.

Horizontal MNEs are the FDI version of intra-industry trade. There are large volumes of "intra-industry FDI" among similar companies that invest in multiple countries. For example, Ford produces cars in both the US and Germany, while Volkswagen produces in both countries as well. Like IIT, horizontal FDI is dominated by two-way investment among MNEs in developed countries, though this is changing as China and other emerging economies become greater sources of FDI.

Vertical integration means producing goods at different stages of an overall production process. Thus, an MNE might extract iron ore in one location, produce steel in another, and assemble cars in a third location. Or it might perform R&D for developing computers in one place, produce components such as semiconductors and glass displays in other countries, and assemble them in yet another location.

Many vertically integrated activities take place within the boundaries of a specific global firm. In this case, the activities are "internalized" within the firm.

However, to the extent that a vertical MNE ships tasks (and jobs) to their affiliates and other firms abroad, they are engaged in *offshoring*. Offshoring refers to producing tasks outside the headquarters country, whether within the MNE at affiliates or with unaffiliated contract producers.

To the extent that an MNE contracts with unrelated firms to provide inputs and services that they might otherwise have done within the firm, they are engaged in *outsourcing*. Such activities are *externalized* outside the firm but subject to contractual relationships. The tasks of producing inputs, assembly, and so on could be outsourced to firms in the headquarters country or to foreign firms as a form of offshoring.

In a way, vertical outsourcing is the opposite of vertically integrated firms because they split up (or "fragment") production stages across borders and among firms, many of which are not affiliates of the parent. In this case, the firm is "externalizing" its production stages.

Some MNEs, such as those in tourism services and consumer goods, are largely horizontally integrated. Others, such as those in mineral extraction, petroleum, and textiles and apparel, are largely vertically integrated.

However, producers of complex goods, such as autos, machinery, and chemicals, engage in both horizontal and vertical production. For example, while it is true that global automobile firms perform final assembly of vehicles in multiple countries (a form of horizontal integration), they also have extensive networks of input suppliers in different locations (a form of vertical integration). For such reasons, economists sometimes refer to the operations of MNEs as *complex integration*.

As discussed in earlier chapters, globalization since the 1990s has encouraged an extreme form of offshoring and outsourcing, called *global supply chains or vertical production networks*. In these chains, the parent company contracts with large numbers of both owned and unaffiliated suppliers at different production stages. More perspective on offshoring and outsourcing through such supply chains is offered later in this chapter.

Study question 1

Which of the following statements about FDI is not true?

A. If a foreign firm acquires at least 10% of an American facility, it is considered FDI under the US definition.
B. Outsourcing is a form of vertical integration within MNEs.
C. An MNE with both horizontal and vertical production is engaged in complex production.
D. Horizontal integration applies mainly to consumer goods and services, such as fast food, tourism, and banking.

Discussion of study question 1

The correct answer is B. Outsourcing is in fact a form of vertical fragmentation, not integration. A is correct under US standards. C is correct, for it describes complex production. D is correct because horizontal integration refers to producing a similar good at multiple locations, generating intra-industry FDI.

Explaining Why There are MNEs

FDI involves high costs

Turn next to the basic question of why multinational enterprises exist at all and the logic underlying foreign direct investment. The answers may seem obvious but in fact are subtle.

Theories of FDI must explain why a firm would engage in FDI and international integration when there are clear cost disadvantages to doing so. These disadvantages include the following, among others:

- high fixed costs of investing in subsidiaries and building plants and distribution systems;
- additional communication and transport costs across distance;

- difficult language barriers and cultural differences;
- the need to pay higher wages to managers from headquarters countries to induce them to move and work abroad;
- limited understanding of local markets, tax laws, regulations, and business practices;
- risks of expropriation, in which the host government takes over or nationalizes your operation, and other forms of policy discrimination;
- risks that local firms in destination countries will imitate the technologies and products offered by MNEs;
- exchange rate volatility, which generates unpredictability in future costs and profits when measured in the parent company's home currency.

Such problems do not face domestic competing firms in the countries where FDI is made to nearly the same extent. So why would MNEs subject themselves to these higher costs and structural problems?

The OLI framework

These extra costs imply that *a necessary condition for a firm to become an MNE is that it has (large) compensating advantages over local firms.* The standard theory that economists use to define and explain these advantages relates to *advantages of ownership, location, and internalization (OLI), as set out by John Dunning in a book titled "International Production and the Multinational Enterprise"* (1981). MNEs can make sufficient profits due to these advantages that it is worthwhile absorbing the additional costs and uncertainties of FDI.

The following notes briefly summarize the OLI framework:

Ownership advantages

Ownership advantages of the MNE refer to some proprietary advantage it owns that a local firm would not have. Ownership advantages are characteristics of the firm.

In the great majority of situations, these refer to some technological advantage, such as a superior production process, better management systems, new products, and a reputation for high quality. These advantages allow MNEs to produce at lower cost than local firms, command market loyalty among consumers, or enjoy the ability to price higher-quality goods at high-profit markups. These advantages are often called *knowledge-based assets* (KBAs). Thus, ownership advantages provide profit margins that permit firms to engage in foreign production and absorb the higher costs of doing so.

Further, these advantages provide some *monopoly power* for MNEs because they may be hard for local firms to imitate. This market power is enhanced to the extent the advantages are protected by local intellectual property rights (IPRs), such as patents, trademarks, and copyrights, and other regulations protecting exclusive rights to use the ownership advantages. These policies raise the costs of copying and imitation by local firms, raising the incentives for MNEs to invest. This logic helps explain why IPRs are so important in the debate over globalization of trade and investment markets.

Here is a critical insight that is the basis for why ownership advantages support MNEs. One major reason for the emergence of MNEs is the fact that "headquarter knowledge services", such as R&D investments, marketing, and engineering, may be performed in one place (or a few places) but the results of those services, such as a blueprint, a formula, a new technology, and new products developed by R&D, may be used in several production locations without having to do the R&D over again.

In economic terms, *R&D is a public input*, in that the knowledge it produces supports production not at one location but rather can be used by many affiliates without diminishing the value of the R&D. In fact, because R&D is privately performed and its results are privately owned, it is often called a "quasi-public input".

This ability to do R&D and other parent company services once and then share the knowledge across affiliates is a huge advantage because it removes the need to replicate those costs in different locations. That generates significant economies of scale for MNEs that do not exist for local firms.

Thus, many MNEs develop new technologies in the headquarters country and then produce in several locations using those technologies. Again, this logic points out that the main economic function of many MNEs is to transfer technology abroad.

Location advantages

Location advantages are features of host countries that make integrated production in those countries more profitable than simply exporting goods to them. Location advantages are characteristics of countries.

The primary location factors that attract FDI, as identified by economists, are the following:

1. Productive inputs that are readily available at low cost. A major reason for vertical integration is that MNEs need secure access to raw materials, say in the mining and chemical sectors, and to inexpensive labor for labor-intensive input production and assembly.

2. Large market size, which could refer to the size of the country where FDI takes place or to that market plus nearby countries where the affiliate could sell its products. For example, a major reason for considerable FDI in Turkey is its proximity to the EU market.

   An obvious variant is that a preferential trade area generates a large joint market size across member countries. This large market size is a significant factor in attracting FDI to Mexico within USMCA (NAFTA), both from the partner countries the US and Canada and from countries outside the agreement.

3. High transport costs and trade barriers can encourage foreign firms to establish or acquire production facilities behind the tariff barriers.

   This "tariff-jumping" was an important reason for American FDI in the Common Market (now EU) in its earlier years, Japanese FDI in the US in the 1980s, and in many other cases. Development economists thought high import barriers would attract FDI in manufacturing sectors to developing countries in the 1960s and 1970s. It is debatable whether attracting FDI through this costly approach was beneficial. The consensus among economists now is that high trade barriers diminish the attractiveness of countries for FDI because they interfere with efficiently trading intermediate inputs in supply chains.

4. Government policies can encourage or discourage FDI. Examples are production subsidies and tax advantages to attract foreign investors. Whether countries competing in this way is beneficial or mutually destructive is an active topic of controversy at the WTO, in the EU, and elsewhere.

For example, US states sometimes pay big subsidies to encourage large international enterprises to invest in their cities and towns. The associated increase in jobs and perhaps tax revenues is seen as a benefit.

However, the evidence from economic studies suggests that there is often little net benefit from doing so. The reason is that states may outbid each other, offering subsidies (which must be paid by raising taxes on other residents and firms) that are larger than potential gains from attracting the FDI. This is an example of what economists call a "prisoner's-dilemma" outcome, in which states pay the costs and MNEs gain the benefits.

Internalization advantages

Recall that to "internalize" global production means to decide to keep production across facilities within the ownership and control of the MNE, rather than to work with independent contractors to outsource ("externalize") production.

Internalization advantages are factors that encourage firms to keep production within their own management and control. They are both country policies and characteristics of technologies. Internalization advantages are the most subtle, but also the most important, issue for explaining why MNEs exist.

Ownership and location advantages could explain why a firm would choose FDI over exporting its goods to a particular market.

But they do not explain why a firm would choose FDI over licensing the rights to use its technology or to make its products to unrelated firms in other countries.

To understand this, note that licensing provides revenues to innovative firms without exposing them to the costs of FDI and foreign production. If technology markets were perfect, the licensing revenues would be the same (in present value terms) as revenues from FDI and should be more profitable. So why is there so much FDI instead of licensing?

The reason is that licensing across borders involves its own difficult problems, primarily in defining and enforcing contracts:

First, it is hard to establish a market price for the license upfront. The firm receiving the license ("licensee") so that it can produce and sell in its own market may not know how much it is willing to pay before it knows how valuable the product is. And the firm selling the license ("licensor") will not reveal the value of its product without an enforceable license. If it did reveal its product or technology, the licensee could copy it without paying market value for the license.

Second, suppose a license is provided. Without well-defined and enforceable contracts, the licensee could "shirk" on the terms of the contract by

- Producing low-quality versions of the product, thereby diminishing the licensor's reputation for quality.
- Invading markets of other licensees, reducing those license fees to the originator.
- Selling the product or technology to other users, or simply copying it for its own use then abandoning the contract.

Such problems reduce the profitability of licensing. They are significant, especially for knowledge-based assets that have been licensed, such as new technologies and the rights to produce high-quality consumer products.

For such reasons, MNEs often find it more advantageous to engage in FDI, which gives them far more management control over local operations than does licensing. That is, they prefer to internalize production rather than outsource it.

This situation also provides an incentive for MNEs to use well-trained managers (often from their headquarters) to run the overseas facilities and to safeguard their technological advantages.

Over time, MNEs tend to train more managers from recipient countries and to make management more localized. This is one reason why MNEs tend to pay higher wages than do local firms producing competing goods. The MNE pays a wage premium to keep its local managers from revealing their technological secrets or starting new firms using that information.

And it explains again why local protection of IPRs is so important for attracting FDI in knowledge-based industries. But note the interesting implication that the stronger the domestic protection for IPRs and contracts, the more likely MNEs are to outsource (externalize) their production.

Study question 2

Indicate whether each of the following is an example of an ownership (*O*), location (*L*), or internalization (*I*) advantage:

A. Country chooses to join a preferential trade agreement _____
B. An MNE has a patent on a new product it can produce in multiple locations _____
C. An MNE in the pharmaceutical industry is concerned that its new medicines will be copied by local firms unless contracts are well enforced _____
D. A country is located far from the MNE's headquarters country _____

Discussion of study question 2

A is a location advantage in that it raises market size. B is an ownership advantage because the MNE can produce cheaply in several locations. C is an internalization advantage where contracts are enforced. D is a location advantage because the high transport costs related to distance encourage more FDI.

Offshoring, Jobs, and Inequality

Basic data

To understand the growth in vertical supply chains, consider trends in employment of foreign affiliates of US-based MNEs. Data from the US Department of Commerce show that over the period 2000–2014, there was relatively little employment growth in Canada and Europe, where FDI is largely horizontal in nature.

However, employment at US-owned affiliates increased by 43% in Mexico, 231% in the rest of Latin America, and 183% in Asia, reflecting the transfer of lower-skilled jobs to those locations within the production structure of vertical MNEs.

Another way to see growing production networks is through the rapid growth of two-way trade (IIT) in Table 12.1. It shows that Germany and Poland dramatically increased IIT in intermediate inputs, as did the US and Mexico, indicating a major growth in vertical supply chains between those pairs of countries.

Table 12.1 Trade growth (EX+IM) and IIT indexes in selected industries, 1995–2016.

	Germany–Poland			US–Mexico		
	Growth (%)	1995 IIT (%)	2016 IIT (%)	Growth (%)	1995 IIT (%)	2016 IIT (%)
Computers (HS 8471)	1523	3.9	93.1	1081	10.8	42.2
Motor Vehicles (HS 8703)	540	66.5	77.9	346	10.3	23.1
Motor Vehicle Parts (HS 8708)	5238	46.5	84.5	523	72.0	82.1

Source: Computed by author from United Nations Commodity Trade Statistics.

Vertical production, offshoring, and inequality

The growth of vertical supply chains is interesting in itself. But another important dimension is its potential impact on inequality.

In Chapter 5, it was noted that since the 1980s, trade liberalization and reduced trade costs have combined with technological change to generate growing income and wage inequality in rich countries. The fact that lower trade barriers and trade costs contribute to inequality in those countries is consistent with the Stolper–Samuelson (SS) theory because more openness to trade raises the real incomes of abundant factors, such as capital and technical skills, while reducing the real wages of scarce factors, such as lower-skilled labor.

However, it was also noted that wage inequality has risen in many developing and emerging countries in the same period, during which those countries also significantly cut their tariffs and other trade barriers. This outcome seems surprising, for the SS theorem should predict an increase in the real wages of low-skilled labor, an abundant factor in poor countries, and a fall in the real incomes of capital and skilled labor, which are scarce.

Several factors could help explain this apparent puzzle. The following notes focus on one critical answer:

The offshoring of employment from rich countries to emerging and developing economies may raise the demand for more skilled workers, compared with less skilled workers, in both regions.

It is possible to understand this outcome by studying a simple model of employment offshoring and labor skills. (As a reminder, "offshoring" means moving economic activity to other countries, whether to foreign affiliates within an MNE or through contracts with unaffiliated foreign suppliers.)

Here is a simple but powerful model that is consistent with data on vertical supply chains, employment, and wage inequality. Consider a complex final good, such as airplanes, automobiles, laptops, or even fashion apparel. These goods are produced with a large range of R&D, engineering, marketing, and management (together called "headquarters services"), raw materials, produced intermediate inputs, and assembly operations.

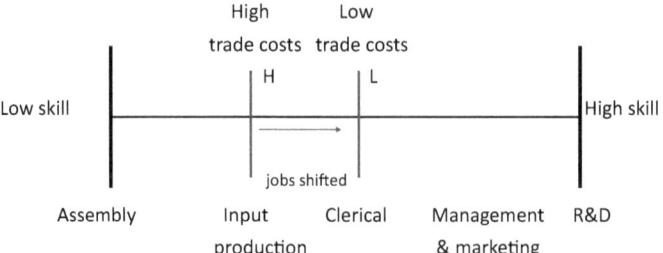

Figure 12.1   The vertical organization of production.

It is reasonable to suppose that these activities can be ranked from the most unskilled labor-intensive, such as sewing on buttons or assembling parts into a cell phone, to the most skilled labor-intensive, such as R&D, management, and marketing. These activities are ranked along a spectrum of skill intensity in Figure 12.1, from least skilled to most skilled.

Now, let there be two countries: high-skill abundant US and low-skill abundant Mexico. Suppose also that initially there are relatively high trade costs, as shown in vertical line H.

A multinational enterprise organizing vertical production would choose a dividing line H between activities that determines which activities will be offshored from the US to Mexico, given relatively high costs of trading goods across borders.

Thus, any job with skill requirements higher than those at H would be located in the US. These would be R&D, management, clerical work, and some medium-skilled component production. Activities with lower skill requirements would be located in Mexico. These would be assembly and somewhat lower-skilled component outputs.

The key thing to understand is that *within each country, the activities located there are still ranked from low-skill-intensive to high-skill-intensive.* They are just different activities within the vertical production chain, with production location determined by skill rankings.

Now, suppose that due to tariff cuts, lower shipping costs, and improved communication technologies, the costs of trading across borders fall to a low level, indicated by vertical line L. This cut in costs would induce the MNE to shift an additional margin of activities, say most clerical work and some management and marketing tasks, from the US to Mexico. This would be the process of offshoring jobs due to lower trade costs.

But the implication is that jobs seen as low-skilled or medium-skilled in the US are shifted to Mexico, where they are at the high end of the skill ranking. The US ends up more specialized in high-skilled activities, which is expected. *But from its standpoint, Mexico also sees employment growth in relatively high-skilled activities.*

In brief, *both countries end up producing a range of activities that are more skill-intensive than they were before the cut in trade costs.* This outcome can be translated into demand for workers of various skill types and the effects on relative wages.

In the US, there is an increase in the demand for high-skilled workers compared to low-skilled and medium-skilled laborers, raising relative wages for skilled employees and reducing them for others. This is a component of growing inequality.

In Mexico, there is an increase in the demand for medium-skilled workers compared to low-skilled workers, but these medium-skilled workers are among the most skilled. Thus, the relative wages of medium-skilled laborers rise there, generating more wage inequality.

Again, the key insight here is that vertical production chains may be organized and ranked from the least-skilled to the most-skilled activities, involving both inputs and outputs. The margin of jobs that is shifted through offshoring is in the middle, raising the skill intensity of production in both countries after tariffs are cut.

This does not happen in the SS model, where both goods are final products produced only by primary inputs (labor and capital). In that theory, there is no R&D, marketing, or trade in intermediate inputs, which together permit vertical organization of production across borders.

Study question 3

Offshoring is the process of moving stages of vertical production chains across borders as the cost of trading goods falls. This transfer can raise wage inequality in both rich countries and developing and emerging countries if:

A. Production is capital-intensive at all stages.
B. The different countries have different rankings of how skill-intensive various production activities are.
C. The chain of activities can be ranked across countries from least skill-intensive to most skill-intensive.
D. Lower trade costs move both types of countries toward more skill-intensive production.
E. Both C and D.

Discussion of study question 3

The answer is E. C must be true for lower trade costs to shift a margin of medium-skilled activities from rich nations to developing nations. But these activities are at the low end of the skill ranking in rich countries and at the high end of the skill ranking in developing countries. And D is the outcome of that process, generating relatively higher wages for more skilled workers in both types of countries.

A is false because activities would vary in capital intensity at different stages. B is false because activities need to have similar skill rankings across activities when compared between countries for offshoring to generate inequality.

Benefits and Costs of FDI

Potential benefits of FDI

FDI and the operations of MNEs have always been a controversial topic. As always in economics, whether they are beneficial or harmful in welfare terms depends on circumstances. Here are some key issues that matter for this question.

The potential gains of FDI to the recipient countries include the following:

- First, FDI brings superior technology. Access to modern international technologies is a key factor in determining the growth rates of developing countries. Solid empirical evidence finds that productivity gains in local subsidiaries and independent firms that supply incoming MNEs with their inputs can amount to more than half the technological improvements of developing countries.
- Second, FDI expands intra-firm trade, meaning more within-MNE trade in R&D, intermediate inputs, and final goods. This possibility allows greater specialization, which is efficient.
- Third, FDI increases competition for local firms and generates dynamic gains from trade and investment. Some firms may shut down, but others become more productive, a rationalization gain.
- Fourth, there are spillover benefits from training technical managers and expanding employment in the formal sector, both of which come with FDI. These workers gain more skills, which can be used more broadly in the economy.
- Fifth, there is the possibility that governments may use policies to attract FDI to achieve certain desirable outcomes, such as regional employment.

Potential costs of FDI

MNEs have long been harshly criticized for their operations in developing countries. This criticism seems largely to be in opposition to large MNEs that exploit local natural resources, without paying much in taxes. Such operations can certainly be harmful.

There are other potential costs:

First, there is the possibility of monopolization by large foreign firms that could charge high prices while refusing to pay extraction fees for natural resources or taxes. Such problems are more likely in small countries with limited abilities to regulate MNEs.

Second, many MNEs may operate in isolation without offering much technical training or knowledge spillovers. This kind of "enclave" production is most likely in extractive industries, such as mining and petroleum. It does not transfer many benefits other than revenues for domestic governments.

Third, MNEs might transfer inappropriate technologies, meaning older or excessively capital-intensive technologies, to poor and labor-abundant nations. This situation may not generate much domestic employment or technology transfer.

Fourth, MNEs are likely to repatriate their profits to shareholders in other countries. In principle, this is not a significant problem because MNEs would not invest if they could not earn some economic returns over the high costs of FDI and those returns ultimately must be paid to shareholders.

However, some MNEs may artificially make profits through the process of transfer pricing, in which artificial within-firm prices are set in order to minimize global tax liabilities. An example would be a firm that charges itself a high price for an input in a high-tax economy in order to make low profits (or even losses) on paper there, incurring a low tax liability. Such practices evade taxes, are inefficient, and cost countries some sovereignty in setting independent tax policies.

Transfer pricing is especially common in industries with extensive intellectual property. US tax law permits companies such as Apple and Microsoft to declare that the tax home of their intellectual property assets is in another country. For example, Ireland is famous for having very low taxes on high-tech production and capital assets. So, these companies can avoid US taxes by declaring another country as their tax base, even if the intellectual property is developed and mostly used in the US. This and similar issues are currently the focus of considerable international policy discussion.

Chapter 13

The Basics of International Finance

International Trade: A Brief Recap

The previous chapter completed the study of international trade in goods and factors. Before moving on, it is useful to summarize the main concepts learned here:

1. Trade exists primarily because of comparative advantage, which depends on the following:

   a. technology and productivity differences;
   b. factor endowment differences;
   c. consumer preferences, such as tastes for variety;
   d. economies of scale.

2. There are many sources of gains from trade and FDI, including efficient specialization, lower import costs, greater variety for consumers, economies of scale, production rationalization, and better access to international technologies.

3. Trade can affect income distribution, making some people better off and some worse off. Mainly, this reflects the fact that trade in goods substitutes for trade in factors: If labor and capital cannot move internationally, exports and imports that heavily embody abundant and scarce factors, respectively, will change the demands for factors.

4. Government policies, such as tariffs and export subsidies, can change trade volumes but do not necessarily raise economic welfare.
5. Trade barriers are usually harmful and redistribute income from consumers and input users to protected producers. Import barriers tend to be regressive by harming lower-income households more than others.
6. Trade barriers are high-cost and indirect policies to achieve non-economic objectives and address market failures.
7. There is a need for multilateral trade rules, such as those established in the WTO and PTAs, to sustain relatively open trade and non-discriminatory policies.
8. PTAs may or may not expand economic welfare when a comparison is made between the gains from trade creation and losses from trade diversion. PTAs may be negotiated for additional reasons that can be beneficial, such as expanding market sizes and encouraging more inward FDI.
9. Labor and capital mobility also generate gains in welfare in both source and destination nations by relocating factors from less productive to more productive countries. But they also may redistribute income between labor and capital in both countries.
10. Multinational enterprises engage in foreign direct investment, which largely shifts technological knowledge abroad, raising global efficiency.
11. Offshoring jobs through FDI can be efficient, but it also redistributes income by reducing the demand for lower-skilled labor in parent countries. It can also raise inequality in countries to which activities are offshored in vertical production networks.

Introduction to International Finance

International finance (also called international monetary economics) studies how global financial markets operate and how macroeconomic factors, including exchange rates and monetary policies, interact across borders.

We study this material to understand several key questions, including the following:

1. Why do countries have trade surpluses and deficits or, more importantly, why do they have "current account" surpluses and deficits?
2. Why and how do countries borrow and lend in international markets? The essential reason is to finance imbalances in the current account, but there are also other important factors.
3. How are exchange rates determined in the short run and long run and how do they affect economic activity?
4. What are the major differences between fixed and floating exchange rates and how do they affect international economic activity?
5. How do governments make macroeconomic policy when there are many interrelated countries—a process called "open economy" policymaking?

Two big issues at the core of international finance are as follows:

1. international borrowing and lending;
2. determination and operation of exchange rates.

Big issue 1: International borrowing and lending

The text so far has considered countries trading goods across borders ("trade across space") within a particular time period, such as a year. The models assumed that a country's trade is balanced in each period in order to avoid incorporating how to pay for a trade deficit. However, the idea that countries have balanced commodity trade in each year is obviously false.

In fact, countries also "trade across time". This means, for example, that a nation may wish in some periods to buy more goods and services than it produces, thereby running current-account (CA) deficits. But this excess consumption today ultimately must be paid for in the future by running CA surpluses. In essence, such countries are borrowing today and repaying later. This idea introduces several important elements.

As noted, countries may import more goods and services (in dollar terms) than they export in a year. This is a CA deficit, which will be studied closely. These CA deficits must be financed by borrowing from abroad, which requires selling more domestic assets to foreign investors than buying foreign assets from them. Other countries are international lenders because they export more goods and services than they import, generating a CA surplus. These CA surpluses arise because an economy earns more income by selling goods and services abroad than it pays to foreigners by purchasing them from abroad. This excess income is lent abroad by virtue of domestic investors purchasing more foreign assets than foreigners purchase of domestic assets.

Keep in mind that it is not actually countries that do this, but the collection of individuals, firms, and organizations (including governments) engaged in buying and selling goods and services that determines whether a country is an international borrower or lender.

Consider some practical examples to help understand these processes:

1. College students typically borrow now to fund their college education. They are making a short-term investment (paying tuition) in order to raise their long-term earnings, permitting repayment of their student loans. Note that the students are consuming goods and services (e.g., education) in excess of their current income. This means they are "importing" (in consumption goods and education) more than they are "exporting" (whatever income they get from working or grants.) Students must finance the difference by borrowing the necessary funds and, at some point, they must pay the funds back.

2. Suppose that a firm wants to build a new factory to use a new technology. It believes that future sales will pay enough to cover these initial costs, so the firm is willing to borrow the funds now and commit to future repayment. If many firms are doing this, the economy would likely need more investment funds than those generated by domestic savings and the economy would have to borrow from foreign markets. The firms may have no idea that

they are using foreign funds because they get loans from their banks, but those banks could be borrowing from foreign savers and financial institutions.

3. In contrast, imagine an economy that is in an economic recession. Domestic firms would not want to expand investments and consumers would reduce their demand for goods and services. Then the demand for funds would be small relative to domestic savings and this economy would be in a position to lend its surplus savings abroad. But that would mean it has a trade (CA) surplus because of its low imports compared to exports.

The essence of these examples is "trade across time". In some years, economies may have good reasons to import more goods and services than they export, running a CA deficit. But that must be financed through current international borrowing.

Other economies in some years may have good reasons to export more goods and services than they import, running a CA surplus. That results in current international lending.

Ultimately, the first group of countries must repay this borrowing by converting to CA surpluses. The second group ultimately will end up being paid back, which means converting to CA deficits. This last concept is sometimes referred to as a country's "intertemporal budget constraint".

This logic means that international finance permits countries to borrow in periods when they need excess funds and lend in periods when they generate excess domestic funds. This process is efficient in moving loanable funds and assets from where they are in surplus to where they are in demand.

Intertemporal trade, reflected in CA deficits and surpluses, and financed by borrowing and lending, makes economies better off for many reasons. Here are three of the main gains from such trade:

1. Countries are not constrained to have balanced trade every period.
2. Rapidly growing economies (e.g., emerging countries) can invest heavily in productive resources in the short run, building future productive capacity and raising incomes and living standards. This would be considerably more difficult if individuals, firms,

and governments in those economies were forced to borrow only from the limited domestic savings pools.

3. International borrowing and lending permit countries to smooth out their consumption over time. If there is a short-term downturn due to a recession or natural disaster in a country, domestic agents can sustain living standards by borrowing from abroad and running a trade deficit.

The task in the following chapters will be to figure out what determines these choices.

Study question 1

The possibility of intertemporal borrowing and lending offers the following benefits to a country except:

A. By borrowing now, a country can invest heavily in production capacity in current periods and generate the ability to pay off those loans later.
B. A country can run CA deficits indefinitely without having to pay off the borrowing those deficits imply.
C. A country can smooth its consumption over time through foreign borrowing and lending.
D. A country with excess domestic funds from savings can lend them productively abroad.

Discussion of question 1

The correct answer is B, a country cannot borrow indefinitely. In principle, a country must eventually pay off the funds it borrows from abroad, by switching from CA deficits to CA surpluses. This is the idea of the intertemporal budget constraint.

A is a true statement, for international financial markets allow high investment needs to be financed by borrowing.

C is a true statement, for a country in an output recession can largely sustain its consumption path by borrowing from abroad.

D is also true for such high-saving countries would be able to lend excess funds to borrowers abroad and expect a return on those loans in future periods.

Big issue 2: Countries have different currencies

The fact that countries have different currencies means that for international trade in goods, services, or financial assets to occur, the currencies must be exchanged for each other.

An *exchange rate* is the price of one country's currency in terms of another country's currency. There are several important concepts of exchange rates. The following definitions are useful at this point:

- The *bilateral exchange rate* is the cost of one currency in units of another. Suppose $1\pounds = \$1.50$. This is the *dollar price of a pound*. Thus, $E = \$1.50/\pounds$ is the price of a pound in terms of dollars. Note that this implies the pound price of the dollar is $1/E = 1/1.50 = \pounds0.67/\$$.
- A trade-weighted exchange rate or an *effective exchange rate* is an index of bilateral exchange rates for a particular currency, with the weights based on a country's trade shares with its trading partner. This is generally a good measure of how expensive or cheap a currency is in world trade, as seen in later notes.
- A *real exchange rate* adjusts bilateral exchange rates (or effective exchange rates) for differences in price levels or differences in inflation rates across countries. This concept is important in comparing the costs of living across countries, as will be studied later.

Other concepts of the exchange rate will be discussed as we move forward.

Also important is the fact that countries must decide whether to permit the value of their currencies to be variable or fixed in terms of other currencies.

A country has a *flexible exchange rate* if the value of its currency is permitted to vary in international financial markets in response to changes in supply and demand for the currency. A country has a *fixed exchange rate* if its policy is to sustain the currency's value rigidly in terms of another currency (e.g., the dollar or euro) or a basket of currencies. Between these extremes are various hybrid policies, such as a *managed exchange rate*, under which a currency's value is permitted to vary within certain limits over time.

Several countries may choose to adopt a policy in which all their currencies are held constant relative to each other. The primary historical example of a *fixed exchange-rate system* was the classical "gold standard" that existed prior to World War 2. In today's world economy, a prominent example is the policy of several European countries jointly to adopt the euro as their common currency.

As will be studied, a country's choice of exchange-rate policy (fixed, flexible, or a mixture) is a critical component of its overall monetary policy. That is, policy decisions to change the money supply can affect currency values, with different outcomes under flexible versus fixed rates.

Basic Facts and Data about Exchange Rates

Bilateral exchange rates

Following are figures and charts of some key bilateral exchange rates with the US$. Some market spot exchange rates as of 6:00 pm Eastern Standard Time January 25, 2022 (*Source*: http://www.x-rates.com/) showing dollar prices for the currencies are given here:

- Canadian dollar (C$) = 0.7918 ($0.7918 per C$) => 1/(0.7918) = C$1.2629/$ is C$ price of $.
- British pound (£) = 1.3505 ($1.3505 per £) => 1/(1.3505) = £0.7405/$ is £ price of $.
- Euro (€) = 1.1302 ($1.1302 per €) => 1/(1.1302) = €0.8848/$ is € price of $.
- Japanese yen (¥) = 0.0088 ($0.0088 per ¥) => 1/0.0088 = ¥113.8699/$ is ¥ price of $.
- Chinese yuan (RMB, or C¥) = 0.1581 ($0.1581 per C¥) => 1/0.1581 = C¥ 6.3264/$ is C¥ price of $. RMB refers to "Renminbi".

If the price of a currency is rising, we call it an *appreciating* currency.

If the price of a currency is falling, we call it a *depreciating* currency.

Note: On June 9, 2020, the yuan rate was C¥ 7.0779/$. Did the yuan appreciate or depreciate relative to the dollar in the period from then to January 25, 2022? (*Answer*: The yuan appreciated because it took fewer yuan to buy a dollar on January 25, 2022. This may be seen also through the dollar price of the yuan, which rose from 1/7.0779 = $0.1413 to $0.1581). Finally, note that if the yuan is appreciating, it means it costs more dollars per yuan. This means that the dollar depreciates at the same time relative to the yuan.

The next three charts show recent variations in certain bilateral exchange rates with the US dollar.

Figure 13.1 shows the weekly average dollar price of the euro, or $/€, from 2017 to early 2022. These currencies are freely flexible

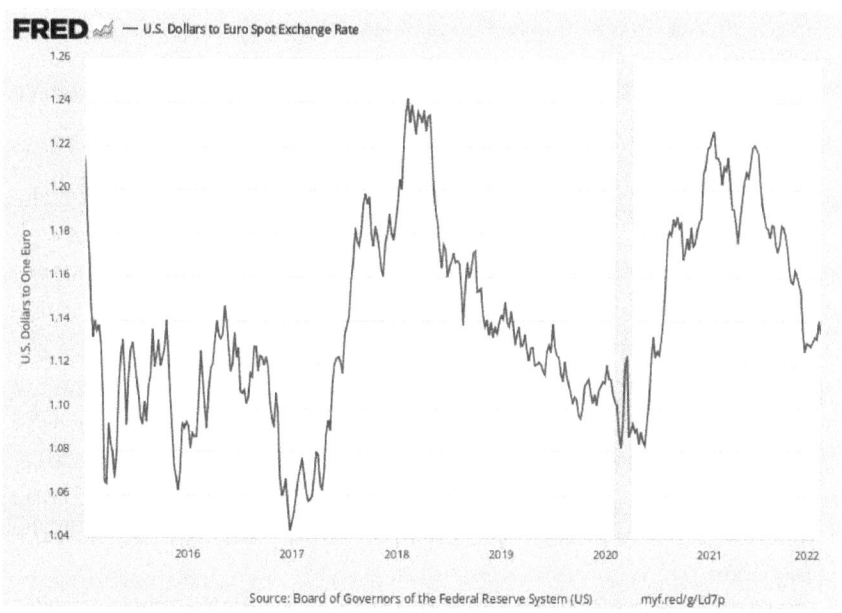

Figure 13.1   The dollar price of the euro, weekly from 2015 to early 2022.

Source: Federal Reserve Bank of St. Louis FRED database, at https://fred. stlouisfed.org/series/DEXUSEU.

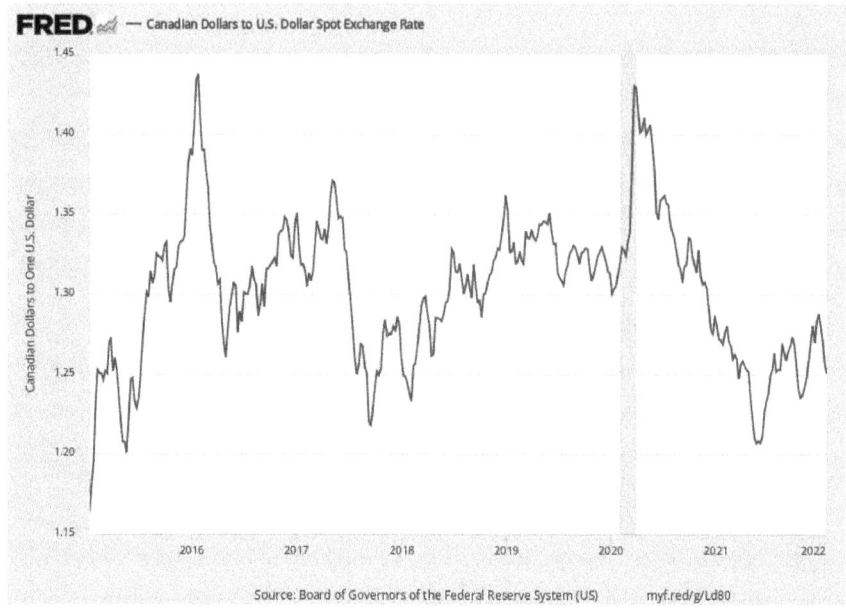

Figure 13.2 The Canadian dollar price of the US dollar, weekly from 2015 to early 2022.

Source: Federal Reserve Bank of St. Louis FRED database, at https://fred. stlouisfed.org/series/DEXCAUS.

against each other. The chart shows a sharp appreciation of the euro in 2017 and 2018, followed by a gradual depreciation through late 2020, and then another appreciation. Later chapters will study why currencies fluctuate like that. Note also there is considerable variability in the weekly exchange rates.

Figure 13.2 shows the weekly price of the US dollar in terms of the Canadian dollar, which float freely against each other. The US$ appreciated dramatically (and the C$ depreciated) in 2015–2016, with the opposite happening in 2021. Note the large appreciation of the US$ in early 2020, corresponding to the onset of the COVID-19 pandemic.

Figure 13.3 depicts the monthly price of the US dollar in terms of the Chinese yuan (RMB). In 1994, the Chinese government announced a substantial devaluation of the yuan, from about 5.7 C¥ per $ to about 8.7 C¥ per $. As will be studied later, this change

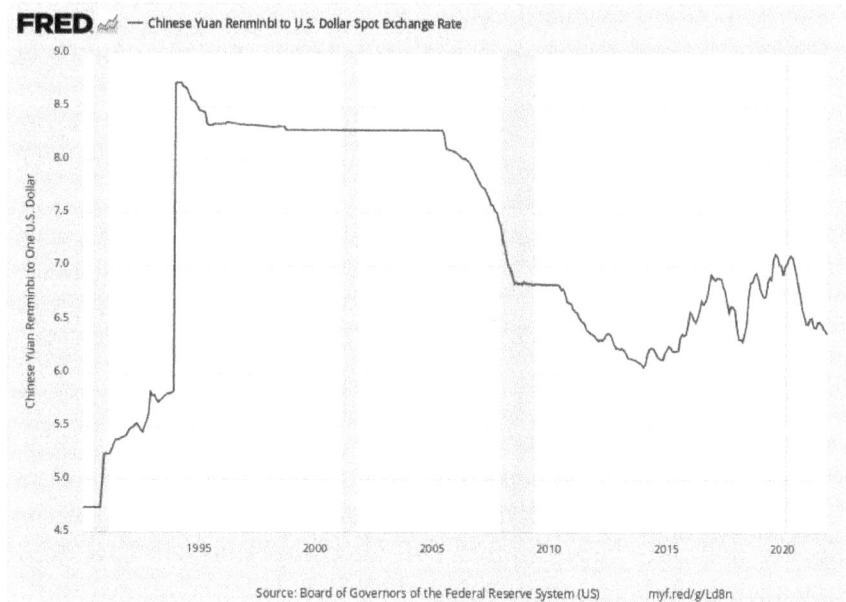

Figure 13.3 Chinese yuan (RMB) per US dollar, monthly from 1990 to early 2022.
Source: Federal Reserve Bank of St. Louis FRED database, at https://fred.stlouisfed.org/series/DEXCHUS.

made Chinese products much cheaper in the US, raising Chinese exports. China sustained a largely fixed rate from 1995 to 2006, after which the yuan appreciated steadily through 2015. Currently, the Chinese policy is to manage changes in the bilateral exchange rate within fairly wide limits.

Effective exchange rates

It is also possible to compute an *effective exchange rate* (EER), which is a weighted average of bilateral exchange rates. Here is a description of how the Federal Reserve does that for the US dollar:

- Choose the countries with which the US has a large volume of trade. Currently, 27 countries or regions are included, with 26 individual countries and the euro area aggregated to one country.

- The weights are usually the shares of each country in the US overall trade with those countries, including both exports and imports of goods and services.
- For each of the 27 countries, multiply the trade weight by the bilateral exchange rate and then add up these products to get the weighted average or EER.
- By convention, for the country being studied (here, the US), each bilateral exchange rate is the price of that country's currency (US$). Since exchange rates aren't comparable in magnitudes (for example, 115 yen/$ isn't comparable to 1.25 C$/$), the computation is an index.

Figure 13.4 shows what has been happening to the effective value of the US$ over time, selecting January 2006 as the base month of the index. An increase in the EER means an appreciation of the effective dollar. A large appreciation happened from 2012 to 2017. Note again the sharp appreciation of the US dollar compared to its major trading partners in the early months of the 2020 COVID-19 pandemic.

Basic Effects of Changes in Exchange Rates

Initial impacts of exchange-rate changes

Consider some preliminary questions and answers about exchange rates that bring in important economic concepts:

Which groups are made better off by a stronger (appreciating) dollar?

- US importers because it makes the foreign-currency prices of imports lower;
- US tourists abroad, who need to spend fewer dollars to buy foreign currency;
- Foreigners holding dollar-denominated assets because their assets are worth more in their own currencies;
- Americans who owe foreign-currency denominated debt, which becomes cheaper.

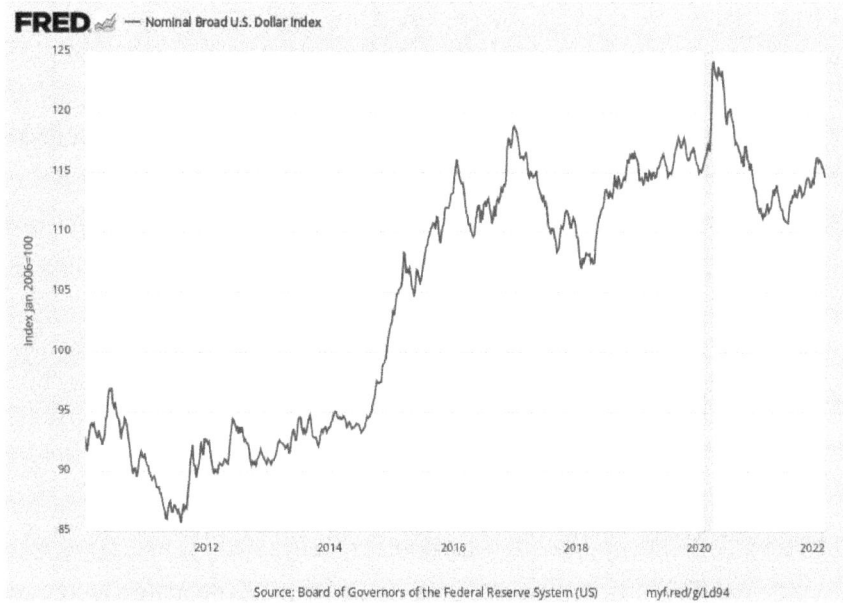

Figure 13.4 Nominal effective value of the US dollar against currencies of 27 major countries/regions, monthly from 2010 to early 2022.

Source: Federal Reserve Bank of St. Louis FRED database, at https://fred. stlouisfed.org/series/DTWEXBGS.

Which groups are made worse off?

- US exporters because their products are more expensive abroad;
- Foreign tourists (and students) in the US, who must pay more for dollars;
- US citizens owning foreign-currency assets, which become less valuable in dollars;
- Foreigners who owe dollar-denominated debt, which becomes more onerous to pay off.

What effect would a large appreciation of the dollar have on the rate of inflation in the US?

Answer: This is a complex question, but at a basic level, a stronger dollar would reduce the dollar price of imports, which should reduce the US inflation rate.

What effect would it have on the ability of developing countries to repay their dollar-based debts?

Answer: A stronger dollar would make it more difficult because firms in those countries would have to earn more in their own currencies to generate the greater number of dollars needed to pay the debts.

Later chapters will study these and other important effects.

Study question 2

Suppose that in April 2020, the exchange rate was US$1 = C$1.25, but in April 2021, it was US$1 = C$1.30. Then all the following statements are true except:

A. The Canadian dollar (C$) depreciated during the year.
B. The US dollar depreciated during the year.
C. The US dollar appreciated during the year.
D. Canadian exports to the US likely rose during the year.

Discussion of question 2

The correct answer is B because the Canadian dollar depreciated (making A true), meaning that the US dollar must have appreciated (making C true).

Answer D is true because a depreciated Canadian dollar would make Canadian exports cheaper in the US, causing them to go up.

Chapter 14

Foreign Exchange Markets and Exchange Rates in the Short Run

The Importance of Foreign Exchange Markets

Introduction

Before analyzing international finance and macroeconomics, it is critical to study and understand foreign exchange (FX) markets. This chapter introduces these markets and then discusses exchange rates as components of asset prices in the short run.

FX markets are important to study for at least three reasons:

1. Doing so introduces the explicit and essential purpose of international finance, which is to facilitate trade in goods and assets across countries and over time. Countries have different currencies, which are traded in FX markets.

   To gain more perspective, there are two fundamental purposes of exchange markets:

   - To facilitate trade across countries at exchange rates determined in FX markets.
   - To facilitate trade over time (international borrowing and lending) through exchanging foreign currency credit and debt instruments. This will lead to studying the relationships between exchange rates and interest rates.

2. Relationships among exchange rates are based on the actions of traders, investors, speculators, arbitragers, banks, and central banks. Their behavior is important in understanding how exchange rates are determined and the effects they have on economies.

3. FX markets are enormous. As of 2019, the estimated daily "turnover" (the dollar value of all FX transactions) was \$6.6 trillion, according to the Bank for International Settlements.

FX Markets: Basic Concepts

FX market basics

The "foreign exchange market" is in fact the collection of all supplies and demands for foreign currencies at a point in time or over a period of time. There is no single location and currency trading happens everywhere, including in small banks, hotels and restaurants that take a foreign currency, and ATMs accessed by tourists abroad.

However, there are several financial centers where large volumes are traded among major corporations and banks, including New York, Toronto, Chicago, San Francisco, Tokyo, Hong Kong, Singapore, Bombay, Zurich, Frankfurt, Paris, and London. There are large advantages to these centralized locations, including the agglomeration of skills, trading techniques, and financial firms.

All major currencies, such as the dollar, euro, RMB, and yen, and most minor ones can be traded on these exchanges. Note that paper currencies can be traded in the FX market, which happens mostly for purposes of tourism and trade in illegal goods. But the vast volume of FX trades involve wire transfers, deposits, overnight loans between banks, and similar financial instruments. Such processes and instruments rarely involve physical currencies, rather they are transacted electronically. These transactions are made by major financial institutions, primarily banks, brokerages, and central banks.

Spot FX rates

There are several types of FX markets, depending on the nature of transactions to be made. Start with the spot FX market, which refers to trades made in which there is immediate delivery of currencies or foreign-currency assets.

Spot FX markets exist primarily to *facilitate international trade in goods and services.* Consider how the FX market facilitates such international trade. Define the spot exchange rate (E) as the dollar price of a foreign currency ($ per unit). Suppose that $E = 0.0091\$/¥ (= 110¥/\$)$ and individuals and companies must pay this price to buy Japanese yen. This is the retail spot rate.

Imagine that Ford, a US auto company, contracts to buy a machine tool from Mitsubishi, a Japanese firm. Mitsubishi's yen price is ¥1.5 m, so Ford would need ¥1.5 m X (0.0091 \$/Y) = \$13,650. From Ford's standpoint, the price of the machine tool is \$13,650. However, as discussed in a later chapter, the contract may be denominated either in yen or dollars, depending on circumstances.

If the contract were denominated in dollars, Ford simply would pay \$13,650. Mitsubishi would convert that sum to ¥ 1.5 m at some bank in order to pay its workers and other costs in Japan.

If it were denominated in yen, Ford would go to its bank and buy ¥1.5 m for \$13,650. It then would pay Mitsubishi the ¥ 1.5 m.

Either way, note that this US import is a supply of dollars and a demand for yen in the spot FX market. It requires an FX transaction to permit the purchase of the machine tool. In the process, both a good (the machine tool) and an asset (the payment for the machine tool) exchange hands.

To see this, let the contract be in yen. Ford would go to its bank, say Chase Bank, which would reduce Ford's account by \$13,650 and give Ford a check or account in the amount ¥ 1.5 m. Ford would send the check (or wire transfer) to Mitsubishi, which would deposit it in its account at a Tokyo bank.

Result: Ford gets its machine tool for $13,650 and Mitsubishi gets ¥ 1.5 million. Chase Bank has reduced its liability to Ford by ¥ 1.5 m, which now sits in an account in Tokyo. (In fact, both banks would charge a small fee to make these trades.) A later chapter discusses how these transactions are recorded in the balance of payments.

Students may wonder at this point where Chase Bank would get the yen it offers to Ford. There are many possible ways:

- Chase could hold yen balances on its own for transaction purposes and for making investments.
- Chase could have customers that export goods and services to Japan, receive yen, and deposit them at Chase in return for dollars.
- Chase could buy yen from other banks in the wholesale or interbank market, which refers to transactions made among major banks and financial firms.

To see this, take the example another step. Suppose Chase bought the ¥ 1.5 m from Sumitomo Bank (SB) for $13,650 (the price would actually be a bit lower in the interbank market). SB would agree because it has customers needing dollars to import or buy dollar-based assets.

Now, suppose a Japanese insurance company wants to buy a $13,650 computer from IBM (and the contract is denominated in dollars). It would buy dollars from SB at a cost of ¥ 1.5 m. In the same way, the insurance company would get its computer and IBM would be paid in dollars.

Note here that IBM wanted to sell a computer and Ford wanted to buy a machine tool. These wants might not be consistent or efficient if made solely within the US economy. But more opportunities exist across borders and the FX market makes possible this trade by linking US suppliers and demanders to foreign suppliers and demanders. *The key point is that FX transactions facilitate trade in goods and services across borders in a process similar to how the dollar-based financial system facilitates trade within the US.*

Study question 1

The spot FX market facilitates trade in goods and services across borders by

A. Permitting buyers and sellers to transact across borders, extending the coincidence of market wants.
B. Converting the prices of goods denominated in one currency to prices in another currency.
C. Ensuring that the demand for foreign currencies, arising from the need to import goods, is met by a ready supply of those currencies.
D. All the above.

Discussion of question 1

The answer is D, all the above. The primary function of foreign exchange markets is to facilitate trade in goods, services, and assets across borders. This is efficient, for it permits sellers and buyers in one country to transact with those in other countries with coincident needs, thereby expanding markets. And the FX markets ensure that currencies are available for these purposes.

Spot-Market Exchange-Rate Consistency through Arbitrage

Spot FX rates and consistency

Table 14.1 shows bilateral spot exchange rates as of February 2, 2022, at 4:30 Eastern Standard Time. These are wholesale spot rates, meaning the exchange rates at which major banks and financial firms transact with each other.

These figures are the price of the row currency in terms of each column currency. For example, at that time, the Australian dollar (AUD) costs 0.906 Canadian dollars (CAD), 0.632 Euros (EUR), and 0.714 US dollars (USD).

Table 14.1 Bilateral wholesale spot exchange rates, 2 February 2022 at 4:30 EST.

	AUD	CAD	CHF	CNY	EUR	GBP	JPY	SGD	USD
AUD		0.905652	0.656777	4.544852	0.632011	0.526790	81.793500	0.962868	0.714485
CAD	1.104177		0.725197	5.018319	0.697852	0.581669	90.314462	1.063176	0.788917
CHF	1.522588	1.378935		6.919936	0.962292	0.802083	124.537793	1.466052	1.087866
CNY	0.220029	0.199270	0.144510		0.139061	0.115909	17.996956	0.211859	0.1572707
EUR	1.582251	1.432969	1.039185	7.191095		0.833513	129.417829	1.523499	1.130494
GBP	1.898291	1.719192	1.246753	8.627452	1.199741		155.267869	1.827804	1.356300
JPY	0.012226	0.011072	0.008030	0.055565	0.007727	0.006440		0.011772	0.008735
SGD	1.038564	0.940578	0.682104	4.720118	0.656384	0.547105	84.947761		0.742038
USD	1.399610	1.267560	0.919231	6.361020	0.884569	0.737300	114.479000	1.347640	

Source: ratesfx.com, https://www.ratesfx.com/rates/crossrates.html.

These rates are bilaterally consistent. For example, the last row shows that \$1 = €0.8846, requiring that €1 = \$1/(0.8846) = \$1.13049. That is indeed the dollar price of the euro, shown in the last cell of the EUR row.

These rates are quoted without reference to market location, such as New York, Toronto, or Tokyo. This suggests that the bilateral exchange rates must be the same across all markets that are open at the same time. This happens through a process of arbitrage, discussed next.

Spot-market arbitrage

Table 14.1 shows bilateral spot exchange rates at a point in time (they change continuously). This raises an obvious question: What makes exchange rates consistent across markets? How do currency traders know that the dollar/yen rate in London is the same as in New York or Tokyo or other financial centers? (Note they may not be during times when one market is closed, but they would immediately come together when that market opens.)

The answer is FX arbitrage, which ensures that there are no differences in spot currency rates across locations. *Arbitrage is the activity of simultaneously buying something at a low price in one location and selling it at a high price in another location to make a riskless profit.*

For purposes of these notes, currency arbitrage is defined to be riskless. However, advanced financial instruments often carry risks for investors who buy and sell assets to arbitrage, or eliminate, differences in anticipated returns.

Arbitrage equalizes the prices of any homogeneous commodity across locations. This is a highly efficient market process because it eliminates the need for market participants to search for the best price, which would be costly.

Foreign currencies are the ultimate homogeneous good (a euro is a euro). Thus, arbitrage will ensure the equality of their prices, except perhaps for very minor transaction costs. This equalization happens instantaneously because currency traders have sophisticated software programs that continuously look for exchange rate differences to arbitrage.

There are two types of arbitrage in spot markets:

1. *Spatial arbitrage* ensures that rates in two or more locations are the same. An example:

   Let a New York (NY) bank sell yen for 0.009$/¥ and a Tokyo bank sell yen for 0.0093$/¥ at the same time.

   Arbitragers (or their software programs) recognize that the yen is cheaper in NY. Thus, they could use, say, $1 m to buy yen in NY to get $1m/(0.0093$/¥) = ¥ 111.11 m.

   At the same time, they could sell those yen (through an electronic contract) to the Tokyo bank and buy dollars, getting ¥111.11 m*(0.0093)$/¥ = $1, 033, 323. This is a *riskless profit* of $33,323 per $1 m. (Or equally, a profit of 0.0003$ per yen traded.) How does arbitrage drive exchange rates together?

   - The $/¥ rate would rise in NY because dollars are sold to buy yen, thereby depreciating the dollar and appreciating the yen.
   - The $/¥ rate would fall in Tokyo, depreciating the yen and appreciating the dollar.
   - This would happen until equality is established in both markets, say at 0.0092 $/¥. (Again, there might be very small differences due to the transaction costs involved.)
   - At this point, no more arbitrage is profitable. We call such an equilibrium a "no arbitrage" condition. What that means is that the $/¥ rate is the same in both Tokyo and NY.

2. *Triangular arbitrage* is more subtle. This process ensures consistency of cross-exchange rates between three or more currencies in a single location. Combining this outcome with spatial arbitrage, there must be consistent cross-exchange rates in all locations. An example:

   Suppose these spot exchange rates exist in New York at a point in time:

   $$E_{\$/C\$} = 0.75\$/C\$ \quad E_{\pounds/C\$} = 0.6\pounds/C\$ \quad E_{\$/\pounds} = 1.3\$/\pounds$$

   (Here, the subscripts on E refer to the price of the second currency in terms of the first. Thus, the first rate is the dollar price of the C$.)

Note that in New York, there are two ways to compute the $£/C\$$ spot rate:

The direct rate $= E_{£/C\$} = 0.6£/C\$$
The cross rate $= (E_{\$/C\$})/(E_{\$/£}) = (0.75)/(1.3) = 0.577£/C\$.$

Note in the cross rate the dollar cancels, leaving a figure that is equivalent to $£/C\$$. This figure $(0.577£/C\$)$ is the *cross-exchange rate* in New York between pounds and C\$.

Students should recognize that C\$ are expensive (in terms of $£$) using the direct rate but cheap using the cross rate. Thus, let arbitragers use $£$ 1m to buy $(£1\,\text{m})*1.3\$/£ = \$1.3\,\text{m}$ in NY and simultaneously sell those dollars to buy $\$1.3\,\text{m}/0.75\$/C\$ = $ C\$1.7333 m.

At the same time, the arbitragers sell those C\$ to buy $(C\$1.7333m) * (0.6£/C\$) = £1.03998$ m in New York. This process earns a riskless profit of $£39,980$ per $1\text{m}£$ arbitraged.

How would this arbitrage affect the spot exchange rates?

As before, the effects will be to drive these direct and cross rates together in NY:

- $E_{\$/£}$ would fall because arbitragers sell pounds to buy dollars (dollar appreciates, pound depreciates).
- $E_{\$/C\$}$ would rise because arbitragers sell dollars to buy C\$ (dollar depreciates, C\$ appreciates).
- $E_{£/C\$}$ would fall because arbitragers buy pounds with C\$ (pound appreciates, C\$ depreciates).

This process continues until equality is reached. In this example, three consistent exchange rates would be

$$E_{\$/C\$} = 0.768\$/C\$ \quad E_{£/C\$} = 0.595£/C\$ \quad E_{\$/£} = 1.29\$/£.$$

As an exercise, show that these bilateral spot rates generate consistent cross-rates. Again, this arbitrage happens both within any market and across all markets. It occurs instantaneously with sophisticated computer software so market participants should never expect to see differences in cross rates.

Are the cross-exchange rates in Table 14.1 consistent?

In the table, $E_{\$/C\$} = 0.788917$; $E_{£/C\$} = 0.581669$; $E_{\$/£} = 1.35630$. Then, the cross rate for $£/C\$ = (0.788917/1.35630) = 0.581669$. This equality is due to instantaneous arbitrage.

The Forward FX Market and Forward Rates

Forward exchange rates

An equally important process is *forward arbitrage*, which links currency markets over time. Crucially, it also links exchange rates to interest rates across countries. As will be seen, the fact that exchange rates and interest rates are closely related means that both are key components of the returns investors make on domestic and foreign financial assets.

First, we need to understand the idea of a *forward exchange rate. Forward rates are exchange rates known today for currency amounts delivered in the future.*

In the forward exchange market, people sign contracts today to deliver currencies in the future at specific times: 30, 60, 90, 180 days in the future. But they do so at a price (forward exchange rate) decided today in the forward FX market. There is no risk involved in the forward market because all currency prices are known today.

Forward FX markets exist primarily to permit firms to manage the risk that would otherwise arise from the fact that goods and services are generally traded in contracts that are executed over a period of time. That is, most international trade (and many asset) transactions happen under contracts signed over a time period, say 30, 60, 90, 180 days or up to a year. Firms could wait until the contract concludes before transacting in the foreign currency needed to pay it off. But this situation raises risks due to unanticipated changes in spot exchange rates.

Imagine that a US firm signs a contract now to accept and pay for imported machinery in 90 days. In the intervening period, the firm would sell some of its own products, hoping to make enough revenues to pay for the imports in 90 days (plus a profit). The foreign exporter would sign the contract now, produce the machinery over 90 days, and hope the agreed sales price covers its costs.

These traders could just wait and see what the spot rate is in 90 days. But a problem arises with flexible exchange rates. They fluctuate over time, making both parties subject to exchange rate risk. There is a possibility of adverse movements in spot rates that lower profits (or cause losses). This truly is risk because the exchange rate could also move in your favor, raising profits.

Risk-loving firms might accept the risk and just wait to settle the contract at the spot exchange rate in 90 days. But most trading firms prefer to reduce or eliminate this risk through *hedging*. They can do this by using the forward market and agreeing now to settle the contract in 90 days but at the current (and therefore known) forward exchange rate.

Definition: To hedge is to eliminate exchange rate risk through buying or selling forward contracts.

Example: Suppose a liquor store in the US decides to buy 500 cases of Heineken beer from the Netherlands, with delivery in 90 days. The euro cost charged by Heineken for these 500 cases is €5,000 in total. Let the current spot E = 1.2$/€. If that rate does not change, then the dollar cost would be $6,000 in 90 days.

However, if the dollar depreciated (the euro rose) to 1.3 $/€ over 90 days, then the dollar cost would rise to $6,500, implying an exchange rate loss of $500 for the liquor store. On the other hand, if it appreciated (the euro fell) to 1.1 $/€, then the dollar cost would fall to $5,500, implying an exchange rate gain of $500.

It is important to note that this risk applies only to the US liquor store because the contract is stated in euros. Heineken has no risk because it would receive €5,000 either way.

It is possible however that the contract was stated in dollars, with an agreed price of $6,000. Then, Heineken would face the risk and the US store would not. In this case, Heineken would like to see the euro depreciate (and the dollar appreciate) because in 90 days when it is paid $6,000 by the US store, the contract would be worth more euros.

An aside: Currency denomination of contracts

This example points to a big issue in international business: the *currency denomination* of trade contracts.

If a contract were stated in a firm's home currency, then the firm bears no risk. It does face risk if the contract were in the other country's currency. Most US export contracts (around 80%) are in dollars and most EU export contracts (around 70%–75%) are in euros. Thus, exporting firms in those places face relatively little currency risk. But importers in each place do because they must pay in the other currency.

Some firms may choose to denominate their exports in a foreign currency, such as the dollar. In this way, they can absorb the risk themselves as a matter of competitive strategy, for doing so helps maintain their market shares abroad. Japanese firms often do this and around 50% of their exports to the US are expressed in dollars.

Firms in emerging and developing countries (EDCs) face a double problem because both their imports and exports are generally in dollar or euro terms or some other major currency, such as the yen or Chinese yuan. This happens because international traders around the world prefer to transact in a major global currency.

As discussed in a later chapter, this is one good reason why many EDCs choose to fix their exchange rates to the currency of their major trading partner. Doing so reduces this risk facing their trading and investing firms.

Hedging exchange rate risk in the forward market

Returning to the example, the US store has what is called an open liability in euros, so it is exposed to exchange rate risk in the spot market. There are a number of ways in which it could hedge, or eliminate, this risk.

1. Bargain over the currency denomination of the contract. The liquor store might ask for the contract to be in dollars, but Heineken, as a major global supplier, is not likely to agree because it would have the greater bargaining power. Heineken might agree to some form of risk-sharing, but that is unlikely since a trade contract with two currencies is awkward and inefficient.
2. The store could simply adjust its retail selling prices. If the store saw the exchange rate go to 1.30 $/€ in 90 days, it could raise the price of Heineken beer in its store to cover the higher costs.

However, because this store would face local competition from other liquor stores and other beer brands, raising the price might cost it some market share. That just means that its sales would be risky rather than the exchange rate, so it merely shifts the type of risk. Moreover, firms rarely want to change their retail prices rapidly due to shifts in exchange rates.

3. Hedge through spot purchases. The liquor store could buy €5,000 today in the spot market for $6,000 and hold on to the euros for 90 days, using them to pay the contract. This scenario faces no exchange rate risk.

In fact, this would be a naïve strategy because firms rarely would let such an asset (the held euros) sit idle. Rather, it would invest them for 90 days in a euro-based asset at an interest rate known today.

Thus, let the 90-day interest rate on euro assets be $i_{€}^{90} = 0.005$. (This would translate to an annual interest rate of 0.02 or 2%.) Then, the liquor store would have (€5,000)*(1.005) = €5,025 in 90 days. It would then pay its €5,000 contract, get the beer, and have €25 of interest returns left over.

While these strategies may be possible, there is a simpler alternative organized in the forward markets. Indeed, forward markets exist largely for the purpose of hedging exchange rate risk. Traders in forward markets agree today to buy or sell foreign currency in the future at a price known today.

Forward hedging

4. The liquor store could hedge its risk through forward market purchases.

It is important to understand that an agreement to exchange currencies today (spot) is different from an agreement to exchange them in 90 days (forward). Thus, there would be different prices (exchange rates) today in the two markets.

Put differently, spot exchange rates are given by the supply and demand for currencies in spot markets, but forward exchange rates are determined by the supply and demand for forward currencies in 30, 60, 90 days, etc.

Let E be the spot exchange rate and F_t be the forward exchange rate over a period (such as 60 days), where both are measured in dollar/foreign currency, e.g., $/€. Since the spot market and the forward markets over varying periods are different, it follows that

$$E \neq F_{30} \neq F_{60} \neq F_{90} \neq F_{180}.$$

Note that if $F_t > E$, we say the foreign currency is at a *forward premium*. As will be discussed, this means that people expect the foreign currency to rise in value over time and participants must pay a premium for it now. If $F_t < E$, the foreign currency is at a *forward discount* and people expect the foreign currency to fall in value over time.

Computing forward premiums and discounts

Suppose that these exchange rates exist close to those in Table 14.1.

$E_{\$/€} = \$/€\,\text{spot} = 1.198$

$F_{30,\$/€} = \$/€\,30\text{-day forward} = 1.196$. Note that $F_{30,\$/€} < E$ so there is a 30-day *forward discount* on the €.

$F_{60,\$/€} = \$/€\,60\text{-day forward} = 1.195$. Again, there is a 60-day forward discount, which is bigger than the 30-day discount.

Define the *forward premium* or *forward discount* as the percentage difference between the forward rate and the spot rate. Forward premiums and discounts will be denoted by f.

For 60 days in this example, we have

$f_{60,\$/\euro} = (1.195 - 1.198)/1.198 = -0.0025$ (or -0.25%). Note that the spot rate is in the denominator of this formula.

The logic mentioned above suggests that market participants expect the euro to depreciate relative to the dollar over 60 days. The notes will return to that idea later.

Forward hedging

Return to the example of the liquor story seeking to hedge (eliminate) its exchange rate risk. Recall in that example that the current spot $E = 1.2\$/\euro$ and the contract comes due in 90 days.

Let $F_{90} = 1.225\$/\euro$. Note the forward premium on the euro is $f_{90} = ((1.225 - 1.2)/1.2) = 0.0208$ or 2.08%.

Then, the forward cost *today* of getting €5,000 in 90 days is $5,000 * 1.225 = \$6,125$. The liquor store could pay this price (exchange rate) now but receive the euros in 90 days at this known dollar price. There is no risk.

Is this smart? If the dollar were to depreciate over 90 days (or to appreciate by less than 2.08%), then yes because the dollar cost of the beer would be lower using this forward hedging transaction. If the dollar were to appreciate by more than 2.08%, then the liquor store would have ended up better off waiting in the spot market.

However, firms that trade goods and services internationally tend to be risk-averse. The liquor store likely would prefer to avoid the risk by transacting now in the forward market.

Study question 2

Suppose the current spot rate on the British pound is $E = 1.25\$/\£$ and the current 30-day forward exchange rate is $F_{30} = 1.22\$/\£$. Then,

A. The pound is trading at a forward premium relative to the dollar.
B. The pound is trading at a forward discount relative to the dollar.
C. The dollar is trading at a forward premium relative to the pound.
D. The dollar is trading at a forward discount relative to the pound.
E. Both B and C.

Discussion of question 2

The correct answer is E because both B and C are true statements. The pound is cheaper in the forward market than in the spot market, so it is trading at a forward discount relative to the dollar. But that implies the dollar must be trading at a forward premium relative to the pound.

To see this, note first that the spot market price of the dollar is $E_{£/\$} = 1/1.25 = 0.8$. The 30-day forward price of the dollar is $1/1.22 = 0.8197$. Thus, the forward premium on the dollar is

$$f_{30,£/\$} = (0.8197 - 0.8)/0.8 = 0.0246(2.46\%).$$

Forward arbitrage: Linking exchange rates and interest rates

It is now possible to consider arbitrage in the forward FX market, which will link exchange rates to interest rates. Let E = spot rate ($\$/€$) and F = forward rate for 90 days. Let $i_\$$ = the US interest rate for 90 days and $i_€$ = the euro interest rate for 90 days. Assume that the investments paying these returns are identical in the US and Europe in terms of risk. For example, they could be bank deposits or 90-day treasury bonds, neither of which would bear any risk. All that matters to investors is the interest return on these investments.

Thus, the spot, forward, and interest transactions are risk-free because all exchange rates and interest rates are quoted (known) now. But future spot rates are not known and are therefore a source of risk.

Now, consider the act of *forward arbitrage*, which is simultaneously operating in (1) the spot market; (2) the forward market; and (3) both the home and foreign investment markets to establish equalized returns on US and euro assets, measured in the same currency. Here is an example.

Suppose that a US investor has $1 m and is looking for the highest risk-free dollar return. She has two options:

1. Invest for 90 days at the US interest rate. Then, the proceeds $= (\$1\,\text{m}) * (1 + i_\$)$ and the return $= (\$1\,\text{m}) * i_\$$.

Example: Let $i_\$ = 0.005 (0.5\%)$, which is an annualized interest rate of $0.005 * 4 = 0.02 (2\%)$. Then, the proceeds $= \$1,000,000 * (1.05) = \$1,005,000$. This investment pays a 90-day return in $\$ = \$5,000 (0.50\%)$.

2. Invest $1m in the asset in the EU, say in Germany. This involves three risk-free steps:

- Buy euros in the spot market now. The euros received $= (\$1\,\text{m}) * (1/E)$.
- Invest the euros received at the German (EU) rate. The proceeds $= (\$1\,\text{m}) * (1/E) * (1 + i_€)$.
- Agree today to sell these euro proceeds forward at the rate F (known today).

Doing all these generates dollar proceeds $= (\$1\,\text{m}) * (1/E) * (1 + i_€) * F$ in 90 days.

Example: Let $E = 1.2\$/€$; $i_\$ = 0.005$, $i_€ = 0.002$, $F = 1.22\$/€$. What does the investor get?

- Buy spot euros and get $(\$1\,\text{m}) * (1/1.2) = €0.8333\,\text{m}$.
- Invest these euros in Germany to earn $(€0.8333\,\text{m}) * (1.002) = €0.835\,\text{m}$.
- Sell these euros in the forward market for dollars, generating dollar proceeds $= (€0.835\,\text{m}) * (1.22) = \$1.0187\,\text{m}$. This investment return $= \$18,700 (1.87\%)$.

Thus, the US return (just the US interest rate) $= 0.50\%$. But the euro return (working through the spot rate, euro interest rate, and forward rate) $= 1.87\%$.

Here, despite having a lower interest rate, Germany (EU) is the better risk-free investment. How can we compare this to see why?

The forward premium on the euro $(f) = (1.22 - 1.20)/(1.20) = 0.0167 (1.67\%)$. Thus, the combined return on the euro investment is $i_€ + f = 0.002 + 0.0167 = 0.0187 (1.87\%)$.

Clearly, 1.87% is much higher than the US return of 0.5%. What would happen? US investors would arbitrage by buying euro investments. This would mean the following:

(1) Investors would sell dollars and buy euros in the spot market. Thus, the spot rate would rise, say, to 1.210.
(2) Investors would buy German investments, meaning funds would flow from the US to Germany. This would cause $i_€$ to fall. It would also cause $i_$$ to rise but the calculations here will ignore that. Thus, suppose that $i_€$ would fall to 0.001 (which is 0.1% for 90 days).
(3) Investors would sell euros and buy dollars in the forward market. Thus, the forward rate on the euro would fall, say, to 1.215. Now, the forward premium is $f = (1.215-1.210)/1.210 = 0.004(0.4\%)$.

The US direct interest return remains 0.005 (0.5%). But the EU total return is now $0.001+0.004 = 0.005(0.5\%)$. Again, the EU return has two components: the interest rate and the forward premium.

We can see that forward arbitrage would bring these two returns together. The mathematical condition for this to happen is called covered interest parity. (The word "covered" means that all risks are covered or hedged away.)

The covered interest parity (CIP) condition:

$$i_$ = i_€ + \frac{(F - E)}{E} = i_\epsilon + f.$$

In words, the interest rate of the home country must equal the interest rate of the foreign country plus the forward premium or discount on the foreign currency. The left side is the return in dollars on US assets, consisting of just the US interest rate. The right side is the return on euro assets, measured in dollars. It has two components: the interest rate in euros and the forward premium or discount on euros.

Both the domestic and foreign returns are completely risk-free. Again, the CIP condition is a "no-arbitrage" condition, meaning that once equilibrium is achieved, no additional arbitrage would be profitable.

To further cement these ideas, go back to an earlier example for the spot and forward rates on the euro. Let spot $E = 1.198$/€$ and forward $F_{60} = 1.195$/€$. Then, the 60-day forward discount on the euro is

$$f_{60} = (1.195 - 1.198)/1.198 = -0.0025 \text{ (or } -0.25\%).$$

It should then be that the 60-day interest rates should follow CIP: $i_\$ = i_€ + f_{60}$. In this case, since $f < 0$, it must be that $i_\$ < i_€$ over 60 days, by 0.25%.

Here is how to think about CIP in this example. Since $f_{60} < 0$ (there is a forward discount on euro), it must be that the US interest rate is lower than the euro interest rate by 0.0025 over 60 days. Put differently, the euro interest rate must be 0.0025 higher than the US interest rate in order to compensate for the forward discount on the euro, thereby equalizing dollar returns on 90-day assets in both countries.

Actually, this is a poor example because there is no single "euro" interest rate. To define something like that, one would consider a weighted average of all the countries using the euro.

But it is worth checking the data using some past figures. On 16 April 2021, the US 60-day Treasury yield was 0.0051, implying an annualized rate $= 0.0051 * 4 = 0.0204$ or 2.04%. The German 60-day government bond yield was 0.0074 or 2.96% annualized.

The CIP condition suggests that $0.0051 = 0.0074 + f => f = -0.0023(-0.23\%)$. This was very close to the actual forward discount on the euro on that date.

Study question 3

The covered interest parity condition states that

A. The returns to identical home and foreign assets over the same time period must be the same when measured in the same currency.

B. The interest rate on home assets must be higher than the interest rate on foreign assets if the foreign currency trades at a forward discount.

C. The spot exchange rate must equal the forward exchange rate.

D. If the foreign currency is at a forward premium, it must go down in value to establish equilibrium.

Discussion of question 3

The correct answer is A, which is a verbal statement of CIP. B is incorrect because in the situation described, the home interest rate would be lower than the foreign interest rate. C is incorrect because CIP can hold when the spot rate and forward rate are different. D is false for the same reason as C.

Why Covered Interest Parity is Critically Important in International Finance

CIP: Important implications

It is crucial to understand that the theory of CIP relies on there being *perfect financial-capital mobility* between countries. That means there are no policy impediments to financial investments flowing between them. In countries sharing perfect capital mobility, an investor in either can very quickly shift investments between them.

For some countries, this may not be true. Emerging and developing countries often impose controls on the inflows and outflows of financial capital. For example, these controls might be taxes on capital inflows or outflows, or limits on how much foreigners may invest domestically, or on how much wealth a household or firm may be able to transfer abroad. In extreme cases, the policy may prevent people from accessing their deposits in order to stop capital outflows. These issues will be discussed further in later chapters.

For now, suppose there is perfect capital mobility between two countries. Then, we see the following:

1. Interest rates and exchange rates are tightly linked across countries through the CIP condition. To restate it, $i_\$ = i_€ + \frac{F-E}{E} = i_€ + f$.

   These variables (the interest rates and the spot and forward exchange rates) are all components of asset prices, and they are all jointly determined. If any of them moves for some reason, so will the others quickly to establish CIP.

For example, suppose the US Federal Reserve Bank announces that it will cut the money supply in order to reduce inflation. That would drive up the US interest rate and would also drive up the euro interest rate and/or appreciate the forward rate on the euro and/or depreciate the spot rate on the euro. All of that would happen very quickly. Students should be sure they understand why these variables would move in those ways as a result of forward arbitrage.

2. A related point is that central banks can use interest rate policy to affect exchange rates and vice-versa. And here is a critical point that is completely fundamental to international finance: *With perfect capital mobility, it is not possible for a country to choose an independent interest-rate target without affecting exchange rates. Monetary policy and exchange rate policy are closely linked to each other.*

3. A country with a fixed exchange rate but very high financial-capital mobility chooses to tie its domestic interest rate to the foreign interest rate.

Consider a developing country with a fixed exchange rate. For example, for decades, Barbados has set the value of the Barbadian dollar to 1B\$ = US\$0.50 or US1\$ = 2B\$. Since there can be no change in the fixed exchange rate, there would be no forward market or forward exchange rates. In that case, $f = 0$ by definition and we must have

$$i_\$ = i_{B\$}.$$

This equality would hold all the time if Barbados is fully open to financial flows to and from the United States.

By using this fixed exchange rate policy, Barbados cannot set its own interest rate and therefore has no independent monetary policy. Here is more perspective to help understand this situation in Barbados.

Suppose for some reason that Barbados decided to set a lower interest rate than the US one but remained committed to sustaining the fixed exchange rate and maintaining free capital mobility. Then, when Barbados tried to lower its interest rate, by having its central bank expand the domestic money supply, there would be heavy outflows of Barbados dollars to the US to take advantage of the higher interest rate there. But that outflow would put upward pressure on $i_{B\$}$. This would continue until these interest rates equalized again, re-establishing CIP.

Alternatively, if Barbados attempted to keep a lower home interest rate, there would be major financial outflows and great pressure on the B\$ to depreciate. To keep the exchange rate fixed, the central bank of Barbados would have to buy B\$ (and sell US\$), causing a quick depletion of its stock of available dollars, also called its FX reserves. This would not be sustainable, and before long, the central bank would have to just let the interest rate in Barbados return to equaling the US interest rate.

In this situation, we refer to the US dollar as the "exchange rate anchor" for Barbados. The values of both Barbados' currency and its interest rate are anchored to those in the United States.

CIP: Summary

Covered interest parity holds whenever two (or more) countries permit full financial-capital mobility between them. It would not hold if some countries establish capital controls that reduce such mobility.

For countries with fully flexible exchange rates, such as the US, Canada, Japan, the UK, the euro area, and Mexico, CIP takes this form:

$$i_A = i_B + \frac{(F - E)}{E} = i_B + f,$$

where A is one country, B is another, and F and E are the forward and spot exchange rates, defined as the price of B's currency in units of A's currency. This relationship means that interest rates and exchange rates are closely linked to each other, though all can move.

In contrast, a country C may choose to fix its spot exchange rate to that of a major currency, such as the dollar or euro. Since the exchange rate is fixed, there would be no need for a forward exchange market, and there would be no forward premium or discount on C's currency. In that case, CIP takes this form:

$$i_A = i_C.$$

In this case, country C's interest rate must equal country A's interest rate and it has no scope for its own monetary policy. If A's interest rate were to rise (e.g., due to a cut in the US money supply), then C's must rise also by the same amount. This situation also means that if A's currency (e.g., the US dollar) were to appreciate relative to another, say the euro, then C's currency would appreciate relative to the euro by the same amount. These issues are fundamental and will be discussed in more detail in later chapters.

Study question 4

Consider three countries, A, B, and C. A and B are large countries with flexible exchange rates between them. C is a small country that fixes its exchange rate to A's currency. All three have full financial-capital mobility. Now, suppose there is a rise in A's domestic interest rate. Which of the following responses would happen?

A. The interest rate in B would fall and B's forward exchange rate would depreciate.
B. The interest rate in C would rise.
C. The spot exchange rates in both A and C would appreciate relative to B's currency.
D. A cannot raise its domestic interest rate because its exchange rate is fixed to C's currency.
E. Both B and C.

Discussion of question 4

The correct answer is E because both B and C are true statements. A is false because the higher interest rate in country A would tend to push up B's interest rate also while causing B's spot rate to depreciate and its forward rate to appreciate compared to A's currency. This is due to forward arbitrage.

D is false because country A has a flexible exchange rate. B is true because country C would see its interest rate rise in lockstep with A's interest rate. C is true because A's currency would appreciate relative to B's due to A's higher interest rate, while C's currency would also appreciate because its currency is fixed to A's.

Expectations about the Future Spot Exchange Rate and Uncovered Interest Parity

The forward rate and the expected future spot rate

Students may wonder at this point about risky speculation in exchange markets rather than riskless forward arbitrage. *Speculation involves accepting a risky position in foreign currencies in the expectation that they will move in the future in a way that generates profits for the speculator.* Of course, speculators could also lose money on such bets. This possibility raises further important points to be made about exchange rates as components of asset returns.

1. *The equality of the forward exchange rate and the expected future spot exchange rate.*

   In an earlier section, the claim was made that if a foreign currency is traded at a premium, it must be that market participants expect the spot exchange rate on that currency to appreciate over time. If it is trading at a discount, it must be that participants expect the spot rate to depreciate over time. Why? The answer is that speculation should establish this equality.

   Consider a currency trader who believes the spot value of the Canadian dollar (C$) will rise compared to the US$ over the next 60 days. This person could speculate simply by buying a large quantity of C$ now in the spot market and waiting to sell them in 60 days.

   If the future spot rate in 60 days turns out higher than the current spot rate, she makes money. If the future spot rate is lower than the current spot rate, she loses money.

A more sophisticated and common way of speculating is by using the riskless forward market in combination with the spot market. Thus, suppose our investor expects the spot rate to rise from a current spot rate of $E = 0.75\$/C\$$ to an expected future spot rate in 60 days of $\exp(E_{60}) = 0.77\$/C\$$. Keep in mind that the expected rate may not turn out to be the actual rate in 60 days, so it is a risky guess.

What the investor can do is compare that expected future rate to the currently known forward rate over 60 days and act on that. There are two possibilities:

If $F_{60} < \exp(E_{60})$, then forward C\$ are cheaper than the expected value. The speculator would agree to buy C\$ in the (cheaper) forward market, then sell them in 60 days on the spot market (where she expects a higher price). She attempts to make a speculative profit by "going short" on the C\$. (Going short means pledging to sell an asset in the future.)

If $F_{60} > \exp(E_{60})$ exp, then the speculator agrees to sell C\$ in the (more expensive) forward market and buy cheaper spot C\$ in 60 days. She makes a speculative profit by "going long" on C\$. (Going long means pledging to buy an asset in the future.)

Example: Let $F_{60} = 0.76\$/C\$$ and $\exp(60) = 0.77\$/C\$$. The speculator could sign a contract to buy \$1m worth of forward C\$, receiving $(\$1\,\mathrm{m})/(0.76\$/C\$) = C\$1,315,789$ in 60 days. The contract would also commit her to sell that amount at whatever the spot rate turned out to be in 60 days. If her expectation were correct, she would receive $C\$1,315,789*0.77\$/C\$ = \$1,013,158$, a speculative profit of \$13,158 per \$1 m invested.

Of course, the actual speculative profit or loss would depend on the actual value of the spot exchange rate after 60 days. The primary point is that if enough speculation happened, it would drive the forward exchange rate to equal the expected future spot rate:

$$\exp(E_{60}) = F_{60}.$$

In the example, the forward rate was less than the expected spot rate. But speculators bought forward C\$, driving up the forward exchange rate. This would happen until equality is achieved. And this will be true for any time period in which speculators can make strong guesses about the future spot rate: 30, 60, 90, 180 days.

This condition alone explains why, if the forward exchange rate is greater than (less than) the current spot rate, it must be that the markets expect the spot rate on a foreign currency to appreciate (depreciate). This is because the statement is equivalent to saying that the expected spot rate is higher (lower) than the current spot rate.

Uncovered interest parity

Recall the CIP condition:

$$i_\$ = i_{C\$} + \frac{(F - E)}{E} = i_{C\$} + f \text{ over some time period, say 60 days.}$$

But by virtue of speculation, in equilibrium, $\exp(E) = F$ over that same period. From these relationships follows the uncovered interest parity (UIP) condition:

$$i_\$ = i_{C\$} + \frac{[\exp(E) - E]}{E} = i_{C\$} + \hat{e},$$

where $\hat{e}$ is the expected percentage appreciation (if $\hat{e}$ is positive) or depreciation (if $\hat{e}$ is negative) of the Canadian dollar.

In words, UIP states that if the US interest rate is above (below) the Canadian interest rate, the C$ is expected to appreciate (depreciate). Note also that these two conditions imply that in equilibrium, the forward premium (discount) on a currency equals its expected percentage appreciation (depreciation).

Implication: Short-run exchange rate volatility

It follows that *anything that changes market expectations about the expected value of the future spot rate will immediately change the forward exchange rate and interest rates in both countries.* In turn, that would mean immediate changes also in the current spot exchange rate to maintain CIP. This implies that in periods of rapid changes in market expectations, the spot exchange rate is likely to be highly volatile.

What would change expectations about the future spot exchange rate?

It would be "news" (unanticipated information) about almost any economic factor, recessions, higher inflation, natural hazard shocks, bad harvests, new innovations (e.g., a vaccine), changes in tax laws, and so on. Any such news shocks to either country would affect market expectations about which way exchange rates will move.

And, in turn, arbitrage that maintains CIP implies that current spot exchange rates can be volatile in the short run as they respond to news events.

Figure 14.1 illustrates these points by tracking the daily spot price of the UK£ in terms of US$:

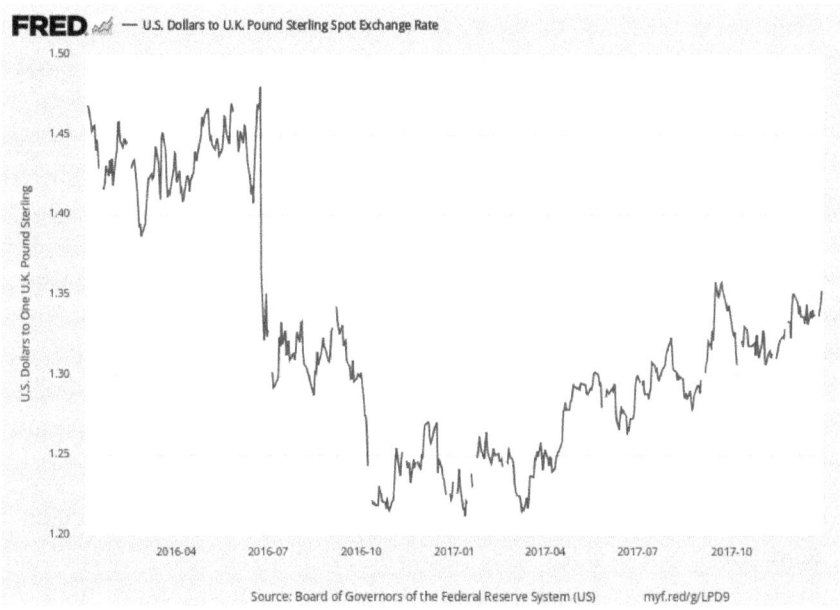

Figure 14.1   Volatility in the daily spot price of the UK pound and the impact of the Brexit vote.

Source: Federal Reserve Bank of St. Louis FRED database, at https://fred.stlouisfed.org/series/DEXUSUK.

1. There is considerable variability in the daily spot exchange rate.
2. On June 23, 2016, British citizens voted to leave the European Union ("Brexit"). This outcome was unexpected and quickly drove the euro down by about 11%.

FX Market Derivatives

These notes have discussed spot markets, forward markets, and hedging, arbitrage and speculation in those markets. That material is sufficient to gain a good understanding of the short-run relationships between exchange rates, interest rates, and expectations.

However, for completeness, it is useful to describe additional types of contracts that are traded in related kinds of FX markets. These contracts are generally referred to as "derivatives", which are extended forms of trading in foreign currencies to manage risk and to speculate for profit.

While there are many forms of derivatives, two general types are commonly used: futures and options contracts. The remaining notes briefly describe these contracts. Students interested in additional analysis should consult advanced financial textbooks.

FX futures contracts

Futures contracts: A trader agrees today to buy or sell a standardized amount of foreign currency at *established future dates*, with those *futures prices* (exchange rates) known today. Thus, a standard contract might be to offer (sell) or take delivery (buy) of £250,000 on June 1 ("June Pound Sterling") at a futures price of the pound known today. Notes:

- These markets operate exactly like futures in agricultural commodities.
- Futures contracts can be bought and sold on an organized futures exchange at any time before the delivery date. Whoever owns the contract on the delivery date must meet its terms.

Why do this? It's another form of hedging a future payment or receipt in a foreign currency.

Example: Suppose in January of some year Microsoft (MS) sells some software and services in France and knows it will be paid €1 million on June 1. It does not want to be exposed to exchange rate risk by waiting until then.

At any point before June 1, it could sell 10 futures contracts of €100,000 each, promising a June 1 delivery for the current day's June 1 futures price. In doing so, MS would receive the (June 1 futures exchange rate)*10* €100,000 in dollars today. For example, if the futures exchange rate were 1.15$/€, it would receive $1.15 m now. But it still must surrender €1 m to whoever buys the futures contracts. On June 1, Microsoft gets paid € 1m for its software and delivers those euros to the owners of the 10 contracts.

FX options contracts

Options contracts: A bank or broker A sells to trader B the option to buy (call) or sell (put) a given quantity of a currency from/to the bank or broker, on or before a specified future date at a set price (exchange rate) known today. B may or may not execute the option, but if B opts to execute the contract, then A must deliver.

FX options can also be bought and sold on organized exchanges. The cost of buying an option contract is the premium paid for it, which rises with the size of the contract.

If on the maturity date of the contract, trading at the spot exchange rate is less profitable than the option price, trader B will exercise the option. Party A must deliver the currency (if B had a call) or buy it back (if B had a put). Otherwise. the contract expires with no value.

Why do this? For firms engaged in trade, it's another form of hedging risk. It is also a way of speculating in the FX market because a trader may have expectations about the future spot rate that differ from the known rate at which the contract would be exercised.

Example: Consider the Microsoft case again. An options contract permits the possibility of both hedging and making a speculative profit.

As noted, MS will receive €1 m on June 1, which is certain. But the risk in waiting is that the euro might depreciate, earning fewer $ on that date. Thus, MS could go to broker *A* on (say) February 15 and buy a put (sell) option on €1 m at an agreed price (exchange rate), paying a small premium for the option of deciding whether to exercise its put later. On June 1, MS compares the spot rate *E* against this put rate.

If the "put" exchange rate is higher than the spot rate on June 1, MS would sell the €1 m to broker *A* at the put price and immediately buy back €1 m in the spot market. Its dollar profit is the (difference between the put exchange rate and the spot rate)*€1 m minus the premium in the options contract.

If the "put" price is below the spot price, MS would not exercise the option and lose only the premium it paid. Its risk is hedged, but in this case, MS might wish it had bought a call option.

This example demonstrates that both futures and options contracts may be used to hedge exchange rate risk. However, such contracts are also useful for speculation to make risky profits in FX markets.

Chapter 15

Exchange Rates in the Long Run and Purchasing Power Parity (PPP)

Introduction: Determining Exchange Rates in the Short Run versus the Long Run

Introduction: Short run versus long run

The last chapter analyzed the role of spot and forward exchange rates as integral components of the returns to assets, as summarized in the CIP and UIP conditions. This is important, for exchange rates and interest rates can vary considerably over short periods of time, which has significant effects on investment flows and asset prices.

In this framework, the "short run" is conceptualized as a period in which exchange rates move only in response to variations in returns to domestic and foreign financial assets. All components of these returns are jointly determined rapidly in FX and asset markets. That means that the only factor that can change these components are unanticipated shocks, or news, which arrive frequently but, by definition, cannot be predicted. To see this, recall the CIP and UIP conditions between two countries A and B:

$$\text{CIP}: \ i_A = i_B + \frac{(F - E)}{E} = i_B + f,$$

$$\text{UIP}: \ i_A = i_B + \frac{[\exp(E) - E]}{E} = i_B + \hat{e}.$$

CIP states that interest rates and the forward premium or discount exist in an equilibrium relationship. However, the only thing that would move these variables to a new equilibrium is a change in the expected future spot rate, as shown in UIP.

Thus, the essence of the short-run theory of exchange rates with perfect capital mobility is the following:

1. Spot rates, forward rates, and interest rates are all components of the financial returns to domestic and foreign assets, and they must move together to establish CIP.
2. Since these components are in equilibrium, they can only change if there is a short-run shock to the system that changes the expected future spot exchange rate.

In effect, this means that short-run changes in exchange rates are unpredictable because they depend on unexpected shocks. While interesting and important, this theory is unsatisfying for failing to relate exchange rates to more fundamental economic variables, which change over a longer time period.

Again, the short run is the period, from hours and days to perhaps a year or two, over which changes in exchange rates are essentially unpredictable. However, over several years, spot exchange rates do seem to trend in more predictable ways. For example, Figure 15.1 shows the daily dollar-per-euro exchange rate from 2012 to early 2022. Note the following:

1. There is rapid short-run variability as seen in the daily movements up or down.
2. However, these fluctuations happen around longer-term trends, such as the substantial appreciation of the dollar over the period.

Chapter 14 was about short-run changes. This chapter analyzes basic economic reasons for the long-run changes in trends. The question now is what determines movements in flexible exchange rates over these longer periods?

The primary answer is that exchange rates move over time in response to differences between countries in fundamental economic variables. While there may be several such variables, they boil

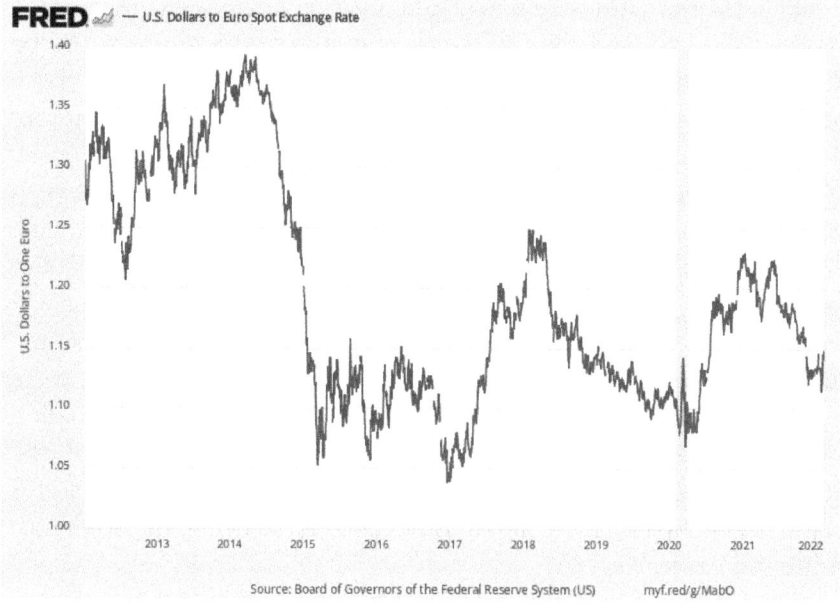

Figure 15.1   The US dollar per euro exchange rate, 2012–2022.

Source: Federal Reserve Bank of St. Louis FRED database, at https://fred.stlouisfed.org/series/DEXUSEU.

down to this prediction: *In the long run, exchange rates ultimately must adjust to reflect changes in the underlying competitiveness of economies.*

A country's macroeconomic competitiveness refers to its aggregate cost of producing goods and services relative to other countries. This cost depends on two key factors at a point in time: the country's aggregate price level and its productivity. Over time, what matters is the country's inflation rate and its growth in productivity, again, relative to other nations.

Intuitive example

The notes will focus primarily on prices and inflation, adding productivity later. Here is the basic intuition for why exchange rates are driven by differences in price inflation.

The United States and Canada have a flexible exchange rate between the US\$ and the C\$, which may move up and down and be volatile over days or months. But suppose that, beginning at some point, over the following five years, the US rate of price inflation were 5% per year and the Canadian rate were 7% per year.

This means, other things equal, that Canadian goods and services would get more expensive every year compared to US products. In turn, people would buy fewer Canadian goods and services and buy more US goods and services. This increase in spending on US products would raise the demand for US\$, while the lower spending on Canadian products would reduce the demand for C\$.

As a result, these shifts would tend to depreciate the Canadian dollar and appreciate the US dollar. In fact, as shown later, the simplest version of the theory predicts in this example that the C\$ would depreciate by 2% compared to the US\$, which is the difference in inflation rates.

Thus, the basic theory is this: Countries with higher inflation rates over time will see their currencies depreciate. Countries with lower inflation rates will see their currencies appreciate.

Prices and the Relative Cost of Living

Introduction to price levels and indexes

Demonstrating and understanding this idea (and related concepts) more fully first requires studying how to compare prices and inflation across countries. The notes begin with price levels (indexes) and then move on to inflation rates.

First, consider how to determine how expensive each country is in terms of its prices, living costs, real wages, and so on. The main way that economists compare price levels across countries is to compute and compare how much it costs to live in various nations.

Let P^{US} be the annual cost to an average household of consuming a basket of goods and services in the US. This is a figure expressed in dollars and is a measure of the cost of living. *The inflation rate* (e.g., the consumer price index) is the year-to-year change in such a basket, as discussed later. This basket would include the cost of a given amount of food of various types, rent or housing costs, medical care, commuting costs, gasoline, entertainment, and other important consumption goods.

One obvious example is the computation of what is called the "poverty line", which is the income needed for a household of four people to purchase a given combination of goods and services that will keep the family fed and healthy. In 2021, the US poverty line was around \$26,500. However, the focus here is on the cost of living for the average or median household, which is the natural way to compare standardized living costs across countries.

Price levels and exchange rates

Again, the basket of consumption goods and services P^{US} is computed using dollar prices. Let P^{UK} be the annual cost for the *identical basket of goods and services* in the UK, a measure of the cost of living there. This is computed using pound ($\pounds$) prices.

To the greatest extent possible, the US and UK baskets should be calculated with the same set of goods and services, in the same quantities, in both countries. The idea is to make them as comparable as possible.

Then, define the *relative cost of living* between these countries as

$$R = \frac{P^{US}}{EP^{UK}}.$$

E is the market spot exchange rate, expressed as the dollar price of the pound ($\$/\pounds$). EP^{UK} is then a measure of the UK cost of living translated to dollars using the market spot rate.

Then, R is a comparison of the relative cost of living for the same basket of goods and services in the US versus the UK, both expressed in dollars (the numerator currency).

Example: Let P^{US} \$60,000 (cost of the standardized basket); $P^{UK} = \pounds50,000$; and $E = 1.35\$/\pounds$. Then, the relative cost of living is

$$R = \$60,000/(\pounds50,000 * 1.35\$/\pounds) = \$60,000/\$67,500 = 0.89.$$

This means that it is 11% cheaper to live in the US than in the UK, expressed in dollar terms.

Note that similar calculations can be used to compute how much a given basket of inputs (labor, capital prices, and intermediate inputs like chemicals and machinery) costs in one country versus another, converted to the same currency. In this case, R would be a measure of *relative cost competitiveness* in trade for two (or many) countries.

For example, central banks and economists spend a lot of time calculating how much the average wage in manufacturing is in one country versus another. Then, $R = \frac{W^{US}}{EW^{UK}}$ would be a measure of how expensive US labor is in manufacturing relative to the UK.

Returning to the example, if R were to rise, it would mean that the relative living costs of the US have increased. For example, if R rose from 0.89 to 0.95, US prices and costs must have gone up six percentage points relative to UK prices and costs.

Economists often refer to an increase in R as being equivalent to a *real appreciation* of the dollar (and a *real depreciation* of the pound) because an appreciation of the dollar would also raise American prices as the British see them. A fall in R would be a *real depreciation* of the dollar.

That is, a *real appreciation* of the dollar (higher R) means the US becomes more expensive relative to the UK. A *real depreciation* of the dollar (lower R) means the US becomes cheaper relative to the UK.

Study question 1

Suppose that a basket of goods and services in Germany costs €80,000 and in Russia, the same basket costs Rb 200,000 (where Rb is the ruble, the Russian currency). Finally, let $E_{\text{€,Rb}} = 0.5$€/Rb. Then, we can conclude that:

A. Expressed in euros, Germany is a more expensive place to live than Russia.
B. Expressed in euros, Russia is a more expensive place to live than Germany.

C. German living costs are 80% of Russian living costs, expressed in euros.
D. Both B and C.

Discussion of question 1

The correct answer is D because both B and C are true statements. To see this, compute the relative living costs in euros:

$$R = \frac{P^G}{E_{€,Rb}P^R} = \frac{80,000}{0.5 * 200,000} = 0.8.$$

This means that, expressed in euros, Germanys' living cost is 80% of Russia's living cost.

Changes in R

What determines changes in these relative costs R? Consider simply the expression for it:

$$R = \frac{P^{US}}{EP^{UK}},$$

where $E = \$/£$ is the bilateral spot exchange rate. Then, we have the following:

1. If P^{US} rises (because of rising US prices of goods and services in the basket), then R rises due to higher US living costs.
2. If P^{UK} falls, then R rises due to lower UK living costs.
3. If E falls (an appreciation of the $ or a depreciation of the £ in the spot market), then R rises because the pound depreciation makes UK costs lower in dollar terms.

Thus, R (the relative cost of living or relative price index) is the *key* international price ratio for comparing costs of living, relative production costs, competitiveness in wages, and so on. It is often called the bilateral *real exchange rate*. With many currencies, economists compare the standardized basket of prices in all countries and combine them with bilateral exchange rates to compute a *real effective exchange rate*. It is important to take a closer look at underlying determinants of these relationships and understand why they are important.

The simplest concept: The law of one price

An initial concept to understand is the law of one price (LOOP). Consider a single good (C) that is (1) freely traded internationally and is (2) completely homogeneous in that products are identical quality no matter where they are produced. Examples might be chemicals, corn, and cabbage. The law of one price says that such goods should have the same price in both (or many) countries when expressed in the same currency.

$$P_C^{US} = \text{EP}_C^{UK}.$$

Note that this equation implies that $R_C = \frac{P_C^{US}}{\text{EP}_C^{UK}} = 1$, where R_C is the relative price of good C in the US versus the UK, expressed in dollars.

Example: Let the price of 1 kg of chemicals $= \$20$ in the US and £17 in the UK, and $E = 1.35\$/£$. Then, $\text{EP}_C^{UK} = 1.35 * 17 = \$21.60$. Chemicals are more expensive in the UK. If there were *perfect and costless movement of goods*, traders would buy C in the US and export them to the UK. Then, the price would rise in the US and fall in the UK. It is also possible that the exchange rate would fall (dollar appreciation) due to greater chemical purchases in the US, though it is unlikely that this would happen due to trade flows in a single commodity.

This *goods arbitrage* would continue until equality of prices is reached. For example, keeping the same exchange rate, let the US price rise to \$20.35 and British price fall to £15.074. Then, the LOOP would hold since \$20.35 = 1.35 * 15.074.

What must be true for LOOP to hold?

1. Goods are homogeneous (identical in quality) and highly tradable.
2. There are no trade barriers or transport costs (including on intermediate inputs used to make the goods).

3. International firms with market power cannot "segment markets" through price discrimination and erect controls preventing goods from being exported from low-priced markets to high-priced markets.

What kinds of goods are homogeneous? This is debatable but we usually think of primary commodities (oil, minerals, gold, and agricultural crops) and simple manufactures, such as toys and clothing. These goods do not need to be differentiated very much and so they have similar characteristics and prices.

But goods that are highly differentiated in quality or branding would not be homogeneous. Cars, sophisticated machinery, cell phones, and so on are not likely to fit the LOOP. This is even more the case because they are produced by large firms with market power, such as GM, VW, Toyota, General Electric, Apple, and Samsung.

Finally, many services are not traded (though there are major exceptions). Thus, it is highly unlikely that the prices of haircuts would be the same across countries. For example, suppose the price of a haircut in the US were $40 and in Mexico were 300 Pesos (Ps). Let $E = 0.067\$/\text{Ps}$ (which is $15\,\text{Ps}/\$$). The dollar price of a haircut in Mexico would be $300 * 0.067 = \$20.10$, which is much cheaper than in the US. But Americans do not flock to Mexico for haircuts because the cost of the trip is not worth it.

Purchasing Power Parity, Living Costs, and Exchange Rates

Purchasing power parity exchange rates

Move now to a more general and powerful concept: the purchasing power parity (PPP) exchange rate. The idea here is to calculate the *exchange rate that would make living costs (or costs of a good) equal in two countries. This exchange rate does not exist in the actual spot markets, so it is unobservable.*

Go back to the definition of R, using total baskets of goods and services:

$$R = \frac{P^{US}}{\text{E}P^{UK}}.$$

The PPP exchange rate would be determined by setting $R = 1$ to equalize the costs of living. Then,

$$E_{PPP} = \frac{P^{US}}{P^{UK}}$$

which is just the ratio of the basket costs in the two countries. In our example above,

$$E_{PPP} = \$60{,}000/£50{,}000 = 1.2\$£.$$

If that were the market spot rate (it would not be), then living costs would be the same in the US and UK, expressed in the same currency, which here is the dollar.

Compare exchange rates: The spot $E = 1.35$ but PPP rate $= 1.2$. That is, the PPP rate would imply a cheaper pound and more expensive dollar. That means that the *market spot rate on the pound is overvalued relative to its PPP rate.*

Consider again the Mexican haircut. The market spot rate is $E = 0.067\,\$/Ps$, but (at least for haircuts) the $E_{PPP} = \$40/300Ps = 0.1333\ \$/Ps$, a more expensive peso. This tells us that the market-based peso is *undervalued* compared to the PPP peso value.

This means that haircuts are really cheap at the market exchange rate compared to the "equal price" or PPP rate. If an American could buy a Mexican haircut for 300 Pesos but had to use the PPP exchange rate of $0.133\$/Ps$, the cost would be $300 * 0.1333 = \$40$, equal to the US price.

What the Mexican haircut example suggests is generally true: services in poor countries (low-wage countries) are typically considerably cheaper than they are in rich countries, when converted at market exchange rates. Why is this?

- Wages are low in poor countries, implying lower costs of non-traded goods, such as personal services.
- Land prices, office rents, taxes, and other business costs tend to be lower also in poor countries than in rich countries. This factor also reduces the relative prices of services.

- In developing economies, many or most services are produced and sold in the informal sector, which lies outside formal markets and is generally unregulated. Such services may not even be measured in the official income statistics.

Why PPP exchange rates are very useful to understand

A really interesting question is whether and how we can measure the true sizes (GDP, GNI) or living standards (GNI per capita) of different countries when we take account of the fact that the prices of goods and especially services really are not the same across countries when converted at market spot rates. PPP exchange rates are designed to make these calculations.

To motivate the concept further, consider the fact that in poor countries, there are considerable amounts of "extreme poverty", a situation in which people live on $2 per day or less. Without question, that level of income is extremely low and the associated living conditions are terrible.

But this metric is not the same as $2 of income in a rich country like the US. *Due to cheap services, people in poor countries can buy more with their incomes than the same income can buy in the US or Europe or Japan.* PPP exchange rates are designed to figure out a "true" comparison of costs and living standards. In addition, it makes sense for some purposes to convert each country's total GNI or GDP into dollars at their PPP exchange rates rather than market rates to see what the effective living standards really are.

Computing these rates is a massive job for economists and accountants (who go out and survey actual prices in all countries). Indeed, there is a massive project funded by the UN and the World Bank called the "International Comparisons Project" that pays for this work.

With these data, the World Bank annually calculates PPP exchange rates, all scaled to the US dollar as the base currency. That is, the analysts ask this question:

"What exchange rate would give the local currency the same purchasing power in a country as the dollar does in the US?" These PPP rates are sometimes referred to as "international dollars".

Table 15.1 illustrates the concept using actual data from 2016.

Computation of PPP exchange rates

The first data column shows the average official market spot exchange rate in 2016 for each country. The second shows GNI using these market rates and the third lists GNI per capita, again with market rates. These figures are what would usually be listed as the standard international income levels. For example, Tanzania had a per-capita GNI of $900 or around $2.50 per day. Tanzania is very poor, to be sure.

Note carefully that each market rate in column 1 is in local currency units per $US, so it is $\frac{1}{E}$ in the notation used in earlier sections. Then, E would be the reciprocal of these figures.

Note an immediate problem with using market exchange rates: the dollar value of GNI and GNI per capita fluctuates with changes in the market rate. For example, in Egypt, the market exchange rate was $10.03\frac{E£}{\$}$ and the dollar value of GNI was $326b. This means that the local currency value of GNI was $326 * 10.03 = 3{,}270 bE£$. Now, suppose the Egyptian currency appreciated to $8\frac{E£\$}{\$}$. Then, the dollar value of GNI would be $3{,}270/8 = \$409$ billion.

Entirely because of the exchange rate change, measured Egyptian GNI went up by 25%, as would measured GNI per capita! This is not a useful way to measure differences in underlying living costs.

The fourth column shows the computed PPP exchange rates, explained in the following paragraph, while the fifth and sixth adjust GNI and GNI per capita using these PPP rates. The final column will be explained in a later paragraph.

Here is how the World Bank computes PPP exchange rates. Since the market exchange rates are defined as $\frac{1}{E}$, the relative price R in Tanzania (using the notation in earlier paragraphs) is

$$R = \frac{P^{US}}{\left[\left(\frac{1}{2,177}\right)P^T\right]}$$

Table 15.1 Computation of PPP exchange rates for selected countries, 2016.

	Market Spot (currency/$)	Market GNI($b)	Market GNI per Person ($)	PPP Rate (currency/$)	PPP GNI ($b)	PPP GNI per Person ($)	Market Rate Over or Under
Tanzania (T shilling)	2,177	49	900	721	148	2,718	undervalued
Egypt (Eg. Pounds)	10.03	326	3,410	3.22	1,051	10,994	undervalued
Vietnam (Dong)	21.935	195	2,060	7,486	571	6,032	undervalued
China (RMB)	6.64	11,374	8,250	3.54	21,324	16,948	undervalued
Mexico (Peso)	18.66	1,154	9,040	9.84	2,189	17,147	undervalued
S. Korea (Won)	1,160	1,414	27,600	875.5	1,874	36,579	undervalued
Japan (Yen)	109	4,817	37,930	94.9	5,529	43,540	undervalued
Germany (Euro)	1.11	3,625	43,940	0.982	4,098	49,673	undervalued
Switzerland (CHF)	0.99	680	81,240	1.261	534	63,797	overvalued
Norway (Krone)	8.40	431	82,390	11.17	324	61,936	overvalued
USA	1.00	18,357	56,810	1.00	18,969	58,700	na

Source: World Bank, World Development Indicators.

In Egypt, it would be

$$R = \frac{P^{US}}{\left[\left(\frac{1}{10.03}\right) P^E\right]},$$

and so on. Thus, these figures essentially tell us what it would cost in these countries to consume the US basket, using market exchange rates.

To get the PPP rate (column 4), the World Bank pays people to go out and compute the prices in local currency of a fixed basket of goods and services, which they then compare to the cost of that basket in the US (in dollars). Then, they divide the US basket price by the local currency basket price (ignoring the market exchange rate), which generates the PPP currency rates in column 4.

In other words, the PPP exchange rates (in local currency per dollar) are the (unobserved) exchange rates at which R would be equal to one in each country. The US and local consumption baskets would cost the same at these (unobserved) PPP exchange rates.

The World Bank does not publish its basket prices. However, it can be inferred from the first row that its procedure raised the PPP-based total GNI in Tanzania from $49 billion to $148 billion. That is, measured at US prices, Tanzania's GNI was worth $148/49 = 3.02$ times what the market-based GNI was. In turn, the PPP exchange rate (local currency per dollar) becomes $(1/E)/3.02 = 2{,}177/3.02 = 721$.

To describe this again, in Tanzania, the spot rate was 2,177 T shillings/$. At that exchange rate, total GNI was $49 billion and GNI per person was $900.

But because services are so cheap, the apparent purchasing power of a Tanzanian (compared to a resident of the US) in 2016 was the PPP-adjusted GNI per person of $2,718, with a total PPI-based GNI of $148 billion. In this sense, people in Tanzania were about three times higher in average incomes than the figures based on the market spot exchange rate would suggest.

The final column shows whether the market exchange rate was overvalued or undervalued in each country in 2016. This is a simple comparison of the market rate with the PPP rate. If the market rate is above the PPP rate (meaning it takes fewer dollars to buy the market-based local currency than it would at the PPP rate), the local currency is undervalued. If the market rate is below the PPP rate, the local currency is overvalued.

Thus, because the market rate of 2,177 TS/$ is cheaper than the PPP rate of 721 TS/$, the Tanzanian shilling is "undervalued" by $(721–2,177)/2,177 = –0.67$ (–67%). In other words, to equalize Tanzania's cost of living with the US cost of living, the T shilling would need to appreciate by 67% relative to the US$. The other PPP rates are computed in the same way.

Computation of PPP exchange rates: Other observations

China's GNI at market rates was $11.37 trillion but at PPP rates was $21.32 trillion, larger than the US economy. *Indeed, in 2014, China passed the US in total GNI (and total GDP) when measured at PPP exchange rates.* Mexico's market exchange rate was undervalued in 2016 by $(9.84 – 18.66)/18.66 = –47\%$, implying that its price-adjusted GNI per capita was over $17,000.

Switzerland and Norway have high incomes at market rates (over $80,000 per capita). But because of high service prices (due to high land costs, high taxes, regulations, and so on), their purchasing power is much lower. The "real" (PPP-adjusted) living standard in Switzerland is $63,797. Again, the way to think about that is that a Swiss person consuming in Switzerland has the same real income as an American who has $63,797 but consumes in the US. Since the US is the comparison country, its income is the same in either computation.

Look again at the last column. "Undervalued" means that the market spot price of the local currency is low compared to the PPP price. China's market rate was 6.64 RMB/$ (0.15 $/RMB), but its PPP rate was 3.54 RMB/$ (0.28 $/RMB). Thus, the RMB (the yuan) was undervalued in the PPP sense by about 47% (computed as $(3.54 – 6.64)/6.64 = –0.467$).

"Overvalued" means just the opposite. In Norway, the market rate was 8.40 Krone/\$ (0.119 \$/Krone), but the PPP rate was 11.17 Krone/\$ (0.09 \$/Krone).

As may be seen, lower-income economies tend to have undervalued market rates and higher-income economies tend to have overvalued market rates. This basically reflects the low wages and costs in the former and high wages and costs in the latter.

Study question 2

Suppose that Argentina's market exchange rate were 15 Argentine Pesos/\$ and the computed PPP rate were 10 Argentine Pesos/\$. Then, which statement is false?

A. The Argentine peso is undervalued at market rates.
B. The Argentine peso is overvalued at market rates.
C. PPP-adjusted GNI per capita in Argentina would be 33% higher than its market-based GNI per capita.
D. An American traveling to Argentina would need to pay 33% more for the Argentine peso than the market rate in order to face the same prices as she does at home.

Discussion of question 2

The correct answer is B, which is a false statement. A is correct because the Argentine peso is undervalued by 33%. Statements C and D are other ways of explaining what it means for the market rate to be undervalued by 33% compared to the PPP rate.

PPP: The Big Mac Index

Another way to see all of this is rather fun. Twice per year, *The Economist* magazine computes its "Big Mac index" for 56 countries. The index compares the price of a McDonald's Big Mac hamburger in dollars at the market exchange rate versus what it would need to be to equal the dollar price in the US. They use this form of a PPP exchange rate to conclude whether the local currency is undervalued or overvalued.

The Big Mac (BM) is an interesting product in this context because it is a homogeneous good wherever it is purchased. But Big Macs are highly localized and are not traded across cities, much less countries. In different cities and countries, local rents and wages are quite different.

As an example, in January 2018, in China (the main Beijing McDonald's), Big Mac data were as follows:

- The local price = 20.4 RMB for a Big Mac.
- Market (official) exchange rate = 6.43 RMB/$(= 0.156$/RMB).
- Market price in US$ = 20.4/6.43 = $3.17. This is what a tourist would pay in dollars by exchanging dollars for RMB in the spot market.
- The US market dollar price = $5.28 (what you would pay at an average US McDonald's).

Then, the implied PPP exchange rate = 20.4RMB/$5.28 = 3.86 RMB/$ (= 0.259$/RMB). Keep in mind that this is the exchange rate that would equalize BM prices in the US and Beijing (but it doesn't exist). Again, in this sense, the RMB was undervalued by $(3.86 - 6.43)/(6.43) = -40\%$. Table 15.2 shows data for other selected countries from the January 2018 edition of *The Economist*.

In Table 15.2, the third column shows the local currency price of a BM, for example, 75 pesos in Argentina and 130 rubles in Russia. The fourth column shows the market exchange rate, for example, 18.94 A pesos per dollar and 56.75 rubles per dollar.

Column 5 computes the dollar price of a BM at the market exchange rate, for example, 75 A pesos/18.94 = $3.96. This was the price a tourist would have paid just by converting dollars to A pesos at the market rate.

Column 6 computes the implied PPP exchange rate, using the US$ price of a BM of $5.28. Thus, in Argentina, the BM-based PPP was 75/5.28 = 14.205 A peso/$. This is the (unobserved) exchange rate that would make an Argentine BM cost the same as a BM in the US.

The final column computes the implied undervaluation (if negative) or overvaluation (if positive) of the local currency based on

Table 15.2   Computation of PPP exchange rates using Big Mac prices.

Country	Local Currency (LCU)	Big Mac LCU Price	Market E Rate LCU per US$	Market US$ Price	PPP E Rate LCU per US$	LCU % Under/Over
Argentina	Argentine Peso	75.00	18.94	3.960	14.205	−24.99
Australia	Australian Dollar	5.90	1.25	4.706	1.117	−10.87
Canada	Canadian Dollar	6.55	1.25	5.257	1.241	−0.43
China	RMB	20.40	6.43	3.172	3.864	−39.93
Egypt	Egyptian Pound	34.21	17.70	1.933	6.479	−63.39
Germany	Euro	3.90	0.82	4.775	0.739	−9.57
Greece	Euro	3.35	0.82	4.101	0.634	−22.33
Hong Kong	HK Dollar	20.50	7.82	2.622	3.883	−50.34
Malaysia	Ringgit	9.00	3.95	2.276	1.705	−56.89
Mexico	Mexican Peso	48.00	18.66	2.572	9.091	−51.29
Norway	Krone	49.00	7.85	6.242	9.280	18.22
Russia	Ruble	130.00	56.75	2.291	24.621	−56.61
Sweden	Kroner	49.10	8.02	6.123	9.299	15.97
Switzerland	Swiss Franc	6.50	0.96	6.765	1.231	28.12
US	US Dollar	5.28	1.00	5.280	1.000	0.00

Source: The Economist magazine, January 2018.

BM prices. For example, the A peso was 25% undervalued and the Russian ruble was 57% undervalued. In brief, it is cheap for tourists to eat in those countries.

In contrast, the Norwegian krone, the Swedish kroner, and the Swiss franc were all overvalued, reflecting the high cost of services and products in those countries. It is expensive for tourists to visit those countries.

Germany and Greece are interesting to note. Both use the euro as their currency, but in January 2018, the euro was about 10% undervalued using the German BM price but 22% undervalued using the Greek BM price. This calculation shows that local Greek service prices and other costs were well below those of Germany.

Levels versus Changes: Absolute and Relative PPP

Absolute versus relative PPP

The PPP exchange rate defined so far is called the *absolute PPP* (APPP) rate. It is the exchange rate that would make living costs equal between countries in the same currency:

$$E_{\text{PPP}} = \frac{P^{US}}{P^{UK}} \text{ (or } R = 1\text{).}$$

This rate is computed by comparing the costs of purchasing a standardized overall basket by a family in the two countries (as in the World Bank project) or, more informally, by the Big Mac index. The terminology that a market exchange rate is undervalued or overvalued might be considered an economic prediction. If it is undervalued, the local currency should appreciate over time in order to move living costs (or production costs) closer to those in the United States. If it is overvalued, it should depreciate. This would happen due to goods being traded from where they are expensive to where they are cheaper, as explained earlier in these notes.

But is it likely that market exchange rates would actually move to this level?

No, because so many goods are non-traded and there are differences in local costs, taxes, rents, and the like. These are structural factors that cannot be much changed simply by trading goods.

Thus, it is unreasonable to expect absolute PPP to hold, and the costs of buying goods really are different across countries for long periods of time. So are differences in wages and other costs due to structural factors. Put another way, some countries have higher price levels than others due to these factors.

And cities within countries have different costs also. For example, there are considerably higher costs in New York than in Tulsa, Oklahoma, in the US. This is because land prices, rents, taxes, and labor costs are higher in New York than in Tulsa.

But even if cost differences persist, perhaps there should be some tendency toward *relative PPP*. This is the idea that over a long period, market exchange rates must move in the direction of differences in inflation rates. That is, a country with high inflation should see a depreciating currency and a country with a low inflation should see an appreciating currency. As explained earlier, high inflation makes a country's products less competitive, reduces exports and raises imports, and thereby reduces the demand for its currency. So, if one country experiences higher inflation than another, the first one will see its currency drop in value to restore its competitiveness in trade.

How is the idea of relative PPP (RPPP) defined? First, while it is unreasonable to think the ratio of living costs should equal $R = 1$ (absolute PPP), the ratio might tend toward a given constant:

$$\frac{P^{US}}{P^{UK}} = \theta.$$

If $\theta > 1$, the US is structurally more expensive than the UK. But if $\theta < 1$, the UK is structurally more expensive.

Then, RPPP is the prediction that percentage changes in the bilateral exchange rate would keep θ constant. Rewrite the equation as

$$P^{US} = \mathrm{E}P^{UK}\theta.$$

Expressed in terms of changes, it follows that

$$\%\Delta P^{US} = \%\Delta E + \%\Delta P^{UK} + \%\Delta\theta$$

(This equation follows from the property of percentages, or really of logarithms, that the logarithmic change of a product is the sum of the logarithmic changes of each part of the product.)

But the θ term in this theory reflects long-lasting differences in structural factors, meaning that it is likely to remain fixed over time, implying that $\%\Delta\theta = 0$. Thus, the RPPP prediction is

$$\%\Delta P^{US} - \%\Delta P^{UK} = \%\Delta E.$$

In words, the difference between US inflation and UK inflation will equal the percentage depreciation or appreciation of the pound relative to the dollar. Then, the proposition of RPPP is simply that the market spot rate adjusts over time to equal differences in inflation rates between countries.

Consider an example, using the US and Canada. At the beginning of some year, let $P^{US} = \$115,000$, $P^C = C\$100,000$, and $E = 0.95\$/C\$$ (price of C\$).

Then, $\frac{P^{US}}{EP^C} = \$115,000/(0.95*C\$100,000) = 1.21 = \theta$. That is, it is initially 21% more expensive to live in the US and this ratio should stay fairly constant over time because it reflects naturally higher costs in the United States. RPPP predicts that the market exchange rate will adjust in the long run (say over 1–2 years or longer) to differences in inflation rates to keep this relative cost stable.

Relative PPP

Thus, let $\%\Delta P^{US} = 3\%$ and $\%\Delta P^C = 5\%$. The US inflation rate (e.g., the consumer price index or producer price index) is 3% and the Canadian inflation rate is 5%. Then, RPPP would mean

$$3\% - 5\% = \%\Delta E = -2\%.$$

That is, faster Canadian inflation should make the C\$ *depreciate* over time, in this case by 2%. This would imply that the new exchange rate would be $E = 0.95*(1 - 0.02) = 0.95*0.98 = 0.93\$/C\$$.

Does this depreciation maintain the same relative living costs? With these inflation rates, we have these new cost bundles: $P^{US} = \$115,000(1.03) = \$118,450$ and $P^C = C\$100,000(1.05) = C\$105,000$. Then, $\$118,450/(0.93*C\$105,000) = 1.21$.

Thus, the differences in the costs of living are sustained, in that it is still 21% more expensive in the US. Again, the idea behind RPPP is that in the long run, E must adjust to reflect changes in the differences in inflation rates.

Is there evidence for this prediction? In fact, evidence shows that among the major industrialized countries with flexible exchange rates, RPPP does hold reasonably well over a 3–5-years horizon, sometimes quicker than that.

Study question 3

Suppose that in 2011, the yen-per-dollar exchange rate was $E_{¥,\$} = 110$. Over the following 10 years, suppose that the Japanese inflation rate was 10% in total (an average of 1.0% per year) and the US inflation rate was 7% in total (an average of 0.7% per year). Then, RPPP would predict all the following except:

A. The dollar became cheaper in terms of the yen-per-dollar rate over the period 2011–2021.
B. The yen depreciated over that period.
C. The exchange rate in 2021 would be 3% higher.
D. The exchange rate in 2021 would be 113.3.

Discussion of question 3

The correct answer is A because it is a false statement. In fact, the dollar would appreciate and become more expensive. B is a true statement because the yen would depreciate according to RPPP. C and D are both true statements and they say the same thing, that the yen-dollar rate would be 3% higher (the yen would depreciate by 3%).

In terms of RPPP, in this example, we would have

$$\%\Delta E_{¥,\$} = \%\Delta P^J - \%\Delta P^{US} = 10 - 7\% = 3\%.$$

Keep in mind that in this example, the exchange rate is the yen price of the dollar rather than the dollar price of the yen.

Relating RPPP to Fundamental Economic Factors: The Monetary Approach to Exchange Rates

Determinants of price inflation

The RPPP theory argues that bilateral exchange-rate changes should track differences in inflation rates between countries over longer time periods. But this begs the following questions: What drives inflation? Why do prices rise faster in some countries than in others? A number of macroeconomic factors could push up prices in a country.

Supply disruptions: At times, there may be disruptions in important sources that supply goods and services, making them scarcer and more expensive. A prominent recent example was the impact of the global COVID-19 pandemic, which diminished labor supplies as workers stayed home and generated multiple shortages in domestic and global supply chains.

Demand shocks: Similarly, at times, there may be increases in aggregate demand, caused by increases in government spending, growth in business investment, sudden wealth increases, or growing consumer confidence.

Both these types of shocks can generate short-term inflation in price levels. However, they typically are temporary in nature as markets adjust. On the supply side, rising prices would induce more production or investments in improved supply chains. Demand shocks may be temporary policy decisions or confidence may wane. Thus, supply and demand shocks tend to have short-term inflationary effects and do not generate sustainable inflation. More relevant for RPPP theory are fundamental, long-term inflation factors, as discussed next.

The monetary theory of inflation and exchange rates

In fact, the basic elements of a long-run macroeconomic model of exchange-rate determination are in place. To recap, using again the US and the UK:

In price levels, we have absolute PPP: $E^{\text{PPP}} = \frac{P^{US}}{P^{UK}}$.

The idea is that in the long run, the exchange rate should tend toward equalizing comparable price levels. As noted, it may be that one country is structurally more expensive, and full APPP is not possible.

In rates of change, we have relative PPP: $\%\Delta E = \%\Delta P^{US} - \%\Delta P^{UK}$.

The idea is that over longer time periods, the depreciation or appreciation of the home currency should equal differences in inflation rates. If the US had higher inflation, E would rise, making the dollar cheaper and the pound more expensive.

Thus, the next task is to develop a theory of how price levels and inflation are determined in two (or many) countries to understand what drives exchange rates over time. In economics, the standard approach is to use a model of the money market in each country, since changes in money supply versus money demand matter for prices and inflation.

An important aside: What is money?

Students may recall discussing the definition of a country's money supply in a prior course in macroeconomics or money and banking. Following is a brief review.

Money is an object that serves three primary functions in an economy:

1. **Store of value:** That is, money is an asset that can be used to buy and sell goods in the future. Items counted as money generally earn very low returns as an asset but are held because market participants are confident that they will retain value.
2. **Unit of account:** The basic monetary unit (e.g., the dollar) is the commodity in which all prices are expressed. Due to this, money is used to measure the relative values of different goods and services. Finally, the price of a unit of money is 1 ($1 is worth $1), permitting money to be the numeraire good in the economy.
3. **Medium of exchange:** To serve as money, the item must be generally accepted as a means of payment for goods and services. This means that money is the most liquid form of payment because it is the asset that is most easily converted into real goods.

Note a critical implication of money. Since all goods and services have prices in terms of money (it's the unit of account) and market agents are willing to accept it (it's the medium of exchange), there is no need for people to engage in barter transactions. Barter means trading one good, such as cattle, for another, such as legal advice, which is extremely costly.

Imagine how difficult it would be to engage in barter across international borders. Thus, the ability of traders to exchange two forms of money (currencies) at a price (the exchange rate) overcomes the need for international barter.

Types of money

Many things have been used as money in history, including seashells, agricultural products, wine, and precious metals.

There are clearly many problems with such commodities as money, including the lack of homogeneity among units, differences in quality, cheating on their intrinsic values, and the simple fact that money supplies would depend on harvests, mining successes, or commercial business decisions rather than policy choices made by monetary authorities.

Today, digital assets such as bitcoins and Ethereum, which are accounted for in decentralized "blockchain" software, are seen by some as potential forms of money. To some degree, they have become a medium of exchange, as certain firms will accept them as payment. However, digital coins themselves are priced in dollars (or euros, etc.) and, therefore, are not a unit of account. Further, their monetary values are highly volatile, making them risky as a store of value. No country yet counts them as part of the formal money supply.

Whether digital assets eventually become a significant form of money remains to be seen. However, it is noteworthy that several countries have begun to issue digital currencies that firms and households may hold in "digital wallets". One example is the "digital RMB" issued by the People's Bank of China. As of 2022, many more countries are considering whether to issue a digital currency. Such assets may become increasingly important elements of the financial system over time.

Monetary categories in modern banking systems

In modern economies, the creation and regulation of the supply of money are the responsibility of *central banks*, such as the US Federal Reserve Bank, the Bank of Japan, and the People's Bank of China. To summarize, the standard forms of money in sophisticated market economies are the following. These categories are based on the functions of central banks and how they affect other forms of money.

1. The *monetary base*, often called $M0$ ("M zero"), is defined as currency in circulation plus reserve deposits of banks held primarily at the central bank. Currency in circulation consists of paper money issued by the government and held outside the central bank. These bills exist to facilitate smaller transactions in the economy.

Larger banks and financial brokers have direct deposits at the central bank. These are called "bank reserves" and, by law, such banks must own at least a minimum amount of them in order to be able to cover unexpectedly large withdrawals of funds by their customers during financially stressful times. These "reserve requirements" help banks remain solvent and stabilize the financial system. Private banks may choose to hold additional reserves, called "excess reserves". These required and excess reserve deposits are the central bank's primary liabilities in its "balance sheet".

2. "**Narrow money**" $M1$ ("M one") is defined as $M0$ + demand deposits.

Demand deposits are checking accounts owned by firms, organizations, and individuals at private banks (i.e., not the central bank). The amounts in those deposits are payable on demand, meaning banks that hold them must process checks or electronic transfers made by the bank customers. They are liabilities of the banks at which they are held.

Students may recall from a money and banking course that the volume of money in $M1$ is the result of banks creating demand deposits from their excess reserves through a "money multiplier" effect. In simple terms, if private banks own more reserves at the central bank than required, they may make loans (in the form of deposits) to borrowers. Those loans may be a large multiple of their excess reserves.

3. "**Broad money**" $M2$ ("M two") is defined as $M1$ + other less liquid assets that serve money functions.

These other less liquid assets primarily include savings accounts, small deposits that mature over time, and money market mutual funds.

The monetary model: The supply of money

Since this is not a course in monetary policy or money and banking, we will make the following very simplified assumption in order to focus on a simple version of the money supply:

Define the nominal money supply as $M1$. In essence, this is the amount of liquid assets that are available to finance transactions in the economy.

Next, assume that a country's central bank (CB) can control the supply of $M1$, making it increase or decrease as a matter of policy. How does this process work?

In fact, the central bank directly controls only part of $M1$, namely the monetary base ($M0$). The primary means of doing so is *open-market purchases of bonds from and sales of bonds to private banks and major financial brokers*. These bonds are typically secure government-issued securities, such as Treasury bills.

It is important to understand that an open-market purchase of bonds by the CB creates more $M0$ because the transaction involves the CB raising private bank reserves (which are part of $M0$) in exchange for the bonds acquired (bonds are not in $M0$). Similarly, an open-market sale reduces the size of $M0$ by releasing bonds (not in $M0$) to private banks in return for reducing those banks' reserves.

However, central banks also can indirectly control $M1$ by influencing the total amount of bank deposits created, which would be ($M1 - M0$). Their tools for doing so include the following, among others:

- Changing the interest rate the CB pays on reserve deposits (e.g., the federal funds interest rate in the US). A lower rate makes it less attractive for banks to hold excess reserves and they will seek to lend them, raising $M1$.
- Changing the reserve requirements imposed on banks. Higher reserve requirements would reduce $M1$ as banks would have fewer excess reserves and would need to make fewer loans.

Monetary policy: Exogenous changes in the money supply

In this context, what is the definition of a country's monetary policy?

The idea in this basic model is that the supply of money ($M1$) is completely under the control of the central bank. It can choose, as a matter of policy, to increase or reduce the money supply. Such changes are *exogenous*, meaning they are controlled by policy and the money supply does not change in response to movements in the economy itself.

In terms of this model, the nominal money supply ($M1$) is exogenous and can be denoted as $M^S = M1$. As will become clear, an increase in the money supply has expansionary effects on the economy (whether in incomes or prices) and a decrease has contractionary effects.

An example: Quantitative easing

"Quantitative easing" was an exceptional effort after the 2008–2009 financial crisis by CBs in the US, the EU, the UK, Japan, and elsewhere to massively increase $M0$ (bank reserves) through purchasing financial assets from banks. The novel element of this policy was that the CBs agreed to buy nearly worthless financial assets, such as collateralized debt obligations and structured debt vehicles from failed housing and commercial real estate markets. In essence, the CBs removed the risk of bankruptcy from these banks and brokers and created reserves for them to own in return.

The expectation was that the banks would quickly lend these excess reserves, expanding $M1$ and encouraging more consumer spending and investment. That is largely what happened in the US and, later, the UK and EU.

This kind of intervention left CBs owning large volumes of additional assets in the process of raising $M0$ and $M1$. For example, Figure 15.2 shows what happened to the Federal Reserve's balance sheet in terms of financial assets owned, which corresponds closely to reserve assets of banks (the Fed's liabilities), which is $M0$. As may be seen, $M0$ doubled from $1 trillion to over $2 trillion in 2009–2010.

The Fed continued to raise $M0$ through about 2018 to support financial markets, before reducing it somewhat. However, to combat the recession of 2020 associated with the COVID-19 pandemic, the Fed dramatically raised the monetary base again, from $4 trillion to $9 trillion.

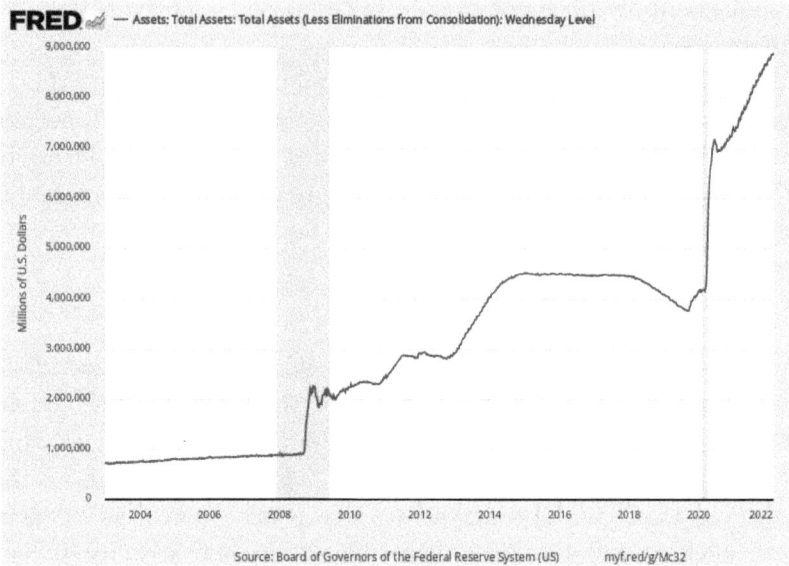

Figure 15.2   The federal reserve balance sheet, 2004–2022.

Source: Federal Reserve Bank of St. Louis FRED database, at https://fred.stlouisfed.org/series/WALCL.

These expansions of the Fed's balance sheet led to large increases in the money supply, as intended. However, many observers feared that it would generate inflationary pressures, as explained next.

The monetary model: Demand for money

To understand why rapid increases in the supply of money could raise prices, it is first important to bring in the demand for money. After all, if the CB supplies money, it must be because there are agents (households, businesses, organizations, and governments) that demand to have it.

To use another simplification, assume that the demand for money is driven only by the need to use money to undertake transactions. Agents may also demand to hold money as a precaution against economic risk and volatility in non-monetary assets but ignore that.

The simplest idea is the familiar *Quantity Theory* of money demand. This states that the volume of transactions in an economy is assumed to be proportional to the dollar value of gross nominal income.

Define gross nominal income as GNI=PY, where P is the aggregate price level and Y is the real income. Real income $Y = $ GNI$/P$ is a measure of the real volume of goods and services that nominal income can purchase at prevailing prices.

Thus, under the quantity theory, the demand for money is

$$M^d = \lambda * PY,$$

where λ is a constant indicating how many dollars people wish to hold for every dollar of nominal income. Thus, if $\lambda = 0.25$, then demand to hold nominal money balances is 25% of GNI. This means that, on average, each dollar demanded would be spent four times $(= 1/0.25)$ during the year to support the nominal GNI.

A critical point is that in this model, money demand would rise in proportion to increases in GNI. If income doubled, whether due to higher prices or higher real GNI, so would M^d.

From this assumption, it immediately follows that the demand to hold real (price-level deflated) money balances is

$$\frac{M^d}{P} = \lambda * Y$$

The left-hand side of this equation measures the real value of the quantity of money demanded. It is proportional to the real volume of goods and services purchased in the economy.

These concepts are confusing in the abstract, so an example will help understand the theory. Suppose that nominal GNI=PY = $18 trillion. Let $\lambda = 0.25$. Then, nominal money demand would be $(0.25)^*($18tr$) = $4.5 trillion.

Suppose also that national accountants decide that the cost of an important basket of goods and services is $P = $100,000$. Then, real income would be $Y = 18 trillion$/$100,000 = 180$ million baskets of goods and services. This concept is the same as the baskets discussed earlier in this set of notes when discussing PPP but now scaled to a measure of the whole economy.

It follows that the real quantity of money needed to buy 180 million baskets would be (4.5 trillion/$100,000) = 45 million. That is exactly enough "real dollars" to buy 180 million baskets in a year. Note that 45m = 0.25*180m. Thus, in holding nominal dollars, people are really demanding 45m real dollars.

What are "real dollars"? They are enough price-adjusted dollars to buy the quantity of real GNI. Both are in the same units.

Practical Note: In practice, dealing with real baskets (other than for calculating PPP exchange rates) is challenging because it would require recalculating the weights assigned to categories of goods and services over time. Thus, instead, economists choose base years in which a price level is set as $P = 1$ (or $P = 100$) so that nominal and real GNIs are the same in that year. Then, changes over time in P would be a price index, such as the CPI, PPI, or GDP deflator used to deflate nominal GNI into real GNI and nominal money demand into real money demand.

The monetary model: Equilibrium

Equilibrium in this model is described in terms of real quantities of money supplied and demanded. On the supply side, nominal $M1$ is assumed to be exogenous and subject to changes due to monetary policy. Denote this as M^S, for money supply. Then, the real money supply is the nominal money ($M1$) divided by the price level: $\frac{M^S}{P}$.

Turning to demand, people wish to hold nominal amounts of money that are proportional to GNI. This means that real demand for money is $\frac{M^d}{P} = \lambda * Y$.

Thus, equilibrium in a country's money market involves having equal real quantities supplied and demanded:

$$\frac{M}{P} = \lambda Y.$$

The left-hand side is the real money supply, and the right-hand side is real money demand. (In equilibrium, the model uses M to indicate both nominal money supply and nominal money demand, which must be equal.)

Here, there is one exogenous variable (the nominal money supply), which is held constant unless the central bank changes it. And λ is a constant parameter. Thus, only P and Y may change endogenously in this equation.

What happens if the money market is not in equilibrium? If real money supply were higher than real money demand, either P would rise to reduce the real money supply or Y would rise to raise real money demand. *Excess money supply causes price inflation or raises real GNI or both.*

If real money supply were below real money demand, then either P would fall or Y would fall. *Deficient money supply generates either price deflation or lower real GNI or both.*

A further important note: The analysis here considers the supply of money to be exogenous. However, it is possible to imagine an exogenous increase in λ, which would be consistent with an exogenous rise in the demand to hold higher real money balances. The result would be excess money demand, causing either price deflation or lower real GNI or both.

Students should keep in mind that higher demand for money is contractionary in the economy. That is because if people wish to hold onto more money, they would be choosing to spend it less frequently, reducing demand for goods and services.

Study question 4

Which of the following assumptions are made in the monetary model?

A. The nominal money supply is exogenously controlled by the central bank.
B. The demand for real money balances is fixed.
C. The nominal demand to hold money is proportional to gross national income.
D. Both A and B.
E. Both A and C.

Discussion of question 4

The correct answer is E because both A and C are assumptions of the model. B is incorrect because real money demand depends on real GNI, which is not a fixed variable.

Exchange rates and PPP in the monetary model

Combine these concepts for the US and a second country, the UK. As noted above, the monetary approach can be used to solve for price levels:

$$P_{US} = \frac{M_{US}}{\lambda_{US} Y_{US}} \quad \text{and} \quad P_{UK} = \frac{M_{UK}}{\lambda_{UK} Y_{UK}}.$$

In each country, *the price level is the ratio of the nominal money supply over real money demand.* The higher is the money supply compared to how much is demanded, the greater must be the price level.

This model assumes that price levels are able to adjust to assure these equilibrium conditions hold. This assumption is reasonable over a sufficient time period. To introduce exchange rates, simply bring in the long-run view of the exchange rate level: APPP.

$$E_{\frac{\$}{\pounds}} = \frac{P_{US}}{P_{UK}} = \frac{M_{US}/\lambda_{US} Y_{US}}{M_{UK}/\lambda_{UK} Y_{UK}} = \frac{M_{US}/M_{UK}}{\lambda_{US} Y_{US}/\lambda_{UK} Y_{UK}}.$$

This fundamental equation predicts that the nominal exchange rate (= APPP rate in the long run) is determined by the *differences in relative money supplies compared to relative real money demands* in two countries.

Intuitively, if the US were rapidly expanding its money supply compared to the UK, and real money demands were not changing by much in either nation, then the dollar would depreciate over time.

But changes in real income also matter. If the US economy were growing rapidly compared to the UK (say, because of improved technology, growth in productivity, tax cuts, or other factors), then the denominator would rise and the dollar would appreciate over time.

The basic idea of the monetary approach to long-run exchange rates is that faster monetary growth at home than abroad should depreciate the home currency, other things equal. Rapid home real income growth should appreciate the home currency, other things equal.

These ideas can be extended to relative PPP. From $P_{US} = \frac{M_{US}}{\lambda_{US} Y_{US}}$ and the idea that λ_{US} is fixed, it follows that the percentage change in the US price level equals the percentage change in the US money supply minus the percentage change in US real income:

$$\% \Delta P_{US} = \% \Delta M_{US} - \% \Delta Y_{US,t}.$$

Similarly, for the UK, $\% \Delta P_{UK} = \% \Delta M_{UK} - \% \Delta Y_{UK}.$

Simply apply relative PPP to explain changes over time in bilateral exchange rates:

$$\% \Delta E_{\$,£} = \% \Delta P_{US} - \% \Delta P_{UK} = (\% \Delta M_{US} - \% \Delta M_{UK})$$
$$- (\% \Delta Y_{US} - \% \Delta Y_{UK}).$$

Thus, if relative PPP holds, then the percentage change in a bilateral exchange rate equals the inflation differential, which in turn is the difference in growth rates in the money supply less the difference in growth rates in real incomes.

As noted earlier, there is considerable empirical evidence that RPPP holds well over longer time periods. This theory indicates that the primary long-run "fundamental" determinants of exchange rates are monetary policy and economic growth rates.

This basic logic is easy to apply in forecasting longer-term exchange rates. Suppose the US was expected to expand its money supply over 10 years by 5% per year and the UK by 4% per year. That factor should depreciate the dollar by 1% per year (on average). Over 10 years, it would imply a 10% dollar depreciation.

But if the US income growth rate were anticipated to be 3% per year and the UK growth rate to be 1.5% per year, then the dollar should appreciate by 1.5% per year (on average) due to this factor. Over 10 years, the total dollar appreciation would be 15% on this score.

Together, these factors would imply a net annual average appreciation of the US\$ of 0.5%: –0.005 = (0.05 – 0.04) – (0.03 – 0.015) on average each year. Over 10 years, this should achieve a total 5% appreciation of the dollar.

The actual path this long-run appreciation would take from month to month or year to year is uncertain due to short-run factors, such as policy shocks and news. But over the ten-year period, it is reasonable to anticipate these fundamentals to dominate.

Study question 5

Consider these data for Sweden (its currency is the Swedish Kroner or SK) and the euro region (its currency is the euro or €):

Sweden expands its money supply by 2% per year and the euro area does so by 5% per year. The Swedish growth rate in real income is 1% per year and the growth rate in the euro area is 2% per year.

Use the monetary model to predict long-run changes in the spot rate, $E_{SK}/€$.

A. The SK would be expected to depreciate by exactly 2% per year over several years.
B. The SK would be expected to appreciate by exactly 2% per year over several years.
C. The SK would be expected to appreciate on average by 2% per year over several years.
D. The euro would be expected to appreciate on average by 2% per year over several years.

Discussion of question 5

The correct answer is C, which is consistent with the monetary model over a decade. A and B are false because the monetary model does not predict equal and precise currency changes in each year (i.e., the short run). D is false because the euro would be expected to depreciate.

Purchasing power parity: Importance and summary

Absolute PPP is a useful concept, for it provides a benchmark definition of an exchange rate that would equalize the costs of living in two or more countries. It can be used to assess whether the market exchange rate is undervalued or overvalued compared to this benchmark.

Relative PPP is fundamentally important in economics because it provides the basic theory of what determines exchange-rate changes in the long run. Consistent with empirical evidence, RPPP is the best predictor of how bilateral exchange rates will move over a period of several years.

As analyzed in Chapter 14, there are large short-run (daily or monthly) variations in exchange rates around longer-term trends. This is because in the short run, exchange rates really are a key component of asset prices. These notes will return to exchange-rate policies in Chapter 17, which considers why countries choose between fixed and flexible rates.

Chapter 16

National Income and the Balance of Payments

Introduction to Accounting for National Income and the Balance of Payments

Primary questions

In this chapter, the text begins developing an understanding of how economies are linked together at the macroeconomic level. The first task is to understand the national accounting concepts that will be essential for understanding aggregate macroeconomic data and how they link countries together.

The primary questions to study include the following:

- How are total national expenditure, output, and income related to international trade and financial flows?
- What are the current account and the current account balance? Why is it different from the more familiar trade deficit or surplus? Which concept is more important for national income?
- Does a trade deficit in goods really mean something negative for welfare, as politicians often suggest?
- What are the primary economic factors determining a country's current account balance?

- How are an economy's choices regarding savings, investments, and government expenditure related to international deficits or surpluses?
- What is a country's "balance of payments" in international finance?
- How do these various concepts relate to changes in an economy's net international wealth?

The macroeconomic circular flow of income in a closed economy

Before analyzing how a country fits into the global macroeconomy, it is important to review the basic concepts in a country that does not engage in trading goods, productive factors, or financial assets. In earlier chapters, such a country was called an autarky, but from now on, refer to it as a closed economy. In any economy, there are three fundamental macroeconomic concepts: expenditure, output, and income, which are now defined and explained.

Gross national expenditure (GNE) is the total spending made by all members of the economy. In a closed economy, individuals and businesses can spend on three broad categories: consumption, investment, and government expenditures. Thus, $GNE = C + I + G$.

Gross domestic product (GDP) is the total value of all *final* goods and services produced in an economy. As seen next, it equals all income earned by primary factors, such as labor, capital, and land.

The concept is limited to "final" goods and services because if we included all transactions in intermediate inputs, we would vastly overstate actual production.

Example: Suppose a car (a final good) sells for $30,000 but its production requires inputs such as glass, steel, leather, semiconductors, and so on worth $20,000. It is incorrect to count all $50,000 (both inputs and output) in GDP because that would count the intermediate inputs twice: once by themselves and once included in the costs of producing the car.

Thus, GDP is correctly measured as all *value added* produced in the economy. Value added is the difference between the price of a good and the costs of its intermediate inputs.

In this example, suppose there were no intermediate inputs required to make the glass, steel, leather, and semiconductors. Then, VA in those intermediate inputs would be $20,000, which is paid to primary factors labor, capital, and land. (In fact, there would be intermediate inputs in glass and so on, which would need to be accounted for.) In turn, VA in the car would be $30,000 − $20,000 = $10,000, which is paid to the primary factors used to produce the car.

Then, total VA in the car and its intermediates is $30,000, or just the price of the car, which is the final output. This illustrates why GDP, which is the total value added, also equals income earned by primary factors. Again, GDP is computed as the value of final goods and services, which is also the total value added.

Gross national income (GNI) is the total income earned by residents of a country, in wages, capital income, and land payments. *In a closed economy, these concepts all equal each other: GNE = GDP = GNI.*

This concept is described in economics as the "circular flow" of income: producing output generates income, which is what's available for spending.

The balance of payments accounts in an open economy

These concepts are now extended to an open economy, meaning a macroeconomy that is open to trade in goods, services, factors, and assets. To do that requires understanding the balance of payments (BOP) and its various components. *The BOP account is a statistical record of the flow of inward receipts and outward payments between residents of one country and the rest of the world in a year.*

Note carefully that this is a statement about flows (new transactions within a year), not stocks (the sum of transactions made in past years). These receipts and payments exist to pay for international trade in goods and services, along with various factor income flows across borders, plus trade in assets. To understand these ideas requires defining some important parts of the BOP.

The balance of trade

The merchandise trade balance is exports of goods minus imports of goods. In this context, "goods" or "merchandise" refers to physical products, such as oil and gas, agricultural products, clothing, furniture, wine, and automobiles.

This concept is commonly referred to as "the trade balance" and is often the balance discussed most widely by the media and policymakers. Indeed, it has considerable influence in political terms.

From an economic standpoint, however, there is little difference between exporting a physical product and exporting a service, such as engineering expertise. Both generate income through exports. There is no good reason to distinguish between goods and services in understanding international trade.

Thus, the better, and correct, concept of "the trade balance" is the *balance of trade in merchandise and services*. This is exports of goods and services minus imports of goods and services.

The trade balance is defined as $TB = X - M$, where X is exports and M is imports, measured in a currency, such as dollars. X and M include both goods and services. The trade balance is sometimes called "net exports" if it is positive and "net imports" if it is negative.

It is useful to keep in mind that, by definition, exports are positive for goods and services in which domestic production exceeds domestic spending, while imports are positive for goods where domestic spending exceeds domestic production. In other words, if $TB = (X - M) > 0$, meaning a trade surplus, the value of output exceeds the value of expenditures. If $TB < 0$, meaning a trade deficit, the value of expenditures is larger than the value of output. The notes will return to this important point later.

Comments on trade in services

The concept of trade in goods or merchandise is obvious. A country may export corn, iron ore, and textiles, while importing machines, chemicals, and construction materials. These things cross borders after being transported on ships, airplanes, trains, and so on.

But how are services traded? The idea of traded services may seem surprising, but many services are traded. Here are some examples:

- tourism services, such as transportation, hotels, meals, and entertainment;
- financial services, such as banking, insurance, legal, and engineering services;
- consulting services;
- education, such as college and university training;
- health services, such as surgery and radiology;
- telecommunication services and software.

It is evident that sometimes goods and services are traded together, as a package. For example, if a company in the US purchases complex machinery from Germany, the contract likely would include the cost of a maintenance contract from the selling firm.

Another major form of services trade is the licensing of intellectual property rights. For example, a firm in Japan may own a technology, on which it registers a patent in another country, such as Korea. The patent-owning firm could choose to license (sell) the rights to produce the good in Korea to a firm located there. The license fees are considered a service export in Japan, because revenues flow to Japan, and a service import in Korea, because the license must be paid for.

A similar transaction is selling the rights to make copies of copyrighted music recordings, movies and television programs, software, and other digital services. A student in Germany who legally downloads a copy of Microsoft Office and pays the fee for doing so is buying a license, making it an import for Germany and an export for the United States. Other prominent examples are licensing the rights to use trademarks to local franchisees in many products and services, such as hotels (e.g., Marriott), fast food (e.g., McDonald's), banks (e.g., JP Morgan Chase), and retail distribution (e.g., Walmart and Ikea).

Transactions in IPR licensing have risen sharply in recent years. For example, US firms earned around $44 b in licensing exports (revenues received) in 1990, which grew to $116 b in 2019. US licensing imports (payments) grew from $16 b to $42 b over that period (*Source*: US Bureau of Economic Analysis, https://www.bea.gov/data/intl-trade-investment/). It is evident from these figures that the US is a significant net exporter of intellectual property, which is unsurprising given the country's relative specialization in technological and creative industries.

It is interesting to explore the channels by which services are actually traded internationally. For this purpose, economists and statisticians at the World Trade Organization define four modes of services trade:

Mode 1 (Cross-border supply): Some services do cross borders, much like trade in goods. Thus, the producers are in one country and the consumers in another. Downloading software from the Internet is an example, as mentioned above.

Mode 2 (Consumption abroad): Many services are used or consumed when the purchaser is abroad, but the service is located there. Examples include a tourist staying in a local hotel, dining in restaurants, and using local transportation.

Mode 3 (Commercial presence): Some services are provided by multinational service enterprises through their affiliates abroad. Thus, foreign branches of US banks sell local financial services and US-owned hotel chains also operate international hotels. By convention, the local sales of foreign affiliates, and the sales of local affiliates of foreign service MNEs, are not included in a country's statistics on trade in services, but implicitly that is what those sales are. In that context, it is interesting that a transaction in which a US tourist pays for a Marriott hotel room in Paris is both a US service import in Mode 2 and a US service export in Mode 3.

Mode 4 (Presence of natural persons): Often, a person travels abroad to provide a service, such as an engineer going temporarily to another country to oversee the installation of a factory or a musician performing a concert overseas. These are service exports for the country of origin and imports in the location where the services are provided.

The current account balance

Return now to components of the balance of payments. The next concept is the *current account* (CA), which includes all transactions made in buying and selling goods and services, plus income payments and receipts. It measures all inflows of revenues minus outflows of payments for "current" transactions, which include anything NOT involving ownable assets. Thus, the CA is the trade balance in merchandise and services (net income from trade) plus "net factor income" plus "net unilateral transfers".

Net factor income (NFI) includes income (receipts) earned by home residents working abroad or owning capital and land abroad, minus income paid (payments) to foreigners working here or owning capital and land here. The top examples include profits earned on capital owned abroad and wages earned by workers abroad.

Net unilateral transfers (NUT) refer to income received from gifts paid to home residents minus gifts sent to foreign residents. The major examples are labor remittances and foreign aid. These are "transfers" in that they are gifts made or received without an income-earning activity involved.

Putting this together, the current account measures net international transactions in current items, which means income received from abroad minus payments made to foreigners for transactions that do not involve assets and liabilities. The CA balance is the sum of these categories:

$$\text{CAB} = (\text{X} - \text{M}) + \text{NFI} + \text{NUT}.$$

The CAB: Data for the US

Figure 16.1 presents figures for components of the US CAB from 1960 to 2016, defined slightly differently from the components above. Data for 2019 for the standard components follow in Table 16.1.

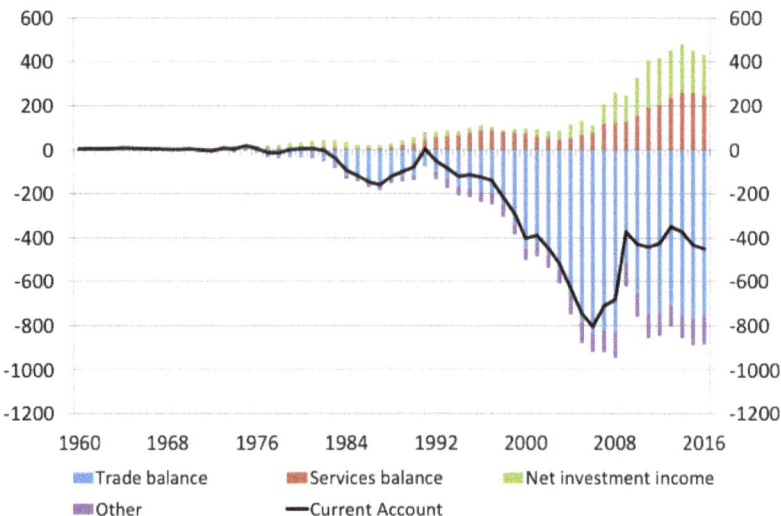

Figure 16.1   Components of the US current account, 1960–2016 ($ billion).
Source: https://voxeu.org/article/external-debt-us-no-cause-concern-yet.

The blue bars show the merchandise trade balance. This balance was nearly zero through the late 1970s and then trended sharply negative, reaching a deficit of nearly −$800 b in 2016. Thus, some factors pushed US expenditure on goods to grow much faster than output of goods after the 1970s. This is an important phenomenon that is addressed in later chapters.

The red bars indicate that there has been a trend increase in net exports of services, reaching over $200 b in 2016. The green bars show the positive and growing amounts of "net investment income", which is the difference between capital income (profits, dividends, and interest) earned by US owners of investments abroad and capital income earned by foreign owners of investments in the US. Net investment income is the largest component of NFI in the US current account, and the US consistently has surpluses in this area. The purple bars show "other" parts of the current account, reflecting net unilateral transfers. These are negative because the US is a source of labor remittances and foreign aid sent abroad.

Finally, the black line shows the current account balance (CAB), which is the sum of these components. While it correlates with the trade deficit, the CA deficit is considerably smaller because of positive net exports of services and net investment income. Again, the CAB is the most relevant measure of the difference between income and payments in current international transactions.

The current account: US data

Table 16.1 shows CA data for the United States in 2019, the last year before the COVID-19 pandemic. Line 1 gives the total of all income earned through exports and receipts of factor income ("primary" income) and inward transfers ("secondary" income). Total income received was $3,763,944 m in 2019. Together, these are "credits" in the current account for reasons discussed later.

In line 3, exports of goods = $1,652,806 m, and in line 33, imports of goods = $2,519,049 m. Thus, the merchandise trade balance = $1,652,806 - 2,519,049 = -$866,244 m (line 103). This is the *trade deficit in goods*.

In line 13, exports of services = $845,228 m, and in line 42, imports of services = $595,409 m. Then, the balance on services = +$249,819 m. The US consistently has a trade surplus in services.

The trade balance (goods and services) = $X - M = -866,244$ m + 249,819 m = -$616,425 m (line 102) or around -$616 b. *This is the best and most comprehensive measure of the trade deficit.*

Receipts of factor income (primary receipts) from abroad = $1,123,101 m (line 23). These are mostly income receipts from Americans owning capital abroad, shown as investment income (line 24). There is a small amount of labor income earned by US citizens living and working abroad (line 29).

Payments of factor income (primary payments) to foreigners = $866,105 m (line 52). Again, this is mostly capital income paid abroad but a larger amount of labor income because there are more foreign workers in the US, working at higher wages, than US workers abroad.

Thus, net factor income = NFI = $1,123,101 - 866,105$ = +$256,997 m. The US has a consistent surplus in NFI.

Table 16.1   US International Transactions: Current Account (Millions of dollars).

Line		2019
	Current account	
1	Exports of goods and services and income receipts (credits)	3,763,944
2	Exports of goods and services	2,498,034
3	Goods	1,652,806
13	Services	845,228
23	Primary income receipts	1,123,101
24	Investment income	1,116,266
29	Compensation of employees	6,835
30	Secondary income (current transfer) receipts[2]	142,809
31	Imports of goods and services and income payments (debits)	4,262,295
32	Imports of goods and services	3,114,459
33	Goods	2,519,049
42	Services	595,409
52	Primary income payments	866,105
53	Investment income	845,785
57	Compensation of employees	20,320
58	Secondary income (current transfer) payments[2]	281,732
101	Balance on current account (line 1 less line 31)[5]	−498,351
102	Balance on goods and services (line 2 less line 32)	−616,425
103	Balance on goods (line 3 less line 33)	−866,244
104	Balance on services (line 13 less line 42)	249,819
105	Balance on primary income (line 23 less line 52)	256,997
106	Balance on secondary income (line 30 less line 58)	−138,923

Source: Adapted from data provided by the US Bureau of Economic Analysis.

Next, in line 30, receipts of income transfers (secondary receipts) from abroad = \$142,809 m. In line 58, payments of income transfers (secondary payments) to foreigners = \$281,732 m.

Thus, net unilateral transfers = NUT = 142,809 − 281,732 = −\$138,923 m (line 106).

Putting this together, the current account balance (CAB) is the sum of these components:

CAB $= (X - M) + $ NFI $+$ NUT $= -\$616{,}425 + \$256{,}997 -$ $\$138{,}923 = -\$498{,}351$ m (line 101) or around $-\$498$ b.

Again, the CAB is the difference between income earned from abroad and payments made to foreign economies for current transactions (exports, imports, factor receipts, and factor payments) and gifts (transfers).

Study question 1

A country's current account balance is the difference between its income earned from abroad and the payments it makes internationally for current transactions. Which of the following concepts is not included in the CAB?

A. The trade balance in goods and services
B. Sales of domestic assets minus purchases of foreign assets
C. Net unilateral transfers
D. Net factor income

Discussion of question 1

The correct answer is B because international trade in the ownership of assets is not a current income-based transaction. Assets and liabilities are included in the capital account, discussed later. A, C, and D are the correct components of the CAB.

The Current Account and National Income

Relating the CAB to macroeconomic totals for an open economy

The notes consider now how the CAB relates to total income and output in an open economy. Recall that in the closed economy, GNE $=$ GDP $=$ GNI. However, the situation is different in the open economy, where these international transactions must be accounted for in the circular flow of expenditures, output and income. GNE remains the same concept because expenditures still are made on three items: GNE $= C + I + G$.

Recall that GDP measures output made in the domestic economy by everyone living there, whether home residents or foreign labor and capital working in the economy. To get from GNE to GDP requires these adjustments:

- GDP includes exports X because that is output made domestically but is not in home expenditure.
- However, imports M are subtracted from GNE because we need to take out of expenditures the amounts spent on imports. Note that C, I, and G all contain some amounts spent on home-produced goods and services, which are part of GDP, and some spent on imported goods, which are not part of GDP.
- Thus, GDP = GNE + $(X - M)$ or GDP = $C + I + G + (X - M)$. GDP is GNE plus the trade balance in goods and services.

This is an accounting identity and is true by definition. It does not mean that if imports go down, then GDP will rise. Nor does it mean that if exports go up then GDP will rise. These components and totals are all determined jointly and 'causal' statements of that kind are not sensible.

Next, consider total income. Note that both NFI and NUT add to domestic income if they are positive and reduce domestic income if they are negative.

Thus, we have GNI = GDP + NFI + NUT. An economy's total income (GNI) is its total output (GDP) plus net inward flows of factor income and transfers. Note that this means GNI > GDP for countries with positive NFI and/or NUT.

Consider Table 16.2, which shows GNI per capita and GDP per capita in 2015 for various nations. Here are some interesting observations from that data:

1. Luxembourg and Ireland have much higher GDP per capita than GNI per capita. The primary reason for Luxembourg is that many highly skilled financial professionals work in the banking industry there but live in neighboring countries. The banking services they produce are in Luxembourg's GDP but the salaries they earn are in their resident countries' GNI. For Ireland, the primary

Table 16.2   Comparisons of GDP per capita and GNI per capita in selected countries, 2015.

Country	Ireland	Luxembourg	Germany	US	El Salvador	Philippines
GDP pc	$62,140	$101,447	$41,324	$56,469	$2,900	$3,027
GNI pc	$51,290	$73,530	$45,790	$56,250	$3,880	$3,520

Source: Adapted from the World Bank, World Development Indicators.

factor is that Ireland has low taxes on foreign capital and the use of intellectual property rights (IPRs, such as patents). This is a major inducement for global software and technology firms to locate facilities there. Again, this means the production value in those foreign-owned facilities is in GDP, but the profits sent abroad are not in Ireland's GNI.

2. The opposite situation holds for El Salvador and the Philippines, where GNI per capita exceeds GDP per capita. This reflects the large number of workers from those countries who work abroad. The remittances (wage incomes) they send back to their families generate positive amounts of NFI in El Salvador and the Philippines.

At this point, we know that GNI = GDP + NFI + NUT. But GDP = $C + I + G + (X - M)$, implying that

$$GNI = C + I + G + (X - M) + NFI + NUT.$$

The first three terms on the right-hand side are GNE (expenditures). The last three terms make up the CAB.

Therefore, and this is fundamental,

$$****\textbf{GNI} = \textbf{GNE} + \textbf{CAB}****.$$

In words: If the economy earns more income (GNI) than it spends (GNE), then it has a current account surplus (CAB > 0). If the economy earns less income than it spends, then it has a current account deficit (CAB < 0).

Again, this is an accounting identity with no causal interpretation.

Saving, investment, and the CAB

It is instructive to see this relationship in another way. To use the usual notation in economics, let Y stand for GNI. Then,

$$Y = C + I + G + \text{CAB}.$$

Thus, if CAB > 0, it must be that $Y > C + I + G$. And if CAB < 0, it must be that $Y < C + I + G$.

This concept can be related to saving and investment in the economy. Define national savings as $S = Y - C - G$. This means that the economy's saving is the difference between its GNI and expenditures on consumption and government spending. This definition relates to saving by private households, ignoring taxes for now. Then, we have

$$S - I = Y - C - G - I = \text{CAB}.$$

Again, this is fundamental,

$${}^{****}S - I = \mathbf{CAB}^{****}.$$

In words, a country with more domestic saving than domestic investment has a CA surplus. A country with less domestic saving than domestic investment has a CA deficit.

It is important to understand what is meant by investment. It is private expenditures on new physical plant and equipment, inventories, structures, and land improvements, plus R&D spending, in a year. It includes business expenditures and household expenditures on new residential construction. Note that investment does not include education expenses, which is odd in economic terms.

As a matter of economic logic, investment should include government investments in roads, ports, education, and so on. However, it generally does not by convention.

Bringing in taxes

Define the economy's *disposable income* as GNI minus taxes. Thus, disposable income $= Y - T$.

Private saving is defined as disposable income that households and businesses do not spend on consumption:

$$S_P = Y - T - C.$$

An important observation is that *taxes are a transfer of income from households and businesses to government.* Thus, we can think of T as income for the government. Then, public (government) savings is just government income minus spending:

$$S_G = T - G.$$

If $S_G > 0$, there is a government **budget surplus** (government is a net saver). If $S_G < 0$, there is a government **budget deficit** (government is a net borrower).

Thus, another way to think of the current account balance is to relate it to saving and investment:

$$\text{CAB} = S - I = S_P + S_G - I.$$

This can be rewritten as

$$\text{CAB} = (S_P - I) + (T - G).$$

In words, the current account balance equals the difference between private saving and investment plus the difference between tax revenues and government spending, or the government budget surplus or deficit. This may be more conveniently stated as the CAB is the sum of private net saving and public net saving.

Since T and G are policy variables, it is possible to state that such policy changes can influence the CAB. That is, other things equal, a larger government budget deficit pushes the economy toward a smaller CA surplus or larger CA deficit.

Study question 2

If a country has a CA surplus, it is the same as saying:

A. Its total expenditure is less than its total income.
B. Its domestic saving exceeds its domestic investment.
C. It will be a net international lender.
D. All the above.

Discussion of question 2

The correct answer is D because statements A, B, and C are all consistent with a CA surplus.

Trade in Assets and Liabilities: The Financial Account

The notes above showed that a country with a CA surplus (which comes from having saving higher than investment and income greater than expenditures) must be a net international lender. A country with a CA deficit must be a net international borrower. The following notes explain in detail what that means and discuss its importance:

The initial task is to understand how trade in assets (investments in stocks, bonds, factories, and so on) enters the BOP. The *financial account* (FA) in the BOP includes all transactions made in buying and selling assets and liabilities between residents of a country and residents of foreign countries in a time period, usually a year. It is supposed to measure international transactions in "capital" items (flows of stocks, bonds, factories, service firms, and all other assets). The financial account balance (FAB) is the difference between assets sold to foreigners (for which domestic residents receive payments) and assets purchased from foreigners (for which domestic residents make payments).

It is important to understand that the assets themselves may not cross borders, but their *ownership* does. That is, if a US-owned firm located in, say, Pennsylvania, were acquired by a foreign investor, the firm itself generally would not move abroad. However, it is now owned by the foreign investor (or perhaps many foreign investors in multiple countries).

For purposes of defining parts of the financial account, national income accountants generally place assets into three categories:

1. There are two types of "non-produced and non-financial assets", which can neither be used for production nor are they financial instruments:

   A. The first is intellectual property rights (IPRs), such as patents, copyrights, and trademarks. These items do not directly produce goods or services but can be bought and sold. Note that this concept refers to ownership of IPRs, rather than the licensing of patents and copyrights to foreigners to permit production, which does not transfer ownership. Revenues received and paid for licensing IPRs are a form of trade in services, as discussed earlier.

B. The second is transfers (gifts) of assets, meaning simply giving ownership of an asset to a foreign resident. The most prominent example of an asset gift is investors in one country forgiving some of a foreign country's debt.

These two assets go into what is called the *capital account* (KA), a component of the FA. But in fact, they are typically very small and are sometimes ignored when discussing the overall financial account.

2. Financial portfolio assets: These are financial instruments, including demand deposits, time deposits, corporate bonds, stocks, mutual funds, financial derivatives, government bonds, and the like.

3. Real production assets, such as real estate, farms, factories, hotels, and the like: International sales and purchases of categories 2 and 3 make up the vast bulk of the financial account, as will be seen in later data.

A note on terminology: If a resident of country A purchases an asset from a resident of country B, the item transacted is referred to as an asset for A but a liability for B. Since they are two sides of the same transaction, the notes will use simply the word asset to describe what is traded, except where it is important to distinguish assets from liabilities.

Here is how asset trades are counted in the balance of payments:

If agents in one country *sell* assets, they are *credits* in that country's BOP and enter positively because there are inward flows of receipts for the assets. But now foreigners own the assets, which is why we say this process is equivalent to domestic agents *borrowing from abroad*.

Here is a simple example: If a US firm borrows money from a British bank, it has in effect sold an asset (the loan) to a foreign investor. Note that this loan is an asset for the British bank but a liability for the US firm.

If agents in one country *buy* foreign assets, they are *debits* in the BOP and enter negatively because there are outward flows of payments for them. But now domestic agents own the assets, which is equivalent to *lending to foreigners.* In the example, the US borrowing from a British bank is an asset sale by the US (and a credit in the US BOP) and an asset purchase by the British bank (and a debit in the UK BOP).

Another example would be a US investor buying a Canadian chemical factory. This would be an asset purchase by the US (a debit in its BOP because funds flow out) and an asset sale by Canada (a credit in its BOP because funds flow in).

The FA balance is then net transfers and gifts in the capital account (KAB) plus net international sales of both financial and real production assets. FAB = KAB + (sales of home-owned assets – purchases of foreign-owned assets). More simply, FAB = KAB + (asset sales – asset purchases). Again, this reflects credits minus debits in international transactions in assets.

With this definition, a country that sells more home-owned assets than it buys of foreign-owned assets has an FA *surplus*. This is referred to as "net foreign inflows of financial capital" because inward receipts exceed outward payments for the assets traded. *But this situation is the same as saying that the country is borrowing from abroad on net because foreign agents end up increasing their ownership of domestic assets by more than domestic agents increase their ownership of foreign assets.*

In the bank loan example above, the US firm "sells" ownership of the loan to the British bank, equivalent to borrowing from that bank. Similarly, a country that buys more foreign-owned assets than it sells of domestic-owned assets has an *FA deficit.*

Recall from earlier in this chapter that a country with a current account deficit must finance that deficit by borrowing from abroad (that is, selling more assets than it buys). The opposite holds for a country with a CA surplus; it is a net international lender.

It is evident that there must be a relationship between the FAB and the CAB. To understand it requires thinking through the mechanics of how the BOP accounts really work.

Study question 3

Which of the following statements about the financial account is false?

A. A country's interest and profits earned on the assets it owns abroad are included in the financial account.
B. The financial account is a record of all international transactions in assets that a country makes in a period of time.
C. A country with a financial account surplus is an international borrower.
D. A gift of the ownership of an asset made by citizens in one country to citizens in another country is measured in the capital account.

Discussion of question 3

A is the correct answer because it is a false statement. Interest and profits on assets owned abroad are accounted for in net factor income (NFI) in the current account. B is the definition of the financial account. C is a true statement because an FA surplus means more receipts coming in for selling assets than going out for buying assets, which is equivalent to net borrowing from abroad. D is true because gifts of assets are included in the KA, which itself is a small entry in the FA.

Balance of Payments Accounting: Credits, Debits, and Double-Entry Bookkeeping

Accounting for the balance of payments

It is important to understand how the BOP is computed and what relationships must hold among its components and definitions. This is because changes in its components are important in understanding how exchange rates move, analyzing changes in monetary policy arising from international transactions, and assessing what might happen to growth, employment, and other variables.

Start with the basic accounting principles. BOP accounting uses *double-entry bookkeeping*. This means that every transaction is both a debit and credit (see the rule in the following).

To keep it simple, a *credit* is something (goods, services, and assets) the country sells to foreigners. It enters as a positive item in the BOP because receipts enter the economy from abroad.

A *debit* is something the country buys from foreigners. It enters as a negative item in the BOP because payments leave the country and go abroad.

This double-entry approach implies that, when fully accounted for, the BOP must sum to zero because credits (+) will add up to equal debits (−). Thus, in principle, BOP = CAB + FAB = 0, as an overall accounting definition. But economists also talk about BOP surpluses and deficits, meaning that there are additional concepts to understand.

Examples of double-entry bookkeeping

These examples will consider different transactions and whether they enter the current account (CA) or the financial account (FA) of the United States.

Example 1: Suppose that Levi's (a US company) sells $2 m of jeans to French buyers, who pay with $2 m drawn on a dollar-based checking account in a New York bank.

US BOP Entries	Debit	Credit	CA or FA?
Jeans export		$2 m	CA (exports)
French payment	$2 m		FA

The French payment is a US debit because a US entity (Levi's) effectively purchases a French asset (the French buyer's deposit at a NY bank).

To put it differently, the US has reduced the assets owned by French residents in the US by $2 m. The transaction transfers ownership of this asset (the demand deposit) from France to the US

(Levi's). This is a short-term bank claim in the FA. To summarize, jeans have been exported by the US (credit) and $2 m ownership of a checking account has been imported by the US (debit).

Example 2: Suppose that a US investor buys a Japanese $1 m corporate bond. It pays with dollars and the Japanese corporation deposits the check in a US bank. This is a payment to Japan in return for the bond, which is an asset.

US BOP Entries	Debit	Credit	CA or FA?
Bond purchase	$1 m		FA
US payment		$1 m	FA

Again, why is the US payment a US credit? Here, the US payment is a US credit because, in effect, the US investor has sold an asset (the bank deposit) to a Japanese agent. Here, one asset has been bought (the bond) and another has been sold (the deposit in the US owned by the Japanese corporation).

In computing the BOP, we assign a (+) to credits and a (−) to debits. *Do not confuse these signs with being better off or worse off; they are just ways of recording transactions.*

In the two cases above, credits = +$3 m, debits = −$3 m, and the overall BOP = 0, as noted earlier. Put differently, grouping CA transactions and then FA transactions,

$$\text{CAB} = +\$2\,\text{m} \quad \text{FAB} = -\$2\,\text{m} - \$1\,\text{m} + \$1\,\text{m} = -\$2\,\text{m}.$$

This logic can get confusing without a basic rule for identifying debits and credits. Here is a useful principle for doing so:

1. Identify the *independently motivated (or "autonomous") transaction* (here those are the jeans export and the bond purchase) and figure out if it is a US sale (credit) or purchase (debit). The payment for that transaction is the offsetting transaction in the double-entry.
2. Place the autonomous transaction into the CA if it refers to trade in current goods and services or is an income transaction. Put it in the FA if it is a transaction in assets. Note that the offsetting

payment virtually always goes into the FA since it is a financial payment, in essence, an international exchange of asset ownership.

More examples

Now, students can use these simple rules to identify the nature of BOP transactions. Here are more examples, again considering the US BOP:

Example 3: US tourists buy $10 m in souvenirs in Thailand, paying cash.

US BOP Entries	D	C	CA or FA
Souvenirs	$10 m		CA (imports)
Cash		$10 m	FA

Souvenirs are a US import of current goods and so is a debit in the CA. The cash (e.g., withdrawals from ATMs in Thailand) payment is a transfer (sale) of a US-owned asset (currency) to Thai ownership and so is a credit in the FA.

Example 4: A US engineering company does consulting work in Saudi Arabia for six months, for which it is paid $20 m.

US BOP Entries	D	C	CA or FA
Engineering services		$20 m	CA (income receipt in NFI)
Saudi payment	$20 m		FA

Example 5: A US company buys a Mexican textile factory for $10 m and pays with some equity (stocks) in its own company.

US BOP Entries	D	C	CA or FA
Factory purchase	$10 m		FA
Stocks transferred to Mexico		$10 m	FA

Now, in these five examples, note the following:

In the CA, credits = +2 + 20 = +$22 m and debits = −$10 m. Thus, CAB = +$12 m. This is a current account surplus.

In the FA, credits $= +1 + 10 + 10 = +\$21\,$m and debits $= -2 - 1 - 20 - 10 = -\$33\,$m. Thus, FAB $= -\$12\,$m. This is a financial account deficit.

In this sense, the BOP $=$ CAB $+$ FAB $= 0$. Think of this as the "accounting" BOP, which must add to zero because of double-entry accounting. Despite that, there is a CA surplus and an FA deficit.

The Economic BOP and the FX Market

The economic BOP and the supply of and demand for foreign currencies

The zero accounting BOP is simply mechanical. How does the BOP relate to fundamental economic concepts? There are three primary concepts to understand clearly:

1. *The CAB determines whether a country is an international borrower or lender.*
2. *The autonomous transactions (defined above) determine the supply of, and demand for, both dollars and foreign currencies in the foreign exchange market.*
3. *The supply of, and demand for, currencies has important implications for whether they change in value (under flexible exchange rates) or are held constant by policy (under fixed exchange rates).*

Consider point 2 first. The supply of, and demand for, dollars (\$) is generated by the independently motivated transactions, ignoring the offsetting settlement payments. In the examples above, what are these autonomous transactions?

- In example 1, it was US jeans export (CA, $+\$2\,$m). But this is both a *demand* for dollars and a *supply* of foreign currency (euros) because the French buyer had to sell euros and buy dollars to purchase the jeans.
- In example 2, it was the US bond purchase (FA, $-\$1\,$m). This is a *supply* of dollars and a *demand* for foreign currency (yen).
- In example 3, it was the souvenir purchase (CA, $-\$10\,$m). This is a *supply* of dollars and *demand* for foreign currency (baht).

- In example 4, it was the US engineering export (CA, +$20 m). This is a *demand* for dollars and a *supply* of foreign currency (rials).
- In example 5, it was the US factory purchase (FA, –$10 m). This is a *supply* of dollars and a *demand* for foreign currency (pesos).

In our five examples, the *autonomous* CAB = +$12 m and the *autonomous* FAB = –$11 m. It follows that the *autonomous* CAB + *autonomous* FAB = +$1 m.

Economists think of this sum as the "economic" BOP surplus because it reflects what participants in FX markets wish to buy and sell across borders, in terms of goods, services, and assets. This economic BOP is generally what is meant when observers say a country has a BOP surplus or deficit.

In this example, the positive BOP means that in terms of autonomous transactions, there is an *excess demand* for dollars since the sum of these transactions is positive. This may be seen in the prior paragraph because the demand for dollars adds to $22 m, arising from the autonomous CA and FA credits, while the supply sums to $21 m, coming from the autonomous CA and FA debits.

That is, in the examples, the US sells $1 m more goods, services, and assets to foreigners than it buys from foreigners with respect to these autonomous transactions. That is the essence of the economic BOP deficit or surplus, which translates immediately into excess supply of the home currency (due to a BOP deficit) or excess demand for the home currency (due to a BOP surplus).

The official settlements balance (OSB) and its role in FX markets

To summarize, there is a close connection between the BOP and supply and demand for domestic and foreign currencies. For the United States, we have the following:

Autonomous credit transactions (CA or FA) are a *demand for dollars* because they are purchases by foreigners of US goods, services, and assets. They are also a *supply of foreign currencies*.

Autonomous debit transactions are a *supply of dollars* because they are purchases by US residents of foreign goods, services, and assets. They are also a *demand for foreign currencies.*

In the examples, the autonomous or economic BOP was a surplus of +$1m. Again, that is the sum of the autonomous CAB and the autonomous FAB.

To avoid confusion, call this "autonomous" FAB the "private" FAB (or pFAB). It captures all asset transactions that involve market participants other that the central bank (such as the Federal Reserve in the US). These participants include tourists, firms, investors, banks, brokers, and government agencies other than the central bank.

Actions of the central bank (CB) are broken out separately because it plays a unique role in FX markets. Specifically, it may buy or sell *foreign reserves* in order to influence changes in exchange rates, as discussed in later notes. Foreign reserves are major foreign currencies, gold, and some other items mentioned later.

Such transactions made by the CB are placed into the "Official Settlements Balance" or OSB. But because reserves are assets, they must be accounted for in the financial account. Thus, the full financial account of a country has two types of transactions: private and official.

$$FAB = pFAB + OSB.$$

Study question 4

Which of the following statements is FALSE about accounting for the balance of payments?

A. The economic BOP is the sum of all autonomous ("private") transactions in the current account and financial account.
B. The total financial account balance includes both private transactions in the FA and the central bank's official settlements balance (OSB).
C. A country with an economic BOP deficit has an excess demand for its currency.
D. The accounting BOP must sum to zero.

Discussion of question 4

Question C is false, so it is the answer. A country with an economic BOP deficit purchases more foreign goods, services, and assets than it sells to foreigners, which means there is an excess supply of its currency. Questions A, B, and D are all true statements.

A first look at flexible versus fixed exchange rates

Now consider the links among the BOP, the foreign exchange market, and actions of the CB. First, what would happen in the foreign exchange market if the example's economic BOP surplus of +$1 m existed? Would the dollar appreciate or depreciate? The answer would depend on the central bank's (Federal Reserve Bank's) response.

First, the Fed could do nothing. Then, the dollar would be freely flexible, and it would appreciate in value because the BOP surplus implies an excess demand for the dollar.

Note that this appreciation would, in turn, make US goods, services, and assets more expensive, causing exports and asset sales to fall. It would also make foreign goods, services, and assets cheaper, causing imports and asset purchases to rise. *That is, the appreciation would cause autonomous credits to fall (the US would sell less) and autonomous debits to rise (the US would buy more) until the economic (or autonomous) BOP = 0.*

This is the essence of a "flexible" exchange rate system. Under this policy, the central bank does NOT intervene to influence the value of the home currency, which is left to seek an equilibrium in the FX market. Note that because there are no CB purchases or sales of foreign reserves in this case, the OSB = 0 and the FAB consists only of the pFAB: FAB = pFAB.

Second, the Fed could intervene (that is, buy or sell foreign currency reserves) in the FX market to take up the difference between supply and demand and prevent a change in the exchange rate. To do so, the Fed would have to buy $1 m in foreign currencies (FX) and simultaneously sell $1 m in the FX market. How would this work in the BOP?

US BOP Entries	D	C	Account
FRB buys FX	$1 m		Official settlements balance (OSB)
FRB pays in $		$1 m	FA

Note that the Fed gains $1 m worth of foreign exchange reserves (pounds, euros, yen, etc.). But here, the primary FX transaction is a debit, so the OSB $= -\$1$ m. Thus,

$$CAB + pFAB + OSB = 0.$$

The first two components are the autonomous "private" (non-central bank) transactions. The 3d component is the activity of the central bank in buying or selling FX reserves.

This is the essence of a "fixed" (or managed) exchange rate system because the purpose the central bank has in buying foreign exchange reserves (and selling dollars) is to prevent the dollar from appreciating in value.

Showing these processes on a supply and demand diagram

An exchange rate is the price of a currency, so it can be determined like a price using supply and demand. Consider the market for dollars, assuming there are just two currencies (dollars and euros). What are the basic determinants of the demand for, and supply of, dollars in the FX market?

As noted earlier, the supply of dollars depends on the amount of US imports (since importers would buy euros and pay in dollars) and the demand for dollar depends on US exports (since European importers would buy dollars). These decisions depend on factors that determine imports and exports, such as prices of goods and services, preferences, technologies, economic growth rates, and tariffs.

But there are also purchases and sales of assets, which enter supply and demand for currencies in the same way. These decisions depend on financial variables, such as interest rates (in relative terms, meaning the US interest rate versus the euro interest rate), inflation rates (also relative), and expectations about investment returns (also relative).

These concepts may be depicted in Figure 16.2, which shows the market for dollars. That is, the price of dollars (euros/dollar) is on the vertical axis and the quantity of dollars is on the horizontal axis.

The supply of dollars slopes upward because as it gets more expensive (and euros get cheaper), US consumers and firms would buy more foreign goods and assets. The demand for dollars slopes downward because as it gets cheaper (and euros more expensive) foreign consumers and firms buy more US goods and assets.

Suppose that the initial exchange rate were 0.85€/$. In the example from the earlier autonomous transactions, the net quantity demanded of dollars in autonomous (non-central bank) transactions is $12 m (point B) and the net quantity supplied is $11 m (point A). This means there is an excess demand of $1 m at this initial exchange rate. *Distance AB measures the US economic BOP surplus (and the European economic BOP deficit), both in dollars.*

Case 1: Suppose there is no Fed intervention. Then, the OSB = 0 and the dollar would appreciate to 0.90. The market equilibrium is at point F, indicating a flexible exchange rate.

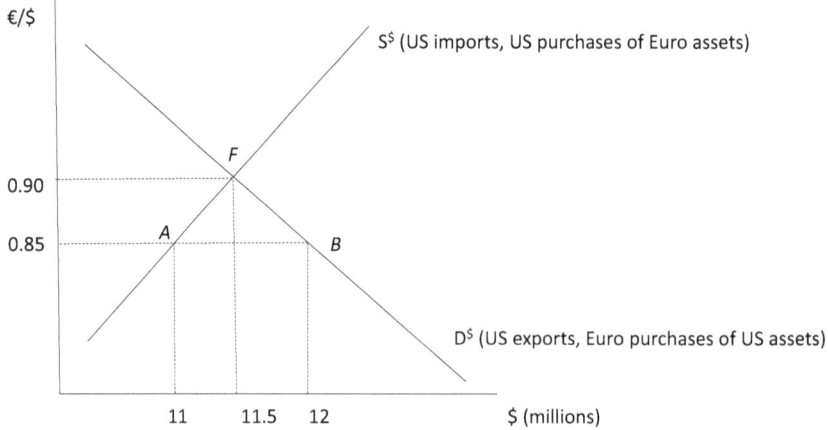

Figure 16.2 The market for dollars and flexible versus fixed exchange rate.

Case 2: Suppose the Fed intervenes to sell $1 m and buy $1 m worth of euro reserves. Then, OSB = –$1 m and the dollar would remain fixed at 0.85. Note that the Fed gains foreign reserves (euros) of 0.85 euros per dollar × $1m = 850,000 euros. Here, the exchange rate is fixed by CB intervention. *In this basic example, the OSB is just the opposite of the economic BOP surplus.*

Actual FA and BOP Data

US data on the FA and balance of payments for 2019

Table 16.1, discussed above, presented figures for the 2019 current account for the United States. To summarize those figures, the CAB was –$498,351 m, which was the sum of the trade balance, NFI, and NUT.

Now consider the financial account in 2019, with the data in Table 16.3. In 2019, there was a tiny capital account (KA) deficit (row 59 minus 60) of –$10 m, which was a net outflow of funds and therefore enters the FA with that negative amount.

The net US acquisition of foreign-owned financial assets = $426,913 m (row 61). Even though they are shown as a positive number here, they are "outflows" (net debits) of funds to buy those assets. Thus, they enter the FA negatively in the BOP.

As accounted for in the FA, these net acquisitions were made up of four categories:

1. $197,670 m in direct investments (FDI), meaning that on net US-based corporations increased their ownership of foreign affiliates by that amount. This is a capital outflow from the US.
2. $35,875 m in net purchases of portfolio assets. This figure may seem small, but it is the overall net amount, meaning gross US purchases minus gross US sales of foreign-issued portfolio investments. The gross figures were much larger. These net purchases are also a capital outflow.
3. Net acquisition of other financial assets of $188,709 m (row 70). These include short-term bank deposits and loans. Again, this is a capital outflow.

Table 16.3   Financial Account and Statistical Discrepancy.

Line	Millions of Dollars	2019
Capital account		
59	Capital transfer receipts and other credits	0
60	Capital transfer payments and other debits	10
Financial account		
61	Net US acquisition of financial assets excluding financial derivatives (net increase in assets/financial outflow (+))	426,913
62	Direct investment assets	197,670
65	Portfolio investment assets	35,875
70	Other investment assets	188,709
75	Reserve assets	4,659
84	Net US incurrence of liabilities excluding financial derivatives (net increase in liabilities/financial inflow (+))	784,440
85	Direct investment liabilities	310,811
88	Portfolio investment liabilities	231,617
93	Other investment liabilities	242,012
99	Financial derivatives other than reserves, net transactions	−38,378
Statistical discrepancy		
100	Statistical discrepancy	102,456

Source: Adapted from data provided by US Bureau of Economic Analysis.

These three areas make up the "private" (non-Central Bank) outflows of funds to buy foreign assets. They sum to $422,254 m as outflows.

4. By convention, the net activities of the central bank are listed in this acquisition component of the FA. As shown, the Federal Reserve bought $4,659 m more in FX reserves than it sold (row 75). Again, this is a capital outflow. In fact, this amount is the OSB = –$4,659 m.

Next, line 84 shows that the net foreign purchases of US-issued assets (called US liabilities) were $784,440 m. This is a capital inflow and recorded as a positive entry in the US financial account. It was made up of the following:

1. net direct investments (FDI) of \$310,811 m;
2. net foreign purchases of portfolio liabilities of \$231,617 m;
3. net foreign purchases of other liabilities of \$242,012 m.

Finally, row 99 breaks out net transactions in certain financial derivatives, which are accounted for separately. Though it is confusing, the figure of $-\$38,378$ m signifies that there was a net inflow of US funds to buy foreign derivatives and therefore enters positively in the FA.

The components of the FA may now be assembled. In terms of "private" (non-Central Bank) transactions, including the small capital account (KA). That is, $pFAB = -\$10 - \$422,254 + \$784,440 + \$38,378 = +\$400,554$ m or about $+\$401$ b.

Recall that $OSB = -\$4,659$ m. Therefore, $FAB = pFAB + OSB = +\$395,895$ m.

Summary and the statistical discrepancy

To summarize, the 2019 data show that $CAB = -\$498,351$ m. This is a CA deficit, which is also called the US "borrowing requirement" because it measures the amount that US traders and investors must borrow from abroad to finance the deficit.

$pFAB = +\$400,554$ m. This is an autonomous FA surplus, and it provides much of the financing for the CA deficit. $OSB = -\$4,659$ m.

The statistical discrepancy
In principle, it should be that $CAB + pFAB + OSB = 0$ due to double-entry bookkeeping. But the data show that this sum equals $-\$102,456$.

Another way of stating this is that the "economic" $BOP = CAB + pFAB = -\$97,797$ m. If that were accurate, it would mean an excess supply of dollars of that amount in the FX markets and the Federal Reserve would have needed to sell net foreign reserves in the same amount to equilibrate the market. But it did not, rather it was a net purchaser of foreign reserves by $4,659 m.

How are these data reconciled? Note that instead of 0, we have CAB + pFAB + OSB = −$102,456 m. In fact, this non-zero sum is simply an error caused by the difficulty in accounting for all international transactions. Many transactions are not recorded, are listed inaccurately, or are subject to other problems. It is impossible to account fully for all such flows of income, payments, and asset trades.

For this reason, BOP accountants add in a "statistical discrepancy" (row 100) of +$102,456 m to make up the difference. That is, the statistical discrepancy (SD) is the amount it must be to make the BOP add up in the accounting sense:

CAB + pFAB + OSB + SD = 0, or SD = −(CAB + pFAB + OSB)

Here, −$498,351 m +$400,554 m −$4,659 m +$102,456 m = 0. The statistical discrepancy is also called "net errors and omissions" to reflect the fact that errors are inevitably made in accounting for international transactions.

Summary of the primary BOP concepts

$$CAB = TB + NFI + NUT.$$

- The CAB measures net income (receipts minus payments) in international income-based transactions.
- But the notes also showed that CAB = GNI − GNE. Thus, the CAB is the difference between a country's income and spending.
- It also was shown that CAB = $S - I = (S_P - I) + (T - G)$. The CAB is also (equivalently) the difference between a country's domestic saving and investment.
- For these reasons, the CAB measures the net international borrowing requirement (if CAB < 0) or lending opportunity (if CAB > 0). The CAB must be financed through international trade in assets.

The KAB is net receipts on small asset gifts. Although in the financial account, in economic analysis, it is typically ignored.

$$FAB = pFAB + OSB.$$

- FAB measures net sales of domestic assets to foreigners minus net purchases of foreign assets. An FAB surplus (FAB > 0) means the country is a net borrower. FAB < 0 means it is a net lender.
- The pFAB measures such transactions by all domestic residents and organizations other than the central bank.
- OSB is net sales minus purchases by the central bank of foreign reserve assets.

It is useful to think of the "economic" BOP as the autonomous income and asset transactions by agents other than the central bank:

- Economic BOP = CAB + pFAB.
- This concept captures what is meant by a "BOP surplus" or "BOP deficit" as an economic conception.
- If the economic BOP > 0, there is an excess demand for the home currency (and an excess supply of foreign currencies) in the FX markets. If the CB does not intervene, the home currency would appreciate. If the CB chooses to fix the exchange rate, it must sell the home currency and buy foreign currencies.
- If the economic BOP < 0, there is an excess supply of the home currency (and an excess demand for foreign currencies) in the FX markets. If the CB does not intervene, the home currency would depreciate. If the CB chooses to fix the exchange rate, it must buy the home currency and sell foreign currencies.

The overall or accounting BOP must add to zero:

- BOP = CAB + FAB = CAB + pFAB + OSB = 0.
- But errors are made so there is a statistical discrepancy: CAB + pFAB + OSB + SD = 0.

For the rest of these notes, it will be assumed that no errors are made so that $SD = 0$.

This means that in principle, $CAB + pFAB = -OSB$. This expression summarizes central bank policy in the foreign exchange markets:

- With a fixed exchange rate, if $CAB + pFAB > 0$ (economic BOP surplus), then the $OSB < 0$ and the central bank must purchase FX reserves.
- With a fixed exchange rate, if $CAB + pFAB < 0$ (economic BOP deficit), then the $OSB > 0$ and the central bank must sell FX reserves.
- With a flexible exchange rate, the central bank does not intervene to buy or sell reserves. Then, $OSB = 0$ and the exchange rate adjusts to set $CAB + pFAB = 0$.

Study question 5

Ignore the KA and assume no errors are made ($SD = 0$). Let $CAB = -\$200\,b$ and $pFAB = +\$150\,b$. Then, we can conclude that

A. This country has an economic BOP deficit.
B. This country's central bank has sold a net $50\,b in foreign reserves.
C. The central bank is managing the exchange rate in order to prevent a depreciation of the home currency.
D. All the above.

Discussion of question 5

The answer is D, all the above. The economic BOP is $-\$50\,b$, making A correct. If there is no SD, then the OSB must exactly offset this deficit, meaning it must be $+\$50\,b$. That implies that the central bank sold $50\,b in foreign reserves in order to prevent the economy's currency from depreciating. Therefore, B and C are also correct.

A Country's External Wealth

The BOP and external wealth

There is another important reason for studying the BOP of a country, which is that the BOP accounts are used to compute changes over time in a country's *external wealth*. *A country's external wealth is the monetary value of the stock of foreign assets owned by home residents minus the stock of home assets owned by foreign residents.* A simpler way to state this is that it is the difference between the value of home residents' ownership of foreign-issued assets (that is, foreign liabilities) and the value of the liabilities they owe to foreigners.

It is really a measure of an economy's "net worth" or the stock of net assets it owns, if external wealth is positive, or the stock of net liabilities it owes to foreigners, if external wealth is negative, at any point in time. *Thus, an economy with positive external wealth is a net creditor in the global economy and an economy with negative external wealth is a net debtor.* External wealth is a stock measure because it adds up the net contributions to such ownership and debt over time.

To illustrate, what is a family's net worth? It is the value of the assets the family owns (such as its house, financial investments, perhaps a business it owns, and so on) minus the debt obligations it owes (such as its mortgage, student debt, medical and credit card debt, and so on). A similar concept applies to countries whose net worth is measured by external wealth.

The key point to understand is the following. If a country must borrow from abroad year after year because it runs a CA deficit requiring a FA surplus, or capital inflow, to finance it, it is reducing its net ownership of foreign assets or raising foreign net ownership of home assets. Chronic CA deficits over time turn the economy into a net international debtor.

If a country must lend to foreign countries year after year because it runs a CA surplus, meaning it must have an FA deficit, or capital outflow, it is increasing its net ownership of foreign assets or reducing foreign net ownership of home assets. Thus, chronic CA surpluses move the economy into a position of being a net international creditor.

This impact on national external wealth is a major reason why the CA balance, and the offsetting FA balance, is a critical concept for governments and investors to monitor and measure. Understanding this concept better requires breaking down the word "assets" (which has been used so far in the treatment of the FA) into "assets" and "liabilities" as seen by the home economy.

In terms of wealth, think of assets (A) as assets (stocks, bonds, loans, factories, and so on) owned by domestic agents but sold to them by foreign agents. They are claims on foreigners and therefore are domestic assets but foreign liabilities.

Think of liabilities (L) as assets owned by foreign agents but bought from domestic agents. These are claims on domestic agents and therefore are foreign assets but domestic liabilities.

With this understanding, external wealth (W) is simply foreign assets owned by home entities minus home liabilities owned by foreign entities. Thus, $W = A - L$, where W, A, and L are measured in value terms (that is, in dollars, euros, yen, and so on).

In words, a country's external wealth is the value of its total external assets minus the value of its total external liabilities, both measured in its own currency (e.g., dollars for the United States). It is also called the country's net international investment position (NIIP).

If $W > 0$, the country is a net creditor. Its ownership of external assets is greater than what it owes as external liabilities.

If $W < 0$, the country is a net debtor. Its ownership of external assets is less than what it owes as external liabilities.

Further, FA credits (capital inflows) decrease external wealth, for these imply sales of domestic liabilities, which is the act of incurring debt. And FA debits (capital outflows) increase external wealth, for they involve purchases of foreign assets, which is the act of acquiring wealth.

Study question 6

Which of the following statements is false about the CA, FA, and a country's external wealth?

A. A country with many years of CA deficits will also have FA surpluses and decrease its external wealth.
B. A country with many years of CA deficits will also have FA surpluses and become a net international debtor.
C. A country with many years of CA surpluses will also have FA deficits and become a net international debtor.
D. A country with many years of CA surpluses will also have FA deficits and increase its external wealth.

Discussion of question 6

The correct answer is C, which is a false statement. A and B are two ways of stating the same thing, which is true: If a country has consistent CA deficits, it must finance them with FA surpluses, which means selling domestic liabilities to foreigners on net. That outcome reduces external wealth. D is also a true statement and refers to a country with consistent CA surpluses and FA deficits, which are capital outflows that purchase foreign assets and raise external wealth. C is false because in this situation, the country would become a net international creditor, not debtor.

Changes in external wealth

There are essentially two ways by which a country's wealth (W) changes over time:

1. Through incurring annual CA balances that are positive or negative:
   If the country runs a CA deficit, it must borrow (that is, it sells net liabilities) and it moves toward a greater net debtor position. This situation means that CA < 0 <=> FA > 0 and foreign investors

are buying home assets on net. But that implies that home debt obligations are rising.

If the country runs a CA surplus, it is necessarily a lender (that is, it acquires net assets) and it moves toward a larger net creditor position. This situation means that $CA > 0 <=> FA < 0$ and home investors are buying foreign assets on net. But that implies they are acquiring greater ownership of foreign debt obligations.

2. The second way wealth can change is through capital gains or capital losses on the value of existing external wealth. Even though wealth is measured in the home country's currency, actual assets and liabilities may be denominated in various currencies, which can appreciate or depreciate, changing their value in terms of the home currency.

To see this, it is reasonable to assume that the foreign assets a country owns are denominated in the foreign currencies where they are issued. That is, US investors buy foreign assets that are denominated in euros, pounds, yen, Canadian dollars, and so on.

Capital gains are price increases in foreign assets a country owns when measured in its own currency. This could happen because either

(1) the foreign assets get more valuable in foreign currency terms at a given exchange rate, raising their value in terms of the home country's currency, or

(2) there is an appreciation of the foreign currencies in which the assets are denominated, raising their value in terms of the home currency.

Since either factor raises the value of foreign assets as measured in the home country's currency, they both improve that nation's external wealth position.

Capital losses are price decreases in the foreign assets a country owns when measured in its own currency. This could happen because either

(1) the price of those assets falls in foreign currency terms at a given exchange rate or

(2) there is a depreciation of the foreign currencies in which the assets are denominated.

Either factor reduces the value of foreign assets as measured in the home country's currency and therefore worsens its external wealth position.

These processes work also for liabilities owed by a country. In terms of factor (1), if there are increases (declines) in the dollar prices of US liabilities, then the value of US net liabilities rises (falls), which worsens (improves) the US external wealth position. This situation also improves (worsens) foreign countries' external wealth measured in their own currencies.

There is one major difference, however, which exists because such liabilities may be assumed to be denominated in the home country's currency, as suggested in the prior paragraph. *In this situation, changes in the exchange rate (item (2)) do not change the valuation of external liabilities.* To see that, suppose the US sells dollar-based home liabilities. Then, a depreciation of the dollar is not relevant for the value of those liabilities in dollars and does not affect that side of the valuation of US external wealth. It does worsen foreign countries' external wealth measured in their currencies.

It is important to note that developing economies may not be able to issue liabilities denominated in their own currencies because foreign investors may not be willing to purchase them unless this debt is issued in a global currency, such as dollars or euros. This fact is important for understanding international financial crises, as discussed in Chapter 18.

Changes in external wealth: Examples

1. Consider a US investor who owns a Canadian oil refinery. Let the value of the refinery at the beginning of the year be C$850 m, with an exchange rate of $E_{C\$}/\$ = 1.25$. Thus, in US$ terms, the investment is worth C$850/1.25 = $680 m.

   Now, suppose that at the end of the year, the C$ value of the refinery had gone up to C$900 m, a capital gain of C$50 m.

Translated to US$, this would be a capital gain of +$40 m at the initial exchange rate, making the refinery worth $720 m.

But suppose also that the C$ had depreciated over the year to 1.28, meaning that the refinery was worth C$900/1.28 = $703 m, a capital loss in US$ of −$17 m. The investment value went from $680 m to $703 m over the year, for an overall capital gain of +$23 m, which is +$40 m (local valuation gain) −$17 m (exchange rate loss). It is worth noting that the US investor could try to hedge this exchange-rate risk, but that is a separate issue not considered here.

Here is a question to consider: Suppose that this refinery generated C$25 m = $20 m in profits at the initial exchange rate (or 25/1.28 = $19.5 m at the new rate). Is this profit part of US external wealth?

Answer: No, these profits are accounted as a credit in the US current account as part of net factor income.

2. Suppose that in the current year, a Swiss pension fund buys $100 m in US corporate bonds. These are now Swiss-owned assets and so are contributions to Swiss external wealth. But they are US-issued liabilities and so enter negatively in US external wealth.

Let the exchange rate at the time of this purchase be $E_{\$/CHF} =$ 1.10. Then, this Swiss asset was initially worth $100 m/1.10 = CHF 90.9 m. Switzerland's external wealth is measured in Swiss francs (CHF).

Over the rest of the year, let the bonds go up in value to $125 m. This is a capital gain for the Swiss investor and would add to Swiss wealth. At the same time, it would increase US dollar liabilities, reducing US net external wealth. At the initial exchange rate, the bonds would now be worth $125 m/1.10 = CHF 113.6 m, a Swiss capital gain of (113.6–90.9) = +CHF22.7 m.

Further, let the exchange rate rise over the period to $E_{\$/CHF} =$ 1.12, a depreciation of the dollar and appreciation of the CHF. This new exchange rate would change the ending value of the bonds to $125 m/1.12 = CHF 111.6 m. Thus, the value of the bonds fell from CHF113.6 m to CHF111.6 m, an exchange-rate valuation loss of CHF 2 m.

Note that this depreciation of the dollar is bad news for the Swiss investor. In general, investors who hold foreign assets denominated in foreign currencies would lose (gain) from a depreciation (appreciation) of those currencies.

The current account and changes in external wealth

Putting these concepts together yields the following important relationships:

First, a country's change in external wealth equals its net increase in home external assets minus liabilities plus the net capital gains on external wealth. Again, net capital gains are changes in the value of external assets minus the value of external liabilities associated with price changes and exchange rate movements.

As explained repeatedly, the value of external assets rises due to capital outflows and the value of external liabilities rises due to capital inflow. Moreover, this difference is, by definition, the opposite of the financial account, implying that

$$\Delta W = -FA + \text{net capital gains.}$$

But $-FA = CA$ by the BOP identity (assuming no statistical discrepancy). Thus,

$$\Delta W = CA + \text{net capital gains.}$$

We now see that a CA deficit (surplus) reduces (raises) external wealth, other things equal.

Figure 16.3 shows increases from 2014 to 2023 in the dollar values of US-owned foreign assets and foreign-owned US liabilities. Liabilities grew faster than assets, due to consistent US CA deficits. The bottom of the chart shows the resulting changes in net external wealth (also called the US net international investment position). Wealth grew increasingly more negative and reached around −$16 trillion by early 2023. Figure 16.3 demonstrates starkly that the US is a large net international debtor.

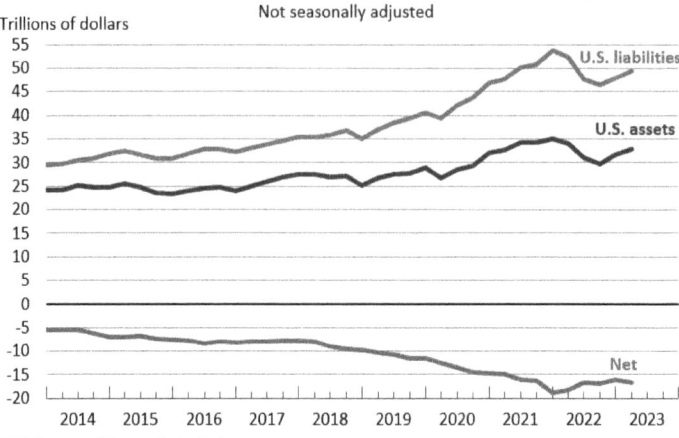

Figure 16.3   Changes in US Foreign Assets and Liabilities, and Changes in US Net International Investment (Net External Wealth), 2014–2023.

Source: US Bureau of Economic Analysis, https://www.bea.gov/data/intl-trade-investment/international-investment-position.

Is growing net external debt a problem?

The key insight to understand is that for every year in which the US runs a CA deficit, it adds to its net international debt. This raises a critical question. Is it possible for the US to sustain this growing debt position for very long?

In fact, most economists believe that *it probably is sustainable for the long term so long as the US economy can service (pay the interest charges) on the debt while continuing to borrow more to pay for the CA deficits.* That is, the US can continue to build debt as long as foreign investors are willing to purchase US liabilities.

On what major factors does this ability to continue to borrow depend?

• First, the expected future interest rates to be paid on US liabilities. If these remain low, then servicing the debt is manageable.
• Second, whether US GDP growth is faster or slower than the growth in foreign interest payments. Put differently, does US

international borrowing finance enough additional productive capacity to service the debt?

- Third, the confidence that foreign investors have in the ability of US debtors (especially the federal government) to service these debts.
- Fourth, the continuing ability of US borrowers to borrow and repay in dollars, which remains largely true. With international debt denominated in the home currency ($), US debtors remain insulated from the risk that the dollar could depreciate and force them to repay in more expensive euros, Swiss francs, and yen.

To date, there are few indications that these factors are worrisome for the United States or will become a problem for many years.

Chapter 17

Fixed and Flexible Exchange Rate Systems

Exchange Rate Choices and Monetary Policy

Introduction: The links between exchange rate policy and monetary policy

The notes in Chapter 14 hinted at an important linkage between a country's exchange rate and its monetary policy. For example, those notes discussed the fact that Barbados has a fixed exchange rate relative to the US dollar. But because Barbados also permits a high degree of capital mobility, it cannot have an interest rate that differs from that in the United States. This implies that Barbados cannot sustain an independent monetary policy.

However, many other countries, such as the US, the UK, Canada, and Japan, have a fully flexible exchange rate system. This system permits the central banks of these countries to sustain different interest rates because the exchange rate can adjust to those differences. In short, they can conduct independent monetary policies.

The Eurozone, in which several countries share the euro as their currency, but the euro is flexible against other currencies, offers a hybrid model. Monetary policy is largely the responsibility of a centralized European Central Bank, not the individual countries as discussed in later notes.

These insights tell us that *exchange rate policy is an essential part of monetary policy for a country*. This chapter explores this fundamental statement and considers the reasons why different countries choose different exchange rate systems.

To begin this exploration, consider the choices various countries make regarding their exchange rate systems. Table 17.1 is adapted from the International Monetary Fund's *Report on Exchange Arrangements 2020*. It shows the "monetary policy framework" by country, which depends crucially on its exchange rate policy, and vice-versa.

Rigidly fixed exchange rates and the absence of independent monetary policy
The first three rows show examples of countries that rigidly fix their exchange rates to a major currency, which is called its "exchange rate anchor". In these cases, a country essentially cannot have any other monetary policy targets. As mentioned already, monetary policy in this situation is entirely aimed at fixing the exchange rate.

Three types of rigidly fixed rates are indicated:

1. "No legal tender" means the economy has taken the dollar, euro, or another major currency as its own currency and the major currency circulates in the economy as the legal tender. This process is often called "dollarization" because, for example, Panama removed its prior currency (the Balboa) and only dollars circulate.
2. A "Currency Board" means the economy has its own currency, such as the Hong Kong dollar, but maintains foreign reserves sufficient to fully back the amount of its currency in circulation with the anchor currency. The central bank (if any) has no role in monetary policy other than converting local currency to dollars on demand.
3. A "conventional peg" means the country's central bank fixes the exchange rate to an anchor currency and buys and sells foreign reserves to achieve the fixed rate. This is the case of Barbados discussed earlier. Denmark pegs the kroner to the euro and Nepal pegs its rupee to the Indian rupee.

Table 17.1 Exchange rate systems and monetary policy frameworks, 2020.

Exchange Rate Arrangement (no. of nations)	Exchange Rate Anchor and Examples				Monetary Policy Frameworks and Example Countries		
	US$ (38)	Euro (25)	Composite (8)	Other (9)	Monetary Aggregate Target (26)	Inflation Target (41)	Other (45)
No Separate Legal Tender (13)	Ecuador, Panama, East Timor	Kosovo, San Marino, Montenegro		Kiribati, Nauru, Tuvalu			
Currency Board (11)	Hong Kong SAR, Dominica	Bulgaria		Brunei			
Conventional Peg (42)	Barbados, Jordan, Saudi Arabia	Denmark, Benin, Chad, WAEMU	Fiji, Kuwait, Libya	Lesotho, Nepal			
Crawling Peg and Other Managed Arrangement (55)	Guyana, Iran, Honduras	Croatia	Morocco, Vietnam, Singapore		Bolivia, China, Nigeria, Bangladesh	Romania, Paraguay	Egypt, Tunisia, Pakistan
Managed Floating (35)					Argentina, Madagascar	Hungary, India, S Korea	Malaysia, Switzerland
Free Floating (31)						Canada, Japan, UK, Russia, Mexico	USA, Eurozone members

Source: IMF, Report on Exchange Arrangements 2020.

Managed exchange rate systems

The fourth row notes that 55 countries actively manage their exchange rates in some way. The IMF recognizes essentially three types of managed systems:

1. Some countries permit their currencies to fluctuate within a narrow band, say plus or minus 1% (a 2% band), around the announced pegged rate.
2. In a "crawling peg", the exchange rate is adjusted in small and announced amounts or changed periodically to reflect fundamentals, such as inflation rate differentials. For example, Singapore manages the value of its dollar relative to a basket ("composite") of major currencies. Thus, its policy target is the effective exchange rate within announced bands over certain time periods.
3. A similar framework is a "stabilized arrangement", in which the currency is allowed to fluctuate within, say, a 2% band for an announced period, such as six months, after which there may be an adjustment in the currency value.

The essential point is that as countries choose more managed exchange rates, they gain some ability to target either the money supply or inflation as the object of monetary policy. For example, China has a managed arrangement in which it pre-announces how much it expects to see the yuan rise or fall relative to the US dollar over certain periods, but within that expectation, it can alter its own money supply and interest rate. Thus, its monetary policy target is the aggregate money supply in China but the managed exchange rate is a tool designed to help achieve that goal.

Floating or flexible rates

Finally, countries may choose flexible exchange rates. The IMF recognizes two such categories:

1. In a managed floating system, the central bank may attempt to influence changes in the exchange rate without having an

announced target. It intervenes in the FX market periodically, perhaps to manage its stock of international reserves or offset unwanted balance-of-payment trends.

2. In a freely floating system, the exchange rate is fully market-driven. The central bank rarely intervenes unless there is a threat of destabilizing fluctuations in the exchange rate.

The primary point is that countries with floating exchange rates get to choose an independent monetary policy, which may be based on inflation targeting, monetary growth targeting, or a mixture of goals. For example, by law, Canada and Japan use changes in the money supply to achieve a targeted rate of price inflation. The US Federal Reserve is directed by law to achieve a mixture of high employment and low inflation.

Key observations

Clearly, there are important empirical regularities regarding the characteristics of countries that choose fixed versus flexible rates.

Fixed-rate countries tend to be

- small and/or poor, such as East Timor and Lesotho;
- economies based on oil or commodity exports, such as Saudi Arabia and Kuwait;
- those with trade (and investment) volumes dominated by the country against which they peg, such as Barbados, Nepal, and Denmark.

Flexible-rate countries tend to be

- larger and highly developed, such as the US, the UK, and Japan;
- linked together in a monetary system, such as the euro area;
- larger and upper-middle-income economies, such as Mexico, Argentina, and Malaysia.

Other countries align somewhere between these extremes in order to attain both some stability in exchange rates and a degree of monetary policy authority.

Choice of the exchange rate regime

Why do these differences exist? The answers are mostly evident from the choices themselves.

A country is likely to adopt a fixed exchange rate under the following conditions:

1. It is small, and its trade and investment flows are dominated by a single major economy or a few such economies. Then, the fixed rate eliminates risks that the exchange rate will be subject to wide swings that deter risk-averse traders and investors. Again, an interesting example is Nepal, which pegs to the Indian rupee. Thus, the anchor country does not need to be a high-income country.
2. Its national income and government revenues are highly dependent on commodity exports, such as oil or minerals. Since the global prices of such commodities are denominated in major foreign currencies, primarily the US dollar, it makes sense to stabilize these revenues through a fixed exchange rate.
3. For various political and economic reasons, the country does not believe it can sustain a stable domestic monetary and fiscal policy for long. Governments always have incentives to inflate their economies through government spending and debt but may have to borrow to pay for that spending in foreign currencies. This process is likely to drive up domestic interest rates (borrowing costs) and inflation. A fixed exchange rate system establishes an anchor that helps prevent the country from having volatile and inflationary macroeconomic policies. This subject will be explored in detail in the following chapter.

A country is likely to adopt a flexible exchange rate under these conditions:

1. It is a high-income economy with diversified trade and investment flows.
2. It has highly developed financial markets that permit its firms and households to hedge risks arising from flexible exchange rates.
3. It is confident that it can sustain an independent fiscal and monetary policy without running into international debt problems.

Again, the euro system is an interesting hybrid of fixed and flexible rates. As a group, these countries exhibit points 1–3 above. But within the system, Eurozone countries wish to avoid exchange rate risk because their trade and investment flows are heavily concentrated within the region.

Denmark is also interesting. It is not in the Euro system but rigidly fixes the kroner to the euro and therefore surrenders its own ability to manage monetary policy.

The great majority of economists favor a flexible exchange rate for advanced countries like the United States, with deep and sophisticated financial markets. However, there are conservative economists and politicians who would like to see the US (and the world) return to a fixed-rate system, as under the classical gold standard, believing it would impose discipline on government policies. Notes on the gold standard follow the first study question.

Study question 1

Countries that choose a monetary system with their currency values fixed to, say, the US dollar are likely to have which of the following characteristics?

A. They are small economies, and their trade and investment flows are dominated by the United States.
B. They have extensive and sophisticated financial markets, including forward and futures markets for their currencies.
C. Their exports are dominated by commodities, such as oil, minerals, and agricultural goods.

D. They are generally not permitted to borrow from abroad using instruments denominated in their own currencies.

E. A, C, and D.

Discussion of study question 1

The correct answer is E because answers A, C, and D are all characteristics that would push a country toward adopting a fixed exchange rate. In contrast, answer B is false because poor countries rarely have such sophisticated financial markets. In particular, countries choosing fixed rates would have no reason for forward and futures exchange markets, which exist only where currencies are flexible.

The Classical Gold Standard of Fixed Exchange Rates

A review of historical fixed exchange rate systems

The analysis to this point has considered why a single country would choose to fix its exchange rate to another currency or perhaps a basket of currencies. Those choices are important components of monetary policy and should be made carefully.

A different, and more general, possibility is that many countries could choose to coordinate with each other in establishing and operating under a system of mutually fixed exchange rates. Rather than individual pegs to, say, the dollar or euro, countries could jointly fix their currency values to something that is not a national currency. Most likely that would be a precious metal, such as gold. If many countries followed this policy, they would effectively establish a regime of bilaterally fixed exchange rates.

In relatively recent history, there have been two major arrangements of this kind. Reviewing that history is informative for understanding fixed exchange rates and monetary policy.

The gold standard

Background on the Gold Standard (pre-World War I).

The classical gold standard was a system in which each participating country fixed its currency value to a particular quantity (1 ounce) of gold. In its fullest realization, it existed from the late 1870s to the early 1920s, and again briefly from the late 1920s to the early 1930s.

Great Britain set the foundation of this system by linking the value of its pound ("pound sterling") to an ounce of gold early in the 19th century. That meant people owning pounds circulating as paper could convert them to gold (and vice-versa) at that rate. Since Britain was the world's dominant trading country at that time, and for many more decades, other major trading countries had strong incentives to adopt similar systems ultimately.

Through much of the 1800s, the US had a "bimetallic" standard in which gold and silver coins were designated as the primary units of currency. The US designated 1 ounce of gold = 15 ounces of silver. Private banks were permitted to issue paper certificates that could be traded for gold and silver coins. The banking system effectively had to own enough gold and silver to make such exchanges on demand. This meant that the supply of money in circulation was tied closely to the stock of gold and silver in the banking system.

After experiencing high price inflation in the Civil War (1861–1865), the US shifted entirely to a gold standard in 1879, setting 1 ounce of gold = \$20.67. The idea was to bring down inflation by reducing the total money supply via eliminating exchanges of currency for silver. This policy destroyed the demand for silver as a circulating coinage material. It also reduced the supply of money in the US and generated pressure for commodity prices to fall, causing real distress in agriculture.

Other major trading countries had either a silver standard or bimetallic standard until the 1870s when most joined the gold standard at defined par values. The gold standard became the dominant international monetary system until it collapsed prior to World War I and again during the Great Depression.

Operation of the gold standard

If the major trading countries fixed the prices of their currencies in terms of gold units, they were explicitly choosing fixed exchange rates. How did the gold standard (GS) work in practice?

1. The finance ministries of these countries, such as the US Treasury, declared a fixed price (called "par value" or "parity") in units of their currency for an ounce of gold. The actual parities as of 1873 were that Great Britain set 1£ sterling = 7.322 grams of pure gold, which worked out to £4.25 per ounce. The US set 1$ = 1.505 grams or $20.67 per ounce of gold. Japan selected 1¥ = 0.75 grams or ¥41.48 per ounce.

    These parities implied that the exchange rates were ($20.67 per ounce)/(£4.25 per ounce) = 4.86$/£ and (¥41.48 per ounce)/($20.67 per ounce) = 2.01¥/$. So long as these parities were maintained, these were rigidly fixed exchange rates. Other countries chose their own parities.

2. The finance ministry promised to buy or sell gold at these fixed parities in any quantity. Banks and individuals could convert paper money into gold, or convert gold into paper, at these parities. But this could work only as long as the finance ministry had a supply of gold. Thus, the country's currency value was backed strictly by gold. The higher the gold stock held by the financial authority, the greater the ability to increase the money supply. These official gold reserves were the "monetary base".

    But the idea was NOT that the finance ministry (such as the US Treasury, or later the Federal Reserve, established in 1913) would try to influence the money supply as a matter of policy by autonomously choosing to change the monetary base. Rather, it passively bought and sold gold as private transactions needed it, meaning that the actual supply of money depended on how much money people needed in circulation.

The gold parity in each country was fixed and not permitted to change. Since there was no expectation of any change, there was no need for any forward markets and only rarely was there any financial speculation against currencies.

To use an example with round figures, suppose that Great Britain set a price of £5 per ounce of gold and the US set a price of $20 per ounce. Then, $4 = £1(E = 4$/£) was the fixed exchange rate or bilateral parity. How was it maintained?

3. Since anyone could buy or sell gold at any participating financial authority, if the bilateral exchange rate in the FX market were different than this parity, a process of arbitrage through gold shipments would move it back to parity.

For example, suppose the market exchange rate were 4.10$/£ so that the market price of a £ is more expensive than the parity price. Suppose for now that gold could be shipped physically at zero cost. Then, for example, currency arbitragers could use $1 million to buy 50,000 ounces of gold at the US Treasury (at a price of $20 per ounce), ship them to the Bank of England to purchase £250,000 (at £5 per ounce), and trade them in the market for £250,000×4.10$/£ = $1,025,000, for a profit of $25,000. However, this process would increase the demand for dollars and raise the supply of euros in the market, driving the market exchange rate back to its parity value of 4$/£. The exchange rate was inherently fixed to the parity value by this process.

Of course, gold is a heavy material with great value and could not be shipped freely. Thus, in practice, the exchange rate in any one country could never get outside a band around the parity value given by the costs of shipping gold back and forth between countries.

Consider this example, using the US and Japan. Suppose the US set $20 = 1 ounce and Japan set ¥40 = 1 ounce. Then, the parity value was 1¥ = $0.50 ($1 = 2¥) in the FX markets. Further, 1¥ = (0.50$/¥)/(4$/£) = £0.125. Exchange rates were fixed among all participating currencies, not just bilaterally.

4. Suppose that a US goods trader or investor wanted to convert an ounce of gold into yen in Tokyo. Then, the trader had to

(1) buy 1 ounce of gold for \$20 at the US Treasury and

(2) ship the ounce to the Bank of Japan and exchange it for yen.

Suppose that it costs \$1.00 per ounce to ship gold between the US and Japan. Note that \$1 is 5% of the fixed gold price of \$20 per ounce. In yen terms, this shipping cost would be ¥2 per ounce, which is 5% of the ¥40 parity.

Thus, the full cost for someone in the US to convert an ounce of gold for ¥40 at the Bank of Japan would be \$21. Then, implicitly, the \$21 was worth ¥40, or \$0.525 = ¥1. Only if the market rate were greater than 0.525\$/¥ would arbitragers ship gold from the US to Japan.

In the other direction, the full cost for someone in Japan to convert an ounce of gold at the US Treasury for \$20 was ¥42 or approximately \$0.475 = ¥1. Only at a market rate below 0.475\$/¥ would arbitragers ship gold from Japan to the US.

Therefore, these shipping costs set up a 5% band above and below the parity rate, within which it did not pay to ship gold back and forth. The 5% margin reflected the cost of shipping an ounce of gold.

Gold export and import points

In this example, the parity value was \$0.50 per yen. But the cost of shipping gold of \$1 per ounce set a 5% band above and below parity (0.475–0.525) within which it would not be profitable to ship and convert gold.

Therefore, if the private market FX equilibrium exchange rate were inside that band, the US Treasury and Bank of Japan do not need to anything because no gold would be offered to or demanded from them. In short, there was no "monetary policy" because these authorities had no ability to issue greater of lower amounts of domestic currency for any other reason.

Now, suppose that in the private FX market, we had E = $0.54 per yen. Then, a trader could profit by shipping gold. Specifically, a trader could

- take $1 million to the US Treasury and buy $1 m/20 = 50,000 ounces of gold;
- ship the gold to Japan at a cost of $50,000, for a total cost of $1,050,000; and
- sell them to the Bank of Japan for 50,000∗40 (yen/ounce) = ¥2 million. At the market exchange rate, these yen would be worth ¥2 m∗0.54 = $1,080,000. The trader would realize a profit of $30,000 per $1 million traded.

This example demonstrates that at any exchange rate above 0.525$/¥, gold would flow from the US to Japan. This exchange rate was called the US "gold export point" (GEP) and the Japanese "gold import point" (GIP).

Similarly, at any exchange rate below 0.475, gold would flow from Japan to the US. This lower rate was called the US "gold import point" and the Japanese "gold export" point.

These flows were closely related to BOP surpluses and deficits of the countries involved, as shown in Figure 17.1. In turn, they had

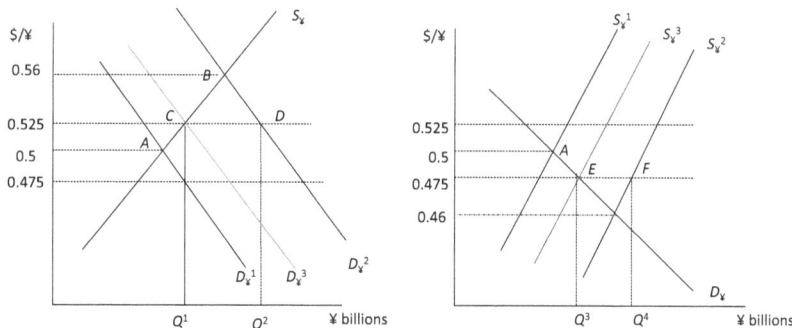

Figure 17.1   Gold flows under the gold standard.
Note: 0.525 = US GEP and Japan GIP; 0.475 = Japan GEP and US GIP.

large impacts on money supplies, affecting the macroeconomies of each country.

The balance of payments and monetary adjustments under the gold standard

Let these diagrams be in billions of yen. Depicted are demand and supply curves for yen.

In the left-hand side diagram, if S and D intersected at point A, the parity value of 0.50 would be the market price of the yen. This exchange rate can fluctuate between 0.475 and 0.525 without any gold flowing.

Suppose instead that S and D for yen intersected at point B, meaning a higher market demand for yen, as given by $D_{¥}^2$. If the exchange rate were flexible, the yen price would rise to 0.56. But the exchange rate could not rise above 0.525 under the GS.

Note that at 0.525 (the US GEP), there would now be an excess demand for yen of distance $CD = Q^1Q^2$ billion yen. As analyzed in earlier notes, this implied that Japan had an economic BOP surplus of CD billion yen, and the US had a BOP deficit of $0.525*CD$ billion dollars. There would still be upward pressure on the yen due to this excess demand.

But if the exchange rate went above 0.525 (say, to 0.53), traders would use dollars to buy gold at the US Treasury, ship the gold to the Bank of Japan, and exchange it for yen at the parity price, making a profit. This is because at this exchange rate, it would be cheaper to get yen through shipping gold than by transacting at the private rate of 0.53 in the FX market.

Key result: Under the GS, if a country had a BOP surplus, gold would flow into its monetary authority. If a country had a BOP deficit, gold would flow out of its monetary authority.

In the right-hand side diagram, again, the parity exchange rate was 0.5. If the S and D for yen intersected at A, that would be the market exchange rate also.

Suppose instead that there was a higher supply of yen, given by curve $S_{¥}^2$. If the exchange rate were flexible, the yen would depreciate to 0.46. But it could not fall below 0.475 (Japan's GEP).

Note that at 0.475, there would be an excess supply of yen, given by $EF = Q^3Q^4$ billion yen. This means Japan had an economic BOP deficit of that amount, and the US had an economic BOP surplus of 0.475*EF billion dollars. There would still be downward pressure on the yen.

At any exchange rate below 0.475, gold would flow from Japan to the United States because getting dollars through the gold channel would be cheaper than getting them in the FX market. Japanese trading firms would buy gold at the Bank of Japan (using yen) and ship it to the US Treasury to get dollars there, making a profit.

Again, gold flows from the country with a BOP deficit to the country with a BOP surplus. The monetary authority in the deficit economy sees gold outflows and the monetary authority in the surplus country sees gold inflows.

How does a BOP surplus or deficit resolve itself in the gold standard system? Consider the first case (left-hand side diagram) in Figure 17.1. Suppose the market exchange rate were 0.53$/¥, which was above the US GEP. What would happen?

Since there would be a Japanese BOP surplus and the exchange rate exceeded the US GEP, Japan would see its stock of gold rise and the US would see its stock of gold fall. This can only continue until the US Treasury risks running out of gold.

But that should not happen. As the gold stock rose in Japan, its money supply also would go up because this gold stock is Japan's monetary base. This would be inflationary and raise Japanese prices, wages, and employment and output. Japanese goods would get more expensive, reducing the demand for yen and eliminating the BOP surplus. This is how the GS was designed to work.

As the gold stock (monetary base) fell in the US, its money supply would go down. This should be deflationary and reduce US prices, wages, employment, and output. This would also reduce the demand for yen. Overall, the demand for yen would shift inward to $D_¥^3$ where the FX market is in balance at the gold export point. This would eliminate both the Japanese BOP surplus and the US BOP deficit.

(*Note*: The supply of yen would also increase (shift to the right) because the Japanese would want to buy cheaper US goods and assets. But it is not necessary to clutter the diagram that way.)

In the second case (right-hand side diagram), the adjustment is shown as a decrease in the supply of yen because as gold flows to the US from Japan, US prices would rise and Japanese prices would fall. This adjustment would eliminate the Japanese BOP deficit and the US BOP surplus.

The essential conclusion is that the gold standard offered an automatic means of correcting BOP surpluses and deficits. Any BOP surplus larger than the one at the gold import point would bring gold into the economy, raising its money supply and prices until the BOP returned to equilibrium. Any BOP deficit larger than the one at the gold export point would take gold out of the economy, reducing its money supply and prices until the BOP returned to equilibrium.

Study question 2

Under the classical gold standard:

A. The money supply of any country depended on its stock of gold.
B. Countries with a BOP surplus would see gold flowing out and prices falling, which would eliminate the surplus.
C. Countries with a BOP deficit would see gold flowing out and prices falling, which would eliminate the deficit.
D. Both A and C.

Discussion of study question 2

The correct answer is D because both A and C are correct statements. An increase in a country's stock of gold would raise its monetary base and therefore its money supply. And if a country had a BOP deficit (above the level consistent with the GEP), it would see gold flowing out, reducing its prices and wages. In turn, that would tend to eliminate the BOP deficit as its exports grew and its imports fell. B is incorrect because BOP surpluses would cause gold to flow in and raise domestic prices and wages.

This process had very large implications for monetary policy.

1. Under the GS, countries with BOP surpluses saw their money supplies rise, which was inflationary. This would make them less competitive and correct the BOP imbalance. Countries with BOP deficits saw their money supplies fall, which was deflationary. This would make them more competitive and correct the imbalance. This "specie flow mechanism" was what corrected imbalances in the BOP.

2. The central banks and finance ministries did nothing here other than just buy and sell gold. There was no independent monetary policy. Rather, the money supplies of countries depended solely on private demands for gold, relative to the existing stock of gold.

3. If there were no monetary policy and no changes in the fixed exchange rate, adjustments to the BOP happened only in terms of internal economic adjustments. Countries with BOP surpluses would see prices rise and there would be more demand for labor, driving up wages (and other costs). Countries with BOP deficits would see deflation and less demand for labor (lower wages and more unemployment).

More comments on the gold standard

It is now possible to see why some conservative economists and politicians may prefer a gold standard to modern systems of flexible exchange rates. The benefits they see include the following:

1. Fixed exchange rates should reduce international exchange rate risk from prices changing due to movements in exchange rates. This should increase international trade and investment.

2. Since the GS would rigidly constrain policymakers, countries would not see their central banks or finance ministries raising or cutting the money supply on their own as a matter of policy. By establishing gold as the "monetary anchor", there would automatically be discipline in the system imposed on policymakers. Perhaps most importantly, governments could not run large and chronic budget deficits and finance them through

inflationary increases in the money supply, as discussed more in the following chapter. Attempts to do so would soon be frustrated by reductions in the money supply through the gold standard.

If those benefits exist, why do the majority of economists prefer flexible exchange rates? What problems would there be with the GS? There are many but here are two main problems to understand:

1. Each country's money supply would depend strictly on its stock of gold. Thus, if there were an exogenous rise in the stock of gold, there would be a rise in the money supply. This would probably generate a BOP deficit and some of this money would go abroad through gold outflows. In short, national and global money supplies would depend heavily on when and where new gold supplies were found and mined.

2. Modern advanced countries do not like the fact that the domestic economy would contract if they have a BOP deficit. In fact, this deflationary pressure under a fixed exchange rate often causes real problems for uncompetitive countries. Countries with high costs and BOP deficits must suffer internal adjustments (deflationary pressures and lower employment) to eliminate those deficits under a fixed exchange rate.

   The best recent example is Greece under the euro system, as described in Chapter 19. The euro is not a gold standard, but it is a common currency, implying effectively a rigid exchange rate for each member country.

   A less painful way of dealing with BOP deficits is simply to permit a depreciation of the home currency, which directly raises exports and reduces imports. In fact, the GS collapsed mainly because certain countries wanted to inflate rapidly through currency depreciation, as was the case with Germany in the 1930s.

3. Most fundamentally, a flexible exchange rate does permit an independent monetary policy, which can have considerable benefits.

The Gold Exchange (Dollar) Standard

Collapse of the gold standard

The gold standard remained in place among major trading economies through the beginning of World War I, a period that put considerable stress on the ability of governments to sustain stable macroeconomic policies, while it also disrupted international trade. High inflation to finance the war made prices in the UK, France, Italy, and elsewhere rise rapidly compared to the United States. Those economies did not have sufficient gold stocks to manage the outflow under the GS, causing them to depart the system during the war. Germany also abandoned it and could not rejoin after the war because of heavy reparations payments imposed on the country. The US remained on the GS and became a significant net creditor as it ran current account surpluses for several years.

Several countries rejoined the GS in the 1920s, hoping it would help stabilize trade and investment flows. Most notably, the UK rejoined in 1925 at the same parity that existed before the war. Combined with the prior high inflation, this exchange rate made British prices and wages uncompetitive, kicking off a deflationary spiral and high unemployment and national labor strikes. Many observers, such as economist John Maynard Keynes, described this decision as a "historic mistake".

Britain's return to the GS, along with several other countries, generated a period of price and wage deflation that became an important contributor to the Great Depression of 1929–1939. During the Depression, countries chose to abandon the system in favor of more flexible exchange rate arrangements. Governments hoped that devaluation of their national currencies would offset deflationary pressures, in excess "exporting unemployment" to others. These mutual competitive devaluations and currency depreciation periods were a major factor underlying the severity and length of the Great Depression, along with the major reduction in global trade associated with rising tariff rates, including the US Smoot–Hawley Tariff Act of 1930.

Brief overview of the gold exchange system (dollar standard)

The *Bretton Woods system and the gold exchange standard (or dollar standard)*

The Great Depression and World War II convinced policymakers that a new system of global institutions was needed to rebuild the world economy after the war.

In 1944, policymakers met at the Bretton Woods Conference in New Hampshire to set out a post-war economic development plan, featuring important and lasting global economic organizations, including the following:

1. the International Monetary Fund (IMF), designed to provide additional liquidity and financial support to countries with balance-of-payments difficulties;
2. the International Bank for Reconstruction and Development (IBRD; known now as the World Bank), charged with providing development loans and financial assistance to developing and emerging countries; and
3. the beginnings of the General Agreement on Tariffs and Trade (GATT; now the WTO), designed to establish rules and guidelines regarding the regulation of trade and to negotiate mutual tariff cuts.

The primary outcome, however, was to establish a new framework of fixed exchange rates under a system called the gold exchange standard (GES) among member countries of the IMF. This arrangement was also called the Bretton Woods system or the dollar standard. The remaining notes explain how that system operated.

The United States, which was by then the major global economic power, was given the primary responsibility to sustain fixed rates. Specifically, it set the gold price at $35 per ounce and the Federal Reserve pledged to buy and sell gold, in return for dollars, at this price. However, it would only do this on behalf of foreign monetary authorities and major banks, not with regular traders.

All other IMF member countries chose an exchange rate fixed to the US dollar and were required to buy and sell their currencies at this rate (within 1% bands) for dollars at the given rate but not gold. Thus, the US dollar became the centerpiece of global finance, rather than gold or other precious metals.

For example, the Japanese yen was set at 360Y/\$(= 0.0028\$/Y) by the US authorities. Students may recall that this exchange rate under the classical gold standard was set at 2.01¥/\$. Thus, the yen was set to be very cheap in this system, which was a deliberate policy to grow Japanese exports and redevelop the economy after its destruction in World War II. The yen remained at that price until 1971.

Operation of the dollar standard

The fixed exchange rate of each currency to the dollar was supposed to have similar effects as the gold standard on domestic economies and to result in similar automatic adjustments to BOP surpluses and deficits. However, rather than gold flowing from a deficit to a surplus country, dollars (as official reserves) would flow.

Countries could also borrow from the IMF to deal with temporary deficit problems. Thus, the IMF became something new in the world: an international organization that could issue money to central banks that needed it. It does this through the issuance of "special drawing rights" (SDRs), which are part of the foreign exchange reserves of central banks that receive them. These issuances are not automatic and must be approved by the IMF board of directors.

Further, countries with chronic BOP deficits were permitted to devalue their currencies on occasion relative to the dollar. For example, in 1949, the British pound sterling was devalued by 30% from its initial parity in the GES of 4.08 \$/£ to 2.80\$/£. The UK further devalued the pound in 1967 to 2.40\$/£, attempting to offset significant BOP deficits arising from high production costs.

Countries with chronic BOP surpluses were permitted to *revalue* their currencies (making them more valuable), as Germany did with the Deutsche mark (DM) a few times. Interestingly, Japan chose not to revalue even though it became highly competitive in the 1970s and 1980s and ran large current account surpluses. Its cheap currency was a big reason for Japanese export growth and became a real irritant with US policymakers.

There are several key points that students should remember about the GES:

- *This entire system was built on the willingness and ability of the United States to sustain its gold price in dollars, which meant it was based on global confidence that the US dollar would not come under pressure to depreciate or appreciate over time.*
- *It was equally built on the willingness and ability of the US to expand its money supply to facilitate the needs of central banks around the world in buying and selling dollars in return for their own currencies. That is, the US had to stand ready to supply dollars as international reserves for other countries.*
- *In turn, that meant that if the US ever tended toward chronic BOP deficits (meaning US households, investors, and the government bought more foreign goods, services, and assets than foreigners bought from the US, implying chronic excess supplies of dollars), foreign traders would take all those excess dollars in the FX market and convert them to local currencies at their central banks.*
- *In turn, these foreign central banks would ask the Federal Reserve to convert their excess dollars into gold and the US gold stock would diminish.*
- *This threat that the US might lose its gold reserves if the country ran BOP deficits was the disciplinary anchor of the system. It limited US monetary and fiscal independence, for the country and central bank could not run an inflationary policy regime for long.*

Collapse of the dollar standard

Why did this system collapse?

- Despite this policy constraint, in the 1960s, the US government felt compelled to run a highly inflationary domestic policy to finance the war in Vietnam and pay for increases in social benefits (the "War on Poverty").

- The US also tended toward large deficits in the current account as imports and payments exceeded exports and receipts. The essential reason was that US households saw their saving rates fall in this period, forcing more borrowing from abroad.

This situation created large US BOP deficits in the 1960s and massive volumes of dollars flowed overseas in FX markets as a result. Foreign trading firms and investors took these dollars to their central banks and converted to local currencies with these impacts:

- Local CBs saw large increases in FX (dollar) reserves.
- These conversions were greatly increasing local money supplies and there was a rise in global inflation. In essence, the United States was "exporting" its inflation through the global monetary system.

By 1969, several foreign central banks saw this system as unsustainable and began to demand gold from the Fed as they brought dollars back to the US. This meant the US gold stock declined rapidly and the US government decided this was unsustainable.

Thus, in 1971, the dollar was devalued from \$35 to \$38 per ounce and then again to \$42.20 in 1972. This is still the US official gold price, though that does not mean anything in the current world of flexible exchange rates.

These devaluations were not enough to restore balance to the international system. In 1973, the US suspended its commitment to buy and sell gold, meaning that it went to a fully floating exchange rate. Other developed countries quickly followed and the major economies have been on fully flexible rates ever since.

As noted in earlier notes, most developing countries keep a fixed exchange rate of some kind, often directly tied to the dollar. But it is the responsibility of those countries' central banks to fix the exchange rate by using their own foreign exchange reserves (dollars, euros, Swiss francs, and other major currencies, plus SDRs) to buy and sell their currencies. It is not the responsibility of the United States.

Study question 3

Which of the following characteristics of the classical gold standard did not happen in the gold exchange (dollar) standard?

A. Gold would flow between countries to correct BOP imbalances.
B. No single country or central bank had the responsibility to sustain stability in the system.
C. Money supplies would rise automatically in countries with BOP surpluses and fall in countries with BOP deficits.
D. Both A and B.

Discussion of question 3

The correct answer is D because both A and B existed under the GS but not under the dollar standard. A did not happen because dollars flowed rather than gold (though foreign central banks could convert dollars to gold if desired). B was not the case because the United States was expected to pursue stable macroeconomic policies and sustain the global monetary system.

 C is an accurate statement, though the difference is that gold flowed in the GS and dollars flowed in the dollar standard. In either case, local FX reserves would go up or down in different countries, which would also raise or lower their domestic money supplies.

Summing Up: Fixed versus Flexible Exchange Rates

Comments on flexible exchange rates

Flexible exchange rates have constituted the basis of the international monetary system among developed economies since 1973 and show no signs of changing. Why do major countries prefer flexible rates?

• A flexible exchange rate permits them to have an independent monetary and macroeconomic policy. That is, if a country wants to stimulate its economy with expansive money growth and budget deficits, it can do that. One important result is likely to be a depreciated currency.

- As a result, the country does not expose its domestic labor and output markets to the pressures of a fixed exchange rate.

All of which means that we should understand why countries choose different systems. With this background, these notes conclude by considering the advantages and disadvantages of fixed and flexible rates.

Fixed versus flexible exchange rates

The case for fixed exchange rates (and against flexible rates)

1. If a country's trade flows are heavily concentrated in a particular foreign currency, it may be wise to fix the rate and avoid facing exchange rate risk, as discussed above.
2. Fixed rates provide greater certainty about the costs of doing business across borders. This advantage is greatest for small, extremely open economies, making them more interested in stable foreign prices than domestic prices.
3. Fixed rates also reduce the risk of international investment.
4. The biggest reason is that fixed rates are a policy "anchor" and countries cannot run an independent macroeconomic policy for long.

These reasons are generally why developing countries peg to the dollar, euro, or other major currency or basket of currencies. They also were the main factors behind the establishment of the euro, which was designed to integrate the European member economies better and reduce currency volatility costs. The euro system is described fully in Chapter 19.

The case for flexible exchange rates (and against fixed rates)

1. Flexible rates permit more independence in monetary and fiscal policy.

   If a country wishes to raise its interest rate in order to dampen the economy, it can do that and permit the *exchange rate* to adjust. Put another way, with a flexible exchange rate, economies are put back into macroeconomic balance through *external adjustments* in the *exchange rate*. The country can have "external balance" achieved without significantly disrupting the "internal balance". This means, for example, that a depreciation of the domestic currency in a country with BOP deficits can help raise aggregate demand without causing higher unemployment.

But it should be noted that policy flexibility is not necessarily the best thing if a country is likely to run highly inflationary macro policies with expansive government spending. Using flexible exchange rates to disguise poorly managed macroeconomic policies is unlikely to work for long.

2. Developed countries with sophisticated financial markets can hedge away exchange rate risk, so the problems with exchange rate variability and instability do not matter as much.

Chapter 18

Exchange Rate Crises

Identifying Exchange Rate Crises

Introduction: What is an exchange rate crisis?

The history of the gold exchange standard offers lessons about why and how there are exchange rate crises. In essence, the anchor economy (the United States) was politically unable to sustain its commitment to the fixed value of the dollar. The inflationary environment pushed the economy toward current account deficits, resulting in trading firms exchanging excess dollars for foreign currencies. In turn, foreign central banks demanded that their growing dollar reserves be converted into gold, eventually depleting the US gold reserves and forcing the country to abandon its fixed exchange rate.

The dollar standard no longer exists, but many emerging and developing countries peg (or manage) their currencies to the dollar or other major currencies. This situation means that there may be periodic episodes in which certain nations find it impossible to maintain the given value of the fixed rate, potentially precipitating a crisis in FX and financial markets.

The term exchange rate (ER) crisis refers to the volatile period just after (1) a pegged exchange rate breaks so that a currency is either permitted to float freely or is devalued to a new peg; and (2) this decision results in a rapid and large depreciation or devaluation of the home currency.

There is no clear definition of how large a depreciation must be to constitute a crisis. But in developing and emerging countries, crises often accompany a depreciation of 20%–25% or higher.

For example, in 1994, the Mexican peso fell almost 60% against the dollar over several months. During the East Asian crisis in the late 1990s, the Korean won fell 50% and the Indonesian rupiah by over 80% before recovering somewhat. In 2002, the Argentine peso fell nearly 90% against the dollar after its fixed rate collapsed. More recently, the Turkish lira fell more than 40% relative to the dollar in late 2021.

Such crises often are followed by large contractions in economic activity before recovery. Typically, emerging countries see a decline in economic growth of several percentage points, or even significant cuts in the level of GDP, for 2–3 years.

In each of these cases, the economy suffering from the crisis had both a fixed exchange rate and few limits on the flows of financial capital into and out of the country. As these notes will discuss, factors emerged causing domestic and foreign investors to move assets out quickly, placing pressure on the local central bank to sell FX reserves and buy the domestic currency to support the peg. At some point, it became impossible to continue this support as FX reserves were depleted.

Since the 1990s, crises of this kind have become more common and more severe. It suggests that fixed exchange rates in emerging countries with high capital mobility may not be sustainable for long if other factors push the currency toward depreciation.

Accompanying financial crises

ER crises are often the result of other macroeconomic and financial problems. Two other kinds of financial crises sometimes happen, often as part of the same process leading to an ER crisis:

1. In a *banking crisis*, domestic banks and other financial institutions in a country may face insolvency and bankruptcy for various reasons, including a recession in which their borrowers default on loans. It is possible that these financial institutions

themselves borrow heavily in foreign currencies. As they head toward bankruptcy, foreign lenders may require rapid repayment, which can generate an ER crisis.

2. In a *sovereign default crisis*, governments essentially go bankrupt and cannot pay off or even service their foreign currency-denominated bonds (debt), causing them to default on those bonds. Again, if this threat seems serious enough, it can spark a crisis in the FX markets, causing the peg to break.

And these events can all work together. If there is an ER crisis and the currency plummets in value, that makes the local currency value of foreign currency debt much higher and can generate a banking crisis and/or a default crisis.

All this makes understanding the sources of ER crises and their impacts a central element of international macroeconomic policy. This analysis will also help students understand better the links between monetary policy and exchange rates.

Central Bank Balance Sheet and Exchange Market Intervention

The mechanics of a fixed ER, monetary policy, and central bank intervention

Earlier notes described in general terms how a CB must buy or sell FX reserves in order to fix its home currency. The discussion here offers more detail, which is helpful for understanding why exchange rate pegs sometimes are abandoned in an ER crisis.

To begin, let a country (say, Argentina) peg to the US dollar, perhaps within a narrow band around the fixed rate. (In fact, currently, Argentina has a managed floating system in which it intervenes to manage the pace of changes in the exchange rate. But this example will illustrate the various issues.)

Let the home currency be the peso, with $\bar{E}_{P/\$} = \bar{E}$. A rise in this rate is a depreciation of the peso.

The essence of monetary policy is that the Argentine central bank (the Bank of Argentina) tries to raise or lower the home money supply by buying and selling financial assets in exchange for pesos, in the domestic financial market. It does this using two types of assets:

1. domestic bonds (think of these as Argentine government bonds), which are issued and denominated in pesos;
2. foreign assets (such as US treasury bonds, gold, or other forms of foreign reserves), which are denominated in dollars.

Students may recall from studying basic macroeconomics or money and banking that if the Argentine CB buys an asset, it does so by selling pesos, which puts more pesos into domestic circulation and increases the Argentine money supply. In this context, "selling pesos" means to create peso-denominated accounts for the banks that provide the asset. These accounts become part of the money supply. Thus, if the CB buys domestic bonds or foreign assets, it raises the Argentine money supply.

Similarly, if the CB wished to reduce the money supply, it would sell bonds or foreign assets to banks and reduce their deposits held at the CB. A CB sale of bonds and foreign assets contracts the money supply.

There is a key difference between transactions in domestic bonds versus foreign bonds. When the CB buys domestic bonds, it spends pesos (now in the money supply) for peso-denominated bonds (which are not money). The exchange is pesos for pesos and there is no direct impact on its FX reserves.

But when it buys foreign assets, the CB spends pesos (now in the money supply) to buy dollar-based assets (which are not money). This transaction increases the CB's foreign reserves, for example, in dollars, but it is pesos for dollars.

Both transactions raise the peso money supply but only the latter changes the stock of FX reserves and directly influences the exchange rate (in this case, to keep the ER fixed by preventing the peso from appreciating).

Similarly, if the CB sells domestic assets (pesos for pesos) or foreign assets (dollars for pesos), it reduces the domestic money supply in either case, by taking pesos out of circulation. But selling foreign bonds reduces the CB's foreign reserves and influences the exchange rate (in this case, to keep the ER fixed by preventing the peso from depreciating).

However, with a fixed ER, the CB also must intervene in FX markets to fix $\bar{E}$, which is part of the monetary policy. It must buy from, and sell to, foreign reserves (dollar assets) to anyone who wishes to do so at the fixed exchange rate. This activity also changes the money supply, as discussed earlier.

The CB can sustain this process so long as it has some foreign reserves (R) available to sell. If it began to run out of R because of large purchases of pesos to prop up the currency, FX market participants would recognize that it cannot sustain the ER much longer. When reserves run out, the CB must abandon the peg and let the currency float.

In most periods, under normal financial and banking conditions, the CB would have enough R and the exchange rate would be seen as credibly fixed. This means that no one would try to speculate against the peso because the CB has enough R to defend it.

Note an important implication: *A country with a flexible ER does not have much need for FX reserves because its CB does not intervene in the currency markets.* This is the situation in most major developed countries with floating rates. But even those CBs might hold some FX reserves balances for various reasons, including making small, short-term interventions to prevent a rapid and destabilizing change in the exchange rate.

Study question 1

Which of the following actions by the Central Bank raises a country's money supply?

A. The CB sells some of its stock of bonds in exchange for domestic currency.
B. The CB buys foreign reserves from a participant bank, giving that bank a deposit in local currency.
C. The CB sells foreign currency bonds to a participant bank, reducing the bank's deposit in local currency.
D. Both B and C.

Discussion of question 1

The correct answer is B. When the CB buys foreign reserves and expands local currency deposits, the local money supply increases. Both A and C are incorrect because in each case, the CB sells something that is not money (domestic bonds or foreign reserves) and takes local currency or deposits out of circulation, which cuts the money supply.

The central bank balance sheet

It will aid in understanding exchange rate intervention and crises to relate these concepts to the central bank's balance sheet. This *balance sheet* accounts for the CB's assets and liabilities, which are directly related to the domestic money supply.

Thus, CB assets are made up of the financial assets it purchases and owns:

1. Let the CB own a quantity B of domestic peso-denominated bonds. This is called *domestic credit* or the bank's *domestic assets*. When purchased by the CB, these bonds create money, so B is part of the money supply.
2. Let the CB own a quantity R (in dollars) of foreign reserves. As we know, this is called *reserves* or the central bank's *foreign assets*. These are also part of the money supply, though valued in pesos at the fixed exchange rate $\bar{E}$. Then, $\bar{E}R$ is the value of reserves in pesos.

As noted in Chapter 15 of the notes, the deposits that private banks own at the CB are called the monetary base (which also includes currency in circulation, which will be ignored here for simplicity). Think of the monetary base as the actual money supply, which is appropriate for the analysis here. Then, the total money supply (in pesos) is the sum of the CB's assets (domestic credit plus reserves) because these items make up those deposits: $M = B + \bar{E}R$.

From that expression, we have $\Delta M = \Delta B + \Delta(\bar{E}R)$. This equation says that the *MS changes if the CB raises or lowers either its domestic credit or reserves.*

As with any balance sheet, the CB must have assets = liabilities. Its liabilities are the deposits created in the act of purchasing domestic credit and reserves. It follows that *the economy's money supply is defined as the stock of CB liabilities.* When the CB chooses to increase its purchases of domestic bonds or foreign assets, it is the same as raising its liabilities and increasing the money supply.

Here is an illustrative example of the basic balance sheet of the Argentine CB, determining the money supply. Assume the CB has purchased Pesos 1,500 billion in $\bar{E}R$ and 2,000 billion in B. Also, let $\bar{E} = 10$ pesos per dollar in order to keep track of foreign reserves in dollars.

Argentina CB Balance Sheet (billion pesos)

Assets		Liabilities	
Reserves $\bar{E}R$	1,500	Money Supply M	3,500
Domestic credit B	2,000		

Note that the value of reserves in dollars is $1,500/10 = \$150$ billion.

Intervention to fix the exchange rate

CB Intervention

It is realistic to assume that the exchange rate can be fixed only if the CB holds positive reserves. Otherwise, it would be floating. That is, the CB must have $\bar{E}R > 0$ to maintain the peg.

From earlier analysis, we know that reserves are the difference between the money supply and domestic credit:

$$\bar{E}R = M - B \quad \text{and} \quad \Delta(\bar{E}R) = \Delta M - \Delta B$$

In words, under a fixed exchange rate, a country's FX reserves must be adjusted to make up the difference between the money supply and domestic credit. But in equilibrium, the supply of money will equal the demand for money (the money balances that residents of Argentina wish to hold for their purposes). Thus, this really says that reserves must make up the difference between the demand for money and domestic credit.

In reality, there are many factors that influence the demand for money in an economy. However, the primary factors are captured by the monetary model in Chapter 15. In that theory, the demand for money depends on the price level, gross national income, and a proportionality factor:

$$M^d = \lambda * PY$$

Then,

$$\bar{E}R = \lambda * PY - B \quad \text{and} \quad \Delta(\bar{E}R) = \Delta(\lambda * PY) - \Delta B$$

What is this proportionality factor λ? It reflects how much money people wish to hold for a given gross national income, PY. Thus, an exogenous rise or fall in the preferences to hold money would raise or reduce λ.

But a more powerful influence is the domestic interest rate, which is paid on interest-earning assets, such as bonds, but not on money. *The interest rate is the opportunity cost of holding money* because a higher rate makes holding money instead of bonds more costly. It follows that *the demand for money goes down as the domestic interest rate rises and goes up as the interest rate falls.*

We can rewrite our equations as

$$M^d = \lambda(i) * PY \quad \text{and} \quad \bar{E}R = \lambda(i) * PY - B$$

These basic equations reflect what the central bank must do to keep the exchange rate fixed if other variables are changing in the economy. In the short run (which is important in financial markets and drives what the CB does), it is appropriate to regard P and Y as exogenous variables from the standpoint of CB intervention.

It is also useful to think of B as the exogenous component of the domestic money supply. That is, the CB can choose the level of domestic credit.

What about $\lambda(i)$? The interest rate ordinarily would be considered an endogenous variable because it would change to balance the money market. For example, if the money supply were to rise above the existing level of money demand, the interest rate would have to fall to make people hold the additional amount of money.

However, this is not the case for an economy with a fixed exchange rate and highly mobile international capital flows. Suppose that Argentina permits free international capital mobility and pegs the peso to the dollar.

Recall an important result from Chapter 14: uncovered interest parity. The UIP condition is $\hat{e} = i_\$ - i_P$, where $\hat{e}$ is the expected depreciation (if positive) or appreciation (if negative) of the peso and $i_\$$ and i_P are the interest rates in the US and Argentina, respectively.

UIP says that under a flexible exchange rate, the peso would be expected to depreciate if the US interest rate were higher than the Argentine interest rate because capital would flow from Argentina to the US, generating a BOP deficit that would be corrected by a depreciated peso.

However, Argentina's policy is to fix the exchange rate. This means *that the expected change in $\bar{E}$ is zero* and UIP becomes

$$\text{UIP} : i_P = i_\$$$

That is, by having a fixed ER and a policy of free capital mobility, Argentina is committed to equalizing its interest rate and the US (or world) interest rate in equilibrium. This is like the case of Barbados discussed earlier. It also means that the domestic interest rate is given by the US interest rate and is exogenous as far as the Argentine central bank is concerned.

It is now possible to analyze the effects on CB reserves of any change in these exogenous variables. The key insight is that, in order to fix E, reserves R must be changed by the CB to satisfy this condition for equilibrium in the domestic money market.

$$\bar{E}R = \lambda(i) * PY - B$$

In words, the stock of foreign reserves (in pesos) must equal the difference between the economy's demand for money and its amount

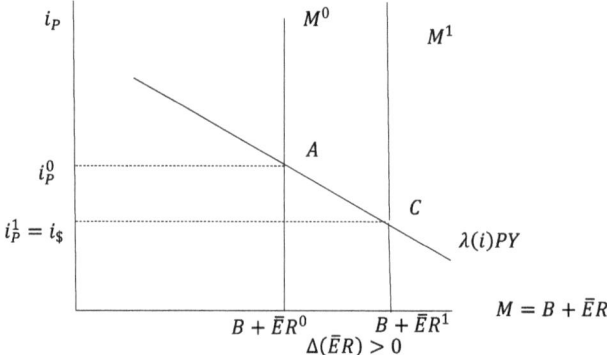

Figure 18.1   Money market equilibrium with a fixed exchange rate.

of domestic credit. Once the CB knows the variables on the right-hand side of the equation, its task is to adjust R to reflect equilibrium. We can think about this in terms of buying or selling FX reserves to achieve money market equilibrium with a fixed exchange rate.

The process is illustrated in Figure 18.1. On the horizontal axis is the stock of money M (domestic credit plus reserves) and on the vertical axis is the domestic interest rate. The downward-sloping curve is the demand for money in Argentina, which increases as the domestic interest rate falls. The vertical lines show two different money supplies. In the diagram, as assumed, the amount of domestic credit B is exogenous and held constant here.

Intervention and the money supply

Consider the situation at point A, where the money supply equals money demand at interest rate i_P^0, which exceeds the US interest rate. This cannot be the equilibrium because, with high capital mobility, investors would move capital into Argentina. But this inflow would tend to appreciate the peso, which the CB must prevent by selling pesos and buying dollar assets, raising the stock of reserves. In turn, the money supply would increase until $i_P^1 = i_\$$ at point C, with the higher money supply M^1.

Note that the change in reserves is $\Delta(\bar{E}R) = \bar{E}R_1 - \bar{E}R_0 = (B + ER_1) - (B + \bar{E}R_0) = M_1 - M_0$. That is, to fix the exchange rate, the CB must increase reserves by enough to raise the money supply and establish equilibrium.

Another way to see this is to imagine that Argentina's CB tried to undertake its own monetary policy to change the domestic interest rate. Suppose that the CB attempted to raise the domestic interest rate by reducing the money supply from M^1 to M^0. The higher interest rate would cause financial capital to flow into Argentina, tending to appreciate the peso. To avoid the appreciation, the CB would have to sell pesos and buy foreign exchange, thereby raising the stock of reserves and returning the supply of money to M^1.

The essential point is that because the CB is required to sustain the fixed exchange rate, its policy must be to buy or sell foreign reserves in sufficient quantities to establish equilibrium consistent with the fixed exchange rate, with equality between the home and US interest rates. *This is what economists mean by stating that a country with a fixed exchange rate does NOT have an independent monetary policy. The CB simply must adjust its reserves as needed, without an ability to alter domestic conditions, such as the interest rate.*

Intervention and fiscal policy versus monetary policy

If monetary policy is ineffective, what about fiscal policy, which means raising government spending or cutting taxes to increase aggregate demand in the economy?

As Figure 18.2 shows, there is an important difference between these policies. In the left-hand side panel, suppose the CB tried to expand the economy by raising the domestic money supply and reducing the domestic interest rate (compare points A and C). It would ordinarily do this by expanding the stock of domestic credit through purchasing domestic bonds, raising domestic credit from B_0 to B_1. Then, the lower interest rate would cause financial capital to flow out of the country, generating downward pressure on the peso exchange rate. To fix the rate, the CB would have to buy pesos and sell reserves, reducing the money supply to where it had been.

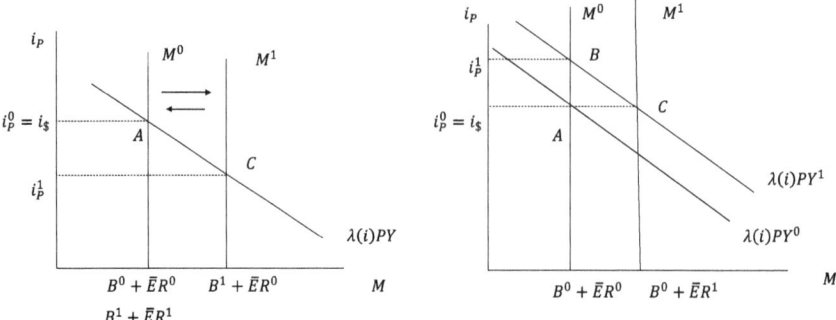

Figure 18.2   Ineffective monetary policy versus effective fiscal policy under a fixed exchange rate.

The interest rate must return to its initial level. *Monetary policy is ineffective at changing interest rates (and aggregate income) under a fixed exchange rate.*

There is an important change, however. The process began by raising domestic credit, which was offset by a decline in foreign reserves. Again, it is the stock of reserves that changes to equilibrate the money market.

What about fiscal policy? The idea is demonstrated in the right-hand side panel. Suppose that gross national income Y goes up from Y^0 to Y^1 because of an increase in government spending. This would increase the demand for money, raising the interest rate in Argentina to i_P^1, illustrated at point B. In turn, capital would flow into the country, which would put pressure on the peso to appreciate.

The CB cannot permit the appreciation, so it must sell peso assets in return for foreign reserves, which go up. In turn, the domestic money supply rises to establish a new equilibrium at C, with a higher money supply. In turn, this supports a higher level of GNI (or P or both). *Thus, it is possible to use fiscal policy to expand or contract the economy under a fixed exchange rate, implying that fiscal policy is an effective macroeconomic policy.*

Note another important difference between these cases. In the left-hand side panel (monetary policy), domestic credit rose but foreign reserves fell. That is, there was a shift in the composition of the money supply (monetary base).

However, in the right-hand side panel (fiscal policy), the CB's stock of foreign reserves goes up at the given amount of domestic credit. The increase in reserves is what permitted the expansion of the money supply. Again, reserves adjust to ensure equilibrium with a fixed exchange rate.

(Author's note of caution: Students should understand that these examples use the money market to illustrate important differences between monetary and fiscal policy. However, they do not show the full equilibrium impacts on GNI, the price level, and other variables.)

Summary

Under a fixed exchange rate, the CB must adjust reserves to establish equilibrium in the domestic money market at the fixed exchange rate. This idea is depicted in the money market by noting that a fixed exchange rate is equivalent to the condition $i_P = i_\$$.

In the process of intervening, reserves $\bar{E}R$ (expressed in pesos) will change (with B held constant or treated as an exogenous variable), causing a shift in both the money supply (monetary base) and the composition of the monetary base between B and ER. Students should now have a better sense of what CB intervention to fix the exchange rate really means.

Note another important point. When economists say that a fixed exchange rate prevents independent monetary policy, what they really mean is the following:

1. The CB can influence domestic credit B by selling and buying domestic bonds.
2. But reserves $\bar{E}R$ must adjust to fix the exchange rate.

Study question 2

Under a fixed exchange rate, which of the following differences between monetary and fiscal policy is or are true?

A. Monetary policy is effective at expanding or contracting the economy, but fiscal policy is ineffective.

B. An attempt to expand the domestic money supply by buying domestic bonds results in higher domestic credit but lower foreign reserves, while expansionary fiscal policy raises foreign reserves.

C. The domestic interest rate cannot differ from the foreign interest rate in equilibrium when using monetary policy but can differ under fiscal policy.

D. Neither monetary nor fiscal policy can change the equilibrium supply of money in the economy.

Discussion of question 2

The correct answer is B as analyzed in Figure 18.2. A is incorrect because the opposite statement is true: monetary policy is ineffective but fiscal policy is effective.

C is false because in equilibrium, the domestic and foreign interest rates must be equal when there is full capital mobility. Note that the "foreign interest rate" refers to the interest rate in the anchor country, that is, the country issuing the currency to which the home exchange rate is fixed.

D is false. As shown in Figure 18.2, the money supply must return to its old level under monetary policy but changes under fiscal policy.

The CB Balance Sheet and Exchange rate Crises

CB balance sheet and changes in the reserve backing ratio

With this additional theory, return to the concept of the CB balance sheet, which shows assets and liabilities, where CB liabilities are the country's money supply. Start with the earlier example:

Argentina CB Balance Sheet (billion pesos)

Assets		Liabilities	
Reserves $\bar{E}R$	1,500	Money Supply M	3,500
Domestic credit B	2,000		

Here, the money supply is 3,500 billion pesos, with 1,500 billion pesos in reserves and 2,000 billion pesos in domestic credit. Recall that reserves measured in dollars are $150 billion.

As should be clear from earlier analysis, the ability of the CB to maintain the fixed exchange rate depends on how high its stock of reserves is compared to the total money supply. In essence, the ability to fix the exchange rate is "backed" by the stock of foreign reserves. This ability is expressed in the "reserve backing ratio" (RBR), which is reserves divided by the money supply.

In this example, RBR = 1,500/3,500 = 0.43. Reserves are 43% of the domestic money supply.

RBR must be positive for the CB to be able to defend the exchange rate. If RBR = 0, it must permit the currency to float.

Now, consider what happens to this ratio when there are changes in the economy:

1. Suppose there were a 20% increase in the demand for money (that is, for pesos) in the economy. As described earlier, this could happen because of a rise in real GNI (Y) or a higher price level (P). Assume this happens here due to a higher real GNI.

   In this case, the CB must raise the money supply to meet this higher demand at the given interest rate (which equals the foreign interest rate). Since the CB is reacting to changes in money demand (rather than using changes in domestic credit), it raises the money supply by purchasing foreign reserves, increasing the stock of pesos in the economy.

   Thus, the new money supply = 3,500*(1.2) = 4,200. The money supply rises by 700 billion pesos. Holding domestic credit (B) constant, this must imply that reserves rise by the same amount, so the new $\bar{E}R = 2,200$.

   New CB balance sheet:

   Argentina CB Balance Sheet (billion pesos)

Assets		Liabilities	
Reserves $\bar{E}R$	2,200	Money Supply M	4,200
Domestic credit B	2,000		

Note something important here: The money supply rose by 20% to meet money demand. However, reserves rose by $\%\Delta(ER) = 700/1,500 = 0.47$ or 47%. In dollars, R rose from $150 b to $220 b, also 47%.

In the first balance sheet, RBR $= 750/1,650 = 0.43(43\%)$. In the new balance sheet, RBR $= 2,200/4,200 = 0.52(52\%)$. It went up, meaning that the CB now has a stronger ability to defend the fixed exchange rate. The RBR increased because all the additional demand for money was met by the CB purchasing more reserves. It should be evident that a reduction in the demand for money would force the CB to remove pesos from circulation by selling foreign reserves, which would reduce RBR.

Exchange rate crises emerging from changes abroad

What are the sources of exchange rate crises in emerging and developing countries with fixed exchange rates? There could be many factors, but two primary ones are *external sources and internal sources*.

External source: A rise in the foreign interest rate

Consider the impact on Argentina's foreign reserves and money supply if there were a sharp increase in the US interest rate. Note that in 2022, the United States pursued a policy of significantly hiking its interest rates in order to reduce domestic inflation.

Suppose that Argentina begins with its initial balance sheet, with reserves of 1,500 pesos, a money supply of 3,500 pesos, and a backing ratio of 0.43. In Figure 18.3, let the US interest rate rise from 0.02(2%) to 0.04(4%). This increase would cause capital to leave Argentina and move to the US, generating a BOP deficit for Argentina and an excess supply of pesos. Suppose that at the new US interest rate, the quantity of pesos demanded falls to 2,600 pesos. Thus, the excess supply would be 900 pesos (compare points B and C).

To fix the exchange rate, the CB must buy those excess pesos by selling foreign reserve assets, denominated in dollars, worth 900 b pesos. (That is, if the exchange rate were 10 pesos per dollar, reserves

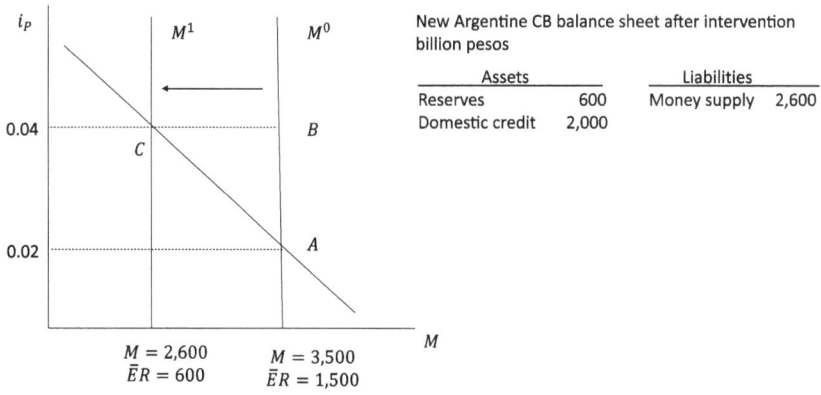

Figure 18.3   A rise in the US interest rate.

of $900/10 = \$90$ b would be sold.) This would reduce the money supply from $3,500$ b pesos to $2,600$ b pesos, with reserves falling from $1,500$ b pesos to 600 b pesos (from $\$150$ b to $\$60$ b in dollars). This is shown in the new balance sheet next to Figure 18.3.

The new reserve backing ratio becomes RBR $= 600/2,600 = 0.23(23\%)$. The need to fix the exchange rate when the US interest rate rises quickly depletes Argentina's foreign reserves. Clearly, if the US interest rate continued to rise, the CB of Argentina could find itself facing a crisis in which it could no longer defend the fixed exchange rate and the peso would need to be floated freely.

Briefly, here are other foreign economic disturbances that could diminish a country's CB foreign reserves and precipitate an exchange rate crisis:

1. Suppose that a developing or emerging economy fixes its currency to the US dollar (or some other major currency, like the euro). If the US dollar (or the euro) enters a period of sustained and rapid appreciation compared to other currencies, the fixed exchange rate implies that the currency of the developing economy automatically appreciates as well, making it less competitive and reducing exports. The ensuing BOP deficit would not be self-correcting, and the CB may have to intervene to buy the local currency, depleting its reserves.

2. A significant global economic recession could depreciate third-country currencies relative to the anchor currency, and therefore against the local currency of the developing economy, resulting in a similar outcome to 1. This situation, where a country's currency appreciates compared to others because of appreciation of the anchor currency, is called the "third currency phenomenon". It can raise comparative costs and generate financial difficulties.

Study question 3

Suppose that Malaysia's currency, the ringgit, were fixed to the US dollar and that capital were allowed to flow fully between the countries. Now, suppose that the US interest rate were to fall. Which of the following statements is false?

A. The Malaysian interest rate would also fall.
B. There would be pressure on the ringgit to appreciate relative to the dollar, leading to a fall in the foreign reserves of the Malaysian CB.
C. The Malaysian money supply would rise.
D. There would be an increase in Malaysia's reserve backing ratio.

Discussion of question 3

The correct answer is B, which is a false statement. The lower US interest rate would make Malaysian assets more attractive, leading to a capital inflow and tending to appreciate the ringgit. To avoid that, the Malaysian CB would sell ringgit assets and buy dollar assets, raising its foreign reserves.

A is true because the fixed exchange rate with high capital mobility would make the two interest rates move together. C is true because the higher stock of foreign reserves would raise the money supply. Finally, D is true because the stock of foreign reserves would rise by the same amount as the money supply but that would raise the RBR. (Students may wish to reinforce this idea by constructing a CB balance sheet for Malaysia.) Note that this situation is the opposite of the Argentine example.

Risk premiums and internal sources of exchange rate crises

Students may have noted that the concept of equal domestic and foreign interest rates is unrealistic in the context of developing countries. Equality follows from three assumptions: (1) fixed exchange rate; (2) free capital mobility; and (3) similar assets in the US and Argentina, such as treasury bonds, are both perfectly safe and not subject to default.

However, countries sometimes default on their bonds during exchange rate or fiscal crises, which makes them different from safe foreign (e.g., US) bonds. Thus, the last concept needed to discuss exchange rate crises is *risk premiums* in the interest rate.

The analysis so far assumed that UIP holds: $i_P = i_\$ + \hat{e}$, where $\hat{e}$ is the expected change in the peso/dollar exchange rate. With an exchange rate that is credibly fixed, meaning the CB has enough foreign reserves to defend it, then this expected change is zero and we get equality of interest rates.

In fact, however, interest rates on similar assets tend to be much higher in developing countries than in developed countries, even where exchange rates are fixed. This must be because investors demand some additional returns, or premiums, to be willing to hold pesos (that is, debt instruments denominated in local currencies).

Evidence on risk premiums

Here are some data from late April of 2018 on the interest rates paid on 10-year government bonds:

US 2.96%   Canada 2.31%   Germany 0.57%   UK 1.43%   Greece 3.92%
India 7.77% Mexico 7.49%   Brazil 9.91%   China 3.69% Hong Kong 2.21%
          Ecuador 7.88%   Venezuela 10.43%

And here are those rates from late April of 2020, along with Standard & Poor's bond creditworthiness ratings:

US 0.60% AA+	Canada 0.59% AAA	Germany −0.47% AAA	UK0.29% AA
Greece 2.31% BB−	India 6.17% BBB−	Mexico 6.82% BBB	Brazil 7.28% BB−
China 2.51% A+	Hong Kong 0.47% AA+	Ecuador 9.87% BBB	
Venezuela 46.52% CCC			

Comments on risk premiums

There are interesting observations to make:

1. Greece shares the euro with Germany and yet its interest rates are considerably higher. Indeed, in April 2020, Germany's 10-year interest rate was negative.
2. Hong Kong has a currency board with its currency fixed to the US$. This means that its monetary authority holds at least one US$ for every Hong Kong dollar in circulation.
3. Ecuador is a dollarized economy and yet its interest rates are higher than those in the US.
4. Venezuela's interest rate rose considerably compared to the US between 2018 and 2020.

What explains these variations are various forms of risk that bondholders face when investing in currencies and countries. There are two primary risks:

First, flexible currencies may be highly volatile, leading to exchange rate risk for traders and investors. This risk also holds for fixed exchange rates when local central banks may not be able to defend the currency value.

Second, national governments may be at risk of default on their debt (bonds) if they cannot obtain enough revenue to repay the interest and principal due on them.

Where these factors exist, traders and lenders will demand a premium in the local interest returns in order to buy and hold domestic bonds. The relationship between the domestic and foreign interest rates becomes

$$i_P = i_\$ + \hat{e} + \text{exchange rate risk premium} + \text{default risk premium}$$

In this equation, the last three terms together explain why the domestic interest rate (e.g., in Argentina or Greece) exceeds the foreign rate (e.g., in the US or Germany). The first two of these three terms together make up the *currency premium* or the additional interest return needed if there is risk in the value of the currency.

With a credibly fixed exchange rate, this sum is zero. But it would be positive (and possibly very high) if investors expect that the currency peg will break, and the home currency will depreciate, perhaps quite rapidly and by a large amount. As noted earlier, depreciations of 60% or more after a fixed exchange rate is abandoned have been common. In those cases, rapid increases in domestic interest rates happened before the exchange rate break.

In the case of Greece, a member of the euro system, these terms would ordinarily be zero. But there were discussions in Greece during the financial crisis of 2008–2014 of leaving the system, which significantly raised that premium in the interest rate. This case will be discussed in detail in the final chapter. This currency premium in interest rates applies also to countries with flexible exchange rates if the currency is volatile and subject to uncertainty.

The last term in the equation has to do with the likelihood that the country's government, firms, or both will default on their foreign debt. It also reflects the risk of asset expropriation, changes in financial regulations and taxes, weak property rights, and other factors affecting financial markets.

It is interesting to note that financial capital generally flows from developed countries to developing countries in volumes that are considerably less than expected by differences in interest returns. In fact, there are often reverse flows from developing nations to developed countries, called "capital flight", when conditions become highly risky in the former. These kinds of institutional problems (currency risk, default risk, expropriation risk, and so on) are a big reason capital does not flow that much to developing countries.

Investment advisors sometimes refer to the *country risk premium* in particular nations. This concept is the same as the default risk premium in the equation above.

The obvious importance of these risk premiums is that domestic interest rates in developing countries can be much higher than world rates, which raises capital costs. For purposes here, the primary lesson is that risk premiums also complicate how central banks must intervene to fix E.

Changes in domestic credit and exchange rate crises

With this background, it is possible to analyze the major domestic, or internal, source of an exchange rate crisis: an unsustainable rise in domestic credit.

Here are primary reasons why domestic credit might rise:

1. The CB could undertake open-market purchases of domestic bonds from private banks.
2. The central government may wish to expand its budget deficit and finance it with additional borrowing. If it cannot readily borrow in the private markets (whether from domestic or foreign investors), it could order the CB to buy its bonds.

The second reason deserves more discussion. In countries where central governments can order the CB to purchase their bonds as a form of deficit (or debt) financing, the result is an expansion of the money supply in a process some call "monetizing the deficit" or "printing money" to finance the deficit. This process can be highly inflationary and destabilizing if it is used extensively to fund excessive government spending. It is the major source of unsustainable rises in domestic credit.

This danger is essentially why developed economies, such as the US, the UK, and Canada, ensure by law that the central bank has independent monetary authority and cannot be ordered to provide such finance. CB independence is a key element of macroeconomic policy stability.

To understand how expansions in domestic credit (B) influence CB intervention and may pressure the fixed exchange rate, consider first how changes in B affect the CB balance sheet. The earlier examples analyzed the effects on the CB balance sheet of a change in domestic money demand and a change in the foreign interest rate. In those cases, the CB had to change the money supply to equilibrate the money market, which caused changes in reserves and the reserve backing ratio.

Now, consider what happens when there is an increase or decrease in the amount of domestic credit B, say, to finance a growing government deficit. With a change like this, the CB usually defends the fixed exchange rate through engaging in what is called *sterilized intervention*. In essence, it buys or sells foreign reserves to just offset the shock to B in order to stabilize the overall money supply.

Going back to the initial example of the Argentine CB balance sheet:

Basic CB Balance Sheet (billion pesos)

Assets		Liabilities	
Reserves $\bar{E}R$	1,500	Money Supply M	3,500
Domestic credit B	2,000		
Dollar reserves $R = \$150$ b			

Now, suppose there were an increase in domestic credit of $+1,000$ billion pesos, say, due to government borrowing. Assume this did *not* affect the demand for money in the economy, so in equilibrium, the money supply must remain the same.

The higher B would raise the money supply initially, tending to depreciate the peso. In that case, the CB would need to reduce its reserves by 1,000 billion pesos (that is, to sell dollar reserves and purchase peso-denominated assets) to keep the money supply, the domestic interest rate, and the exchange rate unchanged.

The new balance sheet would have $\bar{E}R = 500$, $B = 3,000$, and $M = 3,500$. This intervention using reserves to fix the exchange rate when there is a change in domestic credit is called *sterilization in the foreign exchange market to keep the money supply constant*.

Here, it reduces the stock of foreign reserves by 67% and cuts the reserve backing ratio from $1,500/3,500 = 45\%$ to $500/3,500 = 14\%$.

Note that the CB stock of foreign reserves in dollars is now just $50 billion. Clearly, continuing this policy of financing fiscal deficits with sterilized intervention could quickly deplete a central bank's foreign reserves, again forcing the exchange rate to be floated.

Other sources of credit expansion and exchange rate crises

As discussed in the following, excessive government borrowing and the resulting expansion of domestic credit have led to crises in several emerging economies in recent decades. However, there is another major source of financial distress that should be mentioned briefly. It may be the sole source of a crisis or exist together with expansive government borrowing to magnify it.

Specifically, a distressed private banking system may face excessive withdrawals. "Bank runs" are periods in which depositors take their funds out of banks, leading to potential problems of illiquidity and solvency. A banking crisis may emerge, for example, from systemic defaults on bank loans taken out by firms in housing, primary commodities, or other industries, which they are unable to repay because of a recession, higher interest rates, or falling commodity prices.

Many developed economies avoid this risk through federal banking deposit guarantees. However, developing and emerging countries may not have such policies, leaving it to the central bank, as the "lender of last resort", to bail out the banking system. If banks become dangerously short of liquidity, for example, the CB could create deposits for them, raising domestic credit. If banks face insolvency, the CB may purchase some of their assets, especially the unperforming loans on their books, again raising domestic credit.

In such cases, the outcome is similar to that involving CB financing of deficits: Domestic credit expands quickly, and the CB attempts to offset that by selling foreign reserves in order to fix the exchange rate. It may not take long to run out of reserves if the banking crisis is extensive.

Exchange rate crises: Two Examples

The Asian financial crisis: 1997–1998

Several East Asian economies suffered financial distress and significant currency depreciations in 1997–1998. Many found this surprising because those economies had grown rapidly for decades and seemed to have sound macroeconomic policies.

Thailand offers a good example. For many years, Thailand had pegged its currency, the baht, to a basket of major international currencies. By 1997, however, there had been mounting problems in the banking sector, arising from domestic firms becoming increasingly unable to repay massive bank loans, which they took out to finance questionable projects in housing and other sectors. A substantial amount of these loans were borrowed from abroad, requiring repayment in dollars, yen, or euros. This strategy seemed safe under the fixed exchange rate, for there should have been little or no exchange rate risk.

However, as growth slowed and firms started to lose money, they were forced to purchase foreign currencies from the CB in order to service those loans, leading to losses of foreign reserves. By early 1997, it seemed clear to investors that the baht could not be defended much longer and there was massive speculation against it (that is, investors bet that it would go down in value). As its reserves depleted, Thailand was forced to float the baht on July 2, 1997. By the end of that year, the baht had depreciated by more than 50% compared to the dollar. There were also significant bankruptcies, declines in the stock market, and other problems.

There was a rapid spillover (called *financial contagion*) to other countries in the region, including Malaysia, Indonesia, South Korea, and the Philippines, all of which experienced large depreciations of their currencies over several months. There were also large short-term declines in economic output. For example, Indonesia's growth in per-capita GDP fell from around 5% before the crisis to –12% in 1998. In fact, this episode contributed to the collapse of the ruling Suharto regime, which resigned in May 1998.

Collapse of the Argentine currency board: 2001

The Asian financial crisis was an example of an exchange rate crisis arising from the domestic financial and banking system. In contrast, Argentina's history relates primarily to poor domestic macroeconomic policies. Between 1975 and 1990, that country had suffered several periods of high inflation, averaging over 300% per year, reaching a peak of over 5,000% in 1989, a period of what is called hyperinflation. There was a steady decline in per-capita GDP in that period, along with little confidence in the central government and central bank.

These problems stemmed primarily from unsustainable growth in the money supply to create the domestic credit needed to finance large fiscal deficits of as much as 10% of GDP in the 1980s. Argentina was seen as a highly risky economy and foreign investment fell dramatically despite elevated risk premiums on Argentine bonds. Since the government could not borrow much from abroad, it was forced to monetize its deficits through monetary expansion.

In 1990, there was a banking crisis, accompanied by severe financial flight out of the economy, as wealthy citizens sought to hide their assets abroad. This situation was highly unstable and a new government chose to try to impose stability through the combination of fiscal austerity (meaning reduced government spending and higher taxes) and other policies.

An essential policy was to implement a currency board in January 1992. In principle, the currency board was designed to exchange pesos for dollars, one for one, meaning an exchange rate of one peso per dollar. This system was supposed to be backed by enough dollar reserves to cover the full Argentine money supply, meaning an RBR of at least 100%.

Note that this policy represented a radical change in the value of the peso, which had depreciated to a value of 10,028 pesos per dollar by the end of 1991. As explained in earlier notes, the primary objective was to bring inflation down quickly, which it did, falling from over 5,000% in 1989 to 3.4% in 1994. As a result, GDP grew rapidly through most of the 1990s, as did both imports and exports, each tripling in the decade.

These results were impressive in terms of macroeconomic management. However, the austerity, deflation, and import competition also generated large increases in unemployment, which rose to 20% by 2000. The distribution of income and wealth also grew more unequal in the 1990s.

The greatest difficulty was that the government soon abandoned fiscal austerity in favor of rapidly growing deficits. The currency board made it impossible to finance them through monetary expansion, forcing the government to borrow from abroad. Public debt grew much faster than GDP and much of that debt was denominated in foreign currency.

Meanwhile, the US dollar appreciated considerably in the late 1990s, meaning that the peso also appreciated relative to other currencies, reducing exports and employment. This was an example of the "third-currency phenomenon" described earlier.

The result of these factors were higher international debt and a heavily overvalued Argentine peso, especially compared to the Brazilian real (Brazil was a major trading partner), causing a decline in exports, an increase in imports, and growing current account deficits.

By late 2001, the currency board was under severe pressure to sustain the 1 for 1 exchange rate. Most observers realized that it was unsustainable, and investors traded pesos for dollars in order to move their wealth overseas. For a short period, the government issued strict controls on outward financial movements, which was unpopular. In December, the government suspended payments on its foreign debt, a default for which the country is still paying.

In early 2002, the government ended the currency board, abandoned the fixed exchange rate, and permitted the peso to float freely. It depreciated quickly, losing 75% of its value relative to the dollar within months, before stabilizing at 2.9 pesos per dollar in 2003. Since May 2022, the Argentine peso has been subject to a managed float, with the exchange rate rising to over 250 pesos per dollar.

Chapter 19

The Euro System

Introduction to the Euro

Defining the euro

The euro is a currency shared by 20 European countries in what is called the Eurozone. As of 2023, the countries include Austria, Belgium, Croatia, Cyprus, Estonia, Finland, France, Germany, Greece, Ireland, Italy, Latvia, Lithuania, Luxembourg, Malta, the Netherlands, Portugal, Slovakia, Slovenia, and Spain.

Note that there are several countries in the European Union (EU) that do not use the euro, preferring to have their own currencies:

- The Swedish krona, for example, floats freely against the euro. So did the British pound when the UK was an EU member before departing in 2021.
- Denmark is in the EU and pegs its currency, the Danish kroner, tightly to the euro. That means it is effectively in the system and, indeed, euros are widely used within Denmark.
- Other EU members, such as Bulgaria and the Czech Republic, lie somewhere between these extremes.
- Some non-EU members use the euro as their currency, such as San Marino, the Vatican, and Kosovo.

The "Euro system" is essentially the European Central Bank (ECB) and the central banks of the 20 Eurozone countries.

Monetary policy within the Eurozone is supposed to be shared among them, though it is primarily the responsibility of the ECB.

An essential characteristic of the euro is that it is a freely flexible currency and fluctuates relative to the dollar and other major currencies. Thus, it is a hybrid system: an economic area in which all countries share a common currency, which itself floats against other currencies.

Brief history

Begin with a brief history of European economic integration, which has aimed to bind together more tightly the economies of Western Europe (and Central Europe more recently). The essential logic is that if these countries are tightly linked through trade, investment, and monetary relationships, the possibility of military conflict or other forms of domination is minimized. Further, this integration should raise growth rates and prosperity.

There is little doubt that the "European Project" has been a success in this regard. EU countries are generally prosperous and peaceful. But there are some problems with the system, which are discussed after this introduction.

European integration takes three parts: political, economic, and monetary. A reasonable way to conceptualize the overarching objective is to create a "United States of Europe" that is as integrated as American states are in the dollar system.

Political integration

The European Economic Community (EEC), or Common Market, was founded in the 1957 Treaty of Rome, involving six major countries. The EEC expanded to new members through the 1990s. For example, Spain and Portugal joined in 1995.

The 1993 Maastricht Treaty began the process of moving beyond economic integration to political partnerships. It converted the EEC into the European Community, which later became the European Union under terms of the 2009 Lisbon Treaty.

An important institution is the European Court of Justice (ECJ), established in 1952. It was made much more powerful by the Lisbon Treaty and serves essentially as the EU's Supreme Court.

The other main political institutions are the European Commission, which undertakes executive functions, much like the US presidential administration, and the European Parliament, which has authority for legislation. Despite these common institutions, EU member countries retain considerable political autonomy and run their own fiscal policies.

Economic integration

The primary form of economic integration is the trade preferences involved. The EU is a customs union with free factor mobility, meaning that it is properly considered a "common market" in economic terminology.

There is largely free mobility of labor and capital within the EU (and the Eurozone), which remains controversial. Free labor migration was the main impetus for Brexit by the UK, whose voters wished to regain control over immigration. Despite these reservations, studies demonstrate that factor mobility is a major source of prosperity in Europe.

Finally, there is a regulatory element of economic integration. The European Commission issues policy directives aimed at harmonizing regulatory policies within the EU. All members are required to implement these directives, which is also a source of controversy in the region.

Monetary integration

It has long been a goal of those who favor European integration to complete the project by linking European currencies into a single monetary unit and monetary system. In the 1970s, there was a "snake in the tunnel" arrangement, which permitted nine national currencies to fluctuate within a 2.25% band around the US dollar, as an attempt to retain elements of the Bretton Woods system (the dollar standard) that collapsed in 1971. This effectively linked these currencies together within a 4.5% band from the weakest (e.g., the Greek drachma) to the strongest (e.g., the German deutsche mark).

In 1979, the European Monetary System (EMS) was founded. It established the European Currency Unit (ECU), which was a basket of European currencies, meaning a weighted average of their values relative to the dollar. National currencies of the participating countries continued to exist but were tied to the ECU within a 4.5% band.

In 1993, the Maastricht Treaty set the terms for establishing a single currency (the euro) by 1999. These terms involved a set of "convergence criteria" for countries wanting to join. These criteria included the following:

- low national inflation rates;
- low government bond interest rates;
- a federal government deficit below 3% of GDP;
- total public debt below 60% of GDP.

The idea was that countries would feel pressure to adopt the euro in order to integrate with the region. If they could only join after meeting these criteria, the system would involve a common currency among nations with similar macroeconomic conditions and an emphasis on fiscal soundness.

In principle, it would force such countries as Greece and Italy to adopt better and more sustainable fiscal systems. Like Germany, these would involve lower public borrowing, higher taxes and more rational tax systems, and reduced public spending on pension obligations.

It was also thought that monetary integration into the euro would force countries with inflexible labor markets to change their laws, permitting firms to engage in more hiring and firing. This would, in turn, raise productivity and reduce youth unemployment.

Overall, the idea underlying the euro was that countries would benefit from a single currency through greater trade and investment integration. But to be sustainable, the member countries had to have stable and predictable macroeconomic conditions.

Further, advocates of the euro argued that the "Euro-South" countries with high deficits and debt levels (Italy, Spain, Portugal, and Ireland in 1999 at the euro's founding; Greece entered shortly after) would be forced through the Euro system to converge with the low deficits and low debt levels of the "Euro-North" countries (Austria, Germany, the Netherlands, Belgium, France, Finland, and Luxembourg).

The euro was launched (with a phased-in implementation) in 1999–2002 with 11 countries, which has since grown to 20. Those wishing to join must attempt to meet the convergence criteria, which have been relaxed somewhat over time. In fact, the Eurozone members have consistently been lenient about permitting countries to join without meeting the convergence criteria.

An Optimum Currency Area

Is the Eurozone a good idea? The theory of an optimum currency area

The hybrid nature of the Eurozone, with a common internal currency, which is externally flexible, is called by economists a currency area. Like any preferential system, a currency area has benefits and costs.

A useful way to assess the Eurozone (EZ) is to consider whether it constitutes an *optimum currency area* (OCA), meaning one that maximizes net benefits for its members. This old idea in international economics asks the following question: Suppose a set of countries are considering adopting the same currency. What economic characteristics should they have to make this a good policy and achieve an OCA? Following are the key characteristics, explained with reference to the states of the United States, which may be considered a successful OCA. Those states share a common currency, the US dollar.

First, within an OCA, there should be *highly mobile labor and capital among the countries (states) and/or highly flexible labor markets within each member*. The reason is that economic shocks are likely to hit different countries (states) at different times. A big recession or declining job opportunities in the Midwest, for example, would push labor and capital toward the South and West in the United States, which could be expanding. This mobility should help equilibrate local labor markets without suffering high unemployment in specific locations.

Alternatively, if labor markets were flexible, then wages could adjust upward or downward in response to such shocks, resulting in less unemployment. If wages were rigid (meaning they cannot fall) and people were protected by law from layoffs, labor adjustments would be more inflexible. In such countries, there would be more structural unemployment as firms would have weak incentives to hire permanent workers in the first place. Moreover, job protection rules for older workers could raise unemployment among the young.

The main reason that labor mobility and flexibility matter for a currency area is that because US states (and Eurozone countries) do not have their own currencies, there is no possibility for relative costs to be adjusted through appreciation or depreciation within the area. In the example above, fictional midwestern currencies (e.g., the Illinois dollar) could depreciate and western currencies (e.g., the Colorado dollar) could appreciate, which would offset the recession in the Midwest by making its products cheaper and Colorado products costlier. Instead, flexible factor markets permit interregional movements in labor, leaving the common currency to facilitate interregional trade and investment.

Second, there needs to be extensive *fiscal integration* across countries (states). This means that a centralized fiscal authority is responsible for paying a considerable share of local social benefits. Think again of the United States: If a state like Florida had a recession, tax payments from its residents to the federal government would go down, due to lower income, but its receipts from the federal government would go up, due to higher unemployment insurance and food assistance.

These impacts would cushion the downward trend in regional incomes. For example, between 2007 and 2010 (the early years of the fiscal crisis of that period), Florida's payments to the US government fell by \$33 billion and receipts from the government rose by \$7 billion. This total \$40 billion infusion was more than 5% of Florida's gross state product. This is an example of *fiscal federalism*. The reason this structure is important is that it offers an additional automatic regional adjustment system, cushioning recessions in some locations by transferring funds from expanding to contracting areas.

Third, there needs to be a *centralized banking authority that can serve as a lender of last resort* to prop up banks, financial firms, and governments in trouble. In the US, this role is served by the Federal Reserve, but in Europe, the ECB was not permitted to undertake this role until 2012. It still remains somewhat limited in its ability to do so.

This element is important because the centralized banking authority can support banks in trouble in some regions by extending loans and purchasing assets, in effect shifting more liquidity there. National central banks in small countries generally do not have the capacity to play this role because, say, the Belgian central bank would not ordinarily have any authority to purchase Italian bonds.

This problem could be lessened if the private banks and governments in more stable economies, such as Germany and the Netherlands, were prepared to extend such loans and bond purchases across borders in the event of a crisis. But they have not generally been permitted to do this by national law in EU countries. Further, most taxpayers in those countries remain strongly opposed to it, believing that such a system would, in effect, force them to pay for the debts of countries that have less stable macroeconomic conditions and are more likely to experience a financial crisis.

Fourth, it is important within an OCA to have *centralized bank deposit guarantees*, as exist in the US through the Federal Deposit Insurance Corporation (FDIC). The FDIC replaces bank deposits up to some maximum if a bank closes. In the United States, these guarantees can be financed easily because the federal government can borrow almost without limits and the Fed can create more liquidity to prop up the full national banking system during a crisis. This system is so ingrained that few US bank depositors worry about the security of their bank accounts, greatly reducing the possibility of bank collapses.

In the EU, such guarantees generally have existed only at the national level and were not enough to guarantee all deposits even within national banking systems. Instead, the burden of bailing out banks in the EU fell on national governments, which had to take on more debt to do so, rather than any cross-EU fiscal institution, such as the American FDIC. This need for more domestic public borrowing made dealing with the financial crisis in 2008–2012 difficult for Greece, Spain, Portugal, and Italy.

The terminology used to describe a centralized set of deposit guarantees is a *banking union*. The EU has never been a banking union and it will take some time to achieve the necessary legislative rules to establish one. To get there would require a centralized deposit guarantee agency that is funded by banks from all over the Eurozone, with the authority to stabilize banks anywhere.

The Eurozone Scorecard

Assessing the Eurozone as an OCA

How well do these four characteristics work in the Eurozone?

1. Labor mobility is relatively free but still limited, partly by language and cultural factors. Capital is fully mobile among members.
2. There is no centralized fiscal authority (that is, a central government with taxing and spending powers) within the EU to make cross-border income transfers. That may be politically impossible to achieve for some time.
3. The ECB has become a lender of last resort, but only recently. It was not in this position early in the fiscal crisis.
4. There is, to date, no integrated system of federal deposit guarantees or a banking union. Efforts are being made to move in that direction, in particular, to improve lending flows among Eurozone banks.

The Fiscal Crisis and Response

Factors leading up to the fiscal crisis of 2008–2012

This partially developed system was an important factor in making the financial crisis of 2008–2012 deeper and more prolonged in the Eurozone than in the United States. To understand why, consider the period after Spain and Portugal joined the EU in 1986 and adopted the euro in 1999.

With a rigidly fixed exchange rate (the euro), there were no concerns about exchange rate risk on the part of trading firms and investors, both in those countries and in other European countries seeking to invest there. However, in the 1990s and early 2000s, Spanish, Portuguese, Italian, and Irish banks and construction projects were paying considerably higher interest rates on deposits (banks) and the loans they took out (construction projects) than were German banks and bonds issued in the Euro-North. This meant that investment funds moved rapidly and in high volumes into Spain, Portugal, Italy, and Ireland, generating rapid growth and inflation there.

The situation soon developed a major asset bubble and a housing bubble, much like those in the United States that burst in 2008. There were massive and unsustainable amounts of investments in speculative and high-risk financial derivatives.

Another essential problem here was what economists call a "maturity mismatch". Firms in these Euro-South countries were borrowing at low short-term rates to pay for risky long-term projects that could collapse.

The Eurozone in the financial crisis

What happened in the financial crisis?

- The US housing-finance crisis in 2008 spilled over quickly into a Eurozone crisis, especially for large net debtors in Southern Europe and Ireland.

- There were extensive bank runs (panics) and large increases in national public debts to prop up the larger banks. But this happened at the national level, not at an integrated level within the Eurozone.
- Greece, Portugal, and Spain were forced to borrow from the International Monetary Fund and the ECB, plus from private investors in Germany and other northern European countries. This generated some cross-border funds movement, but the funds were loans at high interest rates (except for those from the IMF) and used to service existing debt, not to support wages or pay for pensions or public services.
- Further, these lenders and bond purchasers demanded that Greece and the others cut government expenses and raise taxes to become more fiscally sound.

As a result, Greece suffered a major drop in real GDP and a rise in unemployment. These variables only returned to pre-crisis levels around 2019, just before the COVID pandemic generated additional problems. The effects of the crisis still generate slower economic growth in Malta, Spain, Portugal, and Italy.

The Eurozone: Longer-term economic impacts

As noted, investors in Germany and other Euro-North countries insisted that the debts of these countries be serviced at least, which required massive cuts in public expenditures and increases in taxes. These cuts generated even larger recessions.

This problem would not be as difficult under flexible exchange rates because then the drachma and lire (if they existed) could depreciate against the deutsche mark and Austrian schilling (if they existed). Again, this would make Greece and Italy more competitive, reducing the severity of their recessions.

But these countries use the euro and therefore this kind of exchange rate-based adjustment was impossible. The only real way to get employment rising again was for real wages to fall enough to make Greek and Italian workers competitive with those in other Eurozone countries. But by law and custom in those countries, nominal wages could not fall much. The outcome was high unemployment, and it took a long time for employment levels and incomes to recover. Thus, this "internal adjustment" was difficult, long-lasting, and painful.

Further, public debt levels continued to grow. For example, Greece's public debt as a percent of GDP increased from 100% in 2006 to 174% in 2019. The corresponding figures for 2019 were 117% in Portugal, 133% in Italy, and 96% in Spain. To date, there are few signs of these debt levels diminishing. It is worth noting that this situation has raised pressures from the political right in several nations against democracy, immigration, and membership in the Eurozone and the EU itself.

Conclusion: The Eurozone is not yet an OCA

What would have happened under a properly structured optimal currency area?

1. There would have been labor migration from Southern and Eastern Europe to Northern Europe. That has happened to some degree but not nearly in enough volume.
2. Centralized fiscal transfers would have automatically cut taxes in Greece, Spain, Italy, and Portugal and increased transfer payments to them. In fact, just the opposite happened as funds left these countries to repay debts.
3. The ECB and a centralized EU financial authority would have paid the costs of bank bailouts and buying and removing bad debt, as happened in the United States with the Federal Reserve and the US Treasury. That did not happen for years. Importantly, later, the ECB was given more authority and took on this role through its own monetary expansion through purchasing bonds from many Eurozone countries.

Thus, the Eurozone does not seem to be a successful OCA to this point.

What would have happened if Greece, Italy, Spain, and Portugal were not in the Eurozone?

1. Without question, their currencies would have depreciated a great deal to reduce their prices and wage costs compared to euro costs in Germany and other Euro-North nations. In turn, their exports would have risen, tending to raise incomes and employment.
2. This "external adjustment" would have been considerably less painful, generating less unemployment and a smaller need to raise taxes and cut expenditure.

The lesson for countries like Greece is that they must choose between the certainty and integration benefits of using the euro versus the adjustment costs during a crisis. It is a difficult choice.

Index

Milton Keynes UK
Ingram Content Group UK Ltd.
UKHW020611231023
431161UK00011B/48